The Cogdill-Woods Debate

A discussion on what constitutes scriptural cooperation between churches of Christ

•

Held at
Phillips High School Auditorium in
Birmingham, Alabama
November 18-23, 1957

•

Participating churches

North Birmingham Church of Christ
Marshall Patton, preacher
and the
Homewood Church of Christ
Jack Meyer, Sr., preacher

Disputants

Roy E. Cogdill, Lufkin, Texas
James W. Adams
Nacogdoches, Texas, Moderator
Guy N. Woods, Memphis, Tennessee
Thos. B. Warren, Ft. Worth, Texas, Moderator

Recorded by Troy C. Irvin, Birmingham, Alabama
Transcribed by L. Wesley and James Jones, Louisville, Ky.
Checked and corrected by the tapes by James W. Adams
Nacogdoches, Texas

© **Guardian of Truth Foundation 1958.** All rights reserved. No part of this book may be reproduced in any form without written permission from the publisher. Printed in the United States of America.

ISBN 1-58427-038-1

Guardian of Truth Foundation
P.O. Box 9670

PUBLISHER'S PREFACE

This book is an exact reproduction of the oral speeches delivered by the principals in a six night debate in Birmingham, Alabama, from November 18 through November 23, 1957. The discussion was held in the Phillips High School Auditorium of that city. Arrangements for the discussion were made by two churches of Christ in Birmingham, The North Birmingham Church with Marshall Patton as preacher, and the Homewood Church with Jack Meyer, Sr., as preacher. These two congregations selected the participants in the debate and made all necessary arrangements. The North Birmingham Church selected Roy E. Cogdill of Lufkin, Texas, as their representative in the discussion and the Homewood Church chose Guy N. Woods of Memphis, Tennessee.

The propositions and agreement which accompanies this preface were worked out and agreed upon between the disputants with the approval of the eldership of the congregations which had chosen them as their representatives. The propositions discussed state clearly the issues between the disputants and between the two congregations presenting them as well as the differences between two great segments of brethren among the churches of Christ from coast to coast and border to border.

The speeches delivered, four each night for six nights, each thirty minutes in length, gave each speaker a liberal amount of time to develop his arguments and present his material. These speeches were recorded on tape and transcribed therefrom and printed in this book without either speaker editing his speeches or making any corrections. Thus we have hoped to bring to the reader as fully and accurately as possible the exact debate as it occurred and as the audiences assembled heard it presented without of course the voice and personality of the speakers.

A large number of charts were introduced in the debate to illustrate the various arguments and points contended for and each chart has been reproduced in the book exactly as it was shown and when it was first introduced. Some of the charts have been inserted more than once but it has not been possible to reproduce them each time they were referred to without making the book too voluminous and costly. They are numbered and indexed so as to be easily found for reference whenever needed by the reader.

The issue of "Congregational Cooperation" can be thoroughly studied in this debate from every point of view. Whether churches of Christ cooperate by each acting independently, autonomously under its own elders, directly in the accomplishment of its own program of work and yet concurrently in fulfilling the mission obligatory upon all; or whether such churches of Christ have the right to "build and maintain" human organizations in which to centralize their resources and the control over their work; or whether the "congregational structure" itself can scripturally be made to serve as a "centralized medium" in which churches of Christ may combine their resources and the control over their work are all dealt with in this discussion as to their being a scriptural means of "Congregational Cooperation".

These issues are once again dividing the churches of Christ as they did in the last century. They must be studied again by those interested in truth and righteousness. The publishers present this book with the hope that it will be of great aid in such study by helping to determine the basic principles and attitudes involved in this great conflict as well as serving as a guide in determining what the Word of God really teaches on the questions. It is with a very sincere and fervent desire that each reader will study it carefully and then turn to the truth of God for final decision that we offer this volume. "Ye shall know the truth and the truth shall make you free". Jno. 8:32.

> The Cogdill Foundation
> Box 403, Marion, Indiana 46952

PROPOSITIONS FOR DEBATE

— 1 —

It is contrary to the Scriptures for churches of Christ to build and maintain benevolent organizations for the care of the needy, such as Boles Home, Tipton Home, Tennessee Orphan Home, Childhaven, and other Orphan Homes and Homes for the Aged that are among us.

AFFIRMATIVE: Roy E. Cogdill
NEGATIVE: Guy N. Woods

— 2 —

It is in harmony with the scriptures for churches of Christ to contribute funds from their treasuries in support of the Herald of Truth Radio Program, conducted by the Highland Church of Christ, Abilene, Texas, as a means of cooperating in accomplishing the mission of the Church of the Lord.

AFFIRMATIVE: Guy N. Woods

NEGATIVE: Roy E. Cogdill

Rules:

1. The discussion to be conducted in Birmingham, Ala., at a time and place acceptable to the Homewood and North Birmingham congregations.

2. Three evenings shall be given to each proposition; and each speaker shall alternate with thirty minute speeches until a total of four such speeches have been made each evening, ie., two speeches of this length by each speaker.

3. The speakers recognize each other as brethren, and agree to conduct themselves accordingly.

ACCEPTED: Guy N. Woods
Roy E. Cogdill

INTRODUCTION

The question of "congregational cooperation" has been one of the most difficult and vexing ever to confront the Restoration Movement. It was on this rock that the Movement foundered and split asunder a hundred years ago, the inauguration of the *American Christian Missionary Society* being the formal expression of liberal minded brethren who departed from the hitherto traditionally held attitude toward New Testament authority. When the break between the liberal and conservative elements became final and irrevocable, many conservative brethren breathed a deep sigh of relief that the internal strife was now over, and thought that the problem was settled permanently. They gradually ceased to instruct, or study, or to endoctrinate in the matters of New Testament teaching on the subject. The tragic consequences of that failure have become alarmingly apparent these last few years as the churches have found themselves facing once again the old, old problems over which division came a century ago.

The Birmingham debate between Roy E. Cogdill and Guy N. Woods was, and in its printed form will be for generations yet to come, a classic milestone in the discussion of this problem. The basic question is one of congregational relationships, particularly as they are defined in cooperative endeavors, either benevolent or evangelistic. The fundamental question, for which this debate sought an answer, is whether or not the churches have the right to organize and do their work through societies, associations, or organizations other than the local congregation. These organizations may be either *outside* the framework of the congregation, or *inside* it; but in either instance, they are something other than the congregation.

The spirit of the debate was exemplary in every respect. Both men conducted themselves in the finest tradition of all that is to be desired in such discussions. Each man is truly representative of the point of view defended by him.

Guy N. Woods has been a gospel preacher for thirty years or more, is a staff writer on the *Gospel Advocate,* writes much of the Sunday School literature of that journal, and has held more than a hundred debates. This was his third major debate on the present issues. Probably no man could be found in the entire church more capable of presenting the "federalized cooperation" point of view than he. Trained in the art of debating, he presents his case with skill and resourcefulness. The brethren who agree with his views expressed themselves as feeling that he had presented their case in the very best manner possible.

Roy E. Cogdill has for thirty-five years been recognized as one of the greatest preachers in the church. He has held meetings in every section of the nation, and has done extensive work in Canada as well. His book of Bible studies, "The New Testament Church," has for twenty years been perhaps the most popular and widely accepted book of its kind in use among the Churches of Christ. It has been used as a basic text-book on the subject in several Christian colleges, and has been widely translated into foreign languages for use in the mission fields of the world.

The whole field of Restoration literature will probably not present a more carefully developed and analytical study of the conservative view of "New Testament authority" than is to be found in Cogdill's speeches at Birmingham. His powerful pleas that the organizations and arrangements defended by his opponent are "without Scriptural authority, therefore sinful," will long be remembered by all who heard the discussion, and by all who read this book. Right here, we believe, will be found the permanent and abiding value of this publication. It will furnish the sincere Bible student with a priceless reference book, (not only as concerns congregational cooperation, but in many other questions that may arise in decades yet to come) in the matter of *establishing* Bible authority, and *applying* that authority to specific cases. It is a book to study, to ponder, and to evaluate with an eye not to the temporary questions of the hour but to the final judgment that awaits us all. Cogdill's exposition and defense of the traditional and accepted view of Bible scholars on the subject under discussion will probably do more to unite the churches and bring peace among them than any thing that has been done in recent years. Such will be the hope and the prayer of all those faithful Christians who seek always in all things to be guided by a "thus saith the Lord."

—Fanning Yater Tant

CHURCH OF CHRIST
MOUND AND STARR
NACOGDOCHES, TEXAS

March 26, 1958.

To Whom It May Concern:

      This is to certify that I have carefully checked and corrected the manuscript of the Birmingham, Alabama debate between brethren Roy E. Cogdill of Lufkin, Texas and Guy N. Woods of Memphis, Tennessee. The original manuscript of the discussion was transcribed from tape recordings furnished by Roy E. Cogdill. The transcription was made by Wesley Jones of Louisville, Kentucky. I further certify that this manuscript was checked by me word by word against the tape recordings. I certify further that the final manuscript containing the transcription as it came from Wesley Jones plus my own additions and corrections from the tape recordings is a true and accurate transcription of the Birmingham Debate.

James W. Adams.

James W. Adams,
Box 63,
Nacogdoches, Texas.

April 27, 1958
Louisville, Ky.

To Whom It May Concern:

This is to certify that we prepared the manuscript of the Birmingham Debate, at the request of Roy E. Cogdill. This manuscript was prepared from tape recordings made of the debate; and it is without alteration, being as correct as human accuracy will permit.

James C. Jones
James C. Jones
New Albany, Ind.

L. Wesley Jones
L. Wesley Jones
Louisville, Ky.

STATE OF INDIANA)
COUNTY OF FLOYD)SS

Subscribed and sworn to before me this 5th day of May, 1958.

Vera Ang
Vera Ang, Notary Public

My Commission Expires:
Dec. 19, 1959

FIRST NIGHT

PROPOSITION:

It is contrary to the scriptures for churches of Christ to build and maintain benevolent organizations for the care of the needy, such as Boles Home, Tipton Home, Tennessee Orphan Home, Childhaven, and other Orphan Homes and Homes for the Aged that are among us.

AFFIRMATIVE: Roy E. Cogdill

NEGATIVE: Guy N. Woods

Cogdill's First Affirmative

Gentlemen moderators, brother Woods, ladies and gentlemen:

I am grateful for the good providence of God that has made it possible for us to assemble upon this occasion that we might study together his word. I am also very grateful for the presence of this good audience in spite of the storm and pray that it has done a minimum of damage, especially to those who are of the household of faith. We are glad that you are here and we are grateful for the fact that many brethren have come from all over the country to study these questions with us. Your presence at a sacrifice of time and money upon your part, many of you an extended sacrifice, indicates the great interest that you have in the issues that are involved in this discussion. An interest that I hope and pray is born of a desire to know the truth of Almighty God concerning these issues, that we may stand before him for that which is right and according to truth.

If I know my own heart I'm not interested in a personal victory of any kind over anyone. Neither am I interested in gaining any personal recognition or glory of any sort. I would not participate in such a discussion as this were it not for the fact that in it an opportunity is offered for us to come together and study the Word of God, and therefrom learn the solution to the problems that are involved in the things to be here discussed by us. Our only hope for such a solution as will bring peace and unity, and insure a continuation of fellowship in the service of God among us is for all of us to get together on the word of God. Human wisdom and sophistry will not bring a solution to these problems that will satisfy the hearts of those who respect God's will. Our appeal must not be to such. God's word is truth, and only the truth can make us free. To the truth as it is revealed in the word of God then we must go and from it we must not turn away for a moment's consideration of anything else. The will of God is right. The word of God is truth. The wise man of the Old Testament counseled, "Buy the truth and sell it not." Pay any price for the truth, no matter what it may cost, and when once you possess it refuse to part with it no matter what you may be offered for it.

Every question must be answered, every issue must be resolved, every problem must be settled in the light of God's word. Peter said, "If any man speak, let him speak as the oracles of God; if any man minister, let him do it as of the ability which God giveth: that God in all things may be glorified through Jesus Christ, to whom be praise and dominion for ever and ever. Amen." I Pet. 4:11. We've stated that principle through the years in this fashion—We'll speak where the Bible speaks, and we'll be silent where the Bible is silent. Upon this principle of divine truth we must stand, if God is to be pleased and our souls are to be saved.

The first point that is raised in our proposition as we turn to an analysis of it emphasizes the importance of this. The proposition says, "It is contrary to the scriptures. . ." By the scriptures, we mean, of course, the word of God, particularly the New Testament of God's word, the gospel of Christ, the righteousness of God which is revealed therein. By "contrary to" we mean out of harmony with, not in agreement with, the scriptures, or with the righteousness of God as revealed in them. But how can a thing be contrary to the scriptures and by what means may we determine that such is true? I submit that there are two principle ways for a thing to be contrary to the scriptures. They are, first, where there is an express injunction and a specific prohibition in the word of God violated; second, when there is no scriptural authority for such practice, and doing it requires a "going beyond" the word of the Lord. There are many things wrong in the sight of the Lord for which no specific injunction has been given in the scriptures. God has not said, for example, "Thou shall not have mechanical instruments of music in Christian worship". Or, "Thou shall not put ice cream and cake on the Lord's table." But either of them would be wrong, and we understand why. There is no divine authority for either of them. There is, therefore, no means of establishing that either is the will of God; both are presumptive and are excluded by what God does say.

But how may scriptural authority be established? In order for a thing to be in harmony with the scriptures there must be either; first, an express command or statement; second, an approved example; or third, a necessary inference, in the word of God for it. In other words, it must either specifically be authorized, or included within the scope of the thing that God has authorized. We have long recognized this simple and fundamental fact concerning Bible authority and I'm sure that brother Woods will not dispute or deny it. If there is no authority at all for a thing then it is contrary to the will of God for it to be practiced by the church of our Lord. Without any authority, it is unlawful and therefore sinful because it would be an invasion of the sacred realm of God's silence, and this God has always condemned and cursed. It is the sin of presumption caused by man's reliance upon his own wisdom, and his lack of respect for the will of God. This is true whether it is a matter of doctrine, of worship, or a substitution of man's way for the way of God. It may lie within the realm of general authority and be, therefore, a matter of expediency or of judgment. But it must be included within the thing authorized or it is contrary to the scriptures and displeasing to God. In order that we may be able fully to understand this process of ascertaining whether or not there is divine authority for a thing, we introduce just here a simple chart illustrating the matter. The first one please.

HOW TO ESTABLISH SCRIPTURAL AUTHORITY
THE LORD'S SUPPER

(1) EXPRESS COMMAND — "*This do in remembrance of Me.*"
(Observance)   I COR. 11:23-24.

(2) APPROVED EXAMPLE — "*And upon the first day of the week, when the disciples came together to break bread.*"
(Time of Observance)   ACTS 20:7.

(3) NECESSARY INFERENCE — "*The first day of the week...to break bread.*"
(Frequency of Observance) (*Means as regularly as the day comes,* COMPARE "*The Sabbath day to keep it Holy.*")
HOW OFTEN?

EXPEDIENCY : ANY HOUR WITHIN THE FIRST DAY OF THE WEEK.

2.   1.

This chart is illustrative of the matter of authority by the Lord's Supper. We use the Lord's Supper to illustrate the fact that our practice in such worship is divinely authorized. We have in the scriptures an express command for its observance, for Jesus said, "This do in remembrance of me." I Cor. 11:23,24. He did not expressly stipulate, though, in the record given to us, the specific day, if any, upon which this institution was to be, or is to be, observed. We learn that from the practice of a congregation assembling for such worship in the New Testament. Acts: chapter 20 and verse 7—"And upon the first day of the week, when the disciples came together to break bread, . . ." Here we have the church at Troas assembling to break bread, observe the Lord's Supper, on the first day of the week. Paul was present and took part in that worship.

This is New Testament example. The church of our Lord under apostolic approval and guidance assembled on the first day of the week to break bread. There is no example of them ever assembling upon any other day of the week for this purpose. They assembled only upon the first day of the week to break bread. Hence, we learn that breaking bread in the assembly of the saints, in the worship of God, can be done with divine approval *only* upon the first day of the week.

But neither the express command nor the approved example tell us how often such a practice is to be engaged in. How do we learn the frequency with which we observe the Lord's Supper? The answer is by necessary inference. The clear, unmistakable import of the language used necessarily implies that they observed the Lord's Supper upon the first day of the week as regularly as that day came. We have here a comparison between the command for the observance of the Sabbath and the observance of the Lord's Supper upon the first day of the week. If ". . . the Sabbath day, to keep it holy", meant every Sabbath day as regularly as it came, then "the first day of the week to break bread" means every first day of the week as regularly as it comes. The conclusion is inescapable. It is necessarily implied.

But someone asks, "at what hour upon the first day of the week should the church assemble to break bread?" The answer is obvious: Any hour within the first day of the week is authorized, comes within the scope of authority, is scriptural. The particular hour is not specified, either by express command, approved example, or necessary inference, hence; any hour within the first day that is expedient can be the hour of assembly and there is scriptrual authority for it. However, if there is neither command, approved example nor necessary inference that includes a practice within its scope, that practice is without scriptural authority and anything without scriptural authority is contrary to the scriptures We shall have more to say about this matter later as it applies to the issues at hand in the discussion.

The next statement of our proposition says, ". . . for the

churches of Christ. . .". By this expression we mean congregations of the Lord's people, Christians, using the term in the same sense as it occurs in Romans 16:16, when Paul said "The churches of Christ salute you." This proposition concerns what the churches of Christ can and cannot do scripturally. We're not discussing what Christians as individuals can and cannot do. We may agree on that or there may be some disagreement between us, but it is not a concern of this proposition, or of this debate. For our proposition reads, "churches of Christ".

These churches of Christ are local churches, congregations, planted in their various localities by the same gospel and, therefore, of the same faith and order. What can they do as congregations—as churches of Christ? That is the issue. We're not debating the right of other organizations to do anything at all. We're not concerned in this discussion with what any organization can do except the church of Christ.

The third statement in our proposition is, ". . . to build and maintain. . .". We mean by this, of course, to organize, establish, bring into existence and perpetuate, sustain their order and activity. This would include financing but would not be limited to that. Supplying the means of its existence is only a part of building and maintaining a thing.

The fourth statement of our proposition is, ". . . benevolent organizations for the care of the needy." It becomes obvious from this wording of our proposition that there is involved in this discussion benevolent organizations other than, separate and apart from, the churches of Christ, but built by them for the work of caring for the needy.

We are not discussing the matter of churches of Christ caring for the needy, but their right to build *other* benevolent organizations to care for the needy. It is also obvious that we are not primarily discussing to what extent churches of Christ might use existing agencies aside from these benevolent organizations involved, or whether or not they can; but do churches of Christ have the scriptural right to build organizations through which to do their work of benevolence.

The fifth statement of our proposition is, ". . . such as Boles Home, Tipton Home, Tennessee Orphan Home, Childhaven and other orphan homes and homes for the aged that are among us." This part of our proposition certainly identifies the type of benevolent organizations that this debate is about. They are specfically mentioned and their character is easily determined. There are others, several of them, maybe some of a different type, but those specified in the proposition will identify the kind of an organization that we mean by it. All of these institutions involve two things: First, the organization that characterizes them; second, the work they do. In each instance there is an organization in control of the work, receiving the money, expending it, hiring and firing the superintendent, controlling the program of work in caring for the needy unto whom they minister. We are concerned in this proposition about the organizational structure of the body which has authority to do and control the work that is being done. We are not concerned in this proposition with the mere means or methods which the organization employs or by which it cares, provides care, for the needy or with the doing of the work itself. But with the right of the church to build such organizations to do this work, whatever means or methods might be employed by such organizations. The work done is not the organization which is built. There is no point in trying to confuse the two.

All of us recognize that there are some things essential to any work which can be done. It does not matter whether the work is evangelism, benevolence or edification, there are certain things necessary in order to do it. For example, a place would be required, necessary provisions and facilities must be furnished. Personnel to actually do the work is essential. There is no discussion about this point. This proposition does not primarily involve whether or not a *congregation* can provide whatever is necessary in caring for the needy, such as a place, necessaries of life, care and supervision. I believe it can. Brother Woods may disagree and if he does then we'll differ on that. But the proposition does not necessarily involve that question. It would not necessarily follow that because churches can not build other organizations to do their work of benevolence that the churches themselves cannot make such provision as is necessary.

To illustrate the point, in discussing the right of the churches to build a missionary society, there is not necessarily involved the question of whether the churches themselves can do missionary or evangelistic work. Granting that they can do such work, there is still the question of whether or not they have the right to build other organizations to do it for them. Neither are we discussing in this proposition the specific means or methods that a congregation may use in providing a place for the needy; and necessary provisions and care for them. Because churches do not have the scriptural right to build other organizations to do such work for them, does not necessarily mean that the churches themselves, as organizations, cannot use methods, systematic arrangements, judgment or means of doing their own work of benevolence. To deny the right of the churches of Christ to build other organizations to do their work, does not deny that they can use means in doing it.

To illustrate this, we deny the right of the churches to build other organizations to do their work of teaching in the Bible school. But that does not mean that we are trying to eliminate methods, systematic arrangement, good judgment or to specify the particular way by which it can be accomplished. My proposition obligates me to prove that such organizations as "Boles Home, Tipton Home, Tennessee Orphan Home, Childhaven and other orphan homes and homes for the aged that are among us", are contrary to the scriptures when built and maintained by the churches of Christ. I'm not here to discuss alternatives or to sit in judgment on every kind of a hypothetical proposition that can be imagined and presented. I have a mighty poor estimate of a man that tries to set aside Bible teaching by asking what about the man who makes the confession and starts to the creek to be baptized and a limb falls on him and kills him on the way. What's God going to do with him? Hypothetical cases are invented largely to avoid the truth of God's word. There are many problems in the realm of marriage today, for example, that it would take the wisdom of a Solomon to unravel and to solve. But no set of hypothetical facts can set aside God's law. To properly apply the principles of divine truth, one must know thoroughly the facts as they exist, and be able to exercise wisdom in properly applying the truth to them.

I'm not infallible in my judgment. I've not always made the proper application of the principles of truth for which I have tried to stand. I take it that my opponent would make the same admission. We can know the principles of divine truth though, if we will study the word of God and determine by it alone to be guided. What then is the issue in this discussion? *The issue is not, first, caring for the destitute.* All of us, I take it, believe in that. I cannot conceive of a Christian who doesn't. Second, *the issue is not whether it is the obligation of the church to engage in such work.* Third, *the issue* in this debate *is not the scope of the obligation of the church to engage in such work;* that is, for whom the church should care. Four, *the issue is not the necessity of making adequate provision for* (1) a place for shelter, (2) the necessaries of life, (3) supervision and care. Five, *The issue is not the right of the elders to determine the matters of expediency* involved in the congregation caring for those for whose care it is obligated. Sixth, *the issue is not the use of systematic arrangement in providing for such care. The issue in this discussion is, which organization shall provide for, direct, control such work* as the church is obligated to do in caring for the needy?

We have two organizations under consideration in this discussion. One of them the church of Christ, and the other a corporate body. These two organizations differ in nature in a very marked way. First, one of them is divine in its origin; it originates with God, with the will and wisdom of God. It is the tabernacle which the Lord has pitched. Heb. 8:2. While the other organization, the corporate body, is human in its origin, originating with the will and the wisdom of man, a tabernacle which man has pitched and not God. Second, one of them, the church,

We have the point illustrated here on a chart.

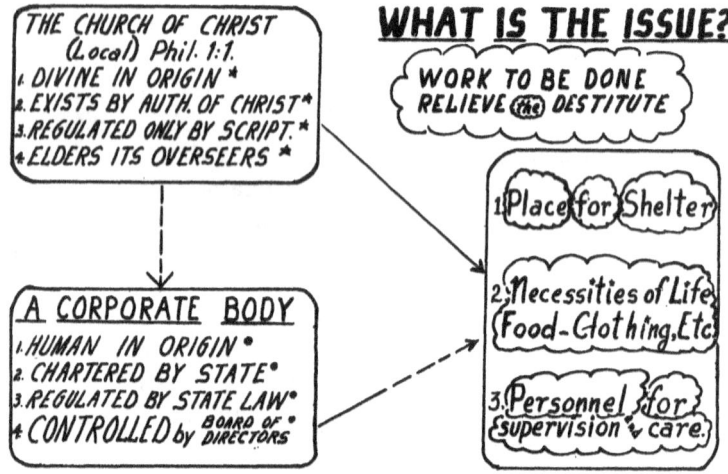

2.

exists by the authority of Christ, chartered by the Lord, while the other is found no where in the word of God, has no divine authority for its existence, but is chartered by the state. Third, one of them, the church of our Lord, is regulated by the gospel of Jesus Christ, by the scriptures that constitute the word of the Lord, derives all of its authority and its direction from New Testament scripture, while the other derives all of its authority and direction from the statutes enacted by the legislature of said state. Fourth, one of the organizations, the church, is under the supervision and oversight of the elders, authorized by the Lord and appointed and directed by his word, also called bishops and pastors; while the other organization, a human arrangement, is controlled by a board of directors, selected and directed by the will of man.

Here is a divine arrangement, the church of our Lord, and a human arrangement, a corporate body, both of them organizations, orderly arrangements; both of them a body of associated persons, separate, distinct and completely independent of each other. On the other hand we have the work to be done, over on this side of the chart. In this instance the work happens to be the relief of the destitute. A Bible command directed to the church of our Lord. Certain destitute that God commands the church to relieve. We mean, of course, by that specific work, or the character of that specific work which God has commanded the church to do, such as is set forth in I Timothy 5:16. "If any man or woman that believeth have widows, let them relieve them, and let not the church be charged; that it", the church, "may relieve them that are widows indeed." Here is a work that the church, by the God of heaven, is specifically authorized to do. Through what organization shall the church accomplish this work? If God had not given the church an organization then perhaps it would be free to fashion one of its own through which to do any of its work. It happens, however, that God has designed an organization. Christ established it, the Holy Spirit reveals it, the word of God authorizes it, through which the church is to do all of its work—the congregation, the local church. Phil. 1:1. "To all the saints in Christ Jesus which are at Philippi, with the bishops and deacons:". We call your attention to the fact that all of the necessary provision in the relief of the destitute can be made by either of these two bodies. (Give me five minute's notice.) Each is entirely capable within the scope of the authority granting them existence and directing their activities of providing all things necessary to the accomplishment of the work under consideration. Either or both of them could provide a place of shelter for the poor; such is within the realm of possibility for both. Either or both of these organizations can provide the necessary things of life for the poor and the destitute. Either or both of them can provide the personnel necessary to supervise and minister to their welfare. All of these things are essential to such work and they can be provided by either organization.

Let me emphasize further that the place, necessaries, and care furnished the destitute is entirely separate from the organization providing it. If the place is the home for the destitute, as we use that word in the sense of a place of residence, or domicile, a place where they live and are cared for, then the home is not the organization, but is provided by the organization. Whether the church provides such a place and thus accomplishes the work, or the place is provided by the corporate body, and thus the work is done, the destitute would have a place for shelter in either event. No one in my acquaintance objects to providing a place for the sheltering of the destitute. It has been not a matter of whether such a work should be done, but a question of which organization shall do it. Which organization shall make such provisions? Which organization shall direct and control the work that is done? It should be carefully observed here that the work done and the place provided are two different things from the organization that is doing it.

To illustrate: The Masonic Lodge provides and maintains institutions for destitute children. That place or home is not the Masonic Lodge. The organization is one thing; the provision it makes for the care of the destitute is another thing. So it is true of the church. If the church makes such provisions as God has commanded that it shall make for the destitute, such an arrangement would not be the church. We all understand that. The same thing exactly is true of the corporate organization when it makes provisions for the care of the destitute. The organization making the provision is one thing, the place, provisions and care furnished is another. The place furnished is not the corporation. It may be owned by the corporation or not. The personnel in the institution are not the corporation; the children are not, neither is the corporation the same thing as the institution or home. Rather it provides such.

(Five minutes.)

It needs further to be noted that the corporation making such provision for the care of the destitute is not the kind of a corporate body that simply holds the title to a property in trust for someone else who is doing the work. The board of directors of this corporate body in question has complete control of the affairs of the institution and are answerable to no one but the law as to how they run it. They receive the money or it is received by their agent. They direct the expenditure of all the money received. They determine what facilities shall be provided, who shall be admitted to the home, and how they shall be cared for. They hire and fire the superintendent and through him as their agent, all other personnel. The work is completely in their charge. This is all true as we shall be abundantly able to show from the charters of these institutions mentioned in our proposition. The actual place of residence, the food furnished, the clothing provided, along with all other essential things, the supervisors and the attendants are all under the control and direction of the board of directors of the incorporated body and those appointed by them as their agents to perform whatever is necessary in making such provisions. This cannot be denied.

It is our contention that the church of our Lord, a divine organization, ought to do the work that God has charged the church with. There isn't anything necessary in caring for the destitute for whom God has charged the church to care that the church as such cannot furnish. The Bible teaches that the church is responsible for doing such work. The organization that God gave the church, and the only one that God ever gave, the local congregation, should do this work, making all necessary provisions itself and exercising the control and the oversight of its work. The congregation, under its elders, can provide whatever is necessary for the care of the destitute as well as any man-made organization. Another organization is not necessary. There is not one thing essential to such a program of relieving the destitute that cannot be provided by the congregation under the oversight of its elders. If so, I want to know what it is. What can this board of directors provide that the elders of the congregation cannot provide? What can this board of directors oversee and control that the elders of the congregation cannot oversee and control that is essential in such a program of work? The answer is absolutely nothing. Where, then, is the wisdom or the right of the church as God designed it and Christ built it, delegating the control over its work, the direction and the doing of the work that God gave it to do, to a human organization? Why should the church contribute its funds to such a human organization and yield the control over the work which God said for the church to do to a human organization? This is the crux of the problem so far as this proposition is concerned. We are to discuss in the second proposition to be debated the question of whether or not one congregation can accomplish and control the work of many churches.

We are interested, in this proposition, in whether or not the church of the Lord has the right to build organizations to do the work God has commanded the church to do. I contend that the church has no such right, scripturally. I believe I can prove it to the satisfaction of every unprejudiced mind. How much time do I have? Fine. Turn another chart for me, will you?

SCRIPTURAL AUTHORITY

Commanded	Generic	Specific
ARK (GEN. 6:14)	WOOD	GOPHER
WATER OF CLEANSING (NUMBERS 19:2)	ANIMAL	RED HEIFER WITHOUT SPOT
PRAISE (EPH. 5:18; COL. 3:16)	MUSIC	SING
EVANGELIZE (I TIM. 3:15; I THESS. 1:7-8)	CHURCH (I THESS. 1:1)	ORGANIZATION (CONGREGATION)(PHIL. 1:1)
EDIFY (EPH. 4:16)	CHURCH	ORGANIZATION (CONGRE.)
RELIEVE (I TIM. 5:16)	CHURCH	ORGANIZATION (CONGRE.)

3.   3

For the churches of Christ to build and maintain other organizations through which to do their work is without divine authority. It is, therefore, a transgression of the law of God and sinful. There is no authority in the scriptures for the churches of Christ to build anything but the church. The law of God does not authorize but one organic structure through which the church accomplishes its work. That is the local church, the congregation. There is, in the word of God, no organization larger, no organization smaller, no organization other than the congregation. Here is God's established order. Phil. 1:1, "Paul and Timotheus, the servants of Jesus Christ, to all the saints in Christ Jesus which are at Philippi, with the bishops and deacons:". Acts 14:23. "And when they had ordained them elders in every church, and had prayed with fasting, they commended them to the Lord, on whom they believed." Here is the authority for the medium through which Christians are to accomplish the mission of the Lord's church. A local congregation of the church of Christ is all and the only organization authorized to carry on Christian work or worship, and such organization excludes each and every other organization for the purpose of carrying on religious work or worship, whether the same be evangelistic, missionary or otherwise. This is the ground upon which we have stood, and upon which we will stand. God has specified the organization of the church as definitely as he has specified the kind of music that we are to use in his praise and the elements of the Lord's table. And for the church to build any other organization is to go beyond divine arrangements and divine authority. "Whosoever transgresseth, and abideth not in the doctrine of Christ, hath not God." II John 9. "Now these things brethren," Paul said, "I have in a figure transferred to myself and Apollos for your sakes; that in us ye might learn not to go beyond the things which are written;". I Cor. 4:6.

WOOD'S FIRST NEGATIVE

Brethren moderators, brother Cogdill, ladies and gentlemen:

I rejoice that in the providence of God and through the invitation of the elders and the preacher of the Homewood congregation in this city that I am privileged to appear before you tonight in the negative of this proposition. I regret exceedingly the tragic incident this afternoon that brought sorrow to people, and I sincerely hope that the suffering may be alleviated, whether it be among Christians or among those who are of the world, immediately.

I concur heartily in the announcements that have been made regarding our conduct here and I can assure you here and now that it's my purpose to conduct my part of this discussion in a fashion which I hope will be edifying and interesting and profitable for all.

With much of brother Cogdill's speech I am in complete agreement. In fact, I should say that the first half of it was largely a waste of his time. No one calls in question these matters which he discussed regarding the authority of the scriptures, the all-sufficiency of the church of our Lord in the matter of performing the work which God gave the church to do. That is not an issue in this debate and will not be. And so he's wasted his time in so far as his discussion of those matters in this particular debate would be concerned.

It is my purpose to get at the issue quickly and I know of no better way to do that than to submit some questions that are calculated to pin-point what is really the issue here. I shall read them and then pass them to him and retain a copy and he may reply to them when and if he sees fit. No. 1. Can all the needs of a fatherless child be adequately supplied without such a child being a part of or having a home? No. 2. Is the congregation the only organization which may scripturally function in benevolence when the means are provided by the church and is the congregation an orphanage and an old-folks home without further organization? No. 3. When the church builds an orphan home for the care of fatherless children, or an old folks home for needy aged people, is it building another church, or a home? No. 4. When the church builds this home and utilizes it in discharging its duty to the fatherless and needy, is it functioning through an organization apart from the church? No. 5. If in such a case the church is functioning through an organization apart from the church, do the elders properly exercise control of this additional organization which is no part of the church? No. 6. If you insist that the church is not functioning through another organization in such a case, give chapter and verse where God authorizes the church to serve as a home. No. 7. When elders place children in a private home already in existence and supports them there, please, tell us whose work is it to provide the actual care; the church or the home? If the home is the church working through another institution, whose obligation is it to control and supervise such children—The home in which they are placed, or the elders of the church who placed them there?

No. 8, and the last: Is there anything inherently sinful in (a) incorporating a church, (b) a business, (c) a home? If no, could the church contribute to an incorporated home which is in need? Now, if the moderator, please, will come and get these so I won't have to leave the microphone, I shall appreciate it. Thank you, sir. These are the questions now, that we shall expect brother Cogdill to deal with when he comes before us.

May I say now, friends, again that there is no issue with reference to what is to be determined in matters of violating the scripture or how to establish scriptural authority. On all of these matters we are agreed, and in so far as his chart was concerned on the Lord's Supper, I accept that without question and there is nothing involved on the chart that is involved in the discussion tonight And the same thing is true with reference to establishing organizations apart from the church to do the work which God gave the church to do as an organization. No question about that at all. As a matter of fact, we may simply discount all of those matters, because that's not an issue.

Now I should like to have his chart, please. What is the issue? That was chart No. 2, I believe, and if I may have it quickly, please, we shall notice here on this.

He has on the chart what the church is, and it's divine in origin, exists by authority of Christ, regulated only by the scriptures, with elders as overseers. And he says it's the obligation of that church now to provide a place for shelter and the necessities of life, such as food and cloth-

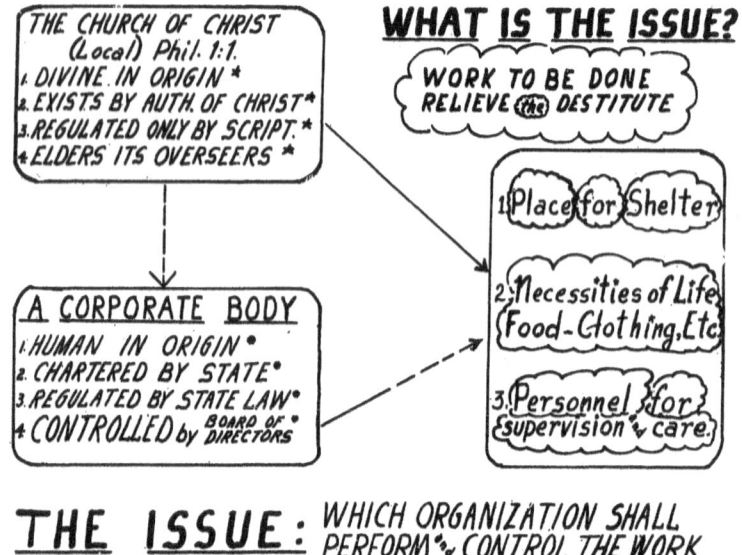

ing and so forth, and the personnel for supervision and care. But now watch, friends, brother Cogdill is doing exactly here that which he is opposing in this debate. He's simply setting up a home which, of necessity, must be operated apart from the church and must possess a license issued it by the state in order to supply that very care. Now I'm going to prove to you that he cannot and will not admit that such is the function of the church as the church.

For example, notice on his chart here he has necessities of life; food, clothing and so forth. Now, under that "so forth" would be included such matters as secular education. Such matters as manual training, or training in the various skills. Brother Cogdill is on record in his book *Contending for the Faith* in which he positively states that the church cannot function in that field. Watch, please, I'll cite his book here *Walking By Faith*, pages 8 and 9, in which he says, "It's not the business of the church to provide and serve as a guide in recreational activity such as church basketball teams, church sponsored skating parties and swimming parties and so on." Then he says further, "The church is not a court or school of domestic relations." And further, "Secular education, the teaching of secular subjects such as Science, Mathematics, History, Literature, does not come within the scope of the mission and work of the church and should be no part of its work." Yet he said it here. Either he must admit that the elders are directing such work, or else he must maintain that it would be wrong to provide orphan children with a secular education. Now I ask him to clarify that. If this is the church here, then it puts the elders in business, and if it's not the church then he's in conflict with his own position. But about that more as we pass along.

Then, next, he informs us that the corporation is not the institution that provides the care. And he says that the home and the institution are two separate and distinct things. I ask you to keep that in mind, please, until we come to these matters on our chart, because we've anticipated that such would be his position and we shall deal with it fully.

Now, let us look at his proposition for a moment. In the first place, note that he affirms nothing. Brother Cogdill is before you tonight making negative speeches in the affirmative. Now, if that surprises you, you may be certain that there would be no other way for him to hold his position and do otherwise, for he offers no plan for church cooperation in benevolence that involves the setting up of a home. He's told you repeatedly in his first speech that only the church may function in that capacity. Watch carefully now this, and I ask him to deal with it when he appears before you. No. 1. He endorses none of the homes that are being cooperatively supported by churches of Christ today. In the second place, he has no plan to establish a home of this nature which he can support and endorse. And while I'm on that question I ask him to designate one place where this situation which he has described tonight exists. No. 3. His position makes such a home impossible.

Now, let it be clearly understood that I'm not before you tonight for the purpose of defending a human institution as opposed to the divine. When brother Cogdill seeks to leave the impression with you that I'm in the defense of human organizations apart from divine ones, he'll be missing the point completely. In the second place, I'm not before you for the purpose of alleging that it's right for a church or churches to delegate any work which God gave the church to do to another organization. In the third place, that the church is inadequate to accomplish any work which God designed for it to do. What are we doing? We are not defending human institutions. We're not arguing that the church may sacrifice its opportunity to perform the work which God gave to the church to do as a church. And we do not claim that the church is inadequate. Get it, friends; the all-sufficiency of the church is not an issue in this debate. Our position, briefly put, which we shall defend, and it will be necessary to make affirmative speeches in the negative, is that the church and home are both divine institutions. That each is all sufficient in the field of activity which God designed for it. And we must not confuse them. This is precisely what brother Cogdill does as we shall now engage to show.

I should like to have the lights dimmed please and my chart No. 1 placed on the screen.

Observe here, we have the distinct realms that are characteristic of the world today. There is the civil government which God designed to function in that capacity and our instruction thereto is set out in Romans 13 particularly. Then, secondly, there is the home and the home may be either a natural home or it may be a legal home. If it's a natural home it has parents over it, and if it's a legal home, it has men who stand in the place of parents, those who are *en loco parentis* to the children. Then, next, there is the spiritual realm, the realm of the church. Observe, please, that in the first realm there is the realm of political activity. Our civil obligation's there. In the second, there is the realm of the family. And in the third, the spiritual realm, which is the realm of the church.

CHART NO. 1

DISTINCT REALMS

STATE

```
CIVIL GOVERNMENT
ROM. 13: 1-7.
```

HOME

```
        FAMILY
PARENTS          BOARD
        GAL. 4: 12.
```

CHURCH

```
SPIRITUAL
MT. 16: 18.
```

Now let's have chart 1A, please.

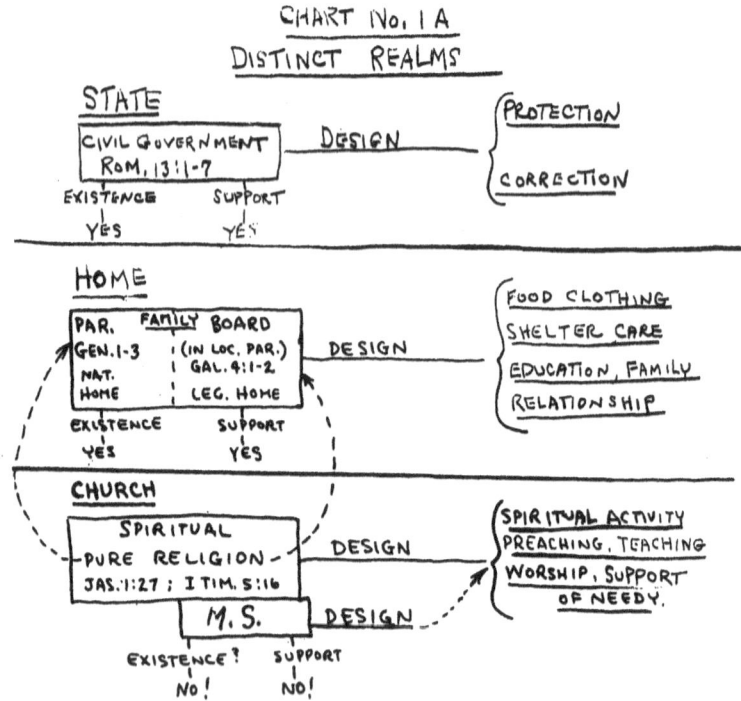

This is a more advanced part on this, more complicated, but it's the same idea. Observe first the civil government and then the home and then the church. It is the function of the civil government to provide protection and correction and its existence is unquestioned. Since its existence is unquestioned then, of course, its right to support is likewise not an issue. The next place, there is the design of the home to supply food and clothing and shelter and care and education and a family relationship and the other intangibles that are characteristic of such a relationship. Now, as we pointed out, it may be a natural home or it may be a restored or re-established home. That is, it may have natural parents or those who stand in the place of them.

Then, next, there is the church of spiritual activity and

BENEVOLENT ORGANIZATIONS 33

it, too, is entitled to support. Its purpose is to provide spiritual activity, preaching, teaching, worship, support of the needy and so on. Now that, friends, will indicate the three realms that are authorized by our Lord, and each of which has a right to exist.

Now then let's have our next chart please; chart No. 3. I want you to note that when these brethren reason with reference to other matters they recognize that distinction. In just a moment we will have that chart, but here, the Church Is Not A Substitute.

CHART NO. 2

CHURCH NOT A SUBSTITUTE

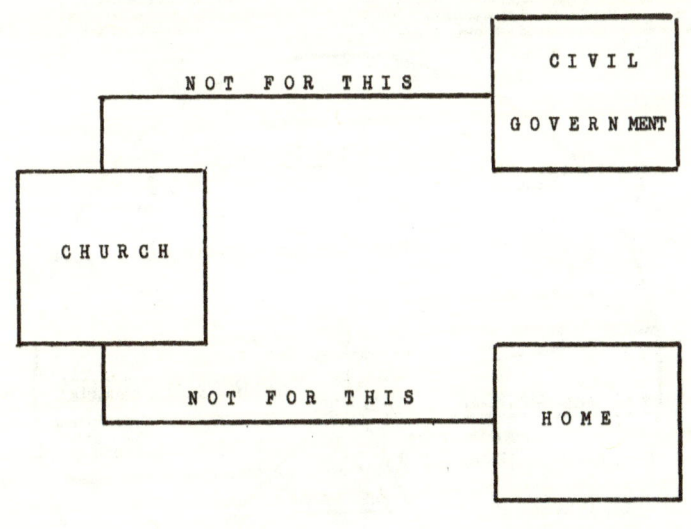

SUBSTITUTE: "A PERSON OR THING PUT IN THE PLACE OF ANOTHER; ONE REPLACING ANOTHER."

It's not a substitute for civil government; it's not a substitute for anything except its own self. It's not a substitute for the home. It's just as wrong, and would be just as wrong to try to make a civil government out of the

CHART NO. 3
Page 24, Gospel Guardian - Special Issue

24 ——— DUTIES AND RESPONSIBILITIES OF EACH ———

THE CHURCH AND THE INDIVIDUAL CHRISTIAN
Robert C. Welch, Louisville, Kentucky

There is needless widespread confusion over the difference between the church and the individual Christian. This confusion does not arise with reference to the primary acts of obedience that salvation might be granted. All seem to agree that the individual must obey whether the church as a whole be right or wrong. The confusion does not exist in the matter of the judgment before Christ. All are agreed that there is a difference, that the individual will stand or fall on his own action or merit even though the church may be just the opposite, that in the judgment the individual's actions will not be judged to be the church in action and the church's actions will not be considered as the individual's actions. See Ephesians 5:25-27; Mark 16:15-16; 1 Corinthians 5:10.

The confusion exists in the realm of the duties, work and organization among Christians and churches. The same theory, though opposed in application, is held by two erroneous and extreme parties within the churches of Christ. Those who advocate that churches fulfil their obligations by contributing to and operating through human institutions base their theory on the proposition that THE CHURCH CAN DO ANYTHING WHICH THE INDIVIDUAL CHRISTIAN CAN DO. The other extreme party contends that individuals cannot contribute to and operate through any human institution which might be classed as religious in nature, basing its contention on the proposition that THE INDIVIDUAL CHRISTIAN CAN DO NOTHING EXCEPT THAT WHICH THE CHURCH CAN DO. The former theory has been promulgated by many, possibly the outstanding promoter being Brother G. C. Brewer. The latter theory has many promoters, possibly the outstanding one of this generation being Brother Carl Ketcherside.

The Christian's Relationships
The individual Christian has many relationships of life ordained of God with conditions and regulations set

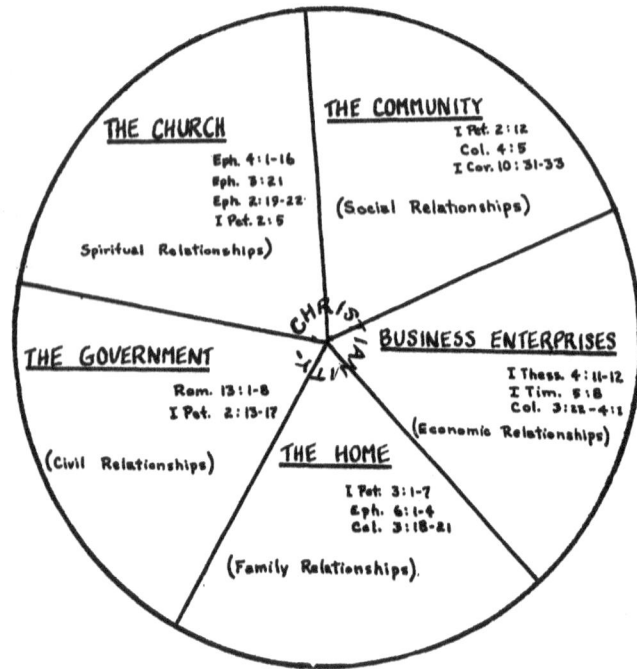

church as it would be to try to make a home out of the church. That is precisely what brother Cogdill and those who stand with him seek to do.

Now let us note our next chart which will indicate to you that even these brethren recognize the distinction. Here is a chart that appeared in the special issue of the *Gospel Guardian* and you will notice that they recognize the distinction between the church and the government and the home. Now when they were writing on this they were dealing with the individual and the church. But that shows they recognize a distinct difference there and yet brother Cogdill has labored tonight to show you that the church may take over the functions of the home and serve as a home. So then observe that distinction.

Now then let's have the lights for a moment. Now, friends, we've shown you that the distinctions that God made must be allowed to exist, that we cannot confuse these distinct realms. I want now to make an argument, and I trust that you will notice these points carefully. I think there's no question but what the obligation to the needy is recognized by all. In James 1:27, which incidentally this special issue of the Guardian says applies to the church, tells us that it's our obligation to "visit the fatherless and widows in their affliction." And in I Timothy 5:16 the apostle Paul plainly and clearly designates the church as obligated in that field.

Now my definition of a home. Here is the Winston Dictionary for Schools, definition: "One's fixed residence or dwelling place; hence, the unit of society formed by a family living together." What is a home: It's a unit of society. Now watch please: A child must be a part of or have a home, either the original or restored, in order to be provided for adequately. (2) These needs include food, clothing, shelter, supervision, medical aid and care, education and spiritual training. No. 3, the church is obligated to supply the funds with which to provide these needs. 4, when these funds have been supplied by the church, the child still needs and must have a home. Now get that, please. When the church has supplied the funds, there is yet all that remains to be done regarding the home. 5th, the church is not a home. It does not perform the functions of a home. When it has done its work, all the work which is characteristic of the home remains to be done. It follows, therefore, that the men who establish the home, though they may serve as elders of the church, do not perform the functions of elders in operating the home which the child must have. Because it's not a function of elders to serve over two divine institutions.

The establishment of the home and its operation are matters of which the state takes cognizance, and it must be done in harmony with existing laws. When such a home has been established, the church may take notice of its needs and assist in supplying them.

Now further, whether the churches does so or not, will be determined by its ability, the needs of the home, and whether such a contribution will be used to the glory of God and the advancement of His cause. Now, friends, I have shown you this: (1) That there are three distinct realms that must be recognized. (2) That one of these realms is the church and the other the home. (3) That they must not be confused. The Catholics seek to turn the church into a civil government. Brother Cogdill would seek to turn the church into a home. God placed elders over only one divine institution, the church. He would put them over two, the church and the home.

Now let us prove the right of the orphan home to exist. Let us please, have chart No. 4. And turn the lights down, please. Thank you.

I should like for my good brethren who write for the Guardian and allege that I change positions from debate to debate to take notice of the fact that this chart has been introduced in every debate that I've held on this, and it's the basic argument that I've introduced. Observe here that the child's original home is on this side.

Then we have the representation there of the broken home. And then, over on the other side, the orphan home which is the restoration of the home that the child had and lost. Now, ladies and gentlemen, if it's right for a child to have a home to start with, and it loses that home,

CHART NO. 4.

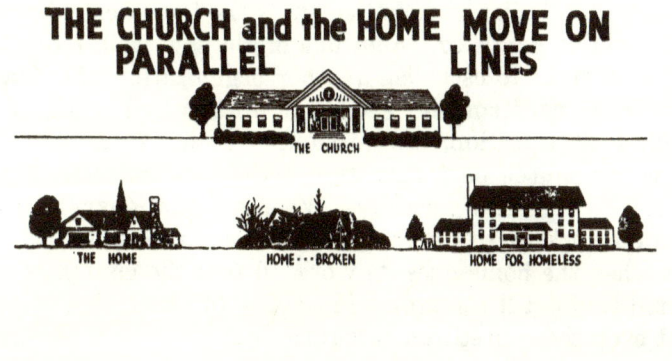

if a group of Christian brethren get together and establish a home for that child, and place it in it and the church recognizes its obligation to support the needy, in that home, then this obligation and the responsibility is exactly the same as it was before the home was destroyed. Get it, please. The child's original home existed by divine authority. Now then when that home is broken, if there are Christian brethren sufficiently interested in the welfare of destitute children to re-establish a home, then the obligation that the church sustains to the original home is the obligation which the church sustains to the re-established home. Get it now, this orphan home that's re-established, is not the church because it's performing the work of a home and not a church. It's strange indeed that brethren cannot see that.

Secondly, observe that it's not in conflict with the church because it's not performing the function of a church as a church. It's performing the function of a home as a home.

It's not in conflict with the home that was destroyed, because that home is gone. What is the orphan home? It is the re-establishment of the home which the child had and lost, established according to state authority and statutes.

Now that, ladies and gentlemen, is the issue here tonight. Let it not be confused. Someone might say, well, all right, if it's all right to establish another organization, the home, in order to perform the benevolent work, why not establish another organization, the missionary society? Simply because the church performs its function and as such serves as its own missionary society. When the missionary society does its work there's nothing else left for the church to do. But when the home does its work all that the church is expected to do still remains. I'm going to prove this to you that even these brethren recognize that.

Now then our next chart. Chart No. 5, please.

CHART #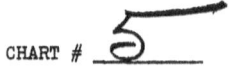

CHART NO. 5
(QUOTATION FROM POTTER HOME MESSENGER)
August, 1957

"Reports from our little girls who are away in private homes are good - four have returned. One family group of four, two boys and two girls, will not return to Potter. They came to us about two years ago, following the death of their mother. They now have a new mother and the family group is happily reunited. Another family group of four children had high hopes of returning to their former home, but the mother's condition was such that the doctor advised against it. Of course, the children are disappointed, but they love their home here and will continue to look forward to the time when their mother will be well and they can be reunited."

Here it is. And I should like for you to read over there that which has been circled around. I cannot see it here close enough to read it. I should like for you to notice that that points out that there were some children in the Potter Home, yes, I think I can see it now. "Reports from our little girls who are away in private homes are good. Four have returned. One family group of four, two boys and two girls will not return to Potters. They came to us about two years of age following the death of their mother. They now have a new mother and the family group is happily reunited. Another family group of four children had high hopes of returning to their former homes but the mother's condition was such that the doctors advised against it. Of course, the children are disappointed, but they love their home here and will continue to look forward to the time when their mother will be well and they can be returned." That, ladies and gentlemen, is basically the purpose of these orphan homes. To replace the home that doesn't exist until such a time as it may be restored.

Now let's have our chart No. 6.

This, friends, will certainly interest you. Here is an editorial from the *Gospel Guardian* which appeared just a few weeks ago. I believe we're not able to get it all on the chart. That is the top where I have the date, I believe. But at any rate that can be checked if you're interested. Let us note now, what is here said. After making an appeal to the brethren for some home to take these children here's what brother Tant says, "Both the mother and the father, who is incapacitated and unable to provide for the children, have already signed the necessary papers committing"—Actually I cannot see it—"committing the children into the custody of the elders of the congregation where they live, to find a proper home. The children are four in number, two boys, age 11 and 6, and two girls, 7 and 4. Once the elders are satisfied as to the ability and character of the prospective parents, the adoption can be arranged legally and swiftly." Then he said, "Let this fact be clear: The purpose of this article is to seek to find a home for all those four children." Now they've got what God provided for them, brother Cogdill. Why if the elders have them, the church has them in its possession. They have everything that you say that the Lord has provided. Here brother Tant is appealing for somebody to come and take these away from God's organization that was designed to provide for them.

Now that, ladies and gentlemen, is the reason we tell you

CHART NO. 6
Editorial Page, Gospel Guardian, Sept. 19, 1957

EDITORIAL

DO YOU WANT A FAMILY

Nearly two years ago we were asked to help find a home for five boys, aged five to twelve, whose mother was dying of cancer and whose father was serving a life term in the penitentiary. A brief notice of the matter was inserted on this page, asking if any of our readers could take one or more of the boys. We stated that it would hardly be likely that anybody would be able to take the entire family, although such would be highly desirable. We underestimated the attitude and ability of our readers. In response to that one request a full dozen families offered to adopt all five boys; and enough others offered to take one or more that, had they been available, more than eighty orphan children could have been placed in Christian homes from this one article.

Subsequent events revealed that even though the father was in the penitentiary, he still had legal custody of his children (after the death of the mother). When it came to a final show-down he refused to permit the children to be adopted, and instead placed them with various members of his family — some of whom were members of the Catholic church and some of whom were members of no church. We were thus thwarted in our desire and effort to place these boys in Christian homes and under the care and control of faithful Christians.

But we shall never forget the thrill that came to us when we saw how generously and how quickly sympathetic Christian people were willing to respond to the needs of these helpless children. Not a single person wrote in suggesting that these unfortunate boys, robbed of their mother by death and of their father by something worse than death, be placed in an institution—regimented, regulated, and life-long stamped for life with the fears, frustrations, and life-long feelings of insecurity which are the inevitable heritage in a greater or lesser degree of every institutionalized child, no matter how great the efforts made to make the institution "home-like".

Once again, we come to our readers with an appeal in behalf of helpless children. This case is similar in some respects to the one of two years ago: a Christian mother is dying of cancer, and before she crosses over she is extremely anxious to see her four sweet children in the home of some Christian father and mother who will love them, shield them, protect them, and care for them as their own. She is not interested merely in knowing that her children will have food and clothes and shelter; there is little chance that any child in America need suffer for lack of these essentials. But it is the other and more important factor that weighs on her heart— the matter of love, Christian teaching, and the normal, happy, secure home life which permits a child to develop into the mature Christian man or woman a devoted mother desires.

Both the mother and the father (who is incapacitated and unable to provide for the children) have already signed the necessary papers, committing the children into the custody of the elders of the congregation where they live to find a proper home. The children are four in number: two boys, aged eleven and six, and two girls, aged seven and four. Once the elders are satisfied as to the ability and character of the prospective parents, the adoption can be arranged legally and swiftly. The children are normal, healthy, and bright. They deserve a home— a home with a loving and tender mother, and a father who is a "father" and not a "superintendent."

Let this fact be clear—the purpose of this article is to seek to find a home for all four children, where they can be kept in a unit, and grow to maturity as a family. There are several faithful Christian couples in the home congregation who are eager to take one or two of the children, but it is desirable, if possible, to keep the family together. At least, the elders are going to make an effort to find some Christian family able to take the entire group. If they fail in that, they will put the children in different homes right in their own congregation, thus allowing them to grow up knowing and associating with one another, even if they cannot be in the same family. If you cannot, therefore, take all four children, do not write!

Have you ever visited an "orphan home"? You ought to do so one day. It will wring your heart unless you are made of stone. The sweet, eager children will swarm around you, clinging to your hands and arms talking to you, competing for your attention, crawling into your lap when you are seated, putting their little arms around your neck, and squeezing with all the strength they can muster. They are usually shy and timid at first, but once you display even the slightest sign of friendliness and interest, they will swarm all over you. They are starved, literally STARVED, for the normal love and affection that is a child's natural heritage. No matron on earth, be she ever so warm-hearted and loving, can take the place of a "mother". And these words are in no sense intended as a criticism of any matron in any orphan home. The matrons we have known are, for the most part, truly consecrated, and are giving their very best for the unfortunate children under their care. The fault lies not with them but with the system under which they are trying to serve. An "institution" is not a home, and never can be. No child in an institution, even the best and finest institution on earth, can have the normal home relationships, the love, the security and feeling of "belonging" that go with a family.

How monstrous the cruelty of a man who would deny to an innocent child the tender love of a mother's kiss, the strong security of a father's arms to protect him—and would place him instead in the impersonal and regimented custody of an institution! His must be a heart that is cold and merciless. We have yet to see one word from any superintendent, matron, or worker in an orphan home

that these brethren can't establish any kind of a home. Because here is the situation that they are faced with. What are they asking for? Somebody to come and get these children. Well, they've got what he said the Lord had provided

BENEVOLENT ORGANIZATIONS

for them. I tell you, ladies and gentlemen, it is the most untenable position that in many years of religious controversy that I have ever met in my life.

Now then let's have chart No. 7.

CHART No. 7

"WHAT THE CHURCH CANNOT DO" — COGDILL
IT CANNOT: (Pg. Nos. from W.B.F.)

1. BUILD ANYTHING EXCEPT ANOTHER CHURCH — PAGE 77.
2. ENGAGE IN BUSINESS, COMMERCE — — — — — — PAGE 8.
3. SUPPLY RECREATION — — — — — — — — — — PAGE 8.
4. TEACH ANY SECULAR SUBJECTS — — — — — — PAGE 8.
5. REAR CHILDREN — — — — — — — — — — — PAGE 31.
6. USE ANY MEDIUM BUT THE CHURCH — — — — — PAGE 33.
7. ACT THROUGH ANY ORGANIZATION EXCEPT THE CONGREGATION — — — — PAGE 34.
8. EXCERCISE CONTROL (THROUGH ITS ELDERS) OVER ANY HOME, SUCH AS "CATHOLICISM" — — — — PAGE 40
9. THROUGH ITS ELDERS, OVERSEE ANYTHING EXCEPT THE CHURCH — — — — — PAGE 42.

I'm going to show you that it's impossible for brother Cogdill to set up any kind of a home, according to his present position. In the first place, he tells us on page 77 *Walking by Faith* and all of those pages now, indications are from that book, that the church cannot build anything except another church. That's on page 77. On page 8 he said the church cannot engage in business or commerce. But it's the function of the home to engage in business. But the church cannot engage in business, therefore, it can't operate as a home. Next, on page 8, he says the church cannot supply recreation, but it's necessary to provide recreation for a home. Therefore, the church cannot provide that which the home needs. In the next place, page 8, it cannot teach any secular subjects, but it's a function and a necessity of the home to teach secular subjects. On page 31, he says the church can't rear children. Can't rear children, mind you, yet he affects to tell us that the church can set up and operate a home as a church without any organization except the church.

Was a man ever more vulnerable in his life than this. Next, page 33, it cannot use any medium but the church throught which to operate. Not only can it not establish any other organization but it can't even use any other medium. Therefore, it can't use the natural home, much less the restablished home. In the next place, page 34, it cannot act through any organization except the congregation. Therefore, it couldn't act through a private home because it's another organization. In the next place, page 40, he says the elders cannot exercise control over any home; that when elders try to exercise control over a home that that's Catholicism. Brother Cogdill, are the elders over this home here? Do these children even have a home that you have set up here? If they do, are the elders over it? And are they acting as Roman Catholics?

And then next, page 42, it cannot let its elders oversee anything except the church. Now then, one of two things are true: Either this is the church or it is not. If it's not the church that he has on this chart here, then it follows that the elders can set up something else besides the church and, if it is the church, then he surrenders the contention that you change the church into a home. That, ladies and gentlemen, is the real issue in this debate. Now let us have the lights, please, and I apologize to brother Cogdill for the fact that it's so dark, and I hope by tomorrow night lights may be provided for your notes. I can recognize the difficulty that's involved here.

Now, friends, let us see what we've shown you. We've shown you that the church is not a home. We've shown you that it sustains an obligation, however, to homes. We've shown you that these homes may be of two classifications, that is, they may be natural or they may be re-established. Now then, in order that you may see that it's necessary for these homes to have state supervision, let me just simply read to you briefly a statement from the minimum standards of the state of Alabama. Inasmuch as we are in Alabama, then, a word with reference to what is required here. Page 9, of this booklet, the Minimum Standards: "All societies, agencies and institutions, public or private, except those under state ownership and control receiving or caring for dependent and neglected or delinquent and minor children, shall be required to obtain annually a license from the state department of public welfare." And that's true even if it were a foster home—Even if it were not a legal home. Even a foster home, if it takes children in and provides 24 hours per day care, even a foster home that doesn't even adopt them must be supplied with a license.

I am in position to establish that by irrefutable evidence. And so, friends, the issue is clearly before you. I thank you.

Cogdill's Second Affirmative

Gentlemen moderators, brother Woods, ladies and gentlemen:

I'm happy to appear before you again to resume the argument that I didn't get through with a while ago but before I get into that, for fear that I might forget them a little later on, I want to give brother Woods an answer to his questions. He likes to ask questions and I like to answer them, so we're both happy.

No. 1, Can all the needs of a fatherless child be adequately supplied without that child having or being a part of a home? One answered: If you mean by a home a place of shelter, No. 2, Is the congregation the only organization which may scripturally function in benevolence when the needs are provided by the church? Is the congregation an orphanage, an old folk's home, without further organization? The congregation is the only organization that can do what God commands the church to do and if, by the home in your question, you mean furnish a place of shelter for the destitute, then the congregation can do that and it's the only organization God ever gave to do it. 3, When the church builds an o r p h a n home for the care of fatherless children or an old folks home for the needy aged people, is it building another church or a home? Well, that depends again on what you mean by a home. You are going to have to define your term home, brother Woods. You shift gears on it. One time you make a home mean a place to stay and another time you make it mean a family or a relationship, an entity. Now tell us what you mean in your questions by a home, if you want the question answered forthrightly.

4, When the church builds this home and utilizes it in discharging its duty to the fatherless and the needy, is it functioning through an organization apart from the church? The functional arrangement is exactly the same as the Bible school arrangement, and I can quote you on that. No. 5, If in such a case the church is functioning through an organization apart from the church, can the elders properly exercise control of this additional organization which is no part of the church? They do exactly like they do the functional arrangements of the Bible school, brother Woods. And again, I give you as my authority on it. No. 6, I Timothy 5:16 is the answer. The church is authorized to relieve the destitute. The question was: If you insist that the churches not function through another organization, in such a case give chapter and verse where God authorizes the church to serve as a home. He commanded the church to provide for, to relieve the destitute. That includes a place, and if that's what you mean by a home, then that's the verse that authorizes it. No. 7, When elders place children in a private home already in existence and support them there, please, tell us; whose work is it to provide the actual care—the church or the home? (b) If the home is the church working through another institution and (c) whose obligation is it to control and supervise such children—The home in which they are placed or the elders of the church who placed them there? The obligation of the church and the elders of the church is to oversee the care for which they are responsible to the destitute and any other work that God commanded the church to do.

No. 8, Is there anything inherently sinful in incorporating a church, a business, a home? If no, could the church contribute to an incorporated home which is in need? It's a sinful thing to organize a corporation and give that corporation control of the work of the church—Any part of the work of the church, brother Woods. And I'll be glad to save brother Warren the trip.

We want to resume now exactly where we left off a while ago, if you will get me my chart on authority. We were pointing out that for the churches of Christ to build and maintain human organizations through which to do their work is without divine authority and, therefore, a transgression of the law of God and sinful. But the only thing God has ever commanded is the congregation. God gave us an organization, gave to the church an organization, specified it, and we have the form of that organization and it's abundantly able to do everything that God commanded the church to do. Brother Woods says that the issue in this debate is not the all-sufficency of the church. We are going to find out before we get through with it that that is the issue. That's exactly what he denies—That the organization that God gave the church is not able to do what God commanded the church to do. And don't forget that that is the issue. It has been all the way through—It is now. And we're not going to let him get away from it.

If he believes that the congregation, the organization that God did give the church, is able to do what God commands the church to do then he has no ground upon which to advocate the church building another organization. And that's what he is advocating. That's exactly what his position is. If the church needs to build and can build another organization, then, brother Woods, the one that God gave is not sufficient. If it needs another it doesn't have enough. If it has enough then it doesn't need another. And that brings the issue right down to the pin-point, so that everybody can understand it. God specified the organization of the church as definitely as he specified the music we are to use in His praise and the elements on the Lord's Table.

And we have that pointed out on the chart on Authority and you don't have the right one yet. All right, scriptural authority.

There are two kinds of scriptural authority in the word of God—Generic and specific. God commanded Noah to build the ark, in Genesis 6:14. If he had commanded him simply to make it out of wood then there would have been

SCRIPTURAL AUTHORITY

Commanded	Generic	Specific
ARK (GEN. 6:14)	WOOD	GOPHER
WATER OF CLEANSING (NUMBERS 19:2)	ANIMAL	RED HEIFER WITHOUT SPOT
PRAISE (EPH. 5:18; COL. 3:16)	MUSIC	SING
EVANGELIZE (I TIM. 3:15; I THESS. 1:7-8)	CHURCH (I THESS. 1:1)	ORGANIZATION (CONGREGATION)(PHIL. 1:1)
EDIFY (EPH. 4:16)	CHURCH	ORGANIZATION (CONGRE.)
RELIEVE (I TIM. 5:16)	CHURCH	ORGANIZATION (CONGRE.)

3.

no way to exclude any kind. He could have chosen any that he saw fit. You're familiar with that argument. But God specified gopher wood and eliminated, excluded, every other kind.

God commanded also the water of cleansing in Num. 19:2. If He had simply said it should be the ashes of an animal, then any animal would have sufficed, any that they might have chosen would have been all right and within the scope of the thing God commanded. But he commanded a red heifer without spot or blemish. A brown one wouldn't do and no other kind of an animal but a heifer would do. God specified, and eliminated every other kind.

Then in praise; Eph. 5:18-19, Col. 3:16, God commanded that we should praise him in the church—By music. If he had simply said music then either kind, instrumental or vocal, would have been within the scope of the thing commanded. But God specified the kind that he wanted and the kind he specified was singing.

Then, again, God commands the church to evangelize.

It's the pillar and ground of the truth. I Timothy 3:15; again I Thess. 1:7-8,—The example of Paul's commendation of the Thessalonian church. The church at Thessalonica carried out God's commandment but God made that commandment a specific one. He didn't simply give it to the church to be carried out in any way that the church saw fit. He specified the organization through which it was to be done and that organization is the congregation. God gave the church an organization, *a specific organization,* to do the thing that he commanded the church to do and that excludes every other organization. The church has no right to build any other organization to do evangelistic work for the reason that God excluded every other.

The same thing exactly is true on edifying. The church is commanded to edify itself in Eph. 4:16. The idea is that God commanded the church to do that but he didn't leave that commandment generic. He gave the church a specific organization through which to do it and that organization is the local congregation. God gave the church another command to relieve the destitute, I Timothy 5:16. But he didn't leave it generically then. He commanded the church to do it, but he specified the organization through which it is to be done and the fact that God specified the organization to do what the church is commanded to do eliminates every other organization just exactly like gopher eliminates every other kind of wood, exactly like ashes of a red heifer eliminates every other kind of animal, exactly like singing eliminates every other kind of music. Help me again there. Let's get the next one.

This time we want to call your attention in the matter of authority to essentials and expedients. The command is to teach, Matt. 28:18-20. God commanded that the gospel should be taught. And any other message is condemned, and the man who teaches it is accursed, but an expedient has left to our choice.

Again, God commands us to baptize. Matt. 28:18-20. That commandment is immersion in water, and any other would be a matter of whether you do it in a class, privately, or publicly. There is a wide deal of difference between the essentials in carrying out the command and that which God

•ESSENTIALS AND EXPEDIENCIES•

Commandment	ESSENTIALS	Expediencies
TEACH MATT. 28:18-20	GOSPEL	CLASS - PRIVATELY PUBLICLY
BAPTIZE MATT. 28:18-20	IMMERSION IN WATER	NATURAL OR ARTIFICIAL POOL
LORD'S SUPPER I COR. 11:23-27	ELEMENTS - Bread and Fruit of Vine	TABLE - CONTAINERS
ASSEMBLY HEB. 10:25	FIRST DAY OF WEEK	HOUR - PLACE
RELIEVE I TIM. 5:16	CHURCH (CONGREGATION)	METHOD-MEANS-MODE Buy, Rent, Gratis

act would be excluded by that very specific thing that God commanded to be baptism. A matter of expediency or choice in the realm of human wisdom or judgment would be whether it would be in a natural or in an artificial pool.

Then we are commanded to observe the Lord's Supper. The elements are the bread and the fruit of the vine. Those elements are specified. They are essential to the observance of the supper. Any other elements would not be the Lord's Supper but whether or not you had it on a table, or what kind of table you put it on, or the number of containers, would certainly be a matter of expediency because God has not specified. That is not a matter of essentiality.

Then again, the assembly over here. Heb. 10:25. God has commanded the church to assemble: To assemble on the first day of the week and not to neglect that assembly. The hour and the place of assembly would be a matter of expediency, but the day is not a matter of expediency.

Finally, God commanded the church to relieve the destitute. The church, the congregation, is the matter of essentiality. God gave the church the organization that's essential. We have no right to substitute anything for it, anymore than we have a right to substitute another day of the week, or the elements on the Lord's table, or another action for baptism, or another message for the gospel. The methods, the means, the mode, whether they buy a place, rent a place, whether it is furnished gratis,—how the church provides the care for the needy or the destitute would be a matter of expediency and we're not going to let brother Woods confuse the expediency of the particular method by which it's done with the organization that does it. We are going to keep him very clearly pointed to that thing all the way through this discussion. Now then, to aids and additions.

· AIDS AND ADDITIONS ·

COMMANDMENT	AIDS	ADDITIONS
SING	BOOKS - LIGHTS LEADER - ETC.	INSTRUMENTAL MUSIC (another KIND of MUSIC)
BAPTIZE	BAPTISTRY	SPRINKLING (another KIND of ACTION)
ASSEMBLE TO BREAK BREAD	BUILDING, LIGHTS SEATS, HEAT, ETC.	SATURDAY (ANOTHER DAY)
PREACH GOSPEL	RADIO - LITERATURE, ETC.	MISSIONARY SOCIETY (ANOTHER ORGANIZATION)
RELIEVE THE DESTITUTE	BUILDING, CARE NECESSARIES	BENEVOLENT SOCIETY (ANOTHER ORGANIZATION)
EDIFY ITSELF	PLACE - FACILITIES TEACHERS	SUN. SCHOOL SOCIETY (ANOTHER ORGANIZATION)
5.		5.

The command is to sing. Aids in that singing would be books, lights, leader, etc. Addition would be instrumental music because you have another kind of music.

The command is to baptize. The aid in carrying out that

command would be a baptistry but an addition would be sprinkling; another kind of action.

The command to assemble and to break bread—The build-and and the lights, the seats, etc., would be aids in executing the thing that God commanded, but Saturday, another day, would be going beyond. It would be an addition to what God said do.

Then again—Preach the gospel. Whether we do it over the radio, by literature, or by word of mouth would be simply a matter of means or aids in carrying out the thing God commanded. But to build a missionary society, another organization, would be to add to what God commanded and, therefore, to transgress God's law.

Then again, God commanded the church to relieve the destitute. The building in which that shelter might be provided, the care or the personnel to care and supervise and to give them the attention that they need and the necessaries of life that have to be furnished and how these things are provided, would all be matters of expediency; aids in executing the commandment. But a benevolent society is another organization that adds to the organization God authorized. Just like the missionary society adds to the organization that God gave the church to preach the gospel.

Again, God commands the church to edify itself. The place where it might carry on that work, the facilities necessary in carrying it on, the teachers to teach; all would be matters, or means, or methods, or aids, in executing the command. But the Sunday School Society would be another organization. What I want to point out to you is that another organization to do benevolent work, when God has given the church an organization, is exactly in the same category with adding instrumental music, with a d d i n g another day, with adding the missionary society, and a Sunday school society. Why, did God give the church the right to build another organization? And we're talking not about what individuals provide, or what the brethren individually might get together and provide. The proposition, brother Woods, reads that "the churches of Christ" have a right to build another organization, a benevolent organization, separate and apart from the church—to build and maintain it.

That's exactly what we're discussing, and that's w h a t you'..e going to discuss with me. Let's just keep that thing clear. We're not talking about what the brethren can get together and do. We're talking about what God gave the church the authority to do and to build. And I'm insisting that God gave the church authority to build nothing except the church. Where is the passage, brother Woods, where God authorized the church of the Lord to build anything or to restore anything but the church? Now give us the passage; that's what we want. And when you find it in the word of God all of your pictures won't be needed. We'll close the debate and go home when you find the passage in which God authorizes the church to build anything but the church; or to restore anything but the church. That's what we want. That's what we want and don't forget it.

What has God commanded the church to do that includes a human organization as a permissible aid; or a necessary or essential element? Why can't a congregation do it? That's the idea. He didn't tell us what the church couldn't furnish. Why, we pointed out to you that the church could furnish a place. And give me my chart on What The Issue Is again.

We pointed out that the church could furnish a place. Does brother Woods mean to say that the congregation under its elders could not rent a house, or buy a house, for the care of the destitute; to furnish them shelter? Is he trying to tell us that the church couldn't buy a home for destitute children, in the sense of a house, or a place, in which to shelter them? Why certainly he woudn't take that kind of a position.

But he gets up here and talks about the home and restoring the home. And one time he makes it mean a place where you live, a domicile, and the next time he makes it mean a relationship, an entity. Well, what is the home anyway? And we'll get to that in a moment.

I call your attention right now on this matter of authority to Matt. 7:21-23. Jesus said, "Not everyone that saith unto me, Lord, Lord, shall enter into the k i n g d o m of heaven; but he that doeth the will of my father which is in heaven. Many will say to me in that day, Lord, Lord, have we not prophesied in thy name? and in thy name have cast out devils? and in thy name done many wonderful works? And then will I profess unto them I never knew you: depart from me, ye that work iniquity." That word, iniquity, Mr. Thayer tells us, the word "anomia", means the condition of 1—"one without law, either because he is ignorant of it or violating it. 2—"A contempt and violation of the law; iniquity or wickedness." Here are men rejected in the judgment—not because they had not worked, but because they had done their works not in harmony with the will of the Lord. They had even professedly worked in his name but they had not worked in accordance with his will and Jesus condemns them for that very reason.

God commands the church, the congregation, to relieve the destitute. I Tim. 5:16. I wonder if there is anything in the divine record that teaches us where the church ever did that. Did the church ever carry on the work of relieving the poor? Well, in Acts, chapter two, I read a very significant passage. The record says, "And all that believed (verse 44) were together, and had all things common; and sold their possessions and goods, and parted them to all men, as every man had need." They took care of the needy in the city of Jerusalem there after the church began, and there isn't anything that indicates that another organization was built by the church to do it. That's what brother Woods is under obligation to find for us, if he's going to defend it by the word of God. Then in Acts 4 beginning with verse 32, "the multitude of them that believed were of one heart and of one soul: neither said any of them that ought of the things which he possessed was his own; but they had all things common. And with great power gave the apostles witness of the resurrection of the Lord Jesus: and great grace was upon them all. Neither was there any among them that lacked: for as many as were possessors of lands or houses sold them, and brought the prices of the things that were sold and laid them down at the apostles' feet: and distribution was made unto every man according as he had need." Who did that? The saints, the church in Jerusalem, took care of their own needy. And there isn't anything to indicate, and by all of the tricks that can be pulled, there can not be injected into that passage anything but the congregation, as a congregation, taking care of its own needy.

Go right on to Acts 6, "And in those days, when the number of the disciples was multiplied, there arose a mumuring of the Grecians against the Hebrews, because their widows were neglected in the daily ministration. Then the twelve called the multitude of the disciples unto them, and said, It is not reason that we should leave the word of God, and serve tables. Wherefore, brethren, look ye out among you seven men of honest report . . ." Notice. Look ye out *among you.* Among whom? The members of the church in the city of Jerusalem. From among your own selves, look ye out seven men. Why, right there among their own members they selected seven men and they were apppointed by the apostles to take care of the matter of serving tables so that the apostles did not have to do it. There the church, again, was taking care of its own as a congregation, without any other organization.

Then right on to Acts 11, "And in those days came prophets from Jerusalem unto Antioch. (Tell me when I have ten minutes). And there stood up one of them named Agabus, and signified by the spirit that there should be great dearth throughout all the world: which came to pass in the days of Claudius Caesar. Then the disciples, every man according to his ability, determined to send relief unto the brethren which dwelt in Judea: Which also they did, and sent it to the elders by the hands of Barnabas and Saul." Here are brethren in need in Judea. The brethren in Antioch sent relief to them. How did they handle it? They delivered it into the hands of the elders. Elders over what? Elders over the congregation. Elders in every church. That's God's word. The distribution of relief in that case was delivered unto the elders and they had charge of its distribution among the needy members of the congregation. Here you have God's order. That's the way it was done in New Testament days, and that's what we're insisting upon now.

But, you know, brother Woods talks a lot about the home. Now I wonder what he means and I'd like for him to tell us.

Do you mean one's legal residence or domicile? That's one definition of home. Why, a man doesn't even have to live there, brother Woods. He can stay in another place and have a legal residence or domicile, or home. Do you mean one's native habitat, his land of nativity, or the place where he dwells? What do you mean by a home anyway? Why, you use the word in first one way and then another; sometimes you make it mean a place; another time you make it mean the family relationship. Well, again, definition of a home is an asylum, an institution for the relief of the destitute or afflicted. Why, that comes from Webster, too. What is it? A home sometimes simply means an asylum, a place of refuge, for the relief of the destitute or afflicted. A fourth definition for a home is the sense in which the Bible uses it. The Bible uses the term "home" one time, or sometimes, as the place where a person lives. Acts 21:6, they returned home. I Cor. 11:34, let him eat at home. Matt. 8:6, a servant lieth sick at home. Sometimes the Bible gives us the description of the ordained relationship that divinely constitutes the home. Now, brother Woods, which is the divine part? Is it the place that's divine? When God ordained the home did he simply build Adam a house? What do you mean by a divine relationship, a divine institution? Or was it the relationship that was divine? I'm insisting that it was the relationship. Matt. 19:4, "He which made them at the beginning, made them male and female." "They shall be one flesh," Gen. 2:24. "What God has joined together let not man put asunder," Matt. 19:6. "The husband is the head of the wife." Eph. 5:23. So you have the husband and wife relationship, Eph. 5:23, I Cor. 14:35, as the basis of the home.

Then the parent and child relationship, Eph. 6:1-5, then the household, servant and master, relationship, I Tim. 5:8, would even include that. The divine relationship is the only part ordained of God as a relationship and is the part of the home that men cannot restore. You don't restore that when you gather up hundreds of children and place them in an institutional home. The divine relationship is not there. You have a poor substitute for it. That's what you have. The house or the place where one lives is not divinely planned and when destroyed the divine relationship is unimpaired. When men provide or restore the place, they restore nothing that is divine in its origin or in its plan.

How much time do I have? I want chart No. 8, please. Not only is brother Woods confused about the home and the lationship of this extra organization to the home, but he's confused also about the matter of the corporate body and what it is. You know the idea of trying to make a corporation a part of something else. By the way, did you notice that in his speech he was careful to say that the thing that has to be obtained is a license. He's been going all over the country preaching and debating, and a lot of the rest of these brethren have, that the law requires an incorporation. Now, brother Woods, I want to join issue with you on that. You've misrepresented that matter all over this country. The law doesn't require anything of the kind and I challenge you to produce the state statute that does require it. Bring it on now and then we'll look at it and see.

What is a corporation anyway? A corporation aggregate is a collection of individuals united by authority of law under a special denomination; with a capacity of perpetual succession and of acting in many respects as an individual. Every corporation aggregate consists of a collection of individuals in a legal entity which is, for many purposes in contemplation of law (get it now), separate and distinct from the members who compose it. A corporation isn't a part of anything, legally, brother Woods. You ought to know that. "A corporation is an ideal body, subsisting only in contemplation of law, which may be composed of members constantly changing; which is deemed for useful purposes to have an existence independently of that of all the members of which it is composed: to be capable of perpetual succession and of acquiring, holding and conveying property." "Pratt vs. Bacon" in the Supreme Court of Massachusetts. Why, from the very nature of a private business corporation, or of any corporation, the stock holders are not the private and joint owners of its properties. It is a real, though artificial person, substituted for the natural person and, under the law, has most of the rights and most of the privileges that any sort or kind of a person has.

Now, concerning your Alabama laws, and he read a moment ago the provision that they must obtain license. But we are joining issue on whether or not they have to incorporate in order to get a license. Listen, here's a letter from the Attorney General of the state of Alabama. "Under the laws of this state it is not necessary to charter a corporation in order to care for needy persons." That's what the Attorney General of this state says. And I'll produce about thirty-nine more from that many different states that say exactly the same thing. It isn't necessary to incorporate. Now with reference to a corporation. What kind of a corporation is it that we want? I'd like the chart. I want No. 9.

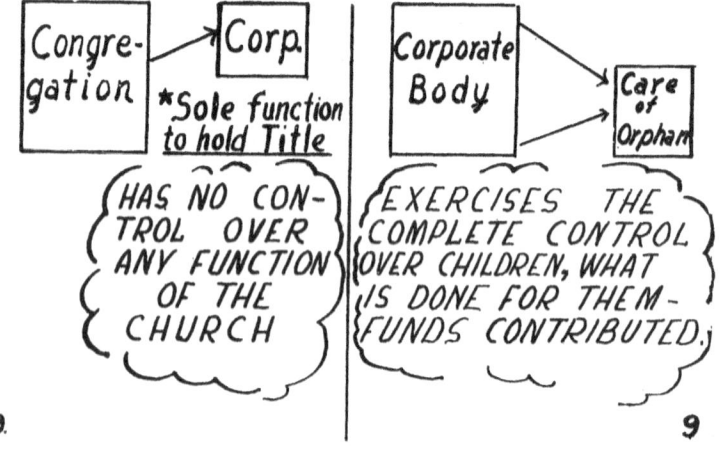

Now, I wonder if brother Woods would endorse a corporation—He asks me some questions about a church corporation, and—is it sinful? Brother Woods, when they form a corporation that controls any part of the work of the church you've sinned. Yes, that's sin. I will oppose any kind of corporation that has any control over the work of the church of the Lord in any phase. I wonder if he would endorse this one. I have here a copy of the article of incorporation of a congregation in California—Burlingame, California. In Section III of Article 4, under board of trustees, "The board of trustees shall have power to call special meetings of the church when they deem it necessary. They shall call a meeting at any time upon written request of the majority of the active members and appoint and remove at their pleasure all officers." They can put elders in and take them out. Do you endorse that kind of a corporation, Guy? Tell these people. That's the kind you've got for your home. Your corporate body, at your home, is in complete control of every phase of the activity of that home. That kind of a church corporation would be just as unscriptural.

Why, this body here can employ. The employees of the church can be removed. They shall prescribe their duties and fix their compensation. Will you endorse it? That's the kind of a corporation you're defending in the work of the church in relieving the destitute. Why, you know the supreme court of the State of Alabama has settled the matter that an incorporated church is two distinct, separate, elements. Let me read it to you. "It has become settled with us, as elsewhere generally, that an incorporated church consists of distinct elements; namely, the church proper and the corporation." There's the Alabama state law. "Bryant vs. 16th Street Baptist Church," 20th Alabama Report 423. Then again, "It is to be observed that these provisions of the code for the incorporation of churches or religious societies, all power conferred thereunder, relate to their properties or temporalities; have no reference to the churches or societies as such; which bodies, as spiritual or ecclesiastical organizations, exist independent of t h e i r charters." Why, brother Woods, a corporation isn't a part of anything. You're supposed to know that. It's a separate entity entirely. Then in Article 1397 and 1398 of the Texas State Statutes there is provided a corporate form for the congregation. But in 1398, Texas law prescribes that that corporation of a congregation shall not have any control over any function of the spiritual body whatever. That isn't the kind of a corporation that you've got over here, brother Woods, and we're not going to let you palm it off on these folks. We're not talking about that kind of a corporation. You're talking over here about a corporation that exercises the complete control over children, over what is done for them, over funds contributed and in that institution—a home that you talk about and that you would compare and confuse with the private home, brother Woods— that corporation has all the control there is and the church has none. And when anybody in the church places a child in that kind of a home, they lose control over it. They can't go back and get it: Not without a court order, if the superintendent isn't willing to release it. No sir. But brother Woods says the church *cannot furnish*, the church cannot furnish the care. All the church can do is furnish the money.

Listen to this. "Thus this writer of the "gospel of common sense", as the epistle of James has so well been described, sets out the practical aspects of pure and undefiled religion as consisting of the following particulars: (1) To visit. (2) To visit the fatherless and widows. (3) To visit the fatherless and widows in their afflictions. The word visit is, of course, used metaphorically and suggests a call made for the purpose of assisting. It is translated from the Greek "episkeptomai"; defined by Mr. Thayer "to look upon to look after, to inspect." And that's Guy N. Woods'. He wrote a book, too. (laughter)

Wood's Second egative

Gentlemen moderators, brother Cogdill, ladies and gentlemen:

I'm sorry that brother Cogdill's time ran out. I think he was doing better on the last than he did at anytime during the speech. I'm sorry that he didn't have a little more time to read it all.

Brother Cogdill, tomorrow night come with the rest of it. Now, friends, all of this business about an incorporation is simply so much matter to confuse the issue. It is thrown up as a smoke screen to keep you off of the real issue. It doesn't make any difference with brother Cogdill whether these homes are incorporated or not. Why bring up the subject of incorporation? His a r g u m e n t is that they are wrong because they are organizations. Now then if they are other organizations, what d i f f e r e n c e does it make whether they are incorporated or unincorporated? All of that is simply so much smoke screen.

Now let's see who's right and who's wrong on this matter of whether or not the incorporation is a part of the home. And while we're on that, and I believe that we can simply turn the lights out over the stage here and leave the others on. We'll try it like that. Let me have, please, chart No. 8, brother Deaver.

CHART NO. 8

PAGE 2, GOSPEL GUARDIAN, APRIL 7, 1955.

In a corporation lawyer's opinion upon the question of the church becoming a different institution when incorporated, the following is his answer:

2. Though this has been called an artificial person, it has many of the powers of an individual - the power to sue, be sued, hold property, pay taxes, be exempt from taxes, and the corporation in this sense is ANOTHER NAME APPLIED TO THE CHURCH OR INSTITUTION. (Emphasis mine, F. E.). Thus the statement that a corporation is an artificial person or entity apart from its members is MERELY A DESCRIPTION IN FIGURATIVE LANGUAGE OF A CORPORATION VIEWED AS A COLLECTIVE BODY. (Emphasis mine. F. E.).

4. A church or the name normally given a church or private institution, and a corporation, if such institution is incorporated, ARE ONE AND THE SAME THING, with the faculty of acting as a unit in respect to all matters within the scope of the purpose for which it was created. (Emphasis mine. F. E.). State vs. Knights of Ku Klux Klan, 232 Pac. 254.

5. Thus a corporation and the institution may be considered SYNONOMOUS. (Emphasis mine. F. E.).

Davidson Bartlett & Walk
By: /s/ W. E. Walk Jr.

Thus, from the standpoint of the law, that should settle the matter. "The corporation and the institution may be considered synonymous." It is "another name applied to the church or institution." It "is merely a description in figurative language of a corporation viewed as a collective body."

published in the brotherhood. "Before the church incorporates, the church exists unincorporated. After it incorporates it no longer exists as the church of Christ unincorporated. Thus, there was one institution before incorporation, and there is one institution after incorporation, and it's the same institution. It's still the church of the Lord." Now somebody here is saying that there's not a separate or extra institution. It's still the same. Now look further here. "The only difference in the church before and after incorporation is that it enjoys a legal entity after incorporation it did not enjoy while unincorporated." Now that's a splendid statement and a correct one.

Now let's see if that's in harmony with accepted authority. Though this has been called an artificial person, it has many powers of the individual. The power to sue, be sued, hold property, pay taxes, be exempt from taxes, and the corporation in this sense is another name applied to the church, or institution. Thus the statement that a corporation is an artificial person or entity apart from its members is merely a description, in figurative language, of the corporation viewed as a collective body." Let's have the top up here, please. "A church, or the name normally given a church, a private institution, and a corporation, if such institution incorporates, are one and the same: with the faculty of acting as a unit with respect to all matters within the scope of the purpose for which it was created." That's a citation from some authority in some case there. "Thus a corporation and the institution may be considered synonymous." Thus, from the standpoint of the law, that should settle the matter. The corporation and the institution may be considered synonymous. It is another name applied to the church or institution. It's merely the description, in figurative language, of a corporation viewed as a collective body. Do you know where that appeared? In the Gospel Guardian. Now I haven't seen any correction of that. Besides that, he cites lawyers in support of it. Not brother Cogdill, but brother Floyd Embree of Ontario, California. Back yonder a few years ago when it was good to argue that they were the same. Now, brother Cogdill is in conflict with his own writers here and with his own paper. And of course, this man is correct here. Because actually a corporation exists only as an intangible being.

Let's see another statement here that will be accepted as authority. Brother Marshall Patton who is present tonight and who is, I believe, the preacher for the congregation that is sponsoring brother Cogdill in this debate, in an article that appeared in the *Gospel Guardian* of sometime back, December 6, 1956, under the title "Authority for Expediences", says, "Brother . . .'s question about the extra organization, legal corporation, which is formed to enable a congregation to buy and hold a meeting house involves a consideration of some legalities with which I am not too familiar. However, I have regarded such a parallel with the church's use of a contracting corporation to build its meeting house. If some states require that legal corporations hold in trust church property, I suppose that some brethren could form such a corporation to hold in trust the property for the church. The church could continue to function in the full discharge of its God-ordained mission irrespective of the legal corporation." Now brother Cogdill, you need to straighten out some of your brethren, both writers, on that matter.

And again now, when you get him straightened out, it still doesn't deal with this issue. It's not—Is there an incorporation? The issue is—Is this church a home? That's the issue in this debate, and we shall not let you forget it.

Now then, friends, we want to deal thoroughly with his speech. And you'll notice now, of course, that he took up every argument I made, didn't he? Every chart that I introduced, he called for it, and he showed you clearly and conclusively that the conclusions set out therein didn't follow, didn't he? He did just as much with it as any man on earth will do, because it's absolutely unanswerable. The only thing he can do is to get up here and introduce an argument and a matter that doesn't even touch the question because, you remember, it's not, is the home incorporated, but, does it have a right to exist, incorporated or unincorporated? That's the issue. If the brethren at Boles home would dissolve their incorporation and continue to operate, unincorporated, would you endorse it, sir? When he answers that, then we'll know just how much importance that we may attach to this subject of incorporation. It is a smoke screen.

Now, friends, let us take up his speech, item by item, and statement by statement. He says the issue is, did God command the church to do something which it can't do? That's not the issue at all. Well, he says, why say that the church has an obligation? The church has an obligation to provide a home for needy people if they aren't able to support themselves. But that doesn't mean that the church takes over that home and operates it as an integral part of the church. There is the issue, friends; whether or not the church is a church or whether or not it is a home.

Now let's have, please, his chart No. 3.

SCRIPTURAL AUTHORITY

Commanded	Generic	Specific
ARK (GEN. 6:14)	WOOD	GOPHER
WATER OF CLEANSING (NUMBERS 19:2)	ANIMAL	RED HEIFER WITHOUT SPOT
PRAISE (EPH. 5:18; COL. 3:16)	MUSIC	SING
EVANGELIZE (I TIM. 3:15; I THESS. 1:7-8)	CHURCH (I THESS. 1:1)	ORGANIZATION (CONGREGATION)(PHIL. 1:1)
EDIFY (EPH. 4:16)	CHURCH	ORGANIZATION (CONGRE.)
RELIEVE (I TIM. 5:16)	CHURCH	ORGANIZATION (CONGRE.)

3.   3.

Scriptural authority—and I'm going to show you here, again, how he misses the point—that he's not dealing with the issue at all. This is a chart on scriptural authority and he has here matters which are not in controversy; that is, the difference between generic and specific and so on, all of which we accept. Now, he comes down here to the question of edification. It is the obligation of the church to edify. Well, does that eliminate, then, any other organization from edifying? Even brother Cogdill doesn't think that it's wrong to have another organization to edify. He's got one of his own, and it's incorporated, too. And it's another organization. Now, friends, he cannot come back up and raise the question of support. The question of support is not under consideration. The question is, does the organization have the right to exist? That's the issue.

Then next here, it's the obligation of the church to relieve the needy. Now his whole point now, if he has any point at all, is to prove to you that the orphan home is wrong because it's another organization. So is the private home. Now, if that has any merit at all, it eliminates the private home. Oh, but he admits that the private home can exist as another organization and the church can support it. Therefore, down goes his contention. Strange, indeed, that a fellow can't see that, as smart as brother Cogdill is.

Chart No. 4, let's have it next.

•ESSENTIALS AND EXPEDIENCIES•

Commandment	ESSENTIALS	Expediencies
TEACH MATT. 28:18-20	GOSPEL	CLASS - PRIVATELY PUBLICLY
BAPTIZE MATT. 28:18-20	IMMERSION IN WATER	NATURAL OR ARTIFICIAL POOL
LORD'S SUPPER I COR. 11:23-27	ELEMENTS - Bread and Fruit of Vine	TABLE - CONTAINERS
ASSEMBLY HEB. 10:25	FIRST DAY OF WEEK	HOUR - PLACE
RELIEVE I TIM. 5:16	CHURCH (CONGREGATION)	METHOD-MEANS-MODE Buy, Rent, Gratis

"Essentials and Expediences". I want you to see that every time that he makes an argument, his logic turns on him with irresistible force. Here it is at the bottom again. All of this, now, with reference to essentials and expediences, we all agree. Yet he eliminates an expediency which he admits, under other circumstances, has a right to exist. What is it? The private home, through which the church may function in benevolence. He hasn't taken the position that the private needy home has no right to exist. Yet the force of his a r g u m e n t is that no organization save the church may function in the matter of relieving people. Why, he either eliminates the private home or he doesn't. If his argument has any merit, the private home must go. But, if the private home may stay and the church function through it, then he's admitted that another organization may perform functions which the church supports.

Let's have his chart No. 5.

• AIDS AND ADDITIONS •

COMMANDMENT	AIDS	ADDITIONS
SING	BOOKS - LIGHTS LEADER - ETC.	INSTRUMENTAL MUSIC (another KIND of MUSIC)
BAPTIZE	BAPTISTRY	SPRINKLING (another KIND of ACTION)
ASSEMBLE TO BREAK BREAD	BUILDING, LIGHTS SEATS, HEAT, ETC.	SATURDAY (ANOTHER DAY)
PREACH GOSPEL	RADIO - LITERATURE, ETC.	MISSIONARY SOCIETY (ANOTHER ORGANIZATION)
RELIEVE THE DESTITUTE	BUILDING, CARE NECESSARIES	BENEVOLENT SOCIETY (ANOTHER ORGANIZATION)
EDIFY ITSELF	PLACE - FACILITIES TEACHERS	SUN. SCHOOL SOCIETY (ANOTHER ORGANIZATION)
5.		5.

I wish he would take up mine as I always do. I do not see why that it wasn't his obligation to try to answer these arguments. Chart No. 5. Again here we have the same difficulty.

Observe here, he says it's wrong to establish the missionary society through which to preach the gospel. I made an argument upon that. I told you that it's wrong for the reason that the missionary society displaces the church. When the missionary society gets through the church hasn't got anything else to do. It has displaced the church. But when the orphan home operates, the church still has all to do it has to do to start with. It doesn't take the place of the church because it's not serving as a church. It's serving as a home. It doesn't take the place of the home that doesn't exist. What is it doing? It's performing the function of a home as a home. And it must be legally operated.

Now he said, he challenged me to prove, that it's necessary to incorporate. There isn't any point in this, but just to show you I can ... He said I had gone all over the country saying it. Well, I'm going to show you that I have good authority for it and, if he produces a letter from somebody, his letter is in conflict with the published statements here. I have here the "Minimum Required, and Desirable Standards, for Child Caring Institutions of the State of Tennessee". And here is what the statement says: "Private institutions offering care to dependent children, M-U-S-T, must be incorporated in accordance with the laws of the state of Tennessee and the scope of the operation must be determined by the purpose set forth in the charter of incorporation."

Cogdill: What's the article?

Woods: Let me finish it ,then I'll read it.

Cogdill: I thought you were through. Pardon me.

Woods: "... must be determined by the purpose set forth in the charter of incorporation. Changes of purpose or program should be provided for in the amendments to the charter." Now look, in the debate I had with brother ...

Cogdill: The article that you're reading?

Woods: I'm reading here from the minimum requirements put out by the Department of Public Welfare of Tennessee, pages 2 and 3, under "Organization And Administration, A., Incorporation, Law or Ordinance", and I'll be glad for you to examine it if you want to. Now, when I met brother Porter, he jumped down two or three paragraphs under "Governing Board", asked the type of governing board and read where it said that church owned and operated institutions may be governed by committees of the board, and tried to make it appear that that was an exception to the rule. That's with reference to the type of board that exists, not on the question of incorporation. This says that under the laws of the state of Tennessee the home M-U-S-T must be incorporated. Now again, what difference does it make? Now, I'll show you that I'm right on that, too.

Where is the passage that authorizes the church to build anything other than a church? I Timothy 5:16, the apostle Paul makes it obligatory upon the church to supply the needs of a destitute widow. Whatever that widow had before and lost then must be restored. I have a chart on that in just a moment which I'll get to. Now he said that the church could buy a place and operate it. The church can supply the means whether it be a natural or a legal home. But the question before us tonight is this: Did God put elders over two institutions? May elders rule a home as well as the church? Elders are over individuals as Christians, in a spiritual sense, but elders are not over people who are not even members of the church. According to this man's views you actually put elders over the bodies of people who are not even in the church and engage in secular activity which is not church activity, such as teaching secular subjects. What did he say about that? As silent as the tomb and he will be from here on out.

Then, next, he cites us to the fact that the disciples of the early church said that none of the things which they possessed were their own, but they had all things common. No one questions that. That isn't the point. I raise this question with reference to that. Did the elders of the Jerusalem church, or even the apostles or anybody else, take over those homes and operate them because they were supplying funds for them? He cites us to the example of Acts 6 which is not a case of benevolence in a true sense at all because, actually, that was a common matter out of which they all lived.

BENEVOLENT ORGANIZATIONS

And then, next, Acts 11:27-30, where from Antioch the funds were sent to Jerusalem or to the elders. And he assumes, therefore, that these elders went into the secular business of operating homes. Of course, the money was sent. But the question before us tonight is this: Did those elders take over those homes and start running them, as elders? That's the question before us and again, we say we'll not let him forget it.

Now, brother Cogdill has the idea that all that's supplied is food and clothing and shelter. Did you notice how that he always dodged some of the other responsibilities? It's just as much the obligation of the home to supply secular education, recreation and so on. That's a part of the work of the home, too. And yet he always dodges that part of it. Now, may the elders provide and oversee such, that is, in the sense of running and operating such? If so, he puts the elders in the recreation business. And we've covered, now, his charts with reference to the corporation. We've shown you it doesn't make any difference in the first place and he's wrong, in the second place.

Now, I want to take up the questions. I asked him this question: Can all the needs of a fatherless child be adequately supplied without such a child being a part of or having a home? He said if I mean by that the matter of having access to these things, No. Well, that's what I've been telling him, that a child must have and be a part of a home. Now, the question before us: Is that home or is it another institution which God ordained to supply that care? No. 2: Is the congregation the only organization which may scripturally function in benevolence when the means are provided by the church, and is the congregation an orphanage and an old folks' home without further organization? He said the congregation is the only organization to do what the church can do. Now that's dodging the point. That's the very point at issue. Is the church set up for, and did God design it in the case of the person who lost his home, to re-establish and restore and operate as a home instead of a church. That's the question before us. I asked him, when the church builds an orphan home for the care of fatherless children or an old folks home for aged needy people, is it building another church, or a home? He said, it depends on what you mean by a home. Said; brother Woods, why don't you define home. I did. I gave you a definition of it, told you exactly what I meant by it. I called your attention to the dictionary definition that it's a unit of society. That's what I mean by a home. And that home may exist either as a natural home or as a re-established home. I asked him, when the church builds this home and utilizes it in discharge of its duty to the fatherless and needy, is it functioning t h r o u g h an organization apart from the church? He didn't answer that. He just came up and said it functioned like the Sunday School. That's not answering my question. Now, brother Cogdill, answer these questions.

Now let's have chart D. Hand that down, please. All right, chart B, please.

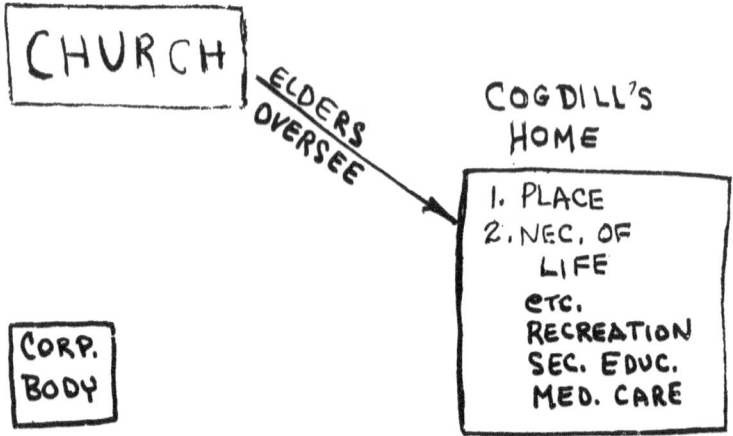

Friends, in the final analysis, this is the position that brother Cogdill finds himself in here. That the church with its elders may oversee it. If brother Cogdill's home were to fall into need, if a catastrophe were to hit him, such as a tornado, it might come to any of us, and if it came necessary

And I want you to see a statement here, and we'll present to what brother Cogdill is, undoubtedly, splendid authority. Now before I tell you where this is from, and that's very good. Just leave it right there, please. Before the church here is an article, now, that appeared in one of the papers for the church to supply need for his home, would they then take over that home and start operating it? They would not, of course. Is it the function of the elders to supply a place for brother Cogdill, the necessities of life, recreation, secular education and medical care? Now that is exactly the position that he's occupying.

Let's have chart No. X.

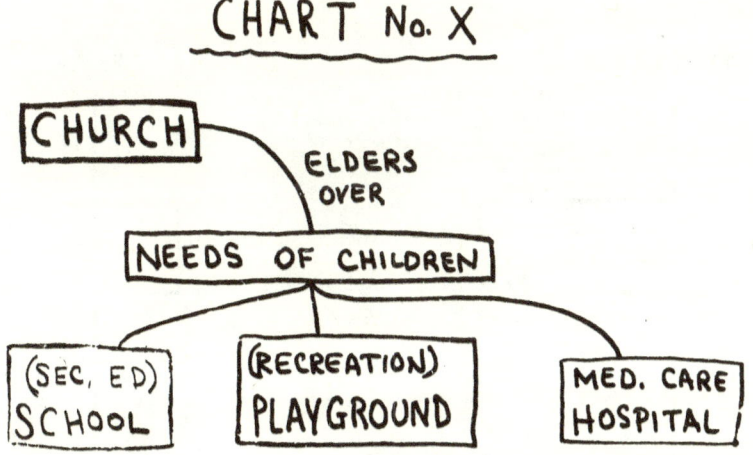

Here, friends, here will get before you clearly what I've been driving at. The needs of children include a great deal more than merely food and clothing and shelter. That is; they need secular education, hence a school. They need recreation: a playground. They need medical care. Does brother Cogdill take the position that the elders, as such, may operate in all of these fields? Now he must do one of two things. He must say that this is the proper function of elders, or he must admit he is wrong. Now, which will he do? Which will he do?

All right, I asked him this: If you insist that the church

is not functioning through another organzation in such a case, give chapter and verse w h e r e God authorizes the church to serve as a home, well he cites us correctly to I Timothy 5:16. That's exactly right. Now lets have chart O, please.

CHART NO. "O"

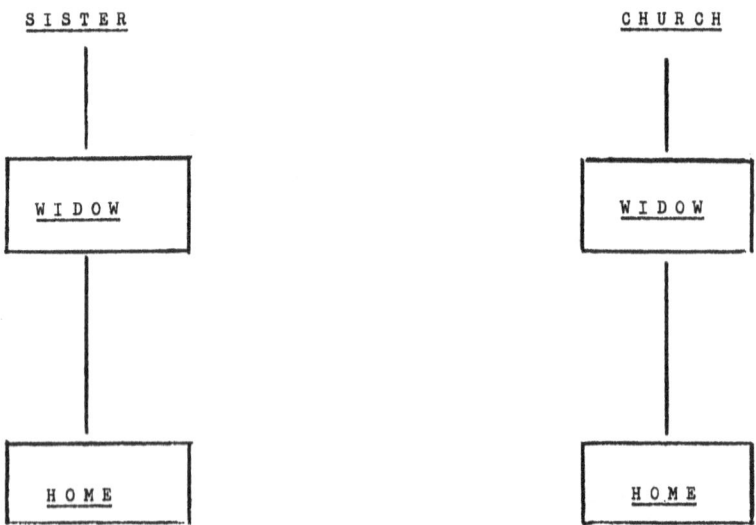

This friends will indicate to you exactly what my position is. In I Timothy 5:16 the apostle Paul discusses the obligation of a woman who has a widow and in which it is the obligation of that widow to supply the needs of her mother. Now, what is it that that sister supplies. She supplies that widow a home. What is the relationship that subsists between this sister and the widow? It is a relationship between a daughter and her mother. Now then what is it that she supplies? She supplies a home. Now watch what the passage says, that if they are women they are to relieve them. Get it now, that the church be not charged. What is it that the sister is to do? She is to supply a home for her widowed mother. What does she supply? She supplies a home. Now get it; that the church be not charged. That eliminates the church from doing that which the sister is supplying. Now watch the next statement. "That it (that is, the church) may care for them that are widows indeed." That the church may do what? May do exactly what the sister was doing, where there is no sister. What is the sister doing? Providing a church for her mother? Brother Cogdill would have you to think so. What is the church doing? Supplying a home. Supplying the very thing that this sister would have supplied if she were still there.

Now that's where the issue and t r a g i c a l l y enough, friends, these brethren are advocating a position that confuses these distinct realms that are characteristic of God's relationship with us today.

Then, next, when elders place children in a private home already in existence and support them there, please tell us, whose work is it to provide the actual care, the church or the home? What did he say about that? If the home is the church working through another institution? What did he say about that? Whose obligation is to control and supervise such children? The home in which they are placed or the elders of the church? He said it was the work of the elders of the church. Work of the elders of the church to supervise the children that are put in a home. Now, friends, I want to ask you in candor, in brother Tant's appeal for some home to take these children off of the hands of these elders that's got the only organization that God provided for the needy, and in its anxiety to get them out of that organization into a home, do you suppose those elders will maintain control over those children after they get in that home? Do you think they will? Now I wonder how ridiculous a fellow can get. That is the issue here tonight. Don't you let him confuse you. And, yet, over this question brethren are pushing their hobbies until the church of our Lord stands today in dire danger of division. Quite correctly, brother Adams, in his introductory remarks, said that this question involves the peace and prosperity of the church. And he's exactly right. Whether or not the church will be reduced to a second rate sect, whether it will terminate its activities that today is carrying the gospel far beyond the bounds ever characteristic of it before, and the basis of the benevolent part of it is whether or not the church is a home. That's the issue.

Is there anything inherently sinful in incorporating a church? A business? A home? If no, could the church contribute to an incorporated home which is in need? Well, now he says it's sinful for it to take control of it. That is, a corporation that takes control of the church and runs it is sinful. And he said: brother Woods, wouldn't you agree? I agree with you. No corporation has the right to usurp and take over the control of any church. I do not hesitate to say that. But now get it. The reason is that there are elders to take care of that work. I say it would be just as wrong to form a corporation and take over the works of parents and usurp them, too. But suppose there are not any parents. Suppose that they are *en loco parentis*, brother Cogdill? Have they taken over and usurped the function of parents? There are not any parents. What are they doing? Serving in the place of parents. That's the purpose of them. Now, friends, why doesn't brother Cogdill deal with the issue? Why get up here and say brother Woods is trying to tell you that the church can't perform the work that God gave the church to do? There have been tens of thousands of words and almost tons of paper used up in quoting statements from me. My brethren who quote me as saying that the church is adequate to accomplish all the work which God gave the church to do, and that the church needs no other organization to do the work which God gave to it. And they seem to think, seem to think that there is something inconsistent in that with the position that I am defending here tonight. Now, you brethren can just save yourself the trouble of further publication along that line, because you see now. And some of you have been seeing it for a long time. Of course, the church is adequate to accomplish all that God expects

BENEVOLENT ORGANIZATIONS 73

the church, as a church, to do. But God doesn't expect the church to serve as a home. And it can't, in the first place. Let's see, I have a chart here that I want to use on that. Let's have chart No. 11.

CHART # 11

IN WHICH OF THE FOLLOWING INSTITUTIONS ARE CHILDREN TO BE CARED FOR:

A CHURCH (Yes) (No)

A HOME (Yes) (No)

A HOME WHICH IS AN INTEGRAL PART OF A CHURCH? (Yes) (No).

Here we are. Which of the following institutions are children to be cared for? A church, brother Cogdill? They have a place now. Kindly designate in your mind and before the audience. A home? A home which is an integral part of the church? Now which? Which of those sets out the situation that God has ordained? Is it a church? Is it a home? Or is it a home which is an integral part of a church? Which? Let him answer that. Let's have chart No. 12.

I want you to see the all-sufficiency of this. I want the brethren who really want to avoid misrepresentation to see it. The church is all-sufficient, to function as a home? Yes, or no. Now, is it all-sufficient to function as a home? The home is all-sufficient to function as a church? Yes or no. Is the church sufficient to function as a church? Is the home sufficient to function as a home? Why, I never believed stronger in my life in the all-sufficiency of the church? But I also believe in the all-sufficiency of the home. And it's just as wrong to usurp the purposes of God's divine institutions and prostitute it to the purposes of another as it would be to try to turn the home into a church.

CHART # 12

1. THE CHURCH IS ALL SUFFICIENT TO FUNCTION AS A HOME (Yes) (No)

    Script. _____

2. THE CHURCH IS ALL SUFFICIENT TO FUNCTION AS A CHURCH (Yes) (No)

    Scrip. _____

1. THE HOME IS ALL SUFFICIENT TO FUNCTION AS A CHURCH   (Yes) (No)

    Scrip. _____

2. THE HOME IS ALL SUFFICIENT TO FUNCTION AS A HOME   (Yes) (No)

    Scrip. _____

Let's have Chart No. 13.

CHART NO. 13
ALL SUFFICIENCY

1. ARE THE CHURCH AND THE HOME, ONE AND THE SAME INSTITUTION? _____

2. IS THE CHURCH ALL-SUFFICIENT TO DO WHAT GOD DESIGNED THE CHURCH TO DO? _____

3. IS THE HOME ALL-SUFFICIENT TO DO WHAT GOD DESIGNED THE HOME TO DO? _____

4. WHICH SCRIPTURE AUTHORIZES A CHURCH TO FUNCTION AS A HOME? _____

5. MAY ELDERS FUNCTIONING AS ELDERS SCRIPTURALLY MANAGE (OVERSEE) A HOME? _____ (SCRIPTURE)

6. MAY PARENTS, FUNCTIONING AS PARENTS, SCRIPTURALLY MANAGE (OVERSEE) A HOME? _____ (SCRIPTURE)

BENEVOLENT ORGANIZATIONS 75

Here are the questions that brother Cogdill must deal with if he wants to grapple with this issue. Are the church and the home one and the same institution? Is the church all-sufficient to do what God designed the church to do? Is the home all-sufficient to do what God designed the home to do? Now, which scripture authorizes the church to function as a home? And may elders function as elders, scripturally manage, oversee, a home? If so, give us the scripture. May parents, functioning as parents, scripturally oversee and manage a church? You just as well put parents over a church as to put elders over a home. Let me have chart No. 17.

CHART No. 17

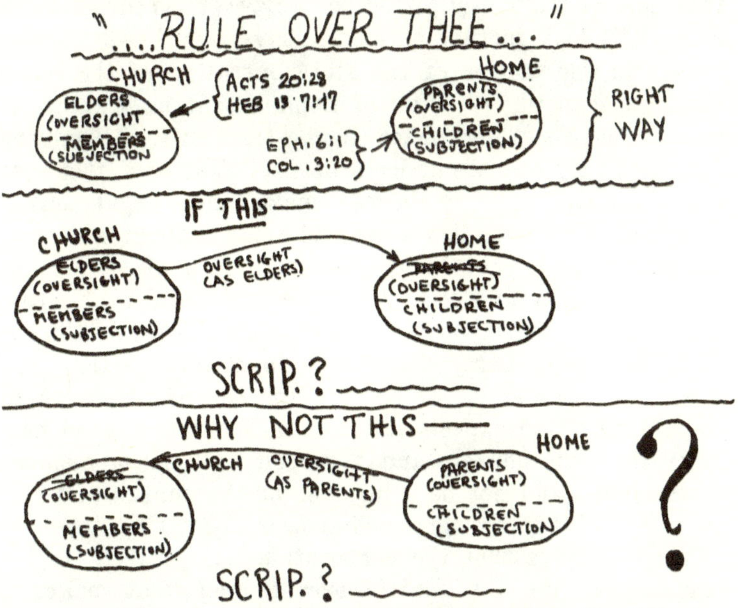

"...RULE OVER THEE..."

RIGHT WAY

CHURCH — ELDERS (OVERSIGHT), MEMBERS (SUBJECTION) — ACTS 20:28; HEB. 13:7,17
HOME — PARENTS (OVERSIGHT), CHILDREN (SUBJECTION) — EPH. 6:1; COL. 3:20

IF THIS —

CHURCH — ELDERS (OVERSIGHT), MEMBERS (SUBJECTION) — OVERSIGHT (AS ELDERS) → HOME — PARENTS (OVERSIGHT), CHILDREN (SUBJECTION)

SCRIP.?

WHY NOT THIS —

CHURCH — ELDERS (OVERSIGHT), MEMBERS (SUBJECTION) — OVERSIGHT (AS PARENTS) → HOME — PARENTS (OVERSIGHT), CHILDREN (SUBJECTION)

SCRIP.?

I have no idea or no expectation of brother Cogdill even remotely dealing with these matters. But you will in your minds and you want to reach a correct conclusion. Here, friends, is the function of the church and its oversight. Elders take the oversight and the members are subject. Over on the other side, parents have the oversight of the home and the children are subjects. Acts 20:28; Heb. 13:

7 designate the function of elders. Eph. 6:1; Col. 3:20, the matter and responsibility of the parents. That's the right way. Now, if, according to brother Cogdill, the church and its elders can take over the home and oversee it and operate it as elders, performing the function of elders of the church, then why not this? The church may be overseen by parents. The parents may usurp and operate the functions of the church as parents. If you can turn a church into a home, why can't you turn a home into a church? Do you think this man will deal with that? There's not one on the top-side of God's earth that can remotely do so. And brother Cogdill will not even attempt to do so, because he can't do it and he knows it.

All he can do is get up here and talk about something that doesn't make any difference anyway? Incorporation. Now, let's look further here. He says that I was careful to say in the matter of the state operation of the home that it's licensed. Well, all of them, so far as I know require a license. That makes them a legal entity. The very fact that they operate under a license. The very fact that they operate under a license makes it a legal entity. You can't even establish a natural home without a license. He objects to it being a legal entity. Even his own home is a legal entity and operates under law. And may I say, friends, that the home is no part, that the establishment of a home is no part, of a church function. It's true that it's the proper spiritual activity for the people to be in the church. God expects it. But the home is a good deal older than the church, and a person could be a member of the home and not be a member of the church and still be in a divine institution: That is in the divine home.

Then he says that the corporation has control. If the corporation has any control over it then that makes it wrong. Well, if it were true that the corporation usurped the functions of the home, as would be the case of a corporation usurping the functions of the church, then there would be some merit to that. But then inasmuch as it isn't in conflict with it, then this point is not well taken. Now, that, friends, covers his speech. Item by item, statement by statement. I want to go back now to brother

Tant's appeal for a home. Beg your pardon? One minute. Right quick, if you can find it there in that time, chart No. 6. Let's see how these brethren try to get children out of God's only organization to care for them. Let this fact be clear. The purpose of this article is to seek to find a home. Find a what? A home! I thank you.

SECOND NIGHT

Cogdill's Third Affirmative

Gentlemen Moderators, Brother Woods, Brethren and Friends:

I'm grateful that by the good providence of God it is possible for us again to assemble in his presence to study his word concerning these things that we believe to be of vital importance to the church of our Lord. If we may have come into the presence of God tonight as brother Puckett has so wonderfully and earnestly prayed, with our minds and our hearts open to the reception of God's truth, I feel certain that an investigation of this kind can but do us good. And I pray earnestly that such may be our attitude, that we may have come without any idols in our hearts to justify, but with the determination to turn to the word of God that we may find the solution to the problems that are confronting us today in the work of the Lord.

I want to begin about where we left off last night in some affirmative work in just a moment. But first of all to give those of you who were not present last night because of the inclement weather perhaps, a little bit of the review of the affirmative material presented leading up to some other matters. We gave emphasis in the beginning of the affirmation last night to the fact that the whole question is a question of divine authority. I believe with all of my heart that what the church can and cannot do always involves the issue of authority. The proposition that we are affirming, that has been read to you, involves what the churches of Christ can do, what they can build, what they can organize, what they can maintain; the kind of institutions that they can bring into existence and be responsible for. It's rather difficult for me to understand how it would be possible for a man to assert that a proposition involving what the churches of Christ can build and maintain is not a matter of authority, and that authority cannot be an issue in it. It seems to me that the fundamental consideration in the whole matter is a matter of authority. Whether or not churches of Christ can build and maintain benevolent organizations to care for the needy depends entirely upon whether or not God has authorized the churches of Christ to build benevolent organizations to care for the needy. This is the issue. The proposition involves what the church has the right to do and what the church does not have the right to do. It isn't a question of the function of the private home. It isn't a question of the function of anything except the church of the Lord in building and maintaining benevolent organizations, to care for the needy. Now that's what we're discussing.

Brother Woods spent almost his entire two speeches trying to confuse you by discussing the private home; and the church and the private home. The private home is not a part of this discussion. This proposition says nothing on earth about what the church can do in or through a private home. This proposition is concerned with the benevolent organizations which the church of our Lord can build, and I'm going to insist on discussing that. That's the proposition that I signed to affirm and that's what I'm going to affirm.

He said something last night about me wasting half of my time. Well, I think I could be a little more generous in my allowance and say that he wasted a whole lot more than half of his trying to confuse the issue as to the private home and the church's relationship to the private home; which concerns not at all the proposition that we have under consideration tonight. He says authority has nothing to do with what the church can build and main-

BENEVOLENT ORGANIZATIONS

tain in the way of benevolent organizations. I shall continue to insist that it has, and I want chart No. 1, if you will, please. How to establish authority for what is done by the church. (And I would like to have a fifteen minute's notice.)

HOW TO ESTABLISH SCRIPTURAL AUTHORITY
THE LORD'S SUPPER

(1) **EXPRESS COMMAND** — "This do in remembrance of Me."
   (Observance)   I COR. 11:23-24.

(2) **APPROVED EXAMPLE** — "And upon the *first day of the week*, when the disciples came together *to break bread*." ACTS 20:7.
   (Time of Observance)

(3) **NECESSARY INFERENCE** — "The first day of the week...to break bread" (Means as regularly as the day comes, COMPARE "The Sabbath day to keep it Holy.")
   (Frequency of Observance)   HOW OFTEN?

EXPEDIENCY : ANY HOUR WITHIN THE FIRST DAY OF THE WEEK.

2.   1.

We pointed out by this chart that there are three ways by which authority can be established in divine affairs—What the church of the Lord can and cannot do. One of them is an express command, as in the case of the Lord's supper. Another one is an approved example, as in the case of the time when the Lord's supper is to be observed. Another one, a necessary inference as to the frequency. These are the methods by which we learn when and how the church of the Lord is to observe the Lord's supper. They are the only three methods by which we can learn what the church can and cannot do about anything. If the passage cannot be found that falls in one of the three categories authorizing the church of the Lord, either generically or specifically, to build benevolent organizations, if brother Woods is unable to show either an express command that includes these benevolent organizations that we are talking about; or an approved example in the New Testament that includes them; or a necessary inference from the word of God, clear and unmistakable, and unavoidable that proves them, then he cannot establish divine authority for the thing that he's undertaking to defend. And if he can't establish divine authority for it, then, friends, they are bound to be wrong in the sight of God, or there isn't anything to divine authority about anything.

We either have to have divine authority for what the church builds or else the church of our Lord is not governed by divine authority. But the Bible teaches that Jesus Christ is "the head over all things to the church which is his body." Eph. 1:23—that all authority is his both in heaven and on earth. The church is a realm of absolute authority subject to Christ. It can do only what he commands, what he authorizes. There must be found within his word either specific authority or a commandment that includes within its scope these benevolent institutions, or all of the contentions that brother Woods makes about the private home and everything else falls by the wayside. We want the passage, the authority from the word of God established by one of these means that gives the churches of Christ the right to build benevolent organizations to care for the needy.

I pointed out to you in consideration of this matter of divine authority that these—the third one, number 3, matters are either generic or specific. God has commanded that the church shall edify itself. The church is to do it, but God didn't just leave it under that general term. He specified the organization in Eph. 4:16. It's the congregation that's to do that. God commands the church to evangelize—to preach the gospel, to be the pillar and the ground of the truth. He specified the congregation that's to do it, or the organization that's to do it. He didn't just command the church to do it and leave it up to the church, but he specified the organization through which the church

Chart No. 3, please.

SCRIPTURAL AUTHORITY

Commanded	Generic	Specific
ARK (GEN. 6:14)	WOOD	GOPHER
WATER OF CLEANSING (NUMBERS 19:2)	ANIMAL	RED HEIFER WITHOUT SPOT
PRAISE (EPH. 5:18; COL. 3:16)	MUSIC	SING
EVANGELIZE (I TIM. 3:15; I THESS. 1:7-8)	CHURCH (I THESS. 1:1)	ORGANIZATION (CONGREGATION)(PHIL. 1:1)
EDIFY (EPH. 4:16)	CHURCH	ORGANIZATION (CONGRE.)
RELIEVE (I TIM. 5:16)	CHURCH	ORGANIZATION (CONGRE.)

3.

is to function in carrying out that mission. God commands the church to relieve the destitute, I Tim. 5:16. And he didn't leave it generic there. It is the congregations, the congregation a specific organization, that God has ordained. No. 4, please.

And that congregation is specific. For the reason that it is specific it excludes every other organization. Exactly like gopher wood excluded all other woods, like the ashes of a red heifer excluded the ashes of every other animal, exactly like sing excludes every other kind of music, so the congregation excludes every other organization to do what God has commanded the church to do.

Then we pointed out to you the difference between essentials and expediencies. In the commandment to teach, the gospel is essential, but classes, privately or publicly, or the methods employed are the expediencies to be used. The choice is left up to us.

God commanded us to baptize. Immersion in water is

•ESSENTIALS AND EXPEDIENCIES•

Commandment	ESSENTIALS	Expediencies
TEACH MATT. 28:18-20	GOSPEL	CLASS - PRIVATELY PUBLICLY
BAPTIZE MATT. 28:18-20	IMMERSION IN WATER	NATURAL OR ARTIFICIAL POOL
LORD'S SUPPER I COR. 11:23-27	ELEMENTS - Bread and Fruit of Vine	TABLE - CONTAINERS
ASSEMBLY HEB. 10:25	FIRST DAY OF WEEK	HOUR - PLACE
RELIEVE I TIM. 5:16	CHURCH (CONGREGATION)	METHOD-MEANS-MODE Buy, Rent, Gratis

the essential. The expediency is whether we do it in a natural or an artificial pool. We have a choice in that matter because it's within the scope of the thing authorized.

The Lord's Supper, I Cor. 11. The elements, the bread and the fruit of the vine—We have no choice about that. God has specified. But he has not specified as to what kind of a table we shall use, or the containers and the number of them that shall be used. They are matters of expediency. They are within the scope of the thing commanded and yet not specified, and therefore, left up to us.

Then in the assembly on the first day of the week we have no choice about when to assemble, to observe the Lord's Supper. But the hour of the first day of the week and the place where we assemble is a matter of expediency.

In the commandment to relieve the destitute, I Tim. 5:16, the church, the congregation, is the essential. The organization is specified. God gave to the church an organization through which to do its work. The methods or the

BENEVOLENT ORGANIZATIONS

means or the mode by which the place is furnished, by which the care and the supervision, the personnel to carry on that work is found and furnished or provided, and by which all of the necessary things of life are furnished would be a matter of expediency. We are not discussing in this debate how these things shall be furnished. That is, as to the specific method that the congregation of the church of the Lord shall use; whether they buy a place, rent it, somebody furnishes it gratis; whether somebody volunteers his service, or help and care is hired and paid for; but we are emphasizing and specifying that God has given the church an organization through which to work. And now No. 5, if you will, please.

• AIDS AND ADDITIONS •

COMMANDMENT	AIDS	ADDITIONS
SING	BOOKS - LIGHTS LEADER - ETC.	INSTRUMENTAL MUSIC (another KIND of MUSIC)
BAPTIZE	BAPTISTRY	SPRINKLING (another KIND of ACTION)
ASSEMBLE TO BREAK BREAD	BUILDING, LIGHTS SEATS, HEAT, ETC.	SATURDAY (ANOTHER DAY)
PREACH GOSPEL	RADIO - LITERATURE, ETC.	MISSIONARY SOCIETY (ANOTHER ORGANIZATION)
RELIEVE THE DESTITUTE	BUILDING, CARE NECESSARIES	BENEVOLENT SOCIETY (ANOTHER ORGANIZATION)
EDIFY ITSELF	PLACE - FACILITIES TEACHERS	SUN. SCHOOL SOCIETY (ANOTHER ORGANIZATION)
5.		5

I Timothy 5:16 does not include the idea of the particular method that the church uses, but it does say that the church is to do it. And when the church does it the church operates through the congregational arrangement that God himself is responsible for. Now brother Woods says that in I Timothy 5:16 is found the home for the widow, but not the organization to control and run that home. Brother Woods, that's what you need to find. Everybody agrees that a destitute widow needs the place for shelter, but where is the organization in I Timothy 5:16 like you have for these institutional homes that the brethren have built; the organization that establishes, that provides, that controls and directs that home for the widow? We all agree that she needs a place to live but not, not on the point are we agreed, that God has given authority for the building of an organization aside from the church, distinct and apart from the church to furnish that place for her to live. That's what you need authority for.

Well, you remember that when he came down to the matter of the organization he said, now, brother Cogdill is doing the very thing that he is trying to condemn. He believes in another organization. Why he believes in the private home. Brother Woods, I'm talking on these charts about another organization that the *church* builds. That's our proposition. That's our proposition. The private home is not an organization that the church builds. And it isn't an organization that comes within the realm, therefore, of an addition that the church makes. The addition is when you build another institution to do the work that God said for the church to do. The private home doesn't fall in that category. And that's a mere dodge that you made and not an answer to the chart and argument at all.

God's command to sing gives us the privilege of using books, lights, leaders and so forth. Instrumental music is another kind of music. Sprinkling another kind of action in baptism. Saturday another day for the assembly of the saints to break bread. The missionary society another organization to preach the gospel. The benevolent society another organization for the relief of the destitute. And the Sunday school society another organization. These organizations to carry on the work that God gave the church to do are as much an addition to God's way and an invasion of the realm of God's silence, therefore, as much a sin of presumption, as to add instrumental music to the worship of God when God specified singing.

There are several things that we want you to notice. First, God has given the church a work to do. Eph. 4:11-12, three things are specified. The church is to evangelize; the church is to minister; the church is to edify itself, and God made no distinction. God made no distinction in those three particular missions that he has assigned the church. In the second place, God has given the church an organization through which to perform its function. That organization, number three, is the congregation; the only organization that God ever gave the church. None larger, none smaller, none other. In the fourth place, that organization is specific in its nature. It is ordained of God and the plan of it is given in God's word. It operates not under a board of directors. It operates not under the arrangements for the private home. No. But it operates under the elders of the church, and God specified elders in every church. Number five, that organization is specific to do what God wants done. And just here I call your attention now to the fact that God has specified the pattern by which the work of the church shall be carried on.

Back in Exodus 25:8-9 God commanded that they should make him a sanctuary. He gave them a pattern of that sanctuary—took Moses into the mountain and gave him a pattern, and all of the instruments thereof. And then commanded him that he should build a tabernacle that he might have a place to dwell among his people. Exodus 26:30, exactly he was commanded or shown that pattern in the mountain. In Exodus 27:8, "as it was shewed thee in the mount, so shall they make it." In the next place we come on down to Solomon's temple in the Old Testament. It was built after divine pattern given by the Lord, I Chronicles 28:9-10 — "And thou, Solomon my son, know thou the God of thy father . . . Take heed now; for the Lord hath chosen thee to build an house for the sanctuary: be strong, and do it." In verses 11 and 12, "Then David gave to Solomon his son the pattern of the porch, and of the houses thereof . . . And the pattern of all that he had by the Spirit." And then in verse 19, "All this, said David, the Lord made me understand in writing by his hand upon me, even all the works of this pattern." It was a divine pattern. God was particular about it. Well, the church today is built after a divine pattern also. For it's God's habitation in the spirit among his people. Eph. 2:22, "In whom ye also are builded together for an habitation of God through the Spirit." Verse 21, "In whom all the building fitly framed together groweth unto an holy temple in the Lord." In Heb. 8:5, "Who serve unto the example and shadow of heavenly things, as Moses was admonished of God when he was about to make the tabernacle: for, See, saith he, that thou make all things according to the pattern shewed to thee in the mount." And he said that the chief point of the things which we are saying is this, that we are talking about a true tabernacle which the Lord pitched and not man. The shadow had a pattern in detail. God gave it. He demanded that it be respected and followed. But concerning the church, his spiritual temple on earth today, he has no pattern, they tell us, and is not concerned. Why the pattern in organization is as plain as the pattern in worship, as the pattern in anything else concerning the church. Phil. 1:1, "all the saints in Christ Jesus which are at Philippi, with the bishops and deacons." Acts 14:23, "And when they had ordained them elders in every church . . ." The jurisdiction of those elders was fixed. I Peter 5:1-2, "The elders which are among you I exhort . . . Feed the flock of God which is among you, taking the oversight thereof." Acts 20:28, "Take heed therefore unto yourselves, and to all the flock, over the which the Holy Ghost hath made you overseers." And then in Acts 2, 4 and 6, and again in Acts 11, we have the pattern as we pointed it out to you last night; the pattern of the congregation in Jerusalem, in those first two references, Acts 2, 4 and 6, where they sold their possessions and made available relief for those who were in need and delivered unto every man, and distributed unto every man as they had need. There was the church, the congregation in Jerusalem, carrying on under the apostles and, by the way, they laid their contribution at the apostles feet. That is, they put it under their control. It was in their charge, and when the time came that a complaint was made in Acts 6, you remember, the apostles said that you are to look out among yourselves—"from among yourselves"—seven men. Now brother Woods says that's not a pattern of benevolence. Well, I'd like to know what it's a pattern of. It's the church relieving the destitute. A congregation taking care of its poor, and it was the congregation that did it. Not some organization built outside of it.

In Acts 11:27-30, the brethren in Antioch determined to send relief unto the brethren which dwelt in Judea. And you remember that they did it. And when they did it, they sent it to the elders. It was placed in the hands of the elders. That's it. Well, what did *they* do with it? They distributed it to those that were in need, or at least had the oversight of it. That's what brother Woods says the church can't do. The church can't take care of the needy. It can't see to it that tables are waited, that food is distributed, that the needy is relieved. Why, you've got to have some other kind of an organization to do that. Brother Woods, you're going to have a hard time finding that other organization in Acts 2, 4, 6 and 11. It just isn't there. The divine pattern holds no sort or kind of a promise either of it.

And you know it's rather remarkable that a man can find another organization in the word of God in passages that don't even remotely hint at it, and then can't see the organization, another organization in the proposition that actually calls for it. Give me the chart on what's the issue. We want to keep that constantly before you. How much time do I have?

The issue in this debate is not the function of the private home. It isn't a matter of what the church and the home in their respective functions are, so far as their relationship to each other is concerned. It's a matter of the church building other organizations. Now brother Woods, if you weren't willing to affirm that the church has the right to build benevolent organizations why did you sign the proposition? Why don't you discuss the proposition that you signed instead of getting up here and talking about the private home? Nobody that I know anything about believes that the church ought to take over anybody's private home. And the only fellows that I know that are advocating that are those that are trying to justify the same kind of institutions that he's arguing for, on the ground that whatever the christian individual can do the church can do.

I've had them contend with me that your home is subject to the elders of the church because whatever the christian individual does the church can do. Well, I don't believe that the home is subject to the elders of the church, from the viewpoint of them having jurisdiction over it and the right to run it. I'm glad to know that Guy Woods doesn't believe that. The Bible doesn't teach it. That would be Catholicism and I'm not advocating that. But I am advocating that the church as a organization, designed by the God of heaven, divine in its origin, ought to do its own work. That's the idea—that the church ought to do its own work. And God has given it an organization sufficient to do its own work. Brother Woods says, Oh, I believe in the all-sufficiency of the church. Then why do you try to justify the church building something besides the church? If you believe in the all-sufficiency of it, why are you interested in justifying the church's building benevolent organizations that are no part of the church? If the church is sufficient and all sufficient to do what God commanded it to do, then it needs nothing else. It needs nothing else, and we are entirely out of place building anything else.

Well, you know he showed us a number of charts. I couldn't see half of them. I couldn't read them even as well as he could, and he couldn't read them too well last night, because it was difficult for us to see. But those charts were not separate arguments. Why that's like a Baptist preacher when he comes along and quotes a lot of passages on faith, and he wants you to deal with each one of them as a separate argument. Why certainly not. They are not separate arguments. He tried to argue last night that the civil government and the home and the church are all separate in their function. I have no quarrel with that. I preach it that way. He leaves out though, the institutional home. He tries to confuse the private

BENEVOLENT ORGANIZATIONS 89

home with the institutional home, this benevolent organization, that he's talking about, and the corporation that controls. Why what he needs to discuss is not the function of the private home. Brother Woods, if you want to get the private home into the discussion, then build you an aid society to take the money of the church and deliver it to the private home and see after its use and control its distribution and run the affairs of that private home. That's what you've got in the institutional home, and that's what you're supposed to be trying to defend. (Five minutes notice, if it hasn't already gone.) He didn't have that thing on his chart. His chart did not correctly represent it.

Well, he said Cogdill's trying to make the church a substitute for the home. I'm trying to do nothing of the sort. I don't believe in doing anything of the sort. I do not believe that the church can function for the home, or the home, the private home, for the church. I tried to get him last night, when he uses the term home, to tell us what he's talking about. Are you talking about the home in the sense of an asylum for the afflicted, for the destitute? That's one definition of the home; an institutional home. Or, are you talking about the divine relationship? I pressed him to tell us, which is it that's restored, brother Woods? Is it the divine relationship, or is it just the place? What is it that's divine about the home anyhow? Is it the house in which the family lives? Or is the family, the relationship? And when you talk about restoring something, what are you talking about restoring? Can the church or anybody else restore that divine relationship that has been destroyed?

Oh, he said Cogdill's got the elders over two institutions. **No,** he hasn't. No, he hasn't. Cogdill's got the elders over only one organization, the congregation. And I'm contending that the congregation, the local church, can furnish everything that is necessary to care for the destitute that God has made it responsible for. I asked brother Woods last night, would you deny that the congregation under its elders can buy or rent a house, a place, for shelter for the destitute? What did he say about it? He conveniently forgot it.

Why friends, is he going to deny that the elders of the church can furnish a house in which the destitute can live? They can for the preacher. They can't furnish his family. They can't furnish the organization that lives in it. But they can furnish the place just like they can furnish the place there, and they can oversee it just like they do the church building. Oh, he said Cogdill's got the church in secular education and he said he didn't believe in that. Why, brother Woods, the church can provide for a destitute child, a child in need, they can provide for the secular education of that child without going into the school business. You know that. What are you trying to put the church in the school business for? They can provide groceries for the hungry without going into the grocery business. They can provide physical education, proper recreation, from that point of view, without building a YMCA. They can hire people who are responsible in matters of that kind and capable of serving in matters of that kind just like they can hire a contractor to build a building without going into the contracting business. And, by the way, they can oversee the work that he does and see that he does it according to contract, too. Yes, the elders of the church can do that. And they can hire a doctor without practicing medicine, and buy drugs without going into the drug store business, and pay the hospital bill when medical attention and care is needed without going into the hospital business. They can oversee the care; and when they place a child in a private home, a destitute child, with the agreement that they will pay that home to take care of that child, the child is still under the control of the elders of the church, and if it isn't properly cared for they can take it out of that home, and put it somewhere where it can be cared for, but they don't have that kind of oversight in the kind of a home you're talking about. When they put a child, or anybody puts one in one of these institutional homes, if the superintendent is not willing to release it, you've got to go to court to get it out, even if it belongs to you, brother Woods.

And there are instances of that kind. There are instances of that kind.

BLACKBOARD DIAGRAM

No, we are not confusing the home and the church. You are trying to get us to do it. That's the point. Then on the matter of incorporation. You know we're making some progress on this corporate business. Brother Woods first argued, in debating this matter, that the corporation was just a means or a method, like the Sunday School that the church uses, a functional arrangement. That was his contention in the debate at Indianapolis. Then in the debate at Paragould he moved that corporation over and he tried to join it on to the home. First, it was a part of the church, and he was trying to tie it on to the church of the Lord. Then in the debate at Paragould he tried to make it an integral part of the home. He's got something there, and doesn't know just exactly where it belongs, or where to put it. And you know, now, it's entirely unimportant. That's what he said about it last night. Well, you've done a lot of preaching and debating about it for it to get so unimportant all of a sudden.

By the way, he said Cogdill's got an organization exactly like the one he's condemning. He's a part of a corporation to edify. I deny that. It's a misrepresentation. It isn't so, brother Woods. The corporation of the Gospel Guardian *Co.* is a business enterprise. It wasn't formed to edify the church. No, that isn't the function of it. It's a business enterprise.

Well, he said that the law requires corporation and he

read from a Tennessee booklet. Brother Woods, listen! That booklet that you had was published in 1952. The law that it cites was enacted in the public acts of Tennessee in 1951. In 1953, every statute cited in that book that you've got was repealed. Every one of them. The last one of them, brother Woods. And here are the public Acts of Tennessee, 1953. Now if you want to borrow this book, find where the statute demands and requires a corporation. You haven't done it yet. The only law you've cited has been repealed, four years ago. You're four years behind time on that.

The idea of a corporation being a part of something else. Why you know he said that Cogdill differs with men in his own company, and writing for his own paper. Well, that's frequently so, and I thank God that's so. You can't differ with the one that Guy Woods is associated with and still be a part of it. If you differ with it you can't write for it any more. Roy Lanier can testify to that as everybody else knows that knows about the arrangement. There are a lot of things in the Guardian that I differ with. I don't differ with what Marshall Patton said. He said exactly what I'm contending for, that a church can have, the members of the congregation, can form a corporation to hold title to property; but the law does not give such a corporation the right to control anything connected with the church. It is simply a trustee arrangement, a permanent trusteeship; and it has no function spiritually whatever, and is precluded by the supreme court of the state of Alabama, and I cited you two or three cases of the supreme court of this state. I could give you the same kind of a citation from nearly every state in the Union, where the law holds, the supreme court holds—I don't care what anybody else says about it. It's a supreme court decision, brother Woods. You can disagree with it if you want to, that the church corporation is separate from the church. A religious or an ecclesiastical society and the corporation that holds title to property are two different things.

And I thank you.

Wood's Third Negative

Brethren Moderators, brother Cogdill, Ladies and Gentlemen:

Again, I rejoice that in the providence of God that I am privileged to appear before you tonight in the negative of the proposition which brother Cogdill seeks to affirm. I should like to call your attention to the fact that fifteen charts which I presented on last evening remain unanswered. Some years ago when brother Porter conducted a debate in this city with Mr. Tingley, I am made to wonder just what the Christians of this community would have thought had brother Porter allowed Mr. Tingley to introduce fifteen charts to which brother Porter made no reference whatsoever. That is not my conception of debating.

Now brother Cogdill has told you that these charts do not teach my position. It is his obligation to take up these matters and show you that they don't. There will be honest and sincere people who will not be satisfied until some effort along that line has been made.

Now I propose to take up his speech item by item and statement by statement because that's my way of doing it. In the first place he told us that I argued that it's not a question of divine authority. I'm unable to know how he drew such a conclusion, because I said nothing of the kind. I said that the arguments that he introduced along that line were not in issue because I accepted them. That's a far cry from saying that the question of divine authority is not involved. It is. But the issue is, what institution has God authorized to perform this work? The work of actual child care? May a church as a church serve as a home? That's the real issue. And you know and I know and brother Roy Cogdill knows that he hasn't met that issue as yet.

He said it's not a question of the private home. He attempted to leave with you the impression that all I argued for last night was the private home. When repeatedly I called your attention to the fact that there are two kinds of homes—private and legal. And I established the divine authority of the private home in order to show that the legal home is simply a reestablishment of the private home that exists by divine authority. What did he do with this? Just like he did with the fifteen charts. Nothing.

Then next he says that the question of authority is involved. Indeed it is! And that question is: What institution is set up for that purpose and performs that work by divine authority? Now I've answered these arguments on his charts. Last night he had chart No. 1, the Lord's Supper. I accept without hesitancy brother Cogdill's views as presented on that chart. He introduced chart No. 3, Scriptural Authority, and there isn't any question at all in this debate as to whether or not the Bible is the source of it, and the question is simply whether or not God has ordained the church as a church to perform these functions.

So also of the matter of essentials and expedients. Now brother Cogdill argues that the church is obligated to perform these obligations. If his argument possesses merit then it's this: That no other organization can exist for the purpose of performing that which God ordained that the church should do. But it's the function of the Gospel Guardian, allegedly, to teach God's word. Now is teaching God's word a function of the church? It is indeed. He told you that the Gospel Guardian doesn't do a work of the church. By which he means, of course, there is no edification for the church in the Guardian. Now I've been knowing that for sometime. (laughter) But I hardly thought he would admit it. Now if his argument possesses any merit then it proves that the Gospel Guardian is unscriptural.

Furthermore, if he argues, yes, that the Gospel Guardian operates on parallel lines with the church, that is it's the function of the Guardian to perform the functions of individuals, then be it so. It's also the function of individuals in an organization which God himself ordained, the church, to perform the functions of child care. And even on that basis we justify it. But now watch, please. Brother Cogdill is arguing like this: That there is a need that is to

BENEVOLENT ORGANIZATIONS

be provided. That is, to relieve the needy. That the church is the organization that is to supply it. That's it. Now then that's the essential. The supplying of the need.

The question of expediency is this: Shall they put them in a private home? Shall they put them in a foster home? Shall we put them in a boarding home? Shall we put them in a home that christian brethren have established for that purpose? There's the real issue. There's where the expediency is. That's it. And hear this, it is the function of the church to supply the need, but it's the function of the home to discharge that need. There is the area of expediency, and brother Cogdill needs to deal with it.

Now he wants to know: Where is the organization in I Tim. 5:16. Let me have chart 0, if you can find it there, please.

This is one of the charts that I introduced on last evening to which no reference was made. In I Tim. 5:16 the apostle Paul points out that a woman that has a widow, now here is a daughter who has a widow, is to provide for that widow that the church be not charged. What is it now that this sister is to provide for her mother? A home, that the church be not charged. Why is that this woman is to do that? In order that the church may not be obligated to provide what would be necessary in the event that there was no such daughter or sister. Now watch, please! What about the absence of such a sister? Get it please. "... that it (that is, the church) may provide for them that are widows indeed." What is that the church is to do? The church is to supply that which the sister would supply were the sister in existence. But since she's not, the church takes over and provides that which the daughter would provide if the daughter existed, but does not.

Now then, according to brother Cogdill's position, what the church is to provide over here is another church, because it can't establish anything else except another church. Now, brother Cogdill, I would say that a little bluster and a little more answering of arguments would be more in order here. He directs our attention to the fact that it's the work of the church to engage in evangelism, and in benevolence and in edification. Does he mean by that that therefore there is no sphere of such activity outside the such activity of the church as an organization? Again, I say that eliminates the Gospel Guardian. He's in the position of having to argue here that even the Gospel Guardian does not perform any function that is parallel to what the church does, or else he must take the position that his own paper occupies the same relationship to the church that the home does.

Now all of this about the pattern, Exodus 25:8,9; 27:8, vs. 26, 30, we accept that without question. We believe that there is a pattern, and that this pattern is exclusive in so far as the church is concerned. But brother Cogdill himself is on record as having said that the Bible is a text book of the church and not a text book of the home. By which, he could not for the life of him give you a detailed pattern of the function of the home as a home in the New Testament.

Then next, he cites us to the chart, No. 2, I believe it is, and here it is on the board. What is the Issue?

Now, on last evening—we answered all of these last evening. This is simply a repetition. I want to prove this question. Here is the church, divine in origin, exists by the authority of Christ, regulated only by the scripture and according to the authority overseeing it. We accept that without question. But he says now, here is the work that is to be done, the necessities of life, shelter, food and clothing. Here is what brother Cogdill is doing. He is simply establishing a home, but he refuses to admit that that's what it is. Now this "and so forth"—you see it out here—that covers a good many things that he hasn't got down here. One of which is secular education. He told you that the elders could not participate in that activity without being disloyal to Christ, that that is a characteristic of the home. He told you that the church could not engage in that. Now, one of two things is true; either it is the church—in which case it is engaging in activities that he says the church can't do, or else it's exactly that which I'm contending for, a home apart from the church. Now which is it, brother Cogdill? I insist that you deal with this part right here, all right, you tell us. You tell the audience when you get up here. Is this right here the church or the home? And, if you say it's the church, you tell us if this work of the church includes such as teaching the children A, B, C's, etc. But, if you say it is the work of the church, then tell us if the elders can serve over two divine institutions as elders. But, if you say it is not the church here and it is the home, then tell us why that you are objecting to another organization besides the church. Do you think he'll deal with that? Now this debate will close and he will never say a word about it, except to make a lot of noise about it.

I do not think that I have ever met a man that was as vulnerable as brother Cogdill in debate. I say that now without any reflection upon him, because I recognize his sincerity. But I have never seen a man that left himself open, and liable to exceptions, more than he. For example, on last evening I introduced a chart with reference to the distinctions between the church and the home. And then tonight, he anticipating difficulties along this line said, I admit the distinctions. Distinction between what? The church and the state and the home. And yet when it comes to this he wants to eliminate the distinctions and make this a part of the framework of the church and put elders over it. I leave it to you to decide whether or not he is confusing them. Then he turns right around and said, and I have his exact quote here, "The church cannot function as a home." Did you hear him say it? The church cannot function as a home . All right then with reference to the etc., as to the necessities of life—food, clothing, shelter, medical attention, supervision, manual training, secular teaching—Is that a function of the church or a function of the home? If he says it's the church, then he's got the church doing that which he says the church can't do. If it's not the church doing that, then he's wrong in his argument. Now get busy on it.

He asked me the question, May the church furnish a house for the needy? Certainly, the church may furnish a place; it may furnish the necessities of life; it may pay the money for the personnel; but when it does that, it has discharged its duty. You get it, ladies and gentlemen, when the church has done all that it's expected to do, all of its work of caring for the needy must yet to be done.

Let me have chart No., just a moment now and let me get the number. It's the one on brother Tant's editorial. While I'm looking it up for the number, maybe you can think of it. No. 6, all right.

This is a very significant thing, friends. Let us have the lights off in the center here, please. Now, friends, brother Tant published an editorial a few weeks ago in which he made an appeal on behalf of some people whose children are in need. He says here, "Both the mother and father, who is incapacitated and unable to provide for the children, have already signed the necessary papers committing the children into the custody of the elders of the congregation where they live for them to find a proper home." He said, "Let this fact be clear—the purpose of this article is to seek to find a home for all four children." What do these children have? They have everything that brother Cogdill says they need. They are in the hands of the elders of the church. The elders have them under their care. Yet here's brother Tant yelling for somebody to provide a home for them. And then get up here and tell us that the church is the only organization that is expected to perform such.

All right, let's have the lights now. Then in his next statement, he absolutely surrendered his entire position. When I asked him the question: May the elders supervise secular education? He said. No, but they can provide it. That's exactly my position. But it's his position, brother Cogdill, that when they supply it, it's the church doing it.

I asked him the question, May the church engage in secular activity? He said it's the duty of the church to provide the food, but not to operate a farm or grocery store or words to that effect. That's my position, but it's his position that all of that is a part of the work of the church and that the elders oversee that. You have just changed sides here in this tonight, sir.

He said the church can supply the clothing, but that doesn't mean they can operate a clothing store. Let me emphasize further that the church can supply supervision, that is, it can supply the money for it; but it's not the function of the elders as elders to act in that capacity, because God didn't put them over two institutions.

Now some of these brethren have been saying around that I take the position that elders cannot serve and that men who are elders, can't serve in this capacity. I've said nothing of the kind. I've said this, then men cannot perform their functions as elders when they are running a home, whether it be a private home, a foster home, a legal home, or whatever type of home it may be. Now the same men who are elders in the church may perform those functions, but they are not performing them as elders. A man may be president of a bank, the head of his house, an elder in the church, and a member of the board of Childhaven, but he's not any one of those in absolute consequence because he's the other. Each one of them involves a separate and a distinct function.

Now finally, and I will have covered all that he said, he said that this statute that I introduced last night has been repealed. Now I wrote to the Bureau of Public Health in Tennessee, last year, 1956. And I asked them for this information and this is what they sent me. Now, brother Cogdill, if there's any deception in the matter, the deception lies with the Department of Public Welfare of the State of Tennessee, because that's what they sent. But what difference does it make, anyway? Brother Cogdill opposes these homes whether they are incorporated or not. Now, brethren, the fact is, I asked him last night this question, Brother Cogdill, would you accept Boles Homes if they dissolved the incorporation? Let's see how much significance he attaches to it. Now we'll see when he answers that whether it's the incorporation or not.

Now, friends, hurriedly, let us look at some matters that we introduced last night before we present some more things. Let me have, please, chart No. 4.

Here is an argument that I have introduced in every debate that I have held on this question. Here is the home that every child is entitled to. Here is the home that results from disease, death, or desertion and divorce, and so on. Here is the home that's restored, or re-established. The church sustains the function to this home if it's in need. The same obligation that's the same here is the same here, when it has been reestablished. If the child had a right to this home to begin with, it has a right to this one to end with. This home and the church are two separate and distinct institutions. The church has its functions. The home has its. The home is re-established. It's not in conflict with the church, because it's not performing the work of the church as the church. It's not in conflict with the home which it replaces because that home has been destroyed. What is the home? It's simply the re-establishment of that which the child had but lost, and it's been restored, and since it must operate under legal supervision, then it's proper for it to be a legal entity, licensed by the state. In fact it's an absolute necessity for such to be. That would be true even of a foster home into which even one child has been taken.

Let us have, please, chart No. 11. Turn the lights back off, please.

In which of the following institutions are children to be cared for? A church, a home, or a home which is an integral part of the church? Now those are questions that were submitted to brother Cogdill last evening. Why doesn't he answer them? Let us have chart No. 12. Thank you.

The church is all-sufficient. Now, brother Cogdill, is it all-sufficient to function as a home? Answer, yes or no. And be sure to give us the scripture. Is it all-sufficient to function as a church?

Then next, the home is all-sufficient to function as a church? Yes or no. Is it all-sufficient to function as a home? The question is, what is the function of the home? What is the function of the church? May they be confused? Brother Cogdill says, Yes.

Now then chart No. 19. And this is to be introduced and hand it to them. This is the first.

Here we are, here are the orphans that are to be provided for. Here is the work of the church. Now according to brother Cogdill this is the relationship that the church sustains to them. The elders oversee a child-care agency Here it is right here on his chart, which he says is scriptur-

CHART NO. 19

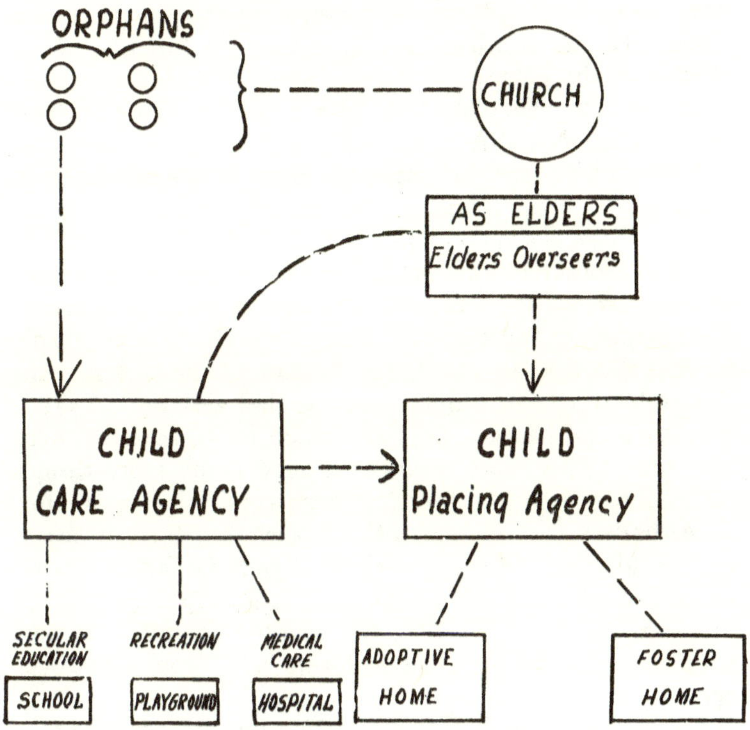

```
ORPHANS
 o o    o o  }------ CHURCH
                        |
                     ┌──┴──────────┐
                     │  AS ELDERS  │
                     │Elders Overseers│
                     └─────────────┘
                        |
   ┌────────────┐    ┌────────────┐
   │   CHILD    │──→ │   CHILD    │
   │CARE AGENCY │    │Placing Agency│
   └────────────┘    └────────────┘
    |     |    \       /      \
 SECULAR RECREATION MEDICAL           
EDUCATION         CARE   ADOPTIVE   FOSTER
 SCHOOL PLAYGROUND HOSPITAL HOME    HOME
```

al. Now then, friends, the function of this. First, to serve in secular education. Second, in recreation, in which case it would have to be a play ground. Then it would be necessary to supply medical care. Then the question of placing these in a child-placing agency would involve the question of whether or not it would be in an adoptive home or a foster home. Now get it, please. Here is the real issue. Is this the function of the church as a church? I say, No, that it's the function of the home as a home. Brother Cogdill says that the church may engage in all of this, until you get down to this, and then he cuts that out. Now how can you operate a home or supply the needs of child-care without supplying the A. B. C., a play-ground, education, medical care, and so on; is that the work of the church as a church? Do elders oversee that as elders? Now one of two things is true: If they do, then they are in the school business, the play-ground recreation business, the hospital business, and so on. They are performing the business of a home. Tell us, brother Cogdill, is that the function of the church or the home?

Let us have chart No. 19A. We'll see what some of that function is. No. 19A.

(How much time do I have?) Here is one of the functions of it. Here is one of the bulletins from one of the homes. Here is a field up here. Bear in mind now that this is what brother Cogdill says. Here is a part of the work of the church. Here is a field involving farming activity. Here is another function of it here. In order to supply a pig for hog killing time. Is that a function of the elders of the church to supply that and to oversee that activity? Take it over to them, please. See how much business the church gets into. This "etc." includes a good many more things. Here is the work of farming here—operating a tractor. Now that's a part of the work of providing for the needy, the actual care. Is the church to engage in this business? I ask you, sir, deal with that. Don't get up here and tell this audience, Oh, we believe the church is qualified to perform these functions. Deal with this "etc." you've got over here, sir.

Then next let's have chart No. 25. Let me know when I have at least three minutes.

Here, friends, is the argument that these brethren have laughed about and made fun of but never have answered. I insist that tonight it's going to take a good deal more than merely brushing it aside to deal with it. Here is my axiom: The whole is equal to the sum of its parts. And I have testimony from the Bible that that's true. Psalm 119:160, "The sum of thy word is truth." That simply means if you've got all of a number of scriptural items, put them all together, and the total constitutes a total situation which is scriptural. Now here is the proof required of my proposition. A home for the homeless provided by the church; secondly, cooperation of churches in supplying the need. Brother Cogdill doesn't deny either one of these, insofar as the work is concerned. Number three, conformity to law in

CHART # 25

WHOLE = SUM OF ITS PARTS

"The Sum of thy word is truth" - Psm. 119:160 (ASV)

PROOF REQUIRED

1. HOME for the HOMELESS supported by the church (James 1:27; 21 Tim. 5:16.)
2. COOPERATION of CHURCHES in supplying the NEED. (Acts 11:27-30)
3. Conformity to law in organization and state control. (Rom. 13)

WILL COGDILL DENY THIS:

   WHATEVER IS ESSENTIAL TO THE DISCHARGE OF THESE OBLIGATIONS

   IS SCRIPTURAL. (Axiomatic)

CHART # 26

ESSENTIAL ITEMS

1. An organization apart from the church and operating as a HOME, and NOT as a CHURCH.
2. A licensed organized institution, supplying proper child-care.

A SYLLOGISM

1. All complete situations, the component parts of which are scriptural, are scriptural situation.
2. The complete situation involved in the establishment, maintenance, and operation of the orphan homes is a complete situation the component parts of which are scriptural.
3. Therefore, the complete situation involved in the establishment, maintenance, and operation of the orphan homes is a complete scriptural situation.x

organization and state control. Now then will brother Cogdill deny this? Whatever is essential to the discharge of these obligations is scriptural. That's Axiomatic. Now let's have the next chart. Chart No. 25. Here's an illustration. No. 24 is actually the one I want, brother Deaver.

Here's an illustration, friends, of what I'm pointing out. This now will show you that brethren have used this argument repeatedly. Here is brother Foy Wallace in the "Bulwarks of the Faith." Listen to it: "A few generations later it fell to such intellects as Barton W. Stone, Thomas and Alexander Campbell, the Scotts and the Creaths, and a legion like them, to launch the mighty plea to abandon party names, party creeds, party organizations, and upon the right creed, the right name, the right doctrine, the right worship, such as taught in the New Testament itself to restore the primitive, apostolic church."

CHART No. 24

BULWARKS OF THE FAITH

spirit, built their protestant foundations on the sands of denominational creeds rather than on the rock of New Testament truth—and their foundations shifted with the crawling sands upon which they were built. Their reformations failed, falling far short of their original purpose.

A few generations later it fell to such intellects as Barton W. Stone, Thomas and Alexander Campbell, the Scotts and the Creaths, and a legion like them, to launch the mighty plea to abandon party names, party creeds, party organizations, and upon the right creed, the right name, the right doctrine, the right worship, such as taught in the New Testament itself, to restore the primitive apostolic church, the which could be neither Catholic nor Protestant, but scriptural, and therefore divine. There is no other basis of Christian unity—scriptural unity. And there is no other way to establish the identity of the primitive apostolic church. The wrong creed, the wrong doctrine, the wrong worship, the wrong organization and the wrong name could not possibly result in the right church. But the right creed, the right doctrine, the right worship, the right organization and the right name, for a like reason, cannot be the wrong church.

Friends of Christ, on this platform we shall stand unshaken and unrelenting. These principles we shall press in the successive services of this meeting. So, in conclusion now, if there are alien friends here this afternoon, as without doubt in scores there must be in this great gathering, we call upon you in the spirit of the gospel invitation to come and stand with us upon the Bible and the Bible alone and join us in the promulgation of these principles. The invitation is yours, with our prayer that you may accept it now, as the song is sung.

—*F. E. Wallace, Jr.*

What is he saying? Right name, doctrine, practice, polity and so on constitutes the church. Why? Because one of those is scriptural. Put them all together and you have a scriptural institution. Now watch: "The wrong creed, the wrong doctrine, the wrong worship, wrong organization and the wrong name could not possibly result in the right church." What is the argument? That the sum of this series of scriptural propositions is itself scriptural .

Now let's have the next chart. No. 26.

CHART No. 26

ESSENTIAL ITEMS

1. AN ORGANIZATION APART FROM THE CHURCH, AND OPERATING AS A HOME, AND NOT AS A CHURCH.

2. A LICENSED ORGANIZED INSTITUTION SUPPLYING PROPER CHILD-CARE

A SYLLOGISM

1. ALL COMPLETE SITUATIONS, THE COMPONENT PARTS OF WHICH ARE SCRIPTURAL, ARE SCRIPTURAL SITUATIONS.

2. THE COMPLETE SITUATION INVOLVED IN THE ESTABLISHMENT, MAINTENANCE, AND OPERATION OF THE ORPHAN HOMES IS A COMPLETE SITUATION THE COMPONENT PARTS OF WHICH ARE SCRIPTURAL.

3. THEREFORE, THE COMPLETE SITUATION INVOLVED IN THE ESTABLISHMENT, MAINTENANCE, AND OPERATION OF THE ORPHAN HOMES IS A COMPLETE SCRIPTURAL SITUATION.

Here are the essential items. An organization apart from the church and operating as a home, not as a church. A licensed, organized institution supplying proper child-care. Now here is the conclusion that's drawn from that —a syllogism: Here's the major premise: All complete situations, the component parts of which are scriptural, are scriptural situations. Two, the complete situation involved in the establishment, maintenance and operation of the orphan homes is a complete situation the component parts of which are scriptural. Here is the irresistible conclusion: Therefore, the complete situation involved in the establishment, maintenance and operation of orphan homes is a complete scriptural situation. Now I challenge him to attack the validity of that or the conclusion that's based upon it.

Now, finally, chart No. 27.

CHART # 27

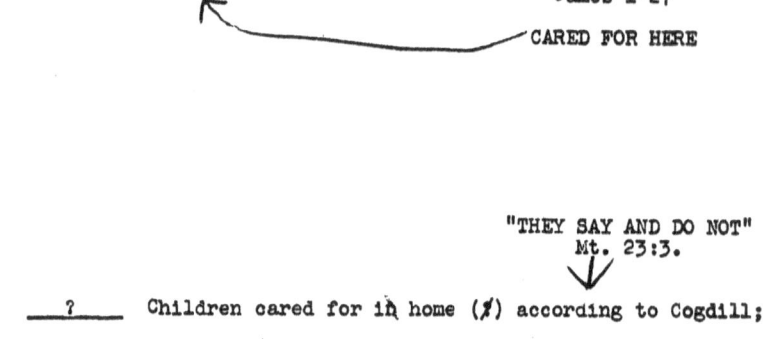

(19 HOMES - 1400 Children)   PURE RELIGION
                                James 1:27
                                CARED FOR HERE

"THEY SAY AND DO NOT"
Mt. 23:3.

___?___ Children cared for in home (#) according to Cogdill;s arrangement, the address of which is _____

I introduce all of these because I want to get them before him before his next speech. Friends, there are nineteen homes that are today being operated by our brethren. And in these nineteen homes there are approximately 1,400 children—one thousand four hundred. There ought to be 14,000 and there would be were it not for the efforts of such men as brother Cogdill. Now then what is it that's being done in these homes? Here we are. The practice of pure and undefiled religion, caring for the needy by the churches of Christ. Get it now: How many children is being cared for in the home which brother Cogdill has on his chart here? And, what is the address of that particular home over there? I want to know how many children are in it, and what the address is. Here, friends, is pure and undefiled religion. Our Lord made a statement regarding some people that say and do not. I'll let you decide tonight whom that description fits insofar as this debate is concerned.

Here is what we're doing. Here is what we're doing—19 of them. I wish there were 199. 1,440 children—the practice of pure and undefiled religion. How many children in Cogdill's foster home that he has set up here? What is it's address? Tell us, brother Cogdill. Tell us.

Now, friends, the issue is before you. It's not is the church sufficient to function as a church. It is, is it sufficient to function as a home.

Cogdill's Fourth Affirmative

Gentlemen Moderators, brother Woods, Ladies and Gentlemen:

It affords me a great deal of pleasure to have the opportunity to come back before you at this time in reply to a speech that you have listened to for the last thirty minutes, and to advance still some further thoughts along the line of our affirmative argument.

I'd like to deal first of all with the point as to the Tennessee Law. I don't know what brother Woods wrote and I don't know how far he'd rely upon the kind of information that he has, but I have here in my hand the public acts of the legislature of Tennessee in 1953. In the preamble to it says, "An act to define child welfare agencies and to provide for the chartering and licensing of said agencies and the standards for such licensing." On down further in the same paragraph it says, "And to repeal section 4520, section 4719." Now, brother Woods, that's the law that you quoted in your sermons up at Cullman when you told the people over the radio up there that in the state of Tennessee the statutes required that a child care institution be incorporated. That's the section that you quoted. I asked you last night when you referred to the Tennessee law for the section, and you gave me everything but the section. But that's the section you referred to in those speeches, that's the law you've been relying on, and this law, 1953, repealed that. So the statute upon which you rely to prove that a corporate body is necessary in order to run a child care institution, has been repealed. It's been repealed for four years, and you don't have a statute on which to rely.

There isn't any in Tennessee or anywhere else and it would be unconstitutional if a legislature tried by law to prescribe the organization for the church of the Lord to do anything. And anybody ought to know that that knows anything about law. It would be unconstitutional on the face of it. The state legislature would not undertake to do so; they wouldn't get by with it if they did. And I wouldn't be willing to comply with it if they tried. If the state law required the formation of a chartered corporation through which the church is to preach the gospel, I'd defy the state law, brother Woods. Would you? Whenever a state law undertakes to interfere with God's principles of divine righteousness, I'm going to obey God rather than man. But you know they've been quoting that matter in these debates, and they've been preaching it all over the country, and making a lot of brethren think you just can't take care of destitute children without forming one of these corporate institutions. And I want this audience to know, and I want this debate to go on record as saying that *that is not so. It ain't so*, with a capital ain't. (laughter). There isn't any such law, and all of these orphan home superintendents that have been saying that you have to do it, they need to produce the statute. They are not good authority on the question.

The next point that I want to deal with in his chart No. 27—Nineteen homes with fourteen hundred children practicing pure and undefiled religion, according to him— James 1:27—cared for in these homes. Matt. 23, "They say and do not." That's Cogdill and that's the group that stands with Cogdill. And he wants the address of congregations over the country that within their own framework as congregations, under the supervision of the elders, are seeing to it that destitute children are cared for. Well, that very Tant editorial that has worried you so much from the *Gospel Guardian* is one instance of where the church is seeing to it that the children are provided for, and they are being provided for under the supervision of the elders of that congregation. And what they were giving people an opportunity to do was to adopt the four children into their own homes, which they considered to be better than any other improvised arrangement that might be made—take them and make them their own children by adoption, and furnish them a private home, not an institutional home, brother Woods.

And if you want the name of that church it's the church at Blytheville, Arkansas, and there are plenty of congregations all around over the country that are doing exactly the same thing. I never knew of a congregation in thirty-five years of gospel preaching that had more dependent children for which it was responsible, or destitute aged people for which it was responsible, than it could take care of, or than it did, for any sustained length of time. I don't know of one that refuses. I certainly wouldn't think much of it as a congregation if it did.

Now he says Cogdill isn't doing anything about it. No, Cogdill hasn't done anything about it for thirty-five years except try to teach congregations everywhere I go that they ought to take care of their own, under their own eldership. That's all I've been doing about it, in addition to taking care of some of them myself. And if you want personal records, I'll compare records with you on that. But, of course, if you don't put children in one of the *institutional* homes and help support them, I don't care if you took a dozen into your own home, and did it out of your own pocket, you don't believe in taking care of destitute children. These brethren have the idol of an institutional home in their hearts that they think there isn't any other kind of benevolence but that. You talk about "hobbyism"—they can't see anything but an institutional orphan home, and they say that it's a matter purely of expediency, but they will tear a church up in order to get it into the budget of that congregation. A matter of expediency, dividing brethren over it.

He made a plea for sympathy last night along the lines that the opposition to these orphan homes are dividing the church. No, it isn't the opposition, brother Woods, it's the introduction of them. It wasn't the opposition to the missionary society that divided the church. It wasn't the opposition to instrumental music that divided the church. It was the introduction of it. It isn't opposition to premillennial teaching or any other kind of false doctrine that creates dissension. It's the introduction of false doctrine. That's the thing that creates the dissension.

Then chart No. 25, the whole is equal to the sum of its parts. "The sum of thy word is truth," and they dote a lot on this argument. The home for the homeless supported by the church—James 1:27 and I Timothy 5:16. Second, Cooperation of churches in supplying the need, Acts 11:27-30. Third, Conformity to the law, an organization and state control, Rom. 13. Will Cogdill deny this? Now that depends entirely on what you mean by these terms. You know what they do? They take a mathematical axiom and move it over into the realm of moral and spiritual truth, and try to make it operate as well in the realm of moral and spiritual truth as it operates in the realm of mathematics. Well, now, when you have a mathematical axiom, the parts, the constituent elements of that whole are fixed and certain. I know how many two plus two plus two are. I know what the parts are. Two is not an indefinite term. But you notice the indefiniteness of his constituent elements here. A home for the homeless and, to save my life, I haven't been able to get him to say yet—I haven't been able to get him to say yet; What part of the home is it that's restored, brother Woods? Is it just the place, or is that entity that you're talking about—The organization, the family, the relationship? What part of it is divine? I've asked him in every speech I've made in this debate. What part of the home is divine anyway? Why he shifts gears on the word home, and uses it in a dual sense, and is as duplicitious about it as he can be. He uses it one time when he means a place. He came over here to the place for shelter and tried to make that a home. Well, I deny that it is. It isn't a relationship. It isn't the divine home, brother Woods. And your institutional home is not a divine home. There isn't any relationship restored there. Why certainly not, as we shall see in just a moment. So your constituent element—your home for the homeless, supported by the church—you're going to have to get a little more definite than that if you're going to get the whole is equal to the sum of its parts to apply.

Then cooperation of churches in supplying the need. And he's going to have to define what kind of cooperation. The relationship of congregations in supplying the need in that cooperation would have a lot to do with it. It would be very vital to it. Then, conformity to law. And you're going to have to find out what the law is before Cogdill will know whether or not he agrees to what you call the law on the matter or not. Definite terms are going to have to be supplied in this matter before your argument is worth the time that it takes to make it. I can take the kind of reasoning that you do on that syllogism and prove anything under God's heaven by it. You leave me that much room to be indefinite as to constituent elements and I'll prove anything just like brother Porter proved to you that the same thing would justify a missionary society. You said it never had been answered. Why he blew that into smithereenes the first time you used it. I heard it done. That there's an obligation to preach the gospel. That the churches can cooperate in preaching the gospel, and nobody denies that. We might have some discussion about what scriptural cooperation in doing it is. Therefore the missionary society is all right. And it proved the missionary society just as easily and just as fully as it proved what you're talking about and what you're trying to prove with it. You know in any kind of a mathematical equation, the constituent elements, the component parts are fixed, and then they have to have the proper equation or relationship. And you don't have either one of them. You don't have fixed constituent elements or component parts, and you haven't even stopped to define the relationship. There isn't anything logical about your argument. It's just like the rest of them, it's pure assumption.

You know he comes up and he says, Now I answered all of these. Well, how did you answer them? Why they didn't have anything to do with the subject. He didn't even show you how it didn't have anything to do with it. Just an assertion, a plain assertion. He has the finest opinion of his assertions and of his "ipse dixit" of nearly anybody I ever heard in a discussion. Why his opponents are always weak and they never answer his arguments no matter what they do to them. And his arguments are never on the issue—To hear him tell it. And he's told you that already over and over in this debate and he'll keep doing it, because that's his style of debating.

Well, now let me tell you that just your assertion that these arguments on authority don't have anything to do with the right of the church to build other organizations is not going to satisfy these people out here that have just as good a thinker as you and I have. They've got something to think with out there, too. And they're not going to take your word for the matter that there isn't anything to anything except what you say.

He says that the essential items in this matter in chart 26, an organization apart from the church, operating as a home and not as a church. And he talks a whole lot about the home operating as a home, and the church operating as a church, and I don't know of anybody that's trying to get the church to operate as a home, or the home to operate as a church. I just don't know of anything that's doing that, unless he is, according to his own position on the matter. Listen to what he had to say about it. "The verb 'visit', James 1:27, is of course, used metaphorically, and suggests a call made for the purpose of assisting. It is translated from the Greek episkeptomai defined by Mr. Thayer: 'To look upon or after, to inspect, examine with the eye, in order to see how he is.'" This eminent lexicographer adds that: "Hebraistically, it means to look upon, to help or benefit; mainly to look after, have a care for, provide for; in this sense it is often used of the bestowal of a blessing both by God and man in sacred writing." Now that simply means that the word "visit", according to brother Woods, and he's just as right about it as he can be, means to care for.

And he made the argument that James 1:27 has to apply to the church or else the church can't practice pure and undefiled religion. Well, we'll grant that for the sake of argument. If the word "visit" means to care for and the church then can't visit, therefore can't practice pure and undefiled religion without caring for, then the church can do it, and you say now it can't. Then you said it could and it had to mean the church; now you say the church can't do it. That if the church wasn't being talked about in James 1:27 that it couldn't practice pure and undefiled r e l i g i o n. Well, brother Woods, can the church visit? In the sense of caring for? Why now his assertion is that all the church can do about it, is simply to raise money.

And while I'm on that give me my chart on the work of the Church. While I continue, find it. I don't have the number on it down. (Right on through the charts on authority.) That's it on the work of the church.

THE WORK OF THE CHURCH

WORK	SCRIPTURE	ESSENTIALS	ORGANIZATION	EXCLUDED
EVANGELIZE	Matt. 28:18-20	PLACE Nec. FACILITIES PERSONNEL	CONGREGATION (Its Own Agency)	EVERY OTHER ORGANIZATION
EDIFY	Eph. 4:16	PLACE Nec. FACILITIES PERSONNEL	CONGREGATION (Its Own Agency)	EVERY OTHER ORGANIZATION
BENEVOLENCE	I Tim. 5:16	PLACE Nec. FACILITIES PERSONNEL	CONGREGATION (Its Own Agency)	EVERY OTHER ORGANIZATION

7.   7.

The congregation is commanded to evangelize, to edify and to carry on the work of benevolence. The essentials in it in either instance is a place, necessary facilities and personnel to carry on the work. Brother Woods says that the church is it's own missionary society but the church is not its own orphan home. Well, I don't know of anybody that ever said that the church is its own orphan home. I don't know of anybody contending for that. But why does he shift gears on us in that statement? Why doesn't he just stay with his parallel? The church is its own missionary society.

Now is the church its own *benevolent society?* There you have a parallel statement. I'm contending that it is. The church is not its own gospel meeting. It isn't even its own preacher. Why you have to have personnel to preach and you have to have a place. You have to have a place and necessary facilities and personnel to carry on the work of the church in any part. You have to have a place and personnel and necessary facilities in order to carry on the work of benevolence. That is necessary in either event. Of course it is. But the congregation in either event is the agency that God has ordained to do it. Brother Woods is in the position of arguing that the church is commanded to do something, that God commands the church to do something that it cannot do, that it cannot fulfil. It doesn't have the means to carry out. Oh, he admits that the church can supply the place and then he tries to get the home and the place the same thing. Well, this place and the relationship are not the same, brother Woods.

Let me show you where he puts the home right along with some other things. "It should be noted that there was no elaborate organization for the discharge of these charitable functions." This is on Acts 11 and the function of the congregation. "The contributions were sent directly to the elders of the churches who raised the offering. This is the New Testament method of functioning. We should be highly suspicious of any scheme that requires the setting up of an organization independent of the church in order to accomplish its work." That is Guy N. Woods. "The self-sufficiency of the church in organization, work, worship, and every function required of it by the Lord should be emphasized. This lesson is much needed today. Religious-secular organizations are always trying to encroach on the functions of the New Testament church, interfere with its obligations and attempt to discharge some of its functions. The church is the only organization authorized to discharge the responsibilities of the Lord's people. When brethren form organizations independently of the church to do the work of the church, however worthy their aims and right their designs, they are engaged in that which is sinful." Why that's as good a speech as I could make on my proposition to save my life. Guy, were you confusing the home and the church when you said all of that? Were you?

Listen again: "Were these churches of Macedonia and Achaia violating the principle of the one body in this arrangement?" Talking about 2 Corinthians 8:8-14. "If no, when the same principle is followed today why make such a charge. The truth is, all of these, the orphan homes, the home for the aged, the Sunday school, are servants of the churches, functional organizations by which the church acts." What is it? The orphan home is a functional organization, just like the Sunday school. Will you endorse the same kind of Sunday school organization that you are contending for in the work of benevolence? If not, then they are not the same kind and you are wrong about it when you wrote that in the *Gospel Advocate*, November 25, 1954, and the other statement was taken from the 1946 Annual Lesson Commentary.

But I want to deal for just a moment with the matter of which part of the home is restored. I've been trying to get him to tell me that. He says that the natural home is broken, now, and then you have it restored. And he had his chart. And I've dealt with it. I've answered every argument that he makes in those charts. I haven't called for them one by one and referred to them because several of them are on exactly the same contention. As I pointed out to you. But there isn't a point in them that has gone by, as he well knows. He says the benevolent home is the natural home restored. I said, brother Woods, do you mean it's the place of shelter, or the divine relationship? And he hasn't said a word in the world about it. I haven't been successful in getting him to answer. If it's the relationship of the home I want to know in what sense has it been restored. Oh, he said they stand *en loco parentis*. Well, *en loco parentis* means in the place of parents. You can't be in the place of parents and at the same time be parents. A thing that is in the place of something is not the thing itself. You haven't restored any parental relationship there. No, sir.

Well, if it's the relationship that's restored when the parents are dead, and you have a substitute therefore, and that's all you have in an institutional home, then I want to know who is the substitute for the parent. Is it the superintendent and his wife? Is it? Every time they change superintendents they'd fire the daddy and mother of the children then, wouldn't they? Why, the children are not even in the legal custody of the superintendent and his wife. Is it the matron? Then every change of matrons would change mothers for the children. Is it the board that is *en loco parentis?* Deal with it, brother Woods. Let's get down to facts in this case. You've talked in generalities and with duplicitous terms long enough. If it's the board then it's not a personal provision at all, for the board doesn't live in the home and doesn't sustain that kind of a relationship with them. Why all they do for the children is to furnish a house for their families and provision, but they won't live with them. What do you think of that kind of a father? Now if you mean that you have something restored in the way of a relationship, suppose you tell us what it is. If the relationship is restored, then why do the homes put the children out when they reach a certain age? I don't want to run my child off when she gets to be 18 years of age. Guy Woods knows that the home is a divine relationship primarily and yet he gets up here and argues that the place is the home, and you let the elders of a congregation furnish the place and they've furnished the home. Oh, no they haven't, and they're not over the home, they are simply over the church. He said Roy Cogdill said that they could provide, but they could not supervise the secular education of the child. Roy Cogdill didn't say it. No, I didn't. I said they could provide and supervise the secular education of the child, but they didn't have to go into the school business in order to do it. Furnishing educational facilities is the function of the state, brother Woods. And when a child is destitute and needs care, needs benevolence, then the church can furnish and see to it, and supervise his getting everything that he's entitled to. And you don't have to go into the hospital business and the school business and the farm business in order to do it.

Why he tries to run hog killing into the home. I've had a home a good many years. I never killed hogs in my life.

(laughter) Hog killing a part of the home. He thinks farming is a function of the home. He doesn't know any more about the home than he does about the church evidently. He's as badly mixed up on the home as he is on the church. No wonder he can't get the two separated. No wonder he's trying to confuse you.

I want in the next place (how much time do I have?) to point out to you another thing or two, concerning this matter of authority. We've emphasized the fact that the authority must come from God or else the church does not have the right to do it. I don't care what it is. If God hasn't authorized the thing that we're talking about and we're not talking about building private homes, that isn't the function of the church. Never has been. We're not talking about restoring the private home. That isn't the function of the church and it never has been. Couldn't do it if it wanted to, without a resurrection from the dead, or without some power to force parents that desert their children to go back to them. It would have to have some kind of authority to do some restoring along that line. It can provide the care that's gone and that's needed, and that's as far as any agency can go in doing it. Unless it's adopted into the home from the viewpoint of law, and that isn't the function of the church. The legal home that you keep talking about is again an arrangement upon the part of the state.

Our proposition doesn't concern these homes. And you know he illustrated it here, a private home, and a foster home and a legal home, and then he finally got around to an institutional home. Do you know the difference between the church placing a child in that private home and paying somebody to take care of it? They still have control of that child. If it isn't properly treated they can take it out of there and put it where it will be. They have control over the work that they are trying to do. The church still retains that control when it hires a private home to take care of a child or an aged person that it's responsible for. But when the church or anybody else puts a child in one of the institutional homes, nobody has any control over it any longer, except that institutional corporation. And they c o u l d starve it to death the next year, and you couldn't do anything but criminally prosecute them. They could teach it any kind of error and you couldn't go get it. Why even a mother can't go get her children out of one unless they're willing for her to have it. The difference, brother Woods, is control over the work that the church is doing.

He said, would Roy Cogdill endorse Boles Home unincorporated? Not in its present organization, No, sir. I don't believe the church had the right to build Boles Home, or any other kind of a human organization to do its work. That's the thing I'm denying. That's exactly it. Any kind of a human organization. Well, what difference does corporation make? I'll tell you. I'll tell you, the difference is, the emphasis that you've placed upon it, and how you've been trying to tell the people that it was necessary when it isn't so. That's one difference it makes. And the next difference it makes is that the corporate form simply makes it easier to prove that there is another organization, and that it's human.

Get me my chart No. 2.

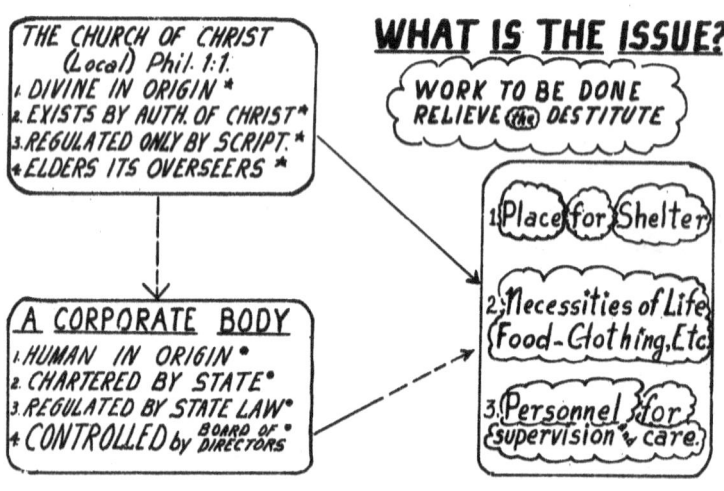

That just makes it easier to prove, that's all. The corporation part of it simply makes it easier to show that what brother Woods denies exists is actually there. Why here we have the work that's being done. You just forget about it being a home. You know a home is a whole lot more than a place to live. Why according to brother Woods these children over here in this crippled children hospital are at home and don't know it. They are getting good attention and good care. When a man goes off from home and stays in a hotel somewhere in order to do his work, and gets so homesick he nearly dies, he's at home and just doesn't know it. He's being taken care of. When the boys go off to some foreign country and are put in barracks and furnished every thing they need, and are well fed and taken care of, and nearly die because of homesickness, they are at home and don't know it. Brother Woods, you don't know what a home is. There's one of your difficulties. You think just a place for shelter is a home, you need to go back and study what the Bible says about the home. It's much more than that. Much more than that. But here's your corporate body over here controlling this work, and all the church can do is just finance it. Just raise the money.

And I want the chart on God's Way versus Man's Way. That corporate body exists, he has to admit that it is human. And there isn't a one of these homes mentioned in this proposition that doesn't have one of them, even the ones that profess to be under the elders, the elders have control over them as the board of directors of the corporation—not as elders of the church. That's true of the last one of them.

Here you have brother Woods' conception of the matter. There's the congregation, the church, with a missionary society or a sponsoring church which we'll discuss before this debate's over, standing in between it and the work of evangelism. There's the congregation, and the old folks home, and the orphans home, corporate institutions, standing in between it and the work of benevolence. And there's the congregation with its edificational society, either a school or a Sunday school organization separate and apart from the church and not a function arrangement of the

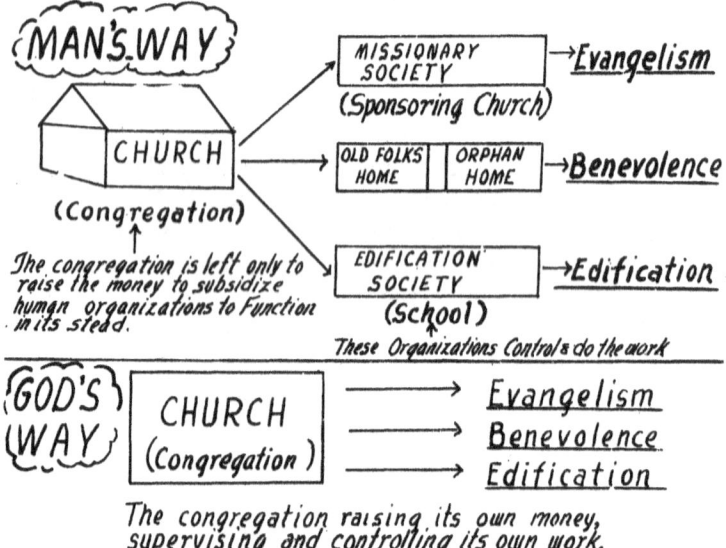

church, standing between it and its work of edification. What can the church do to discharge the work that God has given them? According to Guy N. Woods, all it can do is meet on the first day of the week and break bread and raise money to subsidize these human organizations. Now that's exactly what he's contending for. That's his point on benevolence, and I'm arguing that if it can do that on benevolence, it can do it for the rest of them.

Down there is God's way, the congregation, God's own organization, taking care of its own work under the supervision of its own elders, raising its own money, supervising and controlling its own work.

What did he say about this corporate body here? First, he tried to join it on to the church. Then he had to give that up. He tried over here then to make it an integral part of the home and we've taken that away from him, by supreme court decision. And now all of a sudden the corporate body part of it is terribly unimportant to him. Well, he's been preaching all over the country that it was necessary. I'm glad we've converted him on that.

BLACKBOARD DIAGRAM

You ought to go back up to Cullman and make your radio speeches over and tell them you were wrong about it, brother Woods. And these fellows that have been saying in their debates all over the country that the law requires it, ought to back up and apologize because it ain't so, with a capital ain't again. Produce the statute, that's the best evidence of it as you well know. Find the law that requires it, or else quit insisting on its being necessary. Thank you.

Wood's Fourth Negative

Brethren Moderators, Brother Cogdill, Ladies and Gentlemen:

May I ask if I can be heard in the back of the house when I'm talking about as I am now? Hold up your hand back there if you cannot hear me on the back seat. Would somebody turn up the volume just a little bit on this? I'm not quite as loud as brother Cogdill. What he lacks in lightning he tried to make up in thunder, but I have a little less thunder.

Now, friends, I'm happy to take up this speech, item by item, passage by passage, statement by statment, and deal with it fully. In the first place, brother Cogdill misrepresents me in saying that I introduced the statutes of the Tennessee Code in support of the view that homes must be incorporated. I introduced nothing of the kind. I told him last night that what I have is the booklet that's put out by the Tennessee Department of Welfare. And actually that is the organization that determines what type of organization may exist along that line. Now if he has any quarrel with this matter over its legality, let him deal with this department of health in the State of Tennessee. If brother Cogdill had argued that the incorporation was an essential phase of this debate, I'd think that there was some point in arguing further, and I would show the feasibility of it as well as the necessity of it. But in view of the fact that he admits that he would oppose the homes whether they are incorporated or not, why waste time on that subject? That's what I said. He's admitted that it is easier to prove his proposition by discussing incorporation. Now that's his honest confession to you. That's what he said. He said it was easier to show these things are wrong in this fashion. Well, I knew that was the reason that he was trying to use it. He can't deal with the issue so he deals with a subject which he admits is not pertinent to the argument at all.

Now that's the reason I said Brother Cogdill give us the address of that home that you endorse that is now providing food, clothing, shelter, and so on for their children. He said, I'll tell you where it is; it's in brother Tant's editorial. Do you know what brother Tant's editorial says? A group of elders, which he says are in Blytheville, Arkansas, have a bunch of children, and they are trying their best to get rid of them. Yet, he says that's the scriptural arrangement. They've got them all right but they are trying to get them off their hands. And besides that, they are trying to get them out of their own scope, too, aren't they, because they are advertising through the Gospel Guardian. Why not put it in the church bulletin if they want to keep it in the congregation? Yes, here's an example of sending children out of the scope of the congregation. And another thing, brother Cogdill, you said that the reason you objected to the homes is because the elders do not have or retain control over these children. Said, try to get them out of those homes. Try to get them out of these private homes they are adopted into too.

And another thing, then how much control do those elders have over those children of a family in California should adopt those children as brother Tant suggests? Brother Cogdill, how much control would the elders at Blytheville have over those children if they were sent to California?

Now anybody that can't see that this fellow is floundering helplessly here is in need of more instruction than could be given in one speech. He says he objects to the orphan home because you can't take them out. Can't take them out of the private home they are adopted into either. That is, if they are adopted legally and properly.

Now brother Cogdill has introduced his own experience into this. I can't see that this has any place in this debate. But inasmuch as he has brought it up, he's told us that for thirty-five years he's been urging people, urging the church, to take care of the needy. Well, he's been preaching a little longer than I have. I haven't been preaching for quite thirty-five years. But I'm glad to know that brother Cogdill has been doing this for thirty-five years, urging the church to do it. I have here in my hand a letter addressed to me from brother Gayle Oler of the Boles Home filed with that Home, at least an application of this type, filed with that home by brother Roy E. Cogdill, asking admission of children into Boles Home, in which he signed his name to an application that says in effect that he believes that these children ought to be received into the Boles Home and that it is the responsibility of the churches of Christ to support them there. For thirty-five years he's been talking about it. Now, brother Boles, (laughter) or brother Cogdill, are you still arguing it the same way? Youre the fellow that brought this up. You told us you had been doing it for thirty-five years.

Now let's look at this. If you are wrong now, you were right back there. If you were right back there, you are wrong now. When were you right? And you wanted me to go back up to Cullman. How many have you gone back to and corrected this? You tell me, and I'll get busy and go back to Cullman too. Now, brother Cogdill introduced this.

You remember this. He is the man that brought up the question of having taught these matters for thirty-five years. That doesn't make it right or wrong, but it shows he was doing it a few years ago—what he says is wrong now. I'm s o r r y that he's apostatized from the f a i t h. Brother Cogdill, would you practice this today if you had them under similar circumstances? That's the question.

He says it's the opposition that's dividing the church. Well, I think so too, but brother Cogdill and myself were on the same side of this you remember up until recently. I agree with you brother Cogdill that the opposition to these matters is dividing the church. And I tell you this, ladies and gentlemen, that up until comparatively a few years ago these brethren agreed with me on these matters at issue. Brother Cogdill was utilizing the facilities of Boles Home and saying it was scriptural. Now he's changed his mind. If we're in digression now, he was in digression then. Yet, he tells us that those of us who teach the same thing now are dividing the church. And Brother Cogdill is the man who introduced these matters.

Now he says that all I do is just make assertions. I submit that this audience would bear testimony to the fact that every chart that he introduced, except those in his last speech, I have answered not once but twice. I have taken them up item by item; brother Cogdill yet lacks even making assertions regarding mine. Approximately twenty-three or four charts have been introduced, and he's made the barest mention of just two or three of them. He has not dealt with the issue. Anybody here that thinks he has knows nothing about debating whatsover.

He said that I have moved mathematical truth over into the moral and spiritual realm. Now he says that he knows what two plus two plus two amounts to. But now, when it comes to adding it up, he doesn't know what it adds up to. He can tell you what this and this and this is, but he can't put them all together and add it up. And that's the trouble with him here. He and I agree that two is two, and two is two, and two is two, and we agree that each possesses its own distinct character, but here when you put them all together it doesn't add up to this. What it adds up to, Cecil

Douthitt said, is a "silly-gism." Now that's the answer that these fellows make to that argument.

Brother Cogdill has said in every speech that he's made in answer to me that I have not defined the home. Friends, as a matter of fact, the very first speech that I made I gave him a detailed definition of the home; gave it from the dictionary, told him that that's what I meant by it; that's what I've argued and continued to argue and exactly what I believe about it. And here it is. Now, Sir, get it down in quotation marks. Get it, brother Cogdill: "A unit of society formed by a family relationship, such relationship being either natural or legal." Now that's my definition. I gave that in my very first speech, and he comes up here and says he doesn't know what I mean by the home. Well, he's not listening then. Not listening. That's exactly what we mean by it. What part of the home is restored? The unit of society consisting of the family relationship. That is, consisting of a parent-child relationship, or what is the next best, that which stands in the place of it.

You get this, ladies and gentlemen, suppose for instance that there is a Christian family in this home that has a large house, but they haven't any children—a man and a woman. Now there are three children without a home, and they come to the church here for support. We believe that the elders can take these children and ask the family to take them into their home and to supply them with food and clothing and shelter. Now there's the place. Then he says, there is supervision. That is the parental relationship. And then, the education part of it. All goes to make up the responsibility of caring for a home. Now suppose, instead of having three extra rooms, they have thirty. What difference does it make? Suppose, instead of being a man and a woman, it had been two old maid sisters? Suppose, instead of being two women that's operating this home, suppose it's two brethren? Suppose, instead of being two brethren in the flesh, it's two brethren in the spirit or six brethren in the spirit? What difference does it make? They have simply reestablished the home that was lost. And when you get as many as seven children in it, you've got to have a license.

Let me call your attention to this fact, please. Over at Ft. Smith, Arkansas, when Southern Christian Home started, it started in exactly this way right here. It wasn't but a short time until it had more than three children. It got up above the six or seven required. Those people didn't know that you had to have a license to operate under state control. One day the sheriff came out there and arrested that brother and sister for operating that way—operating without a license. Now, they had been operating a church there for some years. You don't have to license a church, but when you establish a home, you have to license it. It becomes a legal home, and must, therefore, be licensed.

He wanted to know what part is divine. The same part that characterizes the original home those children had but lost. And we restore it, at least as far as it is possible. There now, and this is their only argument, and they've been trying, from one to four articles in practically every issue of the Guardian since I introduced this at Paragould—they've been trying to answer that argument. And here's what they've come up with, and the only thing I've seen, and he's hinting at it tonight: "Unless you have all the elements of the original home, you can't restore it." In which case, a man and woman with three small children, the mother dies, and it becomes necessary for those children to be put out into the homes of relations for a while. In a year or so, the man remarries and brings those children back and reestablishes the family unit. According to these brethren, these children don't have a home any more. One of the constituent elements is missing. They just think they've got a home. That's all. And so brother Cogdill doesn't either.

He says that I'm confusing the home with a place. Well, I've gone into detail on that. I hope that you brethren will work that out tomorrow and not waste time on that any further. He says that brother Porter blew this argument into smithereenes. Well, if brother Porter did, all brother Cogdill would have had to have done tonight is put another fuse under and seen it go up. Do you see any sign of it around here tonight? (A loud noise followed by much laughter. The microphone fell from around Woods' neck to the floor.) All right, friends, that's just like his argument. When you mention it, it goes to the ground.

Now, he says you can prove the missionary society in that fashion. I think that this is the only valid objection these brethren really raise that has any semblance of merit to it. I want to deal with it fully right now. I want to answer every argument that he makes, and I want you to see that he's as wrong as he can be and was right when he was utilizing Boles Home. But now watch: Here is the reason the missionary society is wrong. It displaces God's organization that exists for the purpose of serving as a church. Do you know what a missionary society is? It is another church. It's performing the functions of a church. It actually is doing that which God gave the church to do, that is to serve as an organization for the purpose of propagating the gospel. Now then, if the home, which is established under the conditions which I have outlined, if that home operated in similar competition with the church, which the church establishes, then it would be just as wrong as the missionary society, just as wrong. But watch it now: When the missionary society does its work there isn't any more work the church can do. It has displaced the church. But when the orphan home does its work, then the work of the church still remains—all that the church is expected to do still remains. The part which the orphan home does is simply to take the place of the home which those children had but lost. And so it's not displacing the home, because the home is gone. It's not in competition with the church because it's not performing the work of the church as a church. What is the missionary society? It is a super-organization which displaces the church. What is the orphan home? It's an institution that replaces the home which the child had but lost. There's the distinction, and these brethren never deal with it.

He says nobody is trying to turn the home into a church.

All right then, when brother Cogdill establishes this place or this relationship, it's not a home—not a church, but it's a home. And he told you repeatedly, and he said in his book here, that a church cannot establish anything but another church. Now, one of two things is true: That which the church establishes is another church, and hence it's a church establishing a church for the purpose of performing the work of a home, in which case his statement is wrong; or else, he's wrong when he says the church can't provide the means for another institution. In that fashion, that would eliminate the private home as well.

But he says the word, "visit," means to provide for, in the case of the church. But he thinks the church cannot provide for the needy unless it supplies the organization, in which case, the individual couldn't make a contribution to needy people unless he also supplied them a home. He would have to establish a home in order to "visit." If it works in the case of the church, why not in the case of the individual? He believes that an individual can make a contribution to needy people in their own home without establishing them a home. Yet when he comes to the church, he thinks the only way the church can do it is simply to make it a part of the church itself. Well, again I say, that eliminates the private home.

And then besides that, he said here, he admitted tonight, for the sake of argument. I don't know whether that "for sake of argument" means anything or not. But he said he admitted tonight for the sake of argument that James 1:27 applied to the church, but he denies that in his book. And in the Special Issue of the Gospel Guardian some of them say it applies to the church and some of them say it doesn't. He said tonight he admitted it for sake of argument. If it's not for the sake of argument, maybe he denies it. I don't know how to take him on that. He made an argument here that James 1:27 applies to the church tonight, yet he denies it in his book.

Here, friends, is his chart, "The Work of the Church." Now how's he going to do it? It's the work of the church to evangelize. We agree on that. And it involves a place, and facilities, and personnel. Actually, that place there

Now then, his chart No. 7.

THE WORK OF THE CHURCH

WORK	SCRIPTURE	ESSENTIALS	ORGANIZATION	EXCLUDED
EVANGELIZE	Matt. 28:18-20	PLACE Nec. FACILITIES PERSONNEL	CONGREGATION (Its Own Agency)	EVERY OTHER ORGANIZATION
EDIFY	Eph. 4:16	PLACE Nec. FACILITIES PERSONNEL	CONGREGATION (Its Own Agency)	EVERY OTHER ORGANIZATION
BENEVOLENCE	I Tim. 5:16	PLACE Nec. FACILITIES PERSONNEL	CONGREGATION (Its Own Agency)	EVERY OTHER ORGANIZATION

7.   7.

ought to be under the form of expediency. Of course, a place is involved in it, but then, so far as saying you have to have a place and designating that place, he's wrong about that. And so also with reference to this. But now look, here's the fallacy in this. This point makes the church making a contribution to a private home. Why do I say that? Because the congregation is its own agency in benevolence. Now brother Cogdill's position is that it is wrong for the church to make a contribution to a legal home such as Boles Home or Childhaven because it must contribute only to that which itself operates. But it doesn't operate the private home, hence it is not under its elders and supervision. Then, since the congregation is its own agency and it cannot contribute to anything which it can't run, so it cannot contribute to the natural home unless it takes the home over and runs it. Is it possible that there's anybody here that can't see that?

Now it's strange indeed, when brother Cogdill is as shrewd and smart as he is, and I say that with all sincerity, would make an argument that is as fallacious as that. Let's have his next chart now. Chart No. 8.

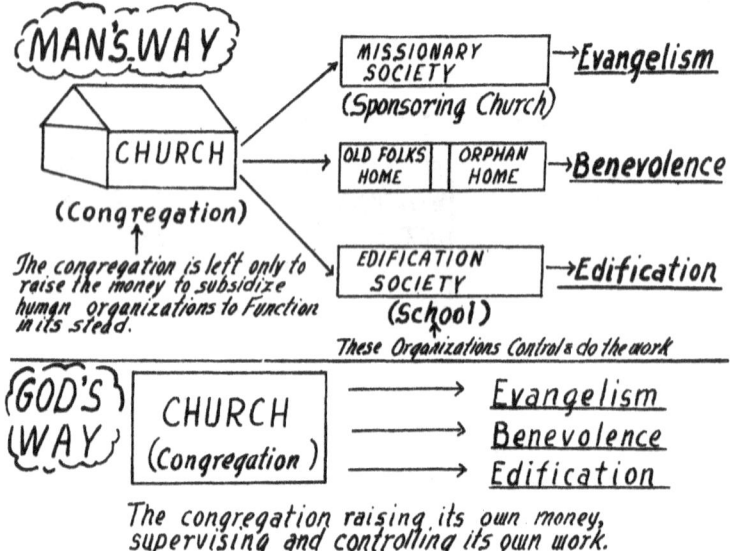

8.

And I do wish he would take up my arguments like this. I would be glad, brother Cogdill, if you would. Chart No. 8: Here is his position. Now, he says, here is man's way, and man's way for doing evangelism is through the missionary society. I agree with him that that's right. Why is the missionary society wrong? Because here is God's missionary society. Now let me call his attention to why the missionary society is wrong on here. Now, brother Cogdill, where is the needy private home on this chart? Where is it, Sir? It's not here because this is parallel to the missionary society. It's not here because this is parallel to the missionary society. It's not here, because he told us a while ago that he didn't believe that the home and the church are the same. I've been charging that he did. But if it's not there, where is the needy private home? This is the congregation. This congregation is left only to raise and give the money to subsidize a different organization to function in its stead. Now, you will have to admit this: that the private home when it is supported by the church—the needy private home—becomes a part of the congregation. In the framework of it, mind you, and its support. In the first place, we are not arguing here that human organizations in opposition to the divine were involved. He knows that they are not.

He said that I take the position that the church cannot do the work which God gave it to do. I said no such thing. That I have taken the position here that the church is not adequate to accomplish that which God has designated the church to do. I never thought of making such an argument. I said that the church is fully sufficient to accomplish all that God intended the church as a church to do. I believe in the all-sufficiency of the church, but I believe just as much in the all-sufficiency of the home.

The Catholics try to make a civil government out of the church. Brother Cogdill is trying to make a home out of the church. He'll not get away with it. He said that the church can't establish anything else—that when it establishes the family relationship of which I have spoken, that it must be another church. In which case, he is confusing the church and the home, and he's putting the elders over two churches. The same elders over two churches when he does it. If he says that this is not the church here, then he is saying that there is a difference between the organization of the church and the home. And, if he admits that that difference exists, then he must admit that it must be legally established.

He said that I made a statement that was inconsistent with my present position. He read from me where I said that any organization independent of the church to perform the work of the church is sinful. Why I believe that with all my heart. I never thought about questioning such a statement. Of course, the church is all-sufficient to perform the work of the church. The question is, brother Cogdill, is it sufficient to perform the work of the home also? You say it is. In which case, you put elders over two institutions as elders. And again, let me say, and I argue and insist that the same men who are elders of the church may operate the home, but they are not performing the functions of elders in so doing. I believe they are at Tipton. It is an expedient arrangement there for those good brethren who are the directors of the home and who are also elders of the church to serve in both capacities, but they are not identical capacities, because the New Testament does not provide for the church to have a president or a corporation.

Then next he said, you can't restore it unless the parents are there. And he objects to the home because the superintendent doesn't live with the children. Now that was the best one he brought up. Some of the brethren back in those days when it was customary to put one of the kids out in a building that was built out apart from the house, that kept him from being in the family at all because he wasn't living under the same roof as the parents did. How ridiculous can you get now? Besides that, up here at Childhaven when I was up there in the Spring, Brother and Sister Brock did live with the children. Do you endorse Childhaven? I didn't think so. We're making a little headway here. Now he was just needing a little time and something to say when he got around there.

And then, he said next, that he won't run the children out of his home. He implied that they run them out of the orphan homes. Said, I won't. You give me a single example of where any child was ever turned away from a home once that child had been received. Naturally, oftentimes they can't take them simply because of the fact that brethren will not open up their purses for the purpose of supporting religion that is pure and undefiled. And much of the reason for it may be charged to my worthy opponent who sits on the other side of the table this evening. There, friends, is the situation. Ah, no these homes do not run them off. They try to make them useful and proper citizens of society and they try to supply them with that which enables them to get out into the world and to make their own home. And be it said to their credit that hundreds of them today are useful and valuable citizens taking their places in the society and the church performing splendid functions for themselves and those about them simply because some people had enough of the milk of human kindness to do something about them. They have a different idea from these elders at Blytheville who've got them on their hands and are trying their best to get rid of them. There is the home that brother Cogdill set up here tonight.

He said he didn't know that hog-killing is a part of home activity. Well, his education has been wonderfully limited. I feel sorry for him that he's been neglected in that particular field. I wonder if he thinks that dish washing is a part of home activity, cooking, sewing, etc.? Now that was just a weak, pitiful dodge. That's all that was. He knows that's a part of child training. He knows that, at least figuratively speaking. (Laughter) Brother Cogdill ought to know that. At least they ought to be able to know what kind of pork chop to buy at the grocery store when they go down there. According to him, it would be wrong for that to be done; or if it is right to be done, then the elders have got supervision over it. They need then to be meat cutters among other things to show them what kind of pork chops to buy.

He says: You're wrong about it, elders can supervise the education of children. Now, friends, I had stated plainly that brother Cogdill had taken the position that the elders of the church and the church itself cannot engage in secular education. I had showed that that was the reason why his position is so inconsistent. Now he comes up here and says: The elders can supervise such activity. You listen here, please, on page 8 of his book here, he says, "The church is not a court or a school of domestic relations." He says, "Secular education and the teaching of secular subjects such as science, mathematics, history and literature does not come within the scope and mission of the work of the church and should be no part of its work." He says here, and I have his exact quote, "Elders can supervise the education of a child." Which time did you state your position, brother Cogdill? He says further here that when elders take the oversight of any program of work such as banking, farming, dairying, real estate, secular education, or anything of that sort outside of the work of the Lord's church, they exercise oversight in another capacity than elders. Which time did you state your position, Sir? One time he says they can take such oversight. Another time, he says they can't. Do you know why he's saying this? Floundering helplessly in this debate, he has to say something. That's the reason.

Yes, he says that he opposed Boles Home whether it was incorporated or unincorporated. That's the reason why that I am not particularly interested in entering into a discussion of this question of incorporation.

Then, he says; What of children in a hospital? There you have food, clothing, and shelter. Yes, they do. The same thing might be said of them in the penitentiary. They've even got a lot of medical care and so on. But listen friends, a home is a unit of society where there is a parent-child relationship or the next best thing to it—where law provides that others stand en loco parentis. There is exactly that the home is. There, if you please, is what I'm defending here tonight. That's what is separate and apart from the church. That's what elders as elders cannot oversee. But that is what the church is obligated to support if it's obligated to support a comparable situation in a needy private home. There are many factors that would enter in as to whether or not there is an obligation. The same thing would be true with reference to a needy private home. But assuming that all other things being equal so far as the obligation is concerned, the parallel is exactly there. I thank you.

THIRD NIGHT

Cogdill's Fifth Affirmative

Gentlemen Moderators, Brother Woods, Ladies and Gentlemen:

I'm grateful again for the good providence of God that makes it possible for us to assemble upon this occasion and study his word concerning issues in which we are all vitally interested as attested by our presence at perhaps a good sacrifice of both time and money for this discussion.

Brother Woods and I cannot decide these matters for you. We can simply point out to you what we believe the word of God teaches. No man ought to be able to make up your mind. You ought simply by a study of the word of God to learn what God himself has said about the matter, reach your own decision upon the basis of what the Bible teaches. That's the only plea that I have to make. I'm not here for the purpose of trying to win any honors debating. I'm not interested in that. I never have been. I am here to try to uphold with all of my power, with all of the sincerity and earnestness that I have, what I believe the word of God to teach, and that's all I'm interested in. To make that just as clear to you as I know how to make it, and to help you, if possible, to come to an understanding of the truth, and the convictions that are based upon it. All other matters fade into insignificance as concerned with that one.

This is our last night on this proposition. In the very beginning this evening, I want to call your attention to a few things concerning some things that were characteristic of the discussion last night lest I forget them later in my speech. First of all I would like to present to you two charts—No. 10, first please—in order that we may deal with a matter that was presented. Brother Woods made the charge that the *Gospel Guardian* is an organization exactly like the orphans home and that it is doing the work of the church, and organized for the purpose of edification, which is the work of the church. That charge is frequently made. It has been made all over the country, both in preaching and in debating, and so we prepared this chart from the point of view from which that charge was first of all presented.

The Gospel Guardian Company, and we have one of our schools with which we are familiar, Abilene Christian College. And, of course, what is characteristic of it is characteristic pretty well of the rest of them. Then an orphan home over here. It wouldn't matter whether it's Childhaven, or whether it's Boles, or which one of these institutional homes it may be. In the first place, the Gospel

Gospel Guardian Co.	Abilene Chr. College	Orphan Home
A CORPORATION NON PROFIT	A CORPORATION NON PROFIT	A CORPORATION NON PROFIT
FURNISHES MEANS OF PREACHING GOSPEL	FURNISHES MEANS OF PREACHING GOSPEL	FURNISHES MEANS OF PREACHING GOSPEL
SUPPORTED BY INDIVIDUALS	SUPPORTED BY INDIVIDUALS	SUPPORTED BY INDIVIDUALS
CHURCH CAN BUY SERVICES	CHURCH CAN BUY SERVICES	CHURCH CAN BUY SERVICES
IN CHURCH BUDGET	IN CHURCH BUDGET	IN CHURCH BUDGET

DOES the PARALLEL GO ALL the WAY??
10.   10.

Guardian Co., is not the paper. The paper is a product of the Gospel Guardian Co. We publish two papers and a number of books and tracts and other things. The company, a corporation, is a non-profit corporation. That doesn't mean that we can't make money. We're like the fellow said that he didn't intend for it to be a non-profit corporation, but it turned out that way. By non-profit corporation we simply mean that under the law there isn't any capital stock, and there aren't any stockholders therefore, and nobody draws any dividends from it. That's what a non-profit corporation is. That doesn't mean that it can't make money, but it can't pay out any dividends. The money that it does make on what it has to sell has to stay in the company, as the law provides.

Well, the same thing, of course, is characteristic of Abilene Christian College, a corporation set up under the same statute; and the orphan homes, the ones that we are concerned about in this proposition in our debate, are likewise non-profit corporations. The Gospel Guardian Co. furnishes means of preaching the gospel, they say. That is, they say that the work in which the company engages is a means of preaching the gospel. Technically, that might be true; grant for the moment that it is, for the sake of comparison. Then they tell us that Abilene Christian College likewise furnishes means of preaching and teaching the word of God. Likewise they justify the operation of the orphan homes on the basis of raising or rearing the children to be Christians. And one of the contentions that has been made in recent debates is that the object of benevolence is in reality evangelism, so the orphan home furnishes a means of preaching the gospel.

Then they tell us that the Gospel Guardian company can be supported by individuals. And that Abilene Christian College can be supported by individuals. That the orphan home is supported by individuals, and that that's all granted, and up to that point they are parallel. That they are parallel again because the church can buy services from the Gospel Guardian Co., and that the church can buy services from Abilene Christian College, Christian education. That the church can buy services from an orphan home, therefore they are parallel. Well, if they are parallel up to that point, and that means, of course, that they are the same kind of institution, all of them existing for the same purpose and doing the work of the church, then if the orphan home has a right in the church budget, Abilene Christian College has a like right in the church budget, and so would the Gospel Guardian Co. have a right in the church budget. If they are parallel institutions and one of them is entitled to participate in the budget and the contributions of the churches around over the country in general, why wouldn't all of them be? Now does brother Woods agree that schools like Abilene Christian College are entitled to church support? The paper for which he writes contends that it is and has for a good long while now. I wonder if he is in harmony and in agreement with the paper that he represents. He claimed that I disagreed with some of the writers for the Guardian, which of course, is the case. We are not agreed about everything. Brother Woods, do you agree with brother Goodpasture and the stand of the Gospel Advocate on putting the schools in the budget of the churches? Or, are you disagreed with the paper with which you're connected?

And if you would rule out putting the schools in the church budget, on what ground would you do it? They are preaching the gospel just like the orphan homes and just like you say the Gospel Guardian Co. is. So the parallel, unless he's willing to go along and put them all in the church budget, and that would certainly solve the problems of printing gospel literature, and the deficit that arises from it. It would sure help our financial problems, if we could convince ourselves and convince the brethren that such would be a good thing to do. But I'm not willing to go along with it.

I want No. 11, now if you will please. While this much of a parallel is often presented to show that they are the same kind, I want to show you by the next chart that they are not parallel.

GOSPEL GUARDIAN CO.	ABILENE CHR. COLLEGE	ORPHAN HOME
ORGANIZED as BUSINESS (Publishing)	ORGANIZED as BUSINESS (School)	ORGANIZED as BUSINESS? (Do not admit it.)
ORGANIZED BY INDIVIDUALS	ORGANIZED BY INDIVIDUALS	ORGANIZED BY CHURCHES
SUSTAINED BY CHARGING FOR SERVICES RENDERED	SUSTAINED BY CHARGING FOR SERVICES RENDERED	IS NOT A SERVICE INSTIT. DOES NOT CHARGE*
COULD BE SELF SUSTAINING	COULD BE SELF SUSTAINING	DEPENDS UPON DONATIONS
RECEIVES NO CONTRIBUTIONS FROM CHURCHES	RECEIVES NO CONTRIBUTIONS FROM CHURCHES	DEPENDS UPON CONTRIBUTIONS FROM CHURCHES

THE PARALLEL FAILS.

11.

The Gospel Guardian Co. is organized for business. We are engaged in the publishing business, not just the printing of a paper. There isn't any point in confusing the paper with the company anymore than there is a point in confusing the place, and the care of children with the corporation. The corporation is one thing and the work that it does is another. So the publishing business is the business for which the company is organized. Abilene Christian College is a business organization, a secular educational institution; primarily it's a business. Nine-tenths of its work is secular education. It's in the school business—in the school business. And the orphan home, is it organized for business? They don't admit it. Seems to be from many points of view a pretty big business in some instances. But they wouldn't admit that that's the purpose for which the orphan home is organized.

Then may I suggest to you that the Gospel Guardian Company was organized by individuals. Abilene Christian College was organized by individuals. But the orphan homes that we're talking about are organized by churches. Now brother Woods shifts gears on us on that, and he talks about what the church can do, and what the brethren do when they set up these homes. We're not debating homes that the brethren have established and the right of the brethren, individually, to establish homes in this proposition. We're debating the right of the churches, *the churches*, to set up and build benevolent organizations. So there's one point of distinction again.

Then the Gospel Guardian Company is sustained by charging for services rendered. We don't print literature and distribute it free. We have to charge for what we print. We do not distribute the Guardian free. Somebody pays for every issue of it that goes out. We don't get to charge as much for it as we would like to. We don't seem to be able to raise the price on religious papers to a justifiable point. But it is sustained, the company is sustained by charging for the merchandise that it sells, the services that it renders. Abilene Christian College is sustained by charging for services rendered, primarily. Tuition is charged the students, and that's their primary source of income so far as the maintenance of the school is concerned. But the orphan home is not a service institution. It does not charge; that is, it isn't supposed to. It's a benevolent organization, and hence, it's not a service institution that charges for its services. I'm talking about these institutional orphan homes that our proposition concerns. The Gospel Guardian Company could be self-sustaining if we could charge enough for the merchandise that we sell. And Abilene Christian College could be self-sustaining if it could charge a sufficient amount of tuition to the students that come. But an orphan home could not be, it theoretically at least must continue to depend upon donations. Our proposition calls for that. Not only the right of the churches to build such institutions and organizations, but to sustain and maintain them. The Gospel Guardian C o m p a n y receives no contributions from churches. It never has taken one to my knowledge and would not with my knowledge or consent; and anything to that effect that has ever been told is a misrepresentation of the facts in the case. We would not receive, our by-laws prohibit the company from receiving a contribution of any kind or character from any congregation. The same thing technically, theoretically at least, is true of Abilene Christian College and of most of the other schools, I take it.

But the orphan home depends upon contributions from churches. So that you can see that the parallel fails at many different points. And they are not the same kind of institutions at all. The church didn't build the Gospel Guardian Company. We're talking in our proposition about Benevolent Organizations that the church does build.

Then last night, he was concerned about and he sort of apologetically introduced the matter of some children being sent up to Boles from Lufkin. Now brother Woods, you don't need to apologize for that in this debate. I knew you would introduce on some pretext or the other before it was over, and I've been expecting it. The only surprise I had in it is that you didn't do it before now. That's all. That thing's been kicked around considerably both in preaching and in debating. Up to this good day I've never seen the statement that I'm purported to have signed. I haven't seen it. I haven't seen my signature on it. I don't know what it contained. I have no rememberance of having signed it. I wouldn't say that I didn't. I will say that if I did, I did what I would not do again. I've repented of that, brother Woods. I wouldn't do it again.

I wouldn't help anybody get any child in any kind of an institution that I believe to be unscriptural. I represented the father of those children in calling brother Oler and when brother Oler learned that the father of those children plead that he would help to support them if he could get them in a home, he wasn't trying to get out of making a living for them—his wife had deserted him and left him with five little boys. He couldn't stay at home and take care of them, and at the same time make a living for them. And so, he came to me and wanted me to help him get them into a home. He went before the judge down at Lufkin and had himself declared incompetent; told me to tell brother Oler, and I told brother Oler over the phone that if they had room for the children and wanted to take them under that circumstance that the father would help support them. That's the basis upon which it was done, and if I signed a statement that said that I endorsed in any way Boles Orphan Home in its organized operation as a church institution I'm sorry that I signed it, I've asked the Lord to forgive me for it; I wouldn't sign another one. It was a form letter. There isn't any secret about the fact that for a good many years I tried to go along with the kind of an orphan home that's operated under an eldership. I haven't denied that. To that extent I've changed. Not that I've changed on any principle that I've ever preached. But that I have changed in the application that I have made of those principles. And when I find out that I'm making a wrong application of any other Bible principle I'll gladly change again, because I'm interested in going to heaven when I die, and I'm going to come just as near as I can to doing what's right about that matter or anything else. Now if I've wronged brother Oler and Boles Home in signing that statement I ask their forgiveness. If I've wronged anybody else I'll be glad to apologize and ask their forgiveness. Now, brother Woods, you're just as welcome as you can be to the incident, the letter, my name to it, if it's there, and everything connected with it. And you preach it and debate it whenever and wherever you get ready and make all of the use of it you want to. You're entirely welcome to it. But tell the truth about my apology for it and the fact that I wouldn't do it again, when you introduce it.

All right, then he says that I haven't in any way referred to his charts. Well now that isn't so. People in this audience know full well that I've mentioned a lot of them specifically. I haven't had them one by one put back up here on this screen and I'm under no obligation to take up my time to let his men hunt for his chart, try to find the right number and get it up here, and then try to read it after I get it up here. I've got something else to do besides look at the pictures that Tom Warren and brother Guy Woods and some of the rest of these brethren can draw. And I'm going to conduct my part of this debate as it pleases me to conduct it, whether Guy Woods likes it or not. And if I don't show all of his charts all over again and he's disappointed in that, I have no apology to make to him.

Now I'll tell you what I will do, you just mention an argument that you have made from any one of those charts that I could hear orally, that I haven't answered, and I'll be glad to pay my respects to it in the next speech. Is that fair enough? I'm interested in answering the arguments that you make and not in dealing with the illustrations of those arguments that you have. Now the difference in his work along that line and mine has been that he's looked at my charts and read them over again, and failed to reply to the argument that's on them. He's answered and dealt with the chart and not with the argument. I've answered the arguments and let him take care of the charts. All right, fine.

He said last night that he did not quote the part of that law that he mentioned as a statute. Well, I want to introduce to you now because it's been referred to, a statement made up here at Cullman. He said, "I have here this statement from the Tennessee Code." This is the literature that they put out. This is the manuscript of his speech mailed out by the church in Cullman for which he held the meeting. Quote, "Upon the filing of an application for license to do business as a private child caring agency, society, institution or maternity home, and upon the presentation by application of satisfactory evidence that such corporation organized as a child caring agency, society or institution, is suitably and properly managed as such, shall issue license, and which license may at any time be revoked by the department of public welfare upon a ninety days written notice being given to the licensee." Then, "Private institutions," quoting again now, "offering care to dependent children must be incorporated in accordance with the laws of the state of Tennessee, and the scope of operation must be determined by the purpose set forth in the charter of the incorporation." Farther on down, commenting upon that, he said, "Further, in Tennessee at least, that this institution must be incorporated." Now what did he cite. Well, introducing the statement he said, "I have here this statement from the Tennessee Code, section 4719, department of public welfare," and then he gave the quotation that I've read to you.

Now, Guy, you did say that it was 4719 in your speech at Cullman, and that's the only statute cited in the book from which you read. The only one, and that has been repealed as this book definitely shows and I read it to you the other night. This is the public acts of the legislature of Tennessee for 1953 and in 1953 the Tennessee state legislature repealed that article 4719. Well, all right, I want in the remaining part of my time tonight, and of course, we'll deal with some other matters that need referring to, in the next speech, but I have another chart that I want to introduce, and this time I want the one on the sufficiency of God's plan.

While the boys are getting it, let me call your attention to the fact that God's plan from eternity centered in Jesus Christ as a saviour and in the gospel as a message of life and salvation and in the church as a sufficient relationship. In Hebrews 2:10, "For it became him for whom are all things and by whom are all things in bringing many sons unto glory to make the captain of their salvation perfect through suffering." Hebrews 5:9, "Being made perfect." 7:25, 27 of the same book of Hebrews, Paul said, "He is able to save unto the uttermost, them that come night unto God, seeing he ever liveth to make

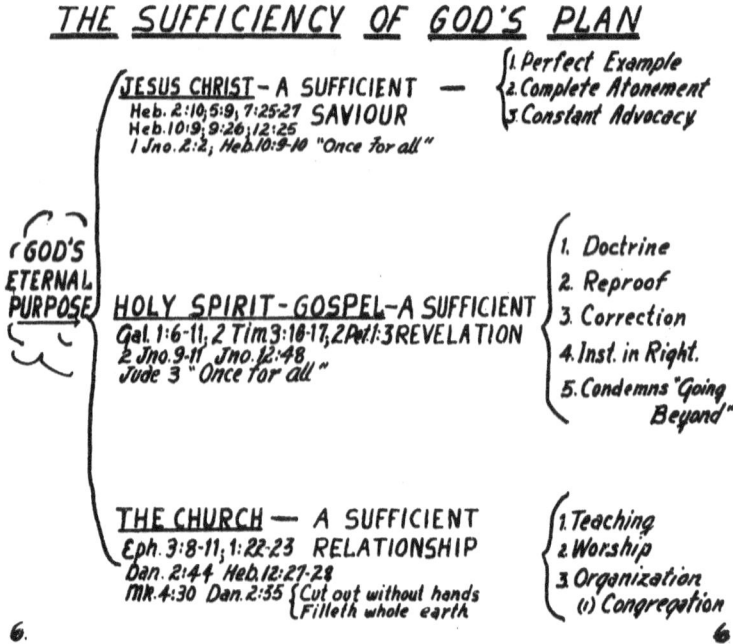

intercession for them." And, "Then for the people's sins he offered up sacrifice once, when he offered up himself." Not only that, but Hebrews 10:10, Christ once for all gave himself that through his body we might be sanctified. Hebrews 9:26, "Once in the end of the ages hath he appeared." The Bible teaches that Jesus Christ is a perfect saviour in the fact that he set a perfect example, made a complete atonement, and is a constant advocate.

The Bible teaches that the Holy Spirit has revealed a perfect and sufficient revelation in the gospel; that it is God' revelation, that "it is profitable for doctrine, for reproof, for correction, for instruction in righteousness," and it condemns "going beyond". Jude said, "Contend earnestly for the faith once for all delivered unto the saints."

Then the same Bible teaches that the church is a sufficient relationship, just as sufficient. In 3:8-11 of the book of Ephesians, that it is God's eternal purpose that his manifold wisdom be made known through the church. Chapter 1, verses 22, 23, the church is the bounty of God's grace, it is the fullness of him that filleth all in all. Daniel 2:44 and Daniel 2:35 in the vision given, and in the interpretation of the dream, it was the little stone cut out of the mountain without hands that filled the whole earth, smote the image upon its feet, destroyed world empires, and filled the whole earth.

In Hebrews 12:28, it is a kingdom that cannot be shaken, one that will stand indeed forever. And Jesus taught that it was as a tiny mustard seed, which when planted grew up into a great tree with its branches reaching out and the birds came and lodged in them. The church is a sufficient relationship in its teaching. It's sufficient to do all of the teaching that God charged the church with doing. It is sufficient in its worship. It has every item in the worship that God intends for the church to engage in. It is sufficient in its organization. It has every feature in its organization to do everything that God commands the church as such to do. That's the whole point. It needs no other organization.

Brother Woods says, "I believe that." Well, if he believes it, he ought not to be debating the proposition that he's debating. Why, he's denying that it is unscriptural, or out of harmony with the scripture, for the churches of Christ to build benevolent organizations. Now brother Woods, by those benevolent organizations do you mean congregations, or do you mean private homes? You've mixed the private home into this discussion. I deny that the church builds a private home. I deny that the church even builds or that it can restore a legal home. That's a matter of law. A private home is brought about by marriage. You enter it by birth. The legal home is prescribed by the law and constituted according to the law. The church can't build either one of them. Hence, that isn't what we're discussing, and you've wasted your time and refused to discuss the real issue in this proposition by spending all of the time that you have spent on the private home. And that's what I've been trying to tell you. It isn't a part of this discussion, and the home that you ought to be defending is not a private home. There isn't anything private about one of these institutional homes—nothing private about it. It isn't on the basis of a private home; it isn't even on the basis of a legal home from an adoptive point of view. No, sir; it is purely a substitute from the viewpoint that it is a place where the destitute children are cared for—and get me my chart on what is the issue—where destitute children are cared for, and where provisions are made for their needs and those needs are supplied, where proper care and supervision is furnished. Chart No. 2.

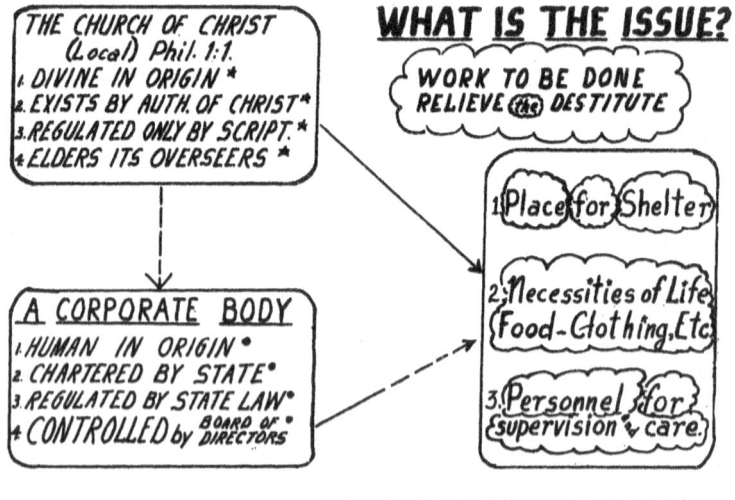

2.   2.

And not only that but it is likewise a place for shelter. It's a home only in the sense that it provides a place just like your crippled children's hospital over here. There isn't any restoration of relationship there. Why certainly not. Why these charters of these institutions, nearly everyone of them says that the board, not the superintendent, these brethren that serve as superintendents are not "en loco parentis," unless they are violating the charter of their institutions. The charter says the board, the corporation, is "en loco parentis."

And I pointed out to him that if the superintendent takes the place of the parent he's himply a hired hand in doing the work that he's doing. He's being paid, and most of them pretty handsomely to do what they're doing for those children. I wouldn't want a "hired daddy," would you? No, sir. Not from that point of view, and I deny that it is the restoration of that relationship. The men who serve on those boards have to serve gratis according to their charter. They are not hired hands, they are doing it out of their interest, no doubt, in the children and their welfare themselves. But they do not live there. They do not administer the care. Why here you have your corporate body providing these things that the church provides. I've challenged him to name the thing necessary over here, a place for shelter, the necessities of life, the personnel to take care of them, that the church cannot furnish. And he hasn't dealt with it.

I have repeatedly affirmed and asked him to deny that the church cannot furnish what the corporate body can furnish. The church can furnish exactly what the corporate body furnishes. Now the trouble with all of his charts is, that he leaves out that institution that he ought to be defending.

Brother Woods, I say again if you weren't willing to defend the corporate organization that provides these homes, that has control over them, if you're not willing to defend it, don't sign the proposition that you signed anymore, and I'm almost sure you won't.

All right, the thing under question in this debate is this human organization over here brethren. Don't let him confuse you. It isn't the private home or the function of a private home. If you call this a home over here, nobody is denying—if you want to use that as a descriptive of it—nobody is denying that a home is supplied *in the sense of a place*. He said, why then a penitentiary would be a home. That's exactly right, according to one of your definitions. And by the way when you re-read that definition last night, you didn't read all of it that you gave the first time. Did you intend to leave part of it out? You left the domicile part of it out when you re-read it. You made it only a relationship. Now you brethren that are defending these institutional homes, one time when you talk about a home and ask a question about a home you're talking about a place, like the residence where the preacher lives, and you compare the institutional orphan home with the house furnished as a place of the preacher's compensation making it mean only a place. The next time, you shift gears and make it mean a family or a relationship. That's the reason I said when you ask a question about a home you ought to say what you're talking about. You use it both ways. Now by a home, if you mean a place for shelter, nobody's opposing it. I'm in favor of it. I said the church can supply it, that God commanded the church to supply it. And I'm sure that there isn't a passage of scripture in the word of God, he hasn't produced one yet, that includes this benevolent organization that runs this institutional home. There's where the issue is. That's what the proposition calls for. Guy N. Woods hasn't touched side, edge nor bottom of it. He's spent his time trying to confuse you, by trying to compare that institutional home with a private home. Now if you're going to make your comparison I pointed out to you last night, if you're going to talk about the relationship of the church and the private home, you're going to have to build you an aid society in here to receive the money from the church and to control the expenditure of it in the private home. That's the only way on earth you can get a parallel of any picture you can draw of what you're trying to defend. And nobody knows that any better than Guy N. Woods, either.

The church is sufficient. It can do as a congregation what God wants it to do, and you've got just as much right to build an organization to take the place of the church preaching the gospel, to take the place of the church in its edification, as you have to build an organization to do the work of the church in relief of the destitute that G o d charged it with.

And you know it just happens that the very same argument that he makes (how much time do I have?) Answer:

Two minutes. That will be enough for this. And turn to my chart on the congregation. The very same argument that he makes to try to justify these homes is the argument that was made to justify the missionary society. I have in my hand Lard's quarterly, Vol. V, I read on page 195, "In considering the merits of these propositions we'll take up the last first. Is it true that the duty of preaching the gospel is by the appointment of God laid on the church? The writer attempts to prove it by sundry quotations from the prophets and the apostles. But this proof comes short of the proposition." Get it now; this is Moses E. Lard. "In the nature of the case it is impossible for a church to preach the gospel. In the secondary sense of illustrating the gospel by example it certainly can, but in the primary sense of the term, preach, it cannot." (The work of the church is the chart I want.) "The church may cause the gospel to be preached. It may furnish food and raiment for the preacher, but it cannot preach." Why that's what Guy says about taking care of the needy. It just can't take care of the needy. That same argument they used to justify the missionary society. He goes right on down, a little later on, and he said, "For it might be that the churches are authorized to employ the societies as their own agents." He says that a missionary society is just another church. I deny it. It's an association of churches and the churches are voluntarily members of it. And they can withdraw from it when they please—when they please. A thousand Christian Churches, Dr. Degroot over at TCU says, within the last few years, have withdrawn from the United Christian Missionary Society. Moses Lard continues, "The duty of preaching the gospel devolves on those who can preach. The duty of sustaining the preachers d e v o l v e s on the churches." So Guy, all that the church can do according to Moses E. Lard and the missionary society people a hundred years ago, is furnish the money and let the human organization distribute it and sustain the preachers. That's your argument to a "T", right up and down the line on the home, and you know it is, and it's the only one you've got, and the only proof you have for it is your assertion.

Who says that the church is it's own missionary society,

but is not its own benevolent society? Guy N. Woods. What does he know about it? Well, not everything, you can be certain of that.

Wood's Fifth Negative

Brethren Moderators, Brother Cogdill, Ladies and Gentlemen:

May I say I'm honored to have the opportunity to be before you again tonight in the negative of this proposition which brother Cogdill has been attempting to affirm. I should like to refer to the last thing that he said in which he was attempting to parallel the missionary society with the orphan home.

It happens that brother Porter, who is sitting at his table, had a debate some time ago, which is published, with Irvin Waters, an anti-Sunday school man, who made exactly the same argument that brother Cogdill has made tonight; only he made it against the Bible School, and brother Porter was on the receiving end. Now I know how brother Porter felt that night. And I might say that brother Waters succeeded just as well as brother Cogdill.

Let me suggest this to you, that this position which he is occupying tonight is the anti-Sunday school position applied to benevolence. I have engaged in numerous debates on the anti-Sunday school question. I have yet to hear these brethren introduce a single argument that Alva Johnson and Van Bonneau, leading anti-Sunday school debaters, didn't use years and years ago. It is then exactly on a par with that hobby and may thus be designated; a hobby which brother Cogdill tonight admits that he has lately espoused, and over which churches are now being divided. This is truly a significant evening in this debate, as we shall in a few moments see.

Now friends, if I know my heart, I have no other purpose in mind in entering a debate except to defend the truth, and error is just as wrong for me to hold and to teach as it is for brother Cogdill. And it's just as objectionable for me to make a mistake as it is for brother Cogdill to make a mistake. I shouldn't condemn him for making an error any more than I would expect him to condemn me. Sometimes we do make mistakes. Sometimes, as for example, in this case of the Tennessee Law it's possible for one to make a mistake. Now brother Cogdill and I both have admissions to the bar. I do not make any claim to being a lawyer. This is no reflection on the law. I recall hearing about some Irishman that was reading inscriptions on a tombstone in a cemetery, and he came to one that said, "Here lies a lawyer and an honest man." And he said, "They sure put two men in that grave, didn't they!" (laughter) But I should like for you to remember please that I have just about as much law as brother Cogdill has. And I think that both of us had better stick to our preaching—that we would be second-rate lawyers at the best.

Now it's been whispered around over town today that brother Woods was dishonest in making the statement that he did regarding the Tennessee Law and that he ought to make a correction on it. And I say, friends, that that's exactly right, if I'm wrong on it. But I want to raise this question: If it should turn out that brother Cogdill is wrong, I wonder if these same brethren would feel that brother Cogdill ought to make a correction too. Now that, friends, we are about to test. May I have chart No. 36, please, and will you turn out the lights.

This morning I called the Mr. H e r s c h e l C. Burkhart, Chief of the Bureau of Child Welfare, of the Tennessee Department of Public Welfare, and I told him what I was engaged in down here; and I told him the nature of the argument that brother Cogdill and I had last night; and I said that brother Cogdill is alleging that because that particular statute was repealed in 1953 that it cancelled out this booklet. I said to him, is it correct that the statute was repealed? He said, yes. But he said it was simply in order to embrace and to extend that which was involved in the original statute. I said to him, Is it true that in Tennessee institutions that supply child care for twenty-four hours a day must be incorporated? He said, Yes. I said to him, would you send me a telegram to that effect? He said, Yes, and here it is. Here is the original and we have one on the chart.

(Wood's chart No. 36)

CT RHB332 33 COLLECT 2 EXTRA=FAX NASHVILLE TENN 20 155PMC=

GUY N WOODS=

BANKHEAD HOTEL ROOM 408 BHAM=

SECTIONS 14-1401 THROUGH 14-1423 TENNESSEE CODE ANNOTATED

REQUIRES THAT PRIVATE CHILDCARING INSTITUTIONS OFFERED

FULL TIME CARE TO CHILDREN OUTSIDE THEIR OWN HOMES MUST

BE INCORPORATED=I

HURSTON C BURKHART CHIEF BUREAU OF CHILD WELFARE

TENNESSEE DEPT OF PUBLIC WELFARE=

Let me read it all: Guy N. Woods, Bankhead Hotel, Birmingham. Sections 1400-1401 through 1423, Tennessee Code Annotated requires that private child caring institutions offering full-time care to children outside their own homes M-U-S-T must be incorporated." Now, of course, this fellow that is the head of that child-welfare bureau may not be a lawyer. He may not know what he is talking about. Now, brother Cogdill, your duty is clear. And I can prove it by a number of interested brethren in this audience tonight. You'll learn, and you brethren might as well learn we don't make statements in debate we can't prove.

Now then, friends, I want to take up his speech, item by item, statement by statement. In the first place brother Cogdill is trying to make him an easy place to land. He's manufacturing arguments from me, and answering the manufactured arguments.

(Do you want this telegram, brother Cogdill? All right, would you come and get it please.)

Now, brother Cogdill is manufacturing arguments. Let

me have this chart please—Chart No. 10. And I might say that brother Cogdill says that I look at his charts, but he doesn't have to look at mine, and he says he hasn't got time for this. Let's have a race here. Let's see which one can get them ready quicker. I'll guarantee that brother Deaver will get my charts ready just as quickly as he will his. Who was it, friends, that argued that there is a parallel between the Gospel Guardian Company, and the orphan home? I haven't. I've never made any such statement as t h a t. Brother Cogdill, you just weren't listening to what I said. Now here's what I said. I said that the incorporation is like the homes. That's what I said. You just weren't listening. I do not believe them to be parallel in every sense. I think there are some parallels. But I think that there are some parallels between the church and the paper. They are both engaged in teaching. I have not made this argument. This is an argument that brother Cogdill has manufactured in order to inject another issue.

Here's what I said: I said that the incorporation of the Gospel Guardian is the same as the home. You know who it is that told me that first? Roy E. Cogdill. I have here his review of the Lufkin Debate, page 30, he says this: We are incorporated under exactly the same statutes as our schools, our orphan homes that operate under a board of directors, and all of our religious publishing houses except those operated for profit." That's what I said. That's all I said. I don't believe there is a parallel there. Why put it up there? Obviously there is not a parallel between institutions that exist for one purpose that is not involved in that which God requires to be done, and an organization that's performing such duty. So he's wasting his time on that. Why answer arguments that have not been introduced.

Same thing is involved in Chart 11. Turn it over. Chart 11. Thank you. Now again here he tries to establish a parallel that nobody's arguing. Brother—Boys, we'll give you time, don't get excited. (laughter) That's mighty fine. All of us together will get it before you, friends. Now, friends, there is no allegation on my part that there is any sort of a parallel that can be drawn out as brother Cogdill has done so. Now I'm not arguing that. My sole point was this: If the incorporation is wrong, then the Gospel Guardian is wrong because brother Cogdill says it's incorporated exactly like the home. That's all I said. Now I don't intend to be led off in any such fashion that way. You brethren better either listen or else stay with the issue.

Then while we're on it, he says here with reference to Chart 11 that we are not discussing setting up of homes by individuals. There isn't any way on earth that a home can actually and literally be set up except by an individual. This chart he introduces which we'll call for in a moment, Chart No. 2, what is the issue. Does he think the church as a church operates literally in the establishment of that? The only way in which a home of any kind can be established, legal, private, foster or otherwise, is by individuals. That's simply dodging.

Now, he said, there's this difference between the Gospel Guardian and the homes, that they receive donations. He says that there's not anything free about the Gospel Guardian. I beg to differ. You send them out all over the country free Cogdill.

Cogdill: No I do not. No, I do not.

Woods: I know you are.

Cogdill: No, I do not.

Woods: You sent them to the students in the colleges free.

Cogdill: They are paid for. Everyone of them.

Woods: Well they are sent to them without paying for them. How about sending me a bunch of books when somebody pays for them?

Cogdill: If you need them I'll be glad to donate them. I think you do.

Woods: Now, friends, don't you see.

Then in the next place he says here with reference to the Gospel Guardian that it exists as a non-profit institution, and yet he told us last night that it was commercialized. That it was a business institution. But now watch: When I showed that in so far as the Guardian was concerned that it's performing the same function allegedly by this charter, as the home, then he comes up here and says, No, it's not performing any work of the church at all—not performing the work of the church at all. Therefore, there's no edification in it for the church. It teaches error. It has by his own admission. It hasn't anything in it that teaches the church or edifies the church, because it's not doing the work of the church at all, and yet he wants the churches to buy services from it when it's offering something the church doesn't need. What on earth do you have to sell, brother Cogdill, that the church needs? It's not a work of the church. It's not edifying the church. Yet, you want the church to buy something that the church doesn't need. Now one of two things is true: Either the Guardian does the work of the church in which case the church is buying something they need, or else you are trying to sell them something that they don't need. Now I want to know why. Now get busy on that, sir.

Now he says he's repented of putting children into Boles Home. I wonder if there's some of the other brethren ready to repent. Brother Oler told me last night after the session that the speaker in this debate on the opposing side had placed these children in the home, that the moderator on the opposing side had put two more in the home, and that one of the brethren who led a prayer last night had used the home as an agency in order to find a child, and had got one out of the home. Well, it looks like they're in business with the home, whether they agree with it or not. Now then are these other brethren ready to make a confession? I'll allow thirty seconds now for an opportunity for another confession here if these brethren are ready to make it. I don't chide them for changing their position. That's—

Adams: Hold his time a minute. Do you want me to read a letter from the District Judge of Gregg County? You asked for me to make a confession.

Woods: Well, are you going to let the judge make it or are you going to make it?

Adams: It's not a confession. It's the judge's statement concerning those two children that brother Oler was talking about.

Woods: Well, you're not ready to make a confession then?

Adams: No.—

Woods: Well, what did you get up here for? Evidently his seat got hot and he just had to say something. That's all I know. I don't see what the judge of some county had to do with whether or not you want to make a confession. If you want to tell me what the judge said why I'll be glad to listen when I'm out of the debate. But then I'm not especially interested just at the moment, brother Adams. It must be very interesting. I'm sure that it's very interesting. But just at the moment I'm not concerned about what the judge said. I merely asked him if he wanted to make a confession.

Now then he says that he's changed his preaching. Well, that's his business. Brother Cogdill is to be honored for that statement, I respect him for it. And I would not reflect upon any man who sincerely sees that he's in error, or thinks that he's in error and changes it and I'll tell what he ought not to do: He ought not to go about over the country leaving the impression like some of them are doing, and I don't say brother Cogdill does. I don't know whether he does or doesn't—some of his cohorts do, that some of the rest of us have lately gone into disgression. When brother Cogdill by his own admission just a few years ago was teaching the same things and practicing the same things for which we contend tonight. And it's good for the audience and for all audiences to know that brother Cogdill has frankly and plainly stated that he's no longer teaching and practicing what he once did. Now it's just a question of whether the churches want to change their course away from that which formerly characterized them into that course of which brother Cogdill is now the recognized champion and leader. That's the question.

All right, further let's have his chart No. 6. Chart No. 6, please.

Now, friends, here is my point, with much that's on that chart, in fact with everything that's on that chart, so far as he emphasizes God's purpose through the Church I am in complete agreement. There isn't any point about our Lord being a perfect Saviour, about the Holy Spirit supplying sufficient revelation, about the church being a sufficient

THE SUFFICIENCY OF GOD'S PLAN

GOD'S ETERNAL PURPOSE:

JESUS CHRIST — A SUFFICIENT SAVIOUR
Heb. 2:10; 5:9; 7:25-27
Heb. 10:9; 9:26; 12:25
1 Jno. 2:2; Heb. 10:9-10 "Once for all"
- 1. Perfect Example
- 2. Complete Atonement
- 3. Constant Advocacy

HOLY SPIRIT - GOSPEL — A SUFFICIENT REVELATION
Gal. 1:6-11; 2 Tim 3:16-17; 2 Pet. 1:3
2 Jno. 9-11 Jno. 12:48
Jude 3 "Once for all"
- 1. Doctrine
- 2. Reproof
- 3. Correction
- 4. Inst. in Right.
- 5. Condemns "Going Beyond"

THE CHURCH — A SUFFICIENT RELATIONSHIP
Eph. 3:8-11; 1:22-23
Dan. 2:44 Heb. 12:27-28
Mk. 4:30 Dan. 2:35 Cut out without hands / Filleth whole earth
- 1. Teaching
- 2. Worship
- 3. Organization
  - (1) Congregation

relationship in that which the church is expected to do. Listen frends, there isn't any place on that chart for the needy private home. Now it doesn't make any difference whether the needy private home is like what I'm defending or not. That's not even the point that I'm getting at. He agrees that the church has an obligation to the needy private home. But where is the needy private home on that chart? It's not there. Hence, he's not correct. Either he thinks that God's plan is not sufficient, because he hasn't got the needy private home indicated on it, or else the needy private home is not a part of the sufficiency of God's plan for the church, and that's my position. Wasn't intended to be a home, it's a church. Isn't it strange, brethren, that these folks confuse the home and the church, and don't know the difference between a home and a church? That seems strange to me.

Next he says friends, that there is no home provided, either legal or private. Let's have now his chart No. 2.

That's the order in which he introduced it. That's the chart on what is the issue. No. 2—One more. Here it is friends. Now then, he says, there isn't any place in God's plan so far as the church is concerned for either the private or the legal home. Well, all right then, what is this right here? What is it? It's a part of the work of the church, he says. But it's not a private home, because there's no place for the private home in connection with the work of the church. It's not a foster home, because he said there's no place for any kind of a home, legal or private.

What is that then? What is that, brother Cogdill? I've told you all along, friends, that he's making this the church and then he tries to put the church in the business of the home, thus he puts elders over the functions of the church, that is, over a home; thus he puts elders over two divine institutions, the home and the church. That is not the elders functions that God gave them. And yet he says that it's Catholicism to put elders over a home.

All right, I've answered his speech now. Item by item, statement by statement, everything that he's introduced tonight. Oh, yes, one other point: He wanted to know, what do I mean by a home. I mean exactly this, in particular if you just spread out this and so forth to include some more that you don't have on there by which I mean, a home may include food and clothing and shelter but also the supervision, education, medical care, and all that goes along with the restoration or re-establishment of a home. That's what I mean by a home. That's exactly it, brother Cogdill. Now look here, friends, this is exactly this legally re-established. Right here what he's got—he's got—And do you know what, last night I asked him, I said, brother Cogdill give me the address of that home you will endorse? Do you know what he did? He did just what he's been doing all the time—he confused the church and the home. I said give me the address of that home that you endorse, and he gave me the address of a church, the Blytheville Church. And they've got some children but they are doing their dead level best to get rid of them. And yet that's his example that he cites here.

BENEVOLENT ORGANIZATIONS 159

Now, friends, that covers his speech item by item. He says he's answered my charts. I will leave it to this intelligent audience to decide whether he's done that. I'm going to run just three or four of them through. Let me know when I have five minutes, and let you decide whether or not he has. Let me have please, chart 18.

CHART NO. 18.

THE HOME

ITS CHARACTER —————————— A Divine Entity Gen. 1:1-3.

ITS DESIGN ——————————— Food, Clothing, Shelter, Education, Medical Care, Security.

ITS DESTRUCTION ——————— Death, Disease, Desertion, Dereliction, Divorce, Dementia.

ITS RESTORATION ——————— Home for the Homeless Supplied by the CHURCHES OF CHRIST.

SEVEN HOMELESS CHILDREN

WHAT IS THE DIFFERENCE?

This is an idea, I introduced this in the debate at Paragould with brother Porter. They've all seen it, and this simply is my argument. Now up at the top there, I have the home is a divine entity, and the authority for it is in Genesis Chapter one to three. The design of this home is to supply food, clothing, shelter, education, medical care, supervision. And sometimes it's destroyed by death, disease, desertion, dereliction, divorce, and dementia. Now its restoration is a home for the homeless supplied and supported by churches of Christ, James 1:27; I Timothy 5:16. What is the difference now? Here is a private home that takes seven homeless children in it. The father and mother serve as the foster parents. When you get more than six children in some states, I believe it's four children in Alabama, though I may have that confused with another state —at any rate it's four to seven in most of the states—California I believe twelve, which is the largest number that I know. But at any way when you get several children in a home then it falls under legal jurisdiction. What then is the difference between a home that had a man and woman married, and they take in these homeless children, and a group of brethren getting together and doing the same thing as they do, conforming to the same law, only instead of having seven, they've got seventy? Or maybe three hundred? Can somebody tell me the difference? Brother Cogdill won't, because there isn't.

Here, friends, is the argument I've made in every speech, in every debate I've held. Now let these good brethren who write for the Guardian take notice of this please. Here is the argument. Here is the home that every child has and is entitled to have. Here is the broken home. There is the home that restores it. What is this home?

It's the home the child had but lost. What's that over there—the restoration of that which the child had but lost. If the church sustains an obligation to this home before it's completely destroyed, which it does, after it is destroyed then it has an obligation to support a restored home as it did this home. This is the child's original home. It's lost. Then it follows that the members of the board who are Christian men who stand en loco parentis, that is in the place of the parents, take the place of the parents and operate the home and the church is obligated to support it.

It's not in conflict with the church because it's not performing the work of the church as a church. It's not in conflict with the home because that home is gone. What is

BENEVOLENT ORGANIZATIONS 161

Let's look please at No. 4. No. 4, please.

CHART NO. 4.

it? It's the home the child had and lost, and it's been restored in the practice of pure and undefiled religion. I'm awful glad I'm defending that, friends, because I believe it with all of my heart to be the truth.

How many minutes? All right, now here, friends, Who is Authorized to Have Oversight? A man, a church, the parents or the elders. Let him give his scripture. Now, brother Cogdill, who is it that's to have oversight of a home? The parents or the elders. I say that we put the elders over the church and we put parents over the home, and it's just as wrong to try to put parents over a church as it would to put elders over a home. (See Chart No. 14, Page 386)

Here we are my friends, here is our authority—We have precept for it James 1:27. He said last night he would ad-

All right, let's have please, No. 30.

CHART NO. 30.

SCRIPTURAL AUTHORITY

FOR ORPHAN HOMES

1. PRECEPT - JAS. 1: 27.

2. NECESSARY INFERENCE: A HOME - 1 TIM. 5: 16; PSM. 68: 5, 6.

3. EXPEDIENCY:
    (1) PRIVATE HOME
    (2) LEGAL HOME - ROM. 13: 1 (LICENSE)
        A. INCORPORATED
        B. UNINCORPORATED.

mit for the sake of argument that it applied to the church. And brother John T. Lewis who is surely an authority in this area says that it has reference to the church in his writings. Here is the necessary inference for it—I Timothy 5:16. There is the supplying of that which the woman had but lost. Psalms 68:5, "God setteth the solitary in families." That says that God puts them, or that it's his desire for them to be put in families; and the Hebrew word there has a wide variety of meanings, but it actually involves and includes a home. Here is the expediency that's involved in it. That is whether it's a private home or a legal home, conforming to state law. Romans 14:1. And whether it is incorporated or unincorporated, that, friends, is a legal affair that does not enter into this question.

Now then my bottom notebook there, please, if I have time, in this remaining moment to introduce one more argument. This I think is an excellent argument and I would like for you to consider it carefully. It's an argument that's based upon Galatians chapter four—Galatians chapter four, and verses one and two. "And I say that the heir as long as he is a child differeth nothing from a servant, though he be Lord of all, but is under tutors and governors until the time appointed by the father." The word "tutor" there is defined to mean, "and the guardian at common law, and he performs the office of a tutor or curator of the Roman civil law, the former of whom had charge of the maintenance and education of a minor, and the latter the care of his fortune." You'll find this in Watts. 330 and 348. And the governor under the Roman civil law was a person who under the Roman law occupied practically the same position with reference to his minor charge as the guardian of the person of an infant occupies toward his ward under our law. And that's in Blackstone Commentaries, page 460; and Blackstone further states on 461, "Guardian of the estate of a minor." Now watch, please. Adm. Clarke says of the first, that is of the tutor, that he is the executor, and the second, the one who superintended the concerns of the family and estate till the heir became of age. (See Chart No. 9, Page 385)

Now let's look at the translations of this. The King James Version says, "but is under tutors and governors until the time appointed of the father." American standard, "but is under guardians and stewards until the day appointed of the father." Revised Standard, "I mean that the heir as long as he is a child is no better than a slave, though he is owner of all the estate, but he is under guardians and trustees until the day set by the father."

Now then friends, here is our argument: The Galatians were in the relationship of minor children answerable to guardians and trustees. Just as such a child was under the control of tutors and governors until the day of his maturity. Paul thus accepted and endorsed the Roman Civil Law touching the control and management of minor children. The superintendents and assistants of the homes have charge of the person of the minor, and the members of the board, directors of affairs financially, and have charge of this estate. The orphan's estate is a term of years, and thus differs not in principle from an estate in fee simple. The board, that is a group of Christian men, standing in the place of the parents, that is en loco parentis, as the tutor and curator, guardian and trustee stood in the place of parents of Paul's day, transacted and direct the business of the minor and hold his property in trust for him. His interest is for a term of years.

Now then it is immaterial whether the trust is set up by will or by gift. In either instance it's held in trust for the use of those for whom it has been provided. It follows then that the orphan homes constitute simply an estate, held in trust for a term of years by the trustees, with the superintendents in charge of education and care of the fatherless. Now that shows that Paul recognized that is the function of people who serve in the place of the parents to take control of it. It matters not whether that estate be by will or by gift. It's exactly the same. It matters not whether it's in fee simple or whether it's a term of years. It happens that in the case of the homes it's for a term of years. And somebody might ask, Well, whom do the orphan homes belong to? They belong to the children, and the board holds the property in trust for the children for a term of years, during which time they enjoy the benefits and the blessings that are characteristic of it. And, beg pardon,

And that it is the function now of the home to supply that and not the church I can prove by another Birmingham preacher. In the Gospel Guardian of September 26, 1957, brother Bob Crawley said this, "Even those brethren who for some purposes such as soliciting from church treasuries for the support of schools and colleges argue that there is no distinction to be made between the work of churches of Christ and the work of individual Christians can see that feet washing is an individual and not a congregational work. We wish they were as perceptive regarding the rearing of children and the lodging of strangers. It is not the responsibility of the churches of Christ to provide day nurseries, youth centers, hobby shops for the social and recreational welfare of children, or older folks either. Providing such things if they are needed is the responsibility of the individual Christian in the sphere of the home." Why I couldn't say it any better than that myself. That's exactly right. And you know what brother Cogdill is trying to do? He wants to make that a church work, and the body of our Lord is dividing over that ridiculous hobby. I'm mighty sorry. I wish brother Cogdill would come back to his first love, and have the courage of conviction and the strength of character to preach that which he formerly preached.

And while we are on the subject of confession, since the publisher of the Gospel Guardian made one, I have a photostatic copy of a letter brother Tant wrote in 1951, in which he said he believed that Tipton Home was a scriptural organization and he would defend it. Now does brother Tant wish to publish it? He may publish it in the next issue of the Guardian.

Cogdill's Sixth Affirmative

GENTLEMEN MODERTORS, Brother Woods, Ladies and Gentlemen:

It's a privilege again to appear before you for the last time on this proposition in the affirmative and to deal with some of the matters that have come before us for consideration.

The very first thing that I want to call to your attention at this time is concerning the Tennessee Statute. He's introduced tonight a telegram from the Chief of the Bureau of Child Welfare of the Tennessee Department of Public Welfare, sighting sections 1400-1401 and 1423 of the Tennessee Code annotated, stating that they require the private child care institution which offers full time care to children outside their own home, must be incorporated. Now he said this man may not be a lawyer. Well, he evidently isn't. He evidently isn't. He's the head of the Child Welfare Bureau, it says, and what I asked Brother Woods for was the statute requiring it, and he cited article 4719 as a statute requiring it. There isn't any statute in the section that this man has cited requiring it. Now brother Woods, I have the entire law, not just what the Chief of the Bureau says must be done. And there's the statutes. That's a copy, and it's by the counsel, the chief of counsel of the state welfare department. That's from a lawyer and it's a copy of the law, and I want you to read in that where the law says it must—not an arbitrary ruling by somebody running some bureau—but where the law says it must. And you know the statute provides for a review of any arbitrary ruling of the department. If they should rule contrary to law, you've got a board of review to reverse them. You don't have to go by what the chief of the bureau might rule on the matter, any more than you have to go by any other bureaucratic form of rule. The best evidence is the statute. And that section specifically provides for licensing, but does not require and it won't say. Now you read it from it—that it must be incorporated, and I'll just admit defeat on the point. But until you do I am not because I'm not wrong about that matter. And there isn't any use in your dodging around any further on it by somebody else saying thus and so about it. They've proved that the law requires a corporate body by everything on earth but the law. They've even proved it by the superintendents of the homes. They've proved it by some of the employees of the welfare bureaus of the various states. But I have about thirty-nine letters from the attorney generals of the states of the United States and not a single solitary one of them says that there is a statute in any of the states that requires a church to incorporate in order to take care of its needy. It would be unconstitutional if they had such a statute on their books.

Why the United States Constitution on the section of religious liberty, in the bill of civil rights, would certainly guarantee the right of any religious body to have any kind of an organization of that religious body to carry on their work. And it would be a violation of the religious liberties in this country for any state law—and I'm saying that you've palmed that law business off on the country long enough. You've quoted it as law and preached it as law; and just don't do that any more now. And you ought to get up here and make a confession about it. If you were as honest in admitting your changes as you compliment me for being, you would do that.

You know he's introduced the matter of a change, and he says now Roy Cogdill ought to come back and preach what he did preach, and then he misrepresented the change I've made. Roy Cogdill has always opposed the home under a board. Always have. I've tried to go along with a home under an eldership. Back as far as the Rice-Oliphant Debate in Dallas, G. A. Dunn and others in this audience will testify to the fact that there was a heated discussion in the day services in Dallas concerning the incorporation of Boles Orphan Home. And then he got back up here in his last speech and wanted to make the impression that the home he is talking and the incorporation are all one and the same thing again. You saw that didn't you—just the home incorporated. Now, brother Wood, I cited you Supreme Court decisions. You won't listen to the court any more than you will to the word of God. You have about as little respect evidently for the Supreme Court of the Country as you do Bible authority. You haven't offered any Bible authority for the thing you're trying to defend. You've tried to prove it by everything else under heaven except the authority from the Word of God. And you haven't given us any of that as we are going to see before this speech is over.

But I want to show you something about some of the changes that Guy Woods has made. Not because it'll prove that anything is right or wrong, but just to show you now, a man that will introduce a matter of that kind who himself has made as radical a change as anybody in the entire church that I know anything about on these questions. Why when he wrote for the Firm Foundation he occupied the Firm Foundation position on the matter. And the Firm Foundation position on the matter was and is today that a church can operate a home. In reply to some questions that were written to him, brother G. H. P. Showalter, back in June 1947, said this: "How may the money be sent? Reason, the Bible, and common sense all agree that it may be sent in any way convenient, in any safe convenient way, and in decency and in order. To whom should the help be sent? It should be sent to the elders of the church where the relief is needed and is dispensed. This would mean that the directors or trustees of the orphan home or any other such home should be the elders of the church where the home is located. They are scriptural ones who are to be entrusted with the use of the relief supplied."

Now Guy N. Woods agreed with that when he was writing for the Firm Foundation. Why hear him saying, back over here, for example, in 1939, when he was at Abilene, talking about some of these very things, making a speech out there, and talking about the tendency toward institutionalism, he said, "The ship of Zion has floundered more than once on the sand-bar of institutionalism. The tendency to organize is characteristic of the age." Then he said further on down in the paragraph, "This writer has ever been unable to appreciate the logic of those who affect to see grave danger in the missionary society but scruple not to form a similar organization for the purpose of caring for orphans, and teaching young men to be gospel preachers. Of course, it is right for the church to care for the fatherless and widows in their affliction, but this work should be done by and through the church, with the elders having the oversight thereof." Guy N. Woods.

Now he says the elders can't have the oversight of it, and still denies that he's changed. Now Guy, you ought to confess that you haven't even told the truth about the change. You not only have changed and ought to confess that, but you've even misrepresented the fact that you h a v e n 't changed, because you have. What does he say? Let me read it again. He said, "Of course, it is right for the church to care for the fatherless and widows in their affliction, but this work should be done by and through the church with the elders having the oversight thereof, and not through boards and conclaves unknown to the New Testament. In this connection it is a pleasure to commend to the Brotherhood Tiptons Orphan Home, Tipton, Oklahoma. The work there is entirely scriptural." Now what made it scriptural? Listen to him now: What made it scriptural? "Being managed and conducted by the elders." Who said that? Guy N. Woods. That was his position in 1939. I can quote him even later on down the line along the very same thing.

For example, I hear him saying over here in the Gospel Advocate in 1954, page 845, "The early church operated a home for destitute widows. In his letter to Timothy Paul wrote," and he quotes I Timothy 5:9, 10, 16, and goes ahead to discuss the matter—"Paul made obligatory the care of widows by the church in this passage. He who denies this repudiates reason, logic and faith." Now, you know he says the business of the church is to furnish money, and the business of the home is to furnish care. And he believes the home ought to do the work of the home and the church ought to do the work of the church. Well, all right if that's the case, and he's reasoning properly, the church can't furnish the care. Yet here he says it can, and he argued it in the same series of articles in the Gospel Advocate concerning James 1:27, when he said the word visit meant to aid, to come to the aid or relief of. I Timothy 5:16 means exactly the same thing. It means to give aid, and he argues that the church is under obligation to give aid to the widows. But he puts the orphans in from James 1:27, into the same arrangement.

And so he said down here on October 28, page 845, in the Advocate, "The church as an organization is obligated to provide for widows, but the same passage of scripture which authorizes care for widows without designating the manner or method, likewise enjoins care for fatherless orphans. James 1:27." Widows are to be cared for by the church—and he's said ever since this debate started that it cannot do it—that the church can't furnish the care. All the church can do is just to furnish the money. Now, Guy, you've changed, and you ought to be man enough to get up here and admit it and make confession and join the change column and the repenting column with a lot of the rest of these fellows that have changed purportedly in the Gospel Advocate. Make your acknowledgement in the Gospel Advocate along with the rest of them. A number of them have and you ought to join the throng.

Well, he said the elders are over the home in my arrangement. Why no. No, they aren't over the kind of a home that he's been talking about—a private home. What kind of a home is it? You know, he said there are four kinds of homes, and he's correct about that. He's correct about it. He says that there is the private home. Well, that's not the kind that we're discussing in this proposition because the church doesn't build that. I've been trying to point that out to him ever since we started. There is the private home, and then he said there is the legal home. Well, the church can't build that. The church can't build the legal home. That's a matter that the law and the state provide for. And then he said there is the foster home and that of course, simply means the parents have taken the place of the parents that are lost, in a private home. That's what he means by that, I suppose. Then there is the institutional home. And I gave him the definition of that from Webster in the very first speech that I made, I believe; at least the first night. And it is, An institution or asylum for the caring for the destitute. Why, that's what it is, like a crippled children's clinic or hospital. They are being cared for. They have a place. They have a place and they have the proper secular education. Well, that's exactly why we put E-T-C. Well, now that E-T-C just accommodated you. You had a lot to say about the proper physical training and the necessaries of life. Now you know he talked about the etc. there. Everything necessary for the proper care and provision of the child. We couldn't put it all on the chart, without making it so big nobody could turn it. So we just put it on there. I believe and I've said all the way through that whatever is necessary for the proper provision of the child and the care of the destitute child, that the church can furnish, but that doesn't put the church in the YMCA business. It doesn't put the church in the baseball business, or the volley ball business. It doesn't put the church in the educational business, and the school business. Why certainly not, anymore than I'm in it when I send a child from my home to a school. The fact of the business is public education in this country is a function of, not the home, but a function of the state. The home simply takes advantage of it—that's the idea—and sends the children to it.

But he wants to know if the elders can be over the home. And he says they can't. Well, let's just look at it a minute. I have a picture here from New Mexico Christian children's home, and they have a sign out in the yard. We don't have it on the projector, but it does say on the sign, and you can examine it if you want to, "Directors, elders of the Fourth Street C h u r c h of Christ." Now, Guy, you o u g h t to straighten them out. You know there's only one home West of the Mississippi river, and the Firm Foundation and the Gospel Advocate have always divided on this matter. Always have. The Firm Foundation and brother Showalter and those who have written for it pretty largely have taken the position that homes ought to be under the elders—whatever size they are—if the church is going to furnish them and the church is going to send money to them, they ought to be under the elders. Well, for a while I said, I tried to go along with that. I don't go along with it anymore. Brotherhood promotions, and the proper application of the principles of truth to them, that we will be discussing for the next three nights, caused me to restudy the application of truth to that matter. That's the respect in which I've changed. The other isn't. I've always opposed any kind of a corporate body under a board of directors overseeing and controlling any of the work of the church—anything that the church does or undertakes to do.

Then down here, the Old Folks Home up at Chapel Avenue Church of Christ, the elders of the Chapel Avenue Church of Christ, it's under their supervision. The very masthead of their official publication says so. Then the children's home down at Lubbock. Why it's under the elders of the church. They don't have an incorporated home. They have an incorporation for the church, yes, to hold title to their property. Five of the elders are its trustees, but they have seventeen elders of that church, and that home is not incorporated as a home, it's under the elders of the Broadway Church at Lubbock. Now, Guy, if they're wrong about it you ought to go to work on them. You say it can't be done. They say we are doing it. Like the fellow that said, they can't put you in jail for that; and the man who had already been put, said, I'm already here

—they have done it. Brethren are doing it, whether it can be done or not.

The Turley Home Charter at Tulsa, Oklahoma, provides within the charter that it is to be under the direction of the elders of the church. Then brother W. D. Rhodes, the superintendent of the home in Wichita, Kansas, in the Home Journal, the officials publication of it, says: "supervised and directed by the elders of the Riverside Church of Christ." Now he gets up here and says that that just can't be done. More than that, in Facts, published by Gayle Oler, February 1, 1952, said, "That as we have published repeatedly before the elders of the church of Christ at Terrell, Texas, have the responsibility of the oversight of Boles home. They appoint a group of men to serve them regularly and properly in the management of the affairs of the home. These men are answerable to the elders." Not members of the Terrell church now, but from churches all over Texas, and they are answerable to the elders of Terrell. "So the criticism that the home at Boles is not under an eldership is untrue." That's 1952, from the pen of Gayle Oler.

While I'm on that let me have your letter from the judge. Brother Oler and the judge don't seem to agree about a matter or two here. "Dear Mr. Adams: I have your letter of October the 25th with reference to the . . . . . matter. I remember you and your connection with this case and will be glad to supply you with a statement from my office as to what occurred. It was the decision of the court that the two children of . . . . . be placed in Boles Orphan Home at Quinlan, Texas. This particular home was specified because it was the choice of the mother, ... It was further decided that the younger child, a baby of three months be put up for adoption. The child could not be placed in Boles Home because the Home did not accept children of that age. I called you on the telephone, asked you if you knew those in charge of Boles Home, to which you replied that you did. I then asked if you would act as an *agent of the court* in contacting the home with reference to placing the two older . . . . . children there, which you agreed to do. I also asked if you would serve as agent of the court in securing an adoption home for the baby, to which you also agreed. The children were then placed in your legal custody by the court with the instructions to place the two older children in the Boles Orphan Home and to find adoptive parents for the baby subject, of course, to the further action of the court. Your only connection with this case was that of agent of the court." Now, brethren, when they bring that kind of a thing up, when a man acts as an agent of the district court, and they bring that up to try to discredit him and reflect upon him, that's stooping to a pretty low level in my judgment. You can think as you please about it. It had no business in this debate to start with.

According to brother Woods position, the churches of Christ can build an organization to care for the needy, but the churches cannot care for the needy. The churches of Christ can build an organization to provide for the destitute but they cannot provide. The churches of Christ can build an organization to build a home, but the churches of Christ cannot build the home. The churches of Christ can build an organization to restore the home, as he calls it, but cannot restore the home. The churches of Christ can build an organization to do all of this, but the churches of Christ can't do any of it. That's Guy N. Woods, and yet he has the audacity to tell an audience of thinking people that he believes in the all-sufficiency of the church. I deny it. He doesn't believe any such thing, or he wouldn't be affirming that the churches of Christ can build other organizations to do the work that God said for the churches of Christ to do. If they are sufficient what do they need with other organizations?

But he said Roy Cogdill and these brethren occupy the anti-Sunday school position. Now, brother Woods, that isn't so either. It's an effort to prejudice. The parallel cannot be shown except in opposition to something. Does he oppose anything? If he does he's an anti. That's all there is to that. Wonder what kind of a benevolent organization he would oppose. Brother Woods, you've still got another speech. I want you to tell us what kind of a benevolent organization that churches of Christ could build to do their work, that would be unscriptural. Tell us what kind of an organization they would have to build in order to have an unscriptural one. That's what we'd like to know.

It is not so that we occupy an anti-school p o s i t i o n. There's no parallel between my position and the anti-Sunday school. It's a misrepresentation because the *anti-Sunday school opposes an organization that does not exist.* And Guy Woods, when he debates them, denies that it does exist as a separate organization; an organization that is mere systematic arrangement for the teaching of the Word of God. *I oppose an organization,* brethren, *that does exist,* and isn't any part of the church, and it isn't any part of the home. And I cited Supreme Court Cases to show you that it isn't a part of either. It's separate and apart from both, its a real, human organization. And he leaves it out of every chart he puts up here.

Where was it on that home restored picture? Here's the private home and the home destroyed, and the home restored. But where is the organization that the church built to restore that home? Brother Woods, that's what you refuse to discuss and that's what your proposition called for. You've refused to discuss the proposition. You ought to admit defeat on your proposition and admit that you haven't discussed it. You haven't touched it side, edge, nor bottom. The organization here is a genuine, real organization, doing what God commanded the church to do. Would you endorse that kind of an organization for the Sunday school?

Then again, *it's separate and apart from the congregation, from the church.* Is the Sunday school such an organization as that? I can quote Guy Woods to the effect that it isn't. Then *the charge assumes the issue of the whole question.* That is *whether or not it's a matter of expediency.* That's begging the issue. He's presuming that this human corporation is a matter of expediency. He hasn't proved it. He hasn't shown us the passage of scripture in which it is incorporated or included within the scope of that passage and it's authority? Turn to my first chart. He hasn't given us the passage yet that includes that human organization that he's arguing that the churches have the right to build. Would he endorse putting all of the Sunday school work under a board of directors—a human organization? We pointed out to you in the beginning of this discussion that this was a matter of authority, that God authorized what he wants the church to do. Our proposition says that it is contrary to the scriptures for the churches of Christ to build benevolent organizations. That's what I've been affirming all the way through. And I repeat he hasn't discussed it. He hasn't represented it on a single one of his charts. Why I pointed out to you just a little while ago in a speech that Guy N. Woods in his first debate on this with brother Porter, up at Indianapolis, tried to fasten that corporate body on to the church. We pointed out that that was his position then. He said that this corporate body was a part of the church. It was just a functional arrangement; and I read the passage the other night in which he said it. It belonged to the church up at Indianapolis. He found out that wouldn't work, so he changed his position on that, and he said down at Paragould that it is an integral part of the home. The corporation, the corporate body and the home are one and the same thing. And he found out that that wouldn't work in this debate because the Supreme Courts of this Country, lawyer or no lawyer, a Supreme Court Decision ought to mean something to a man if he didn't know anything about law—if he didn't know anything about it. The Supreme Court is the highest authority in the state on law. And I cited you the cases where that corporate body is not a part of anything, and when he came up against that, and against the fact that he couldn't produce the statute in any state that requires it as he had been claiming, the corporate body, *the corporate form got mighty unimportant*. We've asked him from the very beginning, Brother Woods, where is any express command, like we have for the Lord's Supper, for the churches of Christ building a benevolent organization? Where is it? Where is the express command, or the approved example like we have for the time of its observance? Now you said you accepted this. Yes, about the Lord's Supper you do, but you won't accept the same principle about these benevolent organizations. That's

HOW TO ESTABLISH SCRIPTURAL AUTHORITY
THE LORD'S SUPPER

(1) **EXPRESS COMMAND** – "*This do in remembrance of Me.*"
(*Observance*) *I COR. 11:23-24.*

(2) **APPROVED EXAMPLE** – "*And upon the first day of the week, When the disciples came together to break bread.*"
(*Time of Observance*) *ACTS 20:7.*

(3) **NECESSARY INFERENCE** – "*The first day of the week...to break bread.*"
(*Frequency of Observance*) (*Means as regularly as the day comes,* COMPARE *"The Sabbath day to keep it Holy."*)
HOW OFTEN?

EXPEDIENCY : *ANY HOUR WITHIN THE FIRST DAY OF THE WEEK.*

1.   1.

where you try to mislead these folks. Sure, you can't deny the Lord's Supper, but what you need to do is put your benevolent organizations on there. Get it in the command, find the example for us that includes the benevolent organization.

The home, yes. The place, yes. For the widow, I Timothy 5:16, to be sure. And you know he talks about the function of the home and the function of the church. Well, in I Timothy 5 they've both got benevolent work to do, and one of them can't do the benevolent work of the other. Paul said, "If any man or woman that believeth have widows let them relieve them," there's your family or home benevolence. I Timothy 5:8, "If a man does not provide for his own household he's worse than an infidel." There's your family or your home benevolence. There's the function of the home in its own benevolent field. But what about the church? "If any man or woman that believeth have widows let them relieve them and let not the church be charged," Why?—"That it"—the church—"may relieve"—the same word exactly—"that it may relieve them that are widows indeed." Why in that passage of scripture there is a benevolent function for the home and a benevolent function for the church, and it's Guy Woods that's mixing them up and trying to confuse you with them. Let the home do its benevolent work; let the church do its benevolent work; and let the church do it and not some human corporation governed by a board of directors that God never said anything about, command, example or necessary inference; and when you don't have it within the scope of that which is authorized, it is not expedient. It's the sin of presumption, like old Nadab and Abibu when they got their fire from the wrong place; like old Uzziah when he went into the temple and burned incense on the altar when he wasn't a priest and turned into a leper for the rest of his life. It's plain presumption, an invasion of the realm of God's silence. We showed you in these other charts over here that it was specifically authorized, that the church of our Lord is specifically authorized, and it has its congregational arrangement—the only organization God ever gave the church.

Now when you send money to Childhaven where do you send it? Do you send it to the elders of the church like they did in Acts 11? If so, what church? Where in one of these institutional homes do you send the relief to the elders? That's what I want to know. Not in these incorporated bodies you don't. No, sir, they designate, and the law requires that they must designate someone as their agent; in that case or in most cases it's the superintendent. But in the New Testament when they sent relief to needy brethren off in another part of the country, they didn't send their needy off somewhere else to be cared for. Oh, no, but when they had more than they could care for and others sent to their relief, they sent it to the elders of the church, and we've given you New Testament example. Acts 2, 4, 6. But where did he produce any example for anything functioning for the church in the field of benevolence—the work that God ordained the church to do. You know how he answered that? He said, brother Cogdill, where is the private home? It isn't on that chart. Well, certainly not. Because the church doesn't build the private home, brother Woods, and that chart's about what the church can build. And that's what we're supposed to be debating about. And you've refused to do it from the beginning. And these people out here know it. Why ask me where is the private home here? Just like over here in this Chart No. 2, what is the Issue? And he said, "well, where is the private home?" It's not the issue. I told you that to start with.

Where is the private home here, he said. It isn't there. It isn't this corporate body, you can guarantee that. That isn't a part of anything the law says. Well, where is the home? Well, the only home there is is the institutional home over here, the kind that he's defending. If that's what he means by home. That's it. And there isn't any authority for this thing down here, the thing that he is supposed to be defending. I want him and I'm begging him for the last time in this debate, brother Woods, be fair enough with these people, prove your propositon. Get on your proposition in your last speech anyway, and produce the passage that authorizes the church to send its money to a human organization to take over and control its work for it. That's what we've been begging you for from the beginning and you've failed, and every thinking person, unprejudiced mind in this audience knows that you've failed; utterly and completely. I knew you would to begin with. I think even you know you have.

And I'm glad for the opportunity of having discussed these matters with you and pray that you'll give them consideration, only in the light of what the Bible teaches. Don't you let Roy Cogdill or Guy Woods either one make up your mind for you, or anybody else, but do it from the word of God.

Wood's Sixth Negative

Brethren Moderators, Brother Cogdill, Ladies and Gentlemen:

I'm now before you for the final thirty minutes of this evening, and I hope that this time may pass rapidly and pleasantly for you. I thought that there was an especially significant statement made by brother Cogdill just as he was closing. And that was that brother Woods was to get on his proposition. I had the impression that brother Cogdill was supposed to be in the affirmative, though I knew that all he was doing was making negative speeches in the affirmative. That is an admission by him that he hasn't got anything positive to set up; that it was my obligation in the negative to prove a positive proposition. Do you know why it is that brother Cogdill stands in that unenviable position tonight? The reason is that there isn't a home in brotherhood, that is a home of the type which we're discussing, which he endorses. He has no plans to start a home that may be operated according to the laws of the state for the purpose of caring for fatherless and destitute children. And he couldn't if he were to try.

For, if he were to establish a home, then the same objections which he levels against Boles and Childhaven and Tennessee Orphan home would apply equally against him. That's the reason why these brethren will never have a home that is supported by the churches of Christ.

It's exactly like the Sunday school position. Those brethren say that we misrepresent them when we say that they do not believe in teaching the Bible in classes. But we just never can find a class that suits them. Now brother Cogdill says that he's not opposed to the church caring for orphan children and providing a home for them and operating that home. But we don't have any to please him. And he has no plans for starting one. And he couldn't start one if he wanted to. Now that's the situation with which we stand in that.

Brother Cogdill tells you that I've failed. Brother Porter and I agree that when somebody starts telling you that, that's a pretty good sign that they're afraid you wouldn't know it. Now I'm perfectly willing for this audience to decide that, brother Cogdill. I think they're intelligent enough to decide whose getting a whipping in this debate. I'm perfectly willing to leave it to them.

I've heard of fellows that would argue with a band-saw. I think I've just about met one of them here tonight. I produced a statement from the head of the department of public health in the state of Tennessee and he informs this gentleman, figuratively speaking, that he doesn't know what he's talking about. Now it's strange that this man is up there in Nashville operating this without the benefit of brother Cogdill's wise counsel. He says, Oh, that's not a ruling of law, and that just shows how little brother Cogdill knows about the law. He says this is an arbitrary statement of some bureau. Well, it so happens that the statute provides that within the frame-work of the statute that this organization shall provide the minimum standards of child care. And so it does partake of the character of law; lawyer Cogdill to the contrary notwithstanding.

Now let's see if it doesn't. Let's see what they say about it. And bear in mind please, that these gentlemen say that instead of these matters being annulled that they were simply enhanced and emphasized. Here is what the official document sent out by the department says: "Private institutions offering care to dependent children must be incorporated in accordance with the laws of the state of Tennessee." The law of the state of Tennessee. Now, of course, those fellows up there are ignorant too.

Now, Brother Cogdill, he tells us that it would be illegal if such were necessary. It isn't illegal to incorporate a church. Brother Cogdill has no objections to preaching for churches that are incorporated, and I can produce him some examples, and I shall be glad to do so, of real institutionalism, right here in this state, of brethren that that are identified with him, and I hope he challenges me to do it. I would just be glad to show him some incorporations here that actually all matters involving things that are wrong. But brother Cogdill doesn't object to an incorporated church. Because he preaches for them. And

BENEVOLENT ORGANIZATIONS

yet when it comes to the matter of the home he says that he objects.

Now he's told you two or three times here that I have three different positions on this question of incorporation, and that's a figment of his imagination. Ever since I stood at law more than twenty years ago, I have had exactly the same idea there because I learned as much about it then as I know now. I learned what the state statute requires on it. He says I took the position up there that it was the church that was incorporated. I have no recollection of that. Why didn't you cite the statement, brother Cogdill? I did nothing of the kind. I think you were just confused and bewildered and just had to say something, because I said nothing about that. I didn't take the position that the relationship of the incorporation is that of a relationship to the church and not the home. And then he says that over at Paragould I took the position that the incorporation is an integral part of the home. Well, I took the position that the incorporation is the thing that exists only in contemplation of the law. And I gave the famous Dartmouth case, the quotation of it that has long stood as a classical definition of that. That it's an invisible, intangible thing, existing only in contemplation of law. That's all it is. It's really just a figment of his imagination.

That's what I've said all along, and he gets up here and tells you or tries to tell you, and of course, you watch the articles spring out of the Guardian telling you that I've taken one position in one debate and another one in another. I don't know what they'd write about if they didn't have some of us as texts.

He said that he tried to go along with homes under elders until he learned better. Brother Cogdill, I thought that that's what you were defending. Isn't this home that you believe in under elders? Now he says he can't go along with the idea of homes being operated under elders. But now he decides and here it is but he doesn't say its a home because the only thing a church can start is another church, so this is not a home here—these situations—but it's not another church because it's not the function of the church to serve as a home. I don't know what that is. Do you? Haven't found out yet, and we're closing the debate on this part of the matter tonight.

He says that I haven't introduced any bible authority for my proposition. Well, you know brother Cogdill has the wonderful fashion of just demolishing arguments by just not paying any attention to them. Not saying one word about them. He just turns them into smithareens by not saying a word about them. I feel sure, friends, that if I were to come to Birmingham and allowed three nights to pass and made no reference to the arguments that had been advanced, or ignored completely the basic matters presented as has brother Cogdill, I feel sure that the brethren whom I represent in this debate and who stand with me on these matters would hang their heads in shame. And rightly so. He tells you that he's answered everything I've presented. What did he say about the chart that I introduced tonight to show that the orphan home is supported by the three kinds of authority that we depend upon. By a direct statement, by an example and by necessary inference. What did he say about that? Let me have that chart. Here it is: By precept, James 1:27.

He said that I didn't give any scriptural authority. I came up here and didn't give any scriptural authority. What did he say about this, friends? What did he say about it? Here is the authority by precept. James 1:27. Here is the necessary inference. 1 Timothy 5:16. And if wants an example of it, I would cite him as an example of it the homes that were provided for by the New Testament church in the matter of the distribution of the needs that was characteristic of the early days after the establishment of the church. Oh, he says that was in the frame-work of the church. It wasn't anything of the kind. The mere fact that this money was supplied by the church doesn't mean that the church took over those homes and operated them. There's the real issue, as we shall, in a few moments show. What did he say about that, ladies and gentlemen? What do you brethren that stand with brother Porter, and with brother Cogdill think about these matters? Be it said to brother Porter's credit, he did try to answer them. Well, brother Porter, would at least say, let's have chart No. 30. All right there it is. Well, that's the same as the next one. All right, we'd put that one on. Then we'd put the next one on. Then he'd say, all right, now that's involved in the third one. Let's have the third one. Then he'd take up the third one. Well, at least he let us look at them. That's one way of dealing with them, and I like his way better than I do Brother Cogdill's. At least I got to look at my charts once in awhile.

Now let's see further, ladies and gentlemen, let's see our chart on Galatians 4. I am sorry brother Warren, but I don't have that number for you. Do you have that there, quickly. All right. Here is another one friends, that I introduced, and I think this is unanswerable. But he made no reference to that. He didn't even cite it under any consideration. What do you brethren think about that? I know you brethren are accustomed to attending debates in which these men debate Baptist preachers, and in which they simply blast them out of existence by taking the New Testament and proving they're wrong. Why don't they do that with me? Why don't they? That's what I would do. Exactly.

Now then, friends, I want to go right along with his speech. Next he said that I have taken a position in this debate that's contrary to my writings in previous years. I don't know why it is that these brethren delight in misrepresenting me. Everytime I meet some fellow that has an anti-position he always cites that Abilene Speech. I met Leroy Garrett and he cited it to prove I didn't believe in located preachers when at the time that I made the speech I was a located preacher at Wellington, Texas. Then later on when I met him on the question of the right of Freed-Hardeman College to exist, he took the position in that debate that in that speech that I was opposed to Christian Colleges, when at that particular time I wasn't in attendance at the school but I had some years before that attended. He cited it to prove, just as Cogdill has tonight, that I was against the orphan home when at that particular time the church was regularly supporting both Tipton and Boles. Now here's the truth of the matter: Back in those days this was never taught by about anybody, except for a few cranks around over the country, and they were up around Indianapolis and St. Louis— And I might say in this connection that I noticed that brother Ketcherside threw out his arms in welcome to brother Porter following the Paragould Debate, and I wonder if he will do the same thing tonight to brother Cogdill. He ought to. He ought, because he made his arguments. In fact, Ketcherside said to me in Paragould that these men are making exactly the same arguments that I made in debate against Rue Porter when I met him. Brother Porter's here tonight and he could testify to that. And so, friends, the truth of the business was that back in those days I was simply opposing organizations that were similar to the Missionary Society and I said so in that very connection. I said when brethren establish organizations similar to the missionary society that they are establishing unscriptural organizations. I believe it just as strongly tonight as I did then. Oh, he said yes, but you said that you endorsed the Tipton Home. I did. I'm endorsing it tonight. I'm defending it here tonight. It's in the proposition. Yes, but you said you endorsed it because it was under the elders. I can prove by brother Porter it's not under the elders. Let me have that top book over there. That one right there. No, the other one. That other one. That one. No the next one. Now, friends, here is the truth of the matter. In Acts chapter 11 and verse 27, we have an account of the disciples sending money to the elders. I am not tonight concerned about who those elders were or where they were. They were elders of a New Testament church. That's sufficient.

Of course, it's right to send money to the elders of the church in an area where there is need. But the question is not: is that money that is sent to those elders to be spent under the direction of those elders by them taking over the management of the homes that are supplied the money; but the question is: did those elders exercise such in Acts 11? Did the elders of Acts 11 take over the homes, the needy homes, and operate them simply because they made a donation to them? That's the issue. I never did think that a home was a church and I didn't believe it in 1939. Yet these brethren have used up reams of paper and gallons of ink all over the country making these statements, trying to make it appear that I do not believe in the all-sufficiency of the church, when I said the church is adequate to accomplish the work which God gave the church to do. Now I believe that, but I believe the home is adequate to accomplish the work that God intended for the home to do. Brother Cogdill does not.

He cites a statement here regarding the Firm Foundation. What has that to do with the question? Let the Firm Foundation defend itself, if it's interested. Brother Showalter, many years ago, when brother J. B. Nelson was selected as superintendent of that commended the trustees, members of the board for the selection of brother Nelson. Now then they say that he changed his position. That's what some of them claim. Maybe he did. Maybe he did. Brother Cogdill did. He says he did. But at any rate, back in the days when brother J. B. Nelson was superintendent of the home brother Showalter endorsed it and he commended it.

Now he said last night and then again tonight, this is the difference between the Firm Foundation and the Gospel Advocate. Well, he said that he objected last night to any paper that would not allow matters to be presented in it except that which one believed. Well, that's a difference between the Gospel Advocate and the Guardian. We believe in teaching people the truth. He admits that he teaches error through his paper. I subscribe to the view that it's just as much the responsibility of an editor—and I rejoice to be under the direction of the distinguished and brilliant editorship of brother B. C. Goodpasture—and I think it's just as much his responsibility to guard the paper against the promulgation of error as it is for a preacher to stand in the pulpit and to guard it. I would not under any circumstance provide a medium for the propagation of error. I remember seeing an editorial that represented two preachers sitting on the front seat in a church building, and a third one standing in the pulpit preaching, and one of the preachers turned to the other and said, "We believe in having both sides heard here." Well, now evidently that's brother Cogdill's idea. I do not subscribe to any such view.

What did he say about his admission along that line? Then next he says here, that the Tipton Home is under elders. Brother Porter doesn't believe it is. Brother Porter doesn't agree with you on that. Brother Porter says the Tipton Home is not under elders. He says it in the Gospel Guardian. He says it in the Gospel Guardian of October the 10th, 1957. He says this about it: "So in the arrangement for Tipton Home we have a human organization, a chartered corporation, set up to provide the home. This corporation which provides the home has a board of directors and one man is the presiding officer of the board." He cites the statement here that brother Earl Todd is the presiding officer. Well, I think he's right. I agree with him, because I don't think it's the function of elders as elders to run a home. I think men who are elders may do it, like they do. He says, Oh, over here at Turley that there the home is operated by the elders. Actually what the bulletin says—and also that from the Riverside Church, and Maude Carpenter Home in Wichita, says that the elders are the directors of the home. That's an eminently fair and fine statement. I said that that doesn't say that the elders are the elders of the home. That's what he wants it to say. It says the elders are the directors of the home. That's what I think they are. They're directors, not elders. That's what they think they are, too. If you don't believe it you ask them. If you don't believe it, you ask them. That's exactly what they think they are. They don't say they are elders of the home, it says they are the directors of the home. The elders are not elders of a home because you can't put elders over a home. You put parents over a home, or their equivalent.

Then next he says that this etc. here includes secular education. Well, that's right. That's what I believe is included in it. All right, one of two things is true. This is either a church or a home. If it's a church, then you've got the church into secular business, and just a few weeks ago I read an article in there—at least with reference to that theme—that the church is not to get into secular business. Brother Earl Dale recently had a lengthy article in the Gospel Guardian against the way that congregations today were getting into secular activity showing that that was not the function of the church. Well, I think so, too. I think it's not, too. I think that etc. there includes a lot of things that the church can't engage in, but the home must. There is the issue, ladies and gentlemen, in this debate.

Then he says further that there's only one home West of the Mississippi River not under a board. He's wrong about that as I've already shown. He says his position is that the elders cannot be over a home. He says he used to try to go along with that idea, that elders might be over a home. A home that's got elders over it, now he can't go along with that. Well, he doesn't go along with this then. It's a home.

Then next here he reads at length from a judge with reference to Brother Adams. Adams was acting as an agent of the court. Could brother Adams have acted as an agent of the court in a matter involving the missionary society? Suppose that it involved activity that had to do with the missionary society. Could he have acted in that capacity? According to brother Cogdill, a man who acts as an official of the court loses his individual character and is not responsible for what he does. If his argument had any merit, that was it. I don't believe that a man can act in any capacity except in his capacity as a Christian. I don't care what the capacity is. He's always a Christian whenever he's in any capacity. And he tried to justify that by making it appear that he was out of his true character as an individual, and was merely an officer of the court, that was it.

Now, friends, before I begin some of the review that I want to leave with you before the discussion closes, I want you to see the miserable perversions of positions and the inconsistencies and contradictions that he's made. Now I say this in all kindness. I do not believe that I ever met a man that was as inconsistent as brother Cogdill. Without any trouble at all I've listed here 20 inconsistencies. Now, I'm going to let you be the judge and you just listen carefully now and see whether or not they're here. Listen carefully: Give me close attention because I'm going to read this rapidly.

He said the only thing a church can build is another church; but that that which the church builds for the benefit of orphan children is not a church. 2. Elders cannot oversee secular education; but elders can provide secular education for orphans and oversee the secular education provided. He has been preaching for thirty-five years that the church can take care of its own orphans; yet he assisted in placing children in Boles Home stating that the churches of Christ should support them there. He admits that the needs of an orphan cannot be met without a home and that the Church is all that is needed in caring for orphans but that the church cannot function as a home. He argues that the needs of an orphan cannot be adequately met without a home, and that the church is the only organization that is needed for such care, yet contends that the church and the home are not the same. He insists that elders must operate the child care agency, that this is not a church, yet denies that elders can oversee anything except the church. He thus fails to recognize that if the church is all the organization that is necessary in caring for orphans either that the needs of an orphan can be adequately met without it having a home, or God put elders over two institutions. He maintains that the church is all that's needed in the care of the orphan, yet he endorses Tant's editorial in which elders make their appeal for a home for orphans which they have in their care. He ridicules the idea that in the care of orphans the church may supply the funds so that the home at Cullman can actually supply the care, yet he thinks the church may send funds to a private home to enable that home to care for orphan children.

He says that the only thing that the elders may scripturally oversee is a church, but the elders may provide and oversee an arrangement for the care of orphans which is not the church. He says that the church is all that is needed in the care of orphans, but that elders may provide an arrangement which is not the church, and yet the only thing they may build is another church. He concedes that a church may send funds to an institution which is not the church to enable that institution to care for orphans, yet objects to a church sending funds to Childhaven and other orphans homes among us because it's an institution which is not the church. He ridicules the idea of meeting legal requirements, yet knows that a child-care institution cannot exist without being legally managed. Of the nineteen homes among us caring for fourteen hundred children there is not one of them which he endorses, yet says he will not discuss alternatives. No. 16, Of the nineteen homes among us with fourteen hundred children, not one of which he endorses, yet he is (a) not attempting to start one he does endorse; (b) he can't start one he can endorse, because the same objection he levels against the nineteen would apply to it. It would be a legal entity, an organization apart from the church doing a work which the church was not organically set up to do. 17. He says that a church can provide food without going into the food business. 18. He says that the Gospel Guardian of which he is publisher is not doing the work of the church, that there is no edification for the church in it, but that it is a purely human enterprise, that error is taught in it, yet urges churches to buy service from it. 19. He admits that it is all right for a church to incorporate but says it is wrong for a home to be incorporated; yet says he opposes the homes whether incorporated or unincorporated, thus showing the incorporation is not as issue. 20. He says that elders can provide and oversee secular education, and yet not be in the school business; that elders can provide and oversee recreation yet not be in the entertainment business; that elders can provide and oversee a farm yet not be in the farming business; But believes that when they provide a preacher and oversee him they are in the preaching business.

Now my friends, there's just a few of them. I never did see when there were more contradictions and inconsistencies involved. Now in so far as the need of homes is concerned it must be recognized that many children are not susceptible of adoption. I couldn't discourage anybody in all their integrity, for any childless family, or any family, for that matter, who have the disposition and the ability to take children into their homes. I say that that is a truly wonderful act. But that's not the church doing it, and if such were done all over the country it still would remain that there are numerous children that are not susceptible of such care and must be provided under some other arrangement. Too many of these brethren forget that there is a legal matter involved. Some folks think that all you've got to do is just go out and get the children and take them into your home. Well, it's not that simple. Remember, please, that a delinquent child is truly a ward of the court, and that it's the court who determines where that child shall be placed. And it's the court that determines whether adoption is feasible or possible or not and there are many children which are not susceptible to adoption. These brethren talk a good bit about its own orphans —the Church's orphans. The church hasn't got any orphans. The church can't have orphans. You can't put orphans in the care of the church. And when these brethren say that those elders over at Blytheville as elders, have the custody of those children, he's just talking through his hat like he was about this matter of incorporation. Because you can't put children into the custody of elders as elders. Now then men who are elders may have the custody of the children, but they are acting as officers of the court, at best guardians, designated as such or else placed in a place of official capacity, being designated such for the time being, by some bureau, such as that which we had under consideration tonight. And in acting in that capacity they are not acting as elders, as elders of the church.

Then on last evening he said that it is impossible for you to get children out of these homes, once they are in them. It is impossible to get them out of these private homes, too. If these children that brother Tant offers through the Guardian, by which I might say he illegally does, and he could be arrested. For attempting to serve as a child placing agency without a license. I'm prepared to prove that, too, if it becomes necessary. If these children were put in these homes he asks for, then it would still follow that you could not get them out of these homes. You can't get them out of a Catholic home, either; if they are put in a Catholic home because of our remissness. These children will not all die—They will not starve to death. Just go to the nearest telephone and call the first Catholic priest, if you don't want them to take care of them. They will be glad to do so. But you can't get them out of the Catholic home, either. You can't get them out of the Methodist or the Baptist home. You can't get them out of hell in eternity either, when they've gone there from a failure of our brethren to provide them with the care and the teaching that would make Christians out of them.

I rejoice tonight to stand before you in defense of these homes and these fourteen hundred children and I can't speak with reference to all of them at the present time. But some time back I was told that all children over twelve years of age in our homes were at that particular time members of the body of Christ; that all of them had obeyed the gospel. Now, of course, from time to time children come and go, for various reasons. But let me further say that they are not driven out. Brother Cogdill owes this audience and owes the brethren that work in this capacity an apology for saying that these homes turn these children away. They do nothing of the kind—that is, that they drive them out. Sometimes they aren't able to receive them because they have no space for them. But they want to, and they would have more space were it not for the fact that some of these brethren go over the country opposing such activity. I'm not able to understand the philosophy of a man that drives a good automobile as I do, wears clothes every thread of which were supplied them by the brethren, and every bite which he eats comes directly or indirectly through the treasury of the church and lives sumptuously in this day, and yet would oppose, and would try to stop, and would if he could kill such activity on the part of providing for the fatherless and the widows. That is, he would stop the church, if he could, from sending contributions to such. I tell you, friends, I reject and repudiate such an attitude. It's not a part of the New Testament teaching, it's contrary to the spirit of Christ, it's anti-ism, it's hobbyism, and it's dividing churches of Christ all over the country; and the sooner the brethren awake to the seriousness of this situation and realize that it is a sword thrust through the heart of our Savior to divide the church over that which these brethren were practicing up until five or six years ago. I say until we awake and become aware of such over the brotherhood, we'll continue to see the tragedies occur as they are occuring throughout the country at this present time. I thank you.

FOURTH NIGHT

PROPOSITION.

It is in harmony with the scriptures for churches of Christ to contribute funds from their treasuries in support of the Herald of Truth Radio Program conducted by the Highland Church of Christ, Abilene Texas, as a means of cooperating in accomplishing the mission of the Church of the Lord.

AFFIRMATIVE: Guy N. Woods

NEGATIVE: Roy E. Cogdill

Wood's First Affirmative

Brethren Moderators, Brother Cogdill, Ladies and Gentlemen:

I am most thankful, that in the providence of God, I am privileged to be before you tonight, in the affirmation of the proposition, which Brother Thomas Warren of Fort Worth, Texas, has just read to you. May I say, before I begin the affirmation of this proposition, that I count myself happy, and am honored by the invitation of the Homewood congregation of this city to affirm what we confidently believe the scriptures teach on this vital and fundamental matter. And I sincerely hope that we can all recognize the importance of this occasion. And that we may have the proper respect for God and His word that would prompt us to respect His teaching and be influenced thereby.

The proposition; it is in harmony with the scriptures for churches of Christ to contribute funds, from their treasuries, in support of the Herald of Truth radio program, conducted by the Highland Church of Christ, Abilene, Texas, as a means of cooperating in accomplishing the mission of the church of the Lord, is that which I am to prove.

May I spend a few moments please, in the definition of the terms of this proposition? By the words, in harmony with the scriptures, I mean in concord with the Bible, that is, both the Old and the New Testaments. By churches of Christ, bodies of baptized believers, over which Christ reigns as head and in which His spirit dwells. And by the phrase, contribute funds from their treasuries, simply to take money from the Lord's day contribution. Support of Herald of Truth radio program, that is, assist in supplying funds to enable it to be carried on a network and over the radio stations which broadcast it. As a means of cooperating in accomplishing the mission of the church of the Lord, in discharge of their duty to Christ, under the Great Commission.

Now, friends, the essence of this proposition is simply this: may a group of New Testament churches cooperate in the preaching of the gospel over the radio and television stations, where one of the participating congregations, takes care of the details? It's just that simple. It just boils down to that, a matter of the churches of our Lord, in their obligation to God, under the Commission, discharging it in preaching the gospel when one of the participating congregations takes care of the details regarding the program in the relationship to the network. Someone might ask, well why is it necessary for one of the congregations to take care of the details? Simply because it is impossible to conduct a network program without one congregation being responsible for the details. For example, Brother John Bannister recently told me regarding the Dallas television program conducted on KRLD-TV; that when they approached the officials of that station intending to buy time, that they were told by the station that the station would not sell them time unless all or a large number of the churches of Christ in the city participated, that they had so many demands for time that they would not sell it simply to one congregation. There are these and many other reasons that operate to make it feasible and necessary for somebody to have the responsibility of taking care of the details. Now, in carrying out these details, it is simply a matter of arranging for and providing the preaching and in the payment for the program, the congregations participate, each discharging its own duty. If there were nothing else in the Bible on this subject save the Great Commission, I would insist that it alone justifies that program and similar cooperative efforts.

I'm going to introduce as my very first chart in the discussion tonight, chart no. 37. And I'm going to ask that we turn the lights out in order that we may be able to see this chart on the screen. Chart no. 37. And here is the copy of it if someone will come for it. Observe

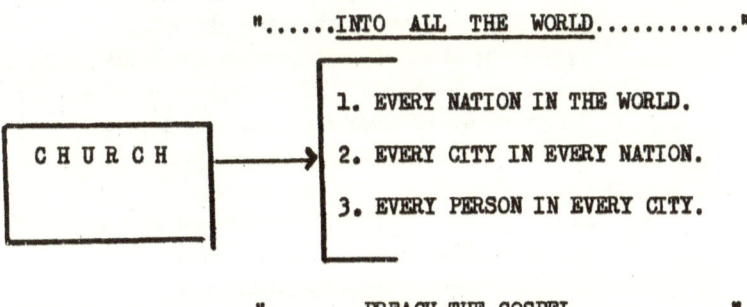

here, Ladies and Gentlemen, that it's the obligation of the church of our Lord to preach the gospel to the whole world. In Mark 16:15, 16, Jesus said, "Go into all the world and preach the gospel to every creature, he that believeth and is baptized shall be saved, he that believeth not shall be damned." Had it ever occurred to you to take notice of what is involved in that proposition? In the first place that necessitates our going to every nation in the world. In going to every nation in the world, it becomes necessary to go to every community in every nation in the world and then secondly to every city in every nation and then to contact every person in every city and to preach the gospel to every person in every city in every nation in all the world.

I want you to see how our obligation is magnified in that command. In the first place, if I came to Birmingham I would have discharged my obligation to come to the city here. But observe step number three, I must then contact every person in Birmingham, which magnifies my obligation 600 thousand fold. So it goes throughout the entire earth. It follows then without some sort of cooperative effort, it is impossible for this commission to be carried out. In fact, friends, it would take more than the resources of the Federal Government of the United States to carry out the obligation that is characteristic of this Commission. And as Brother Tant has said, in some of his writings, that not only is cooperation scriptural, but as he said on one occasion, the New Testament demands it.

Now since the apostolic church did carry the gospel into all the world, and preach the gospel to every creature under heaven, Col. 1:23, it follows that there was cooperative effort on the part of those New Testament churches.

Let us look then. Is there an exclusive pattern of Church cooperation taught in the Bible? Now even if what I have just said is accepted by brother Cogdill, and I presume it will be, it still does not necessarily follow that my proposition is true. If it should develop that there is some exclusive pattern of evangelism and that my proposition involved a type of cooperation that was not embodied in that exclusive type. So it becomes necessary to raise this question: is there an exclusive pattern of church cooperation taught in the Bible? My answer. No. And the evidence of it is right here on this particular chart. Another chart, please.

Observe please, what is here said. When there is but one method or way of doing a thing designated, and we are commanded to do that which is designated, then that becomes an exclusive pattern, and one must follow it in every detail. But if it can be shown that there are a number of types of cooperation taught in the New Testament, then it follows that there is no exclusive method. Observe first, we have examples of cooperation between individuals—2 Timothy 4:9. That involved cooperation between Paul and some of his assistants. Number two, there is an example of one individual and several other individuals co-

SPONSORING CONGREGATIONS

CHART NO. 38.

TYPES OF COOPERATION
IS THERE AN EXCLUSIVE "PATTERN" ?

1. BETWEEN INDIVIDUALS – 2 TIM. 4: 9.
2. ONE INDIVIDUAL AND SEVERAL OTHER INDIVIDUALS – ROM. 16: 1, 2.
3. CHRISTIAN FAMILY AND NEEDY INDIVIDUALS – 1 COR. 16: 15.
4. "DISCIPLES" AND "ELDERS" – ACTS 11: 27-30.
5. CHURCHES AND NEEDY SAINTS IN JERUSALEM – 2 COR. 8, 9.
6. CHURCH AND CHURCH – ACTS 15: 1-32,

WHICH IS THE EXCLUSIVE PATTERN???

operating, Romans 16:1, 2. "Phoebe was a succourer of many." There is a case mentioned in I Cor. 16:15, the household of Stephanas, that had addicted themselves to the ministry of the saints. There, if you please, is the example for the Christian family cooperating with needy individuals. Then Acts 11:27-30. That one tells us about the disciples determining, every man according to his ability, to send relief unto the brethren in Judea, which also they did, sending it to the Elders by the hand of Barnabas and Saul. There is cooperation between disciples and others. Then, 5, we have an example of churches and needy saints in Jerusalem. The churches of Macedonia, and Achaia and Corinth and Galatia in a cooperation involving the great collection of 2nd Corinthians 8 and 9. And then there is the example of the cooperation between churches. The church in Jerusalem, in the matter of the letter that was sent out Acts 15:1-32. Now, Brother Cogdill, when you're on the floor next, tell us which of these is the exclusive pattern that we should follow today. Obviously, friends, there is no such.

The word pattern means this, and here is the dictionary

definition: anything to pose for or worthy of imitation, exemplar, anything designed as a guide or model for making things. Now is anyone of these to be regarded as a guide or model? Obviously not. Simply because there are different types of cooperation here.

Brother Cogdill: Brother Guy, pardon me a m i n u t e. Something's wrong with the speaker. I can't understand a word you're saying over here.

Brother Woods: It seems too loud to me.

Brother Cogdill. Something's wrong with it, it comes on clear one minute and the next minute there is a reverberation in it and you can't hear a word you're saying.

Brother Woods: What about it; is there someone operating the speaker?

Brother Cogdill: Hold his time, until we get it adjusted.

Brother Woods: All right, now, friends, I have shown you that there is no exclusive method of church cooperation taught in the Bible. Now listen to this syllogism please. And I insist that Brother Cogdill shall deal with it. Our major premise is this: All radio programs involving cooperation which violates no fundamental principle of cooperation, are programs which involve scriptural cooperation. Our minor premise is this: The Herald of Truth radio program is a radio program which involves cooperation, which violates no fundamental principle of cooperation. Our conclusion, then is this: Therefore, the Herald of Truth radio program is a radio program involving scriptural cooperation. Now watch carefully, please. The major premise is axiomatic. The minor premise, I am prepared to prove in two different ways: first by showing what kind of a program the Herald of Truth radio program is, and then secondly showing that this is in harmony with one method of New Testament cooperation. And now may I have the lights on please just for a little bit?

I propose to prove what kind of program it is by the statements of those who participate, both contributors and those who are in charge of the program. I have here a letter from the Hillsboro church of Christ, signed by the Elders of that congregation, reading: "That for several years the Hillsboro church has contributed to the Herald of Truth radio and television program. Our contribution for the current year is one thousand dollars. The sole reason for the making of this contribution to the Elders of the Highland congregation, Abilene, Texas was and is the feeling of responsibility which we have to preach the gospel to the whole world. In no sense do we feel that this congregation is relinquishing its responsibility or turning its work over to the Highland Elders."

Secondly, the Garland Road church of Christ in Dallas: "The Garland Road church has for years supported the Herald of Truth because it affords us an opportunity to help carry out the Great Commission of our Lord."

The Broadway church in Lubbock, Texas: "We contribute to the Herald of Truth radio program because we feel that this is a method of preaching the gospel of Christ in an effective manner to many people. When we contribute money to this radio program, we feel that this is a part of our work."

The Union Avenue church of Christ, Memphis, Tenn.: "In reply to your inquiry of October eighth, we wish to state that the Union Avenue church has been contributing to the Herald of Truth radio program for six years. The method of contributions to the Herald of Truth program, the Union Avenue church feels that it is assuming its responsibility under the Great Commission."

The Skillman Avenue church of Christ, Dallas, Texas: "Our Elders decided to contribute to the program because they felt that it was a good work in which they desired to have a part. In making such a contribution, it is my belief that we at Skillman are discharging our own responsibility in doing our own work under the Great Commission."

Now, friends, I submitted a letter to the brethren at Highland. And I have a reply signed by the Elders of that congregation. I asked them with reference to this program: "In the reference to this program in which you speak of it as the work of the Highland church, do you mean that Highland has taken over and is performing the work of each church which contributes to the program? Or do you mean that the work of Highland at Abilene is limited to the production of the program and that each church, which contributes, is doing its own work of evangelism as much so as if it paid the radio bill for its own preaching itself?

Answer: "No! Emphatically. We have never thought, neither has it entered into our minds that we are in anyway, shape, form, or manner performing the work of each congregation, which contributes to the program." They say further, in answer to this question: "Has it ever been the contention of Highland that the congregation which you oversee exercises or has the right to exercise any control over the work of another congregation or congregations, or that you as Elders are performing any function or functions over two or more congregations?" Answer: "We do not exercise any control as Elders of any congregation, other than the 5th and Highland congregation, in Abilene, Texas. We do not believe that we have the right scripturally to exercise any control over any other congregation other than the Highland congregation. We do not believe that we are performing any function or function over any other congregation."

Now what have I done? I have shown you first, what kind of a program it is. That is, it's a program in which contributing churches, recognizing their obligation to God, are putting their resources together for the purpose of paying for a broadcast so that each church may carry out its obligation to God.

I now propose to show that cooperation of this type is scriptural. Let us turn the lights out please and have chart no. 39. In Acts 11: 27-30 we have an account of the disciples in Antioch, determining to send relief unto the people who dwelt in Judea, which also they did, sending it to the hands of the elders. Now, get it friends, while this says that it was the disciples, I have no hesitancy in saying that I regard that it came from the churches. Of course, it's not a pattern because it doesn't say it! It doesn't say that the church sent it, but I have no hesitancy in saying that I'm willing to concede that this came from the church in Antioch. Now what do we have? Here's one congregation sending money to another congregation for the purpose of meeting a need. In this instance the need was physical.

CHART NO. 39.

ACTS 11: 27-30.

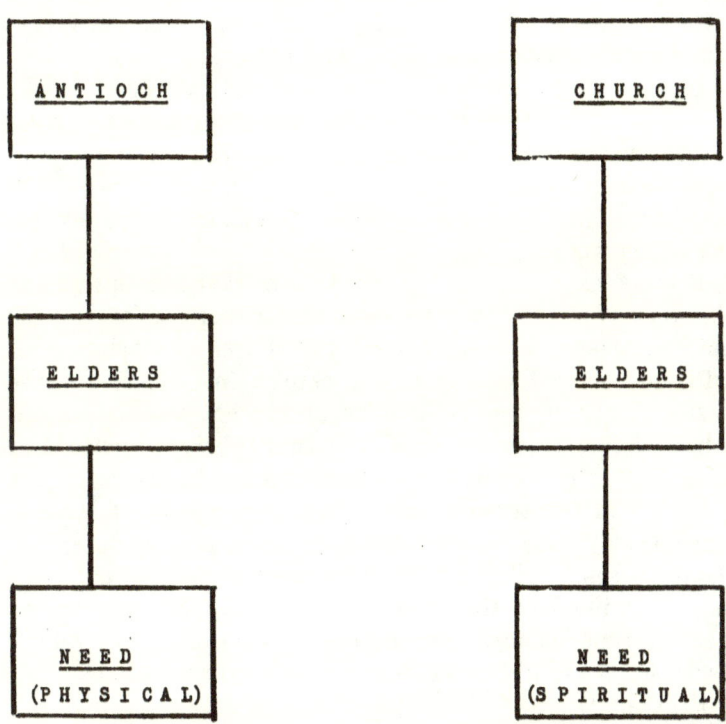

Now, watch, on the other side of the chart I paralleled that with a church sending money to the elders of another church for the purpose of meeting a need which in that case is spiritual. In this case a need is met. It's met in this fashion. In that case the need is met, and it's met in exactly the same fashion. If it's right to meet a physical need in this fashion, it's right to meet a spiritual need in the same fashion unless a man's body is more important than his soul. I wonder if Brother Cogdill will take the position that it's right for churches to cooperate in feeding hungry stomachs, but that it's wrong for churches to cooperate in exactly the same fashion in supplying the need of impoverished souls. That is exactly the matter that is under consideration here tonight. And I insist that that particular point must be met. The objection may be raised: yes, but you're talking about a need in the field of benevolence, and not in evangelism. That is that this situation described here involves a physical need and not a spiritual need, that this has to do with benevolence and not evangelism.

Now, friends, listen carefully, because this is especially relevant and pertinent. The only contribution that is mentioned in the New Testament, as gathered on the Lord's day, was for benevolence. Let us have Chart no. 40. Yet Brother Cogdill uses it as a means of supporting the preaching of the gospel.

Brother Cogdill uses it as a means of carrying out any of the work of the church that requires finances. Now get the pattern please; the members of the church of Corinth contributed to the treasury of the church in Corinth for the needy saints of another congregation; not their own, another. Now, Brother Cogdill says that this is the pattern of New Testament contribution and it may be used for the members of the same congregation, in the field of benevolence, that it may be used for the pupose of preaching, for the purpose of building a church house, in fact for any purpose that involves the need of the church. This is in the field of benevolence. He applies it to the field of evangelism. Someone in the audience: Turn up the volume.

Brother Woods: Yes, turn it up p l e a s e. All right, friends, now let him remember this. Now, I want to show you that this pattern of cooperation has been followed consistently throughout the brotherhood.

For example, the Tabernacle meetings in Nashville, Tennessee, followed this pattern. The Indian work, that was characteristic of the Highland church some years ago in Oneida, Wisconsin, for which Brother Foy Wallace joined me in an appeal to the brethren for assistance, as also did Brother Homer Hailey. There was the Blytheville radio program that for many years was conducted on that same pattern. Our brethren have generally recognized that as a pattern of New Testament cooperation. Now, Brother

CHART NO. 40
1 COR. 16:1, 2.

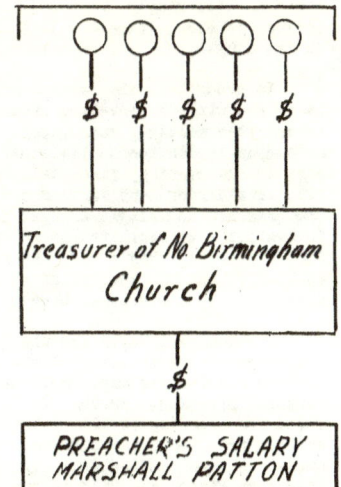

Cogdill has also recognized it. Let us have chart no. 41, please.

On chart no. 41, we have the Music Hall meeting. In this, Brother Cogdill said, "In order that the meeting might be carried on on a scriptural basis, and without provoking criticism, the Norhill congregation decided to sponsor the meeting, guaranteeing all expenses incurred, and simply extend an invitation to the other churches of Christ to have whatever part in the meeting, financially and otherwise, that they wanted to have." And he said further, "Never has an effort of this magnitude been carried to completion

CHART NO. 41
INTRODUCING GOD'S PROPHETIC WORD

During the winter of 1944 and 1945 the Adventists had carried on a campaign in the city of Houston as they had elsewhere, taking advantage of the war situation to arouse interest in their speculative and false doctrines concerning the Second Coming of Christ. They had conducted two or three services weekly in the Music Hall and had carried on an extensive advertising campaign in connection with these services and had attracted quite a lot of attention as a result. The Norhill Church of Christ in Houston thought it proper and wise to follow up this campaign of false teaching with a campaign to preach the gospel on these Bible themes free from speculation and deception. Originally the meeting was arranged with the idea of holding it in the Norhill building but the reception given the idea of such a meeting soon indicated far too great an interest for any one church auditorium in Houston to accommodate the crowds that would want to attend. It was decided, accordingly, to arrange to hold the meeting down in town and invite the cooperation of all the congregations of the Church of Christ in the city.

In order that the meeting might be carried out on a scriptural basis and without provoking criticism, the Norhill Church decided to sponsor the meeting, guaranteeing all expenses incurred, and simply extend an invitation to the other Churches of Christ to have whatever part in the meeting, financially and otherwise, they wanted to have. With this arrangement in mind the Music Hall was contracted for and the preacher and singer engaged for the time decided upon. When the invitation went forth to the other congregations of the city to cooperate in whatever way they could, the response was almost unanimous and was so hearty that the success of the meeting, the first of the kind ever undertaken in the city of Houston, was guaranteed from the beginning.

Brother Jack Meyer and the Heights Church were asked to plan and supervise the advertising of the meeting and that they did their work in fine fashion was amply evidenced by the widespread interest and attendance provoked. Brother F. F. Conley and the Milby Church supervised the ushering at all of the services and received splendid cooperation from the other churches of the city in that work and the large audiences were handled in a fine way. Brother Frank Smith and the church at Pierce and Baldwin had charge of the entertainment of visitors from out of the city and homes were provided for all while attending the meeting. Never has an effort of this magnitude been carried to completion with any better cooperation, finer spirit of unity, or less friction than this one. That was an outstanding feature of the meeting. Twenty churches worked together as one throughout the effort and the Chruches of Christ in Houston demonstrated the practical side of Christian unity and above all sufficiency of the Lord's church in the accomplishment of His work without the interference of human organisations. All of the funds were handled through the treasury of the Norhill church and all the bills incurred paid out of that treasury with a complete report furnished each congregation assisting. That this arrangement worked to the satisfaction of all is attested by the fact that in a city wide gathering of brethren after the meeting was over, the unanimous request of the churches cooperating in the first meeting was that Norhill congregation take the lead in the second meeting to be held the ensuing year.

with any better cooperation, finer spirit of unity or less friction than this one. That was an outstanding feature of the meeting. Twenty churches worked together as one through the effort, and the churches of Christ of Houston demonstrated the practical side of Christian unity and above all the sufficiency of the Lord's church in the accomplishment of its work without the interference of human organization." Now listen. "All of the funds were handled

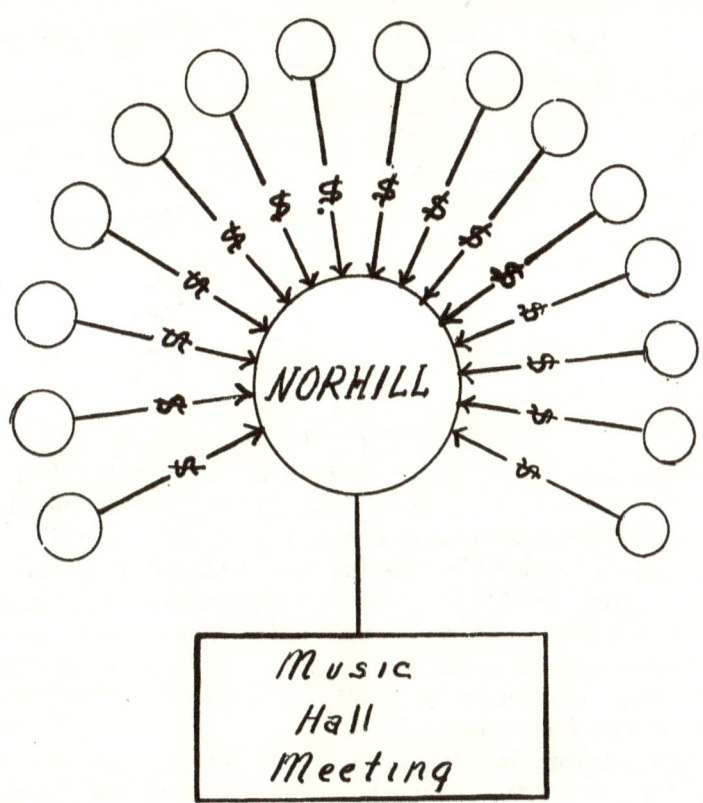

206 COGDILL-WOODS DEBATE

through the treasury of the Norhill church, and all bills incurred paid out of that treasury with a complete report furnished each congregation assisting." Now that friends, is an exact example of that for which I am contending. Let us have chart no. 46 A, please.

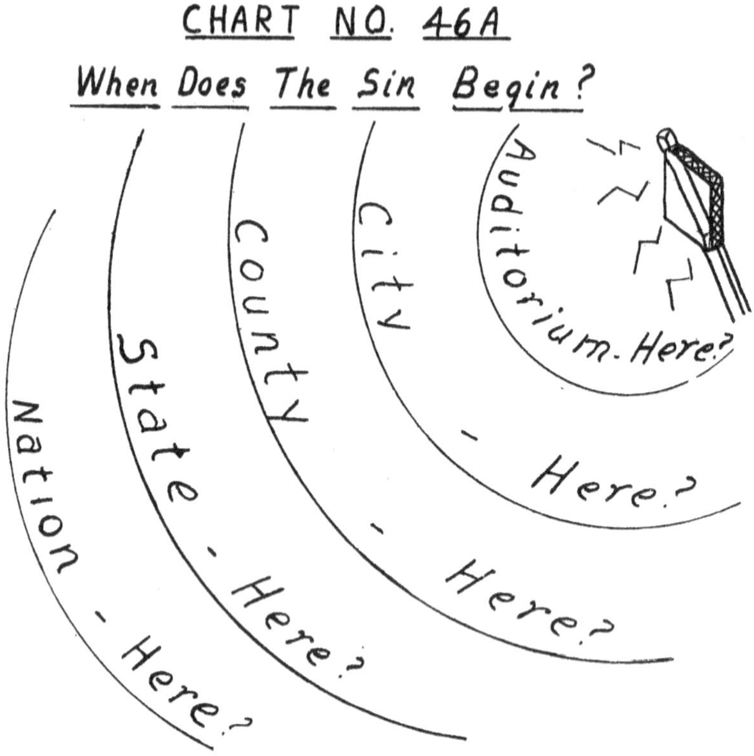

CHART NO. 46A
When Does The Sin Begin?

Nation - Here?
State - Here?
County - Here?
City - Here?
Auditorium - Here?

Chart no. 46 A. Here, friends, is the picture. Just a minute please I . . . Now here, friends, is chart no. 46. Here is the picture that I've just described. Norhill received the funds. The meeting was conducted in the music hall. Here are the 20 churches participating. Let's have the 46 A please. Here, friends, is the situation and I want Brother Cogdill to tell us now when he comes again, that meeting was conducted in that auditorium in Houston. They had, I assume, a public address system, which I hope, worked better than this one. Here's our question: Was it scriptural for these churches to send that gospel to the back of the auditorium. If to the back of the auditorium under those circumstances, suppose that the radio station had been a 250 watt and it had carried to the city limits? It would take one about that strong to serve Houston. Then suppose that there was one large enough to carry it to the

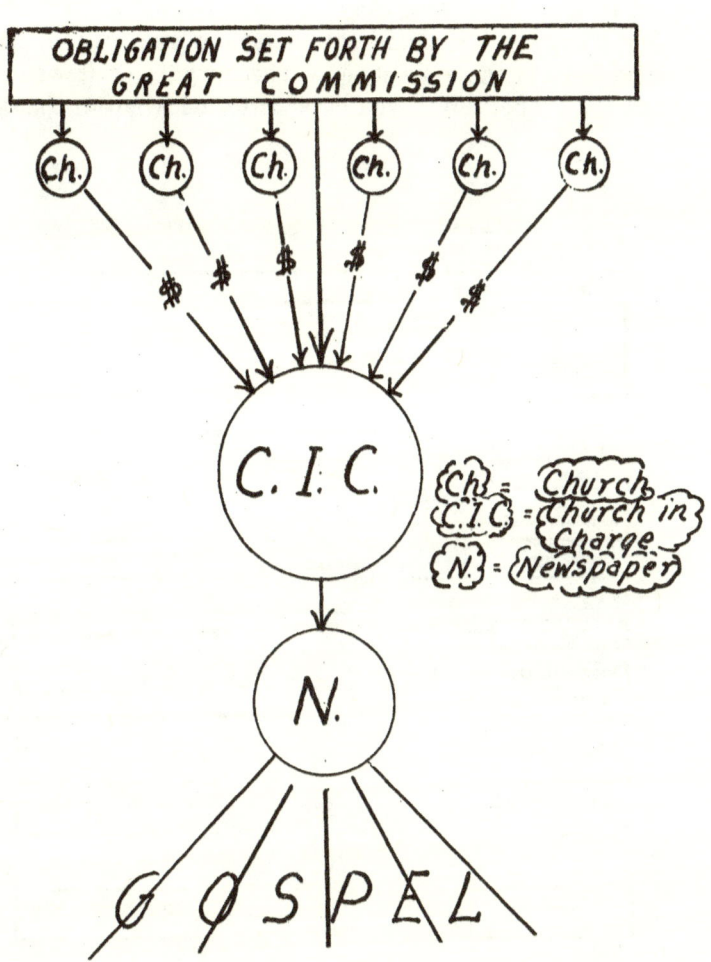

county, or suppose that the power of the station was increased until it covered the state. The same speaker, before the same microphone, increasing the power of the amplifier. Suppose that was increased until it covered the nation. Brother Cogdill, designate at which point sin began.

Now remember that Brother Cogdill is on record as saying that the Houston Music Hall cooperation is scriptural. Let us have chart no. 45.

Here, friends, is the picture; here is Birmingham's newspaper ad cooperation, they are carrying out their obligation set forth in the Great Commission. Here are the contributing churches. Here is the church which was in charge. And here is the newspaper. The purpose of it was to get out the gospel. Will you explain to me wherein the differ-

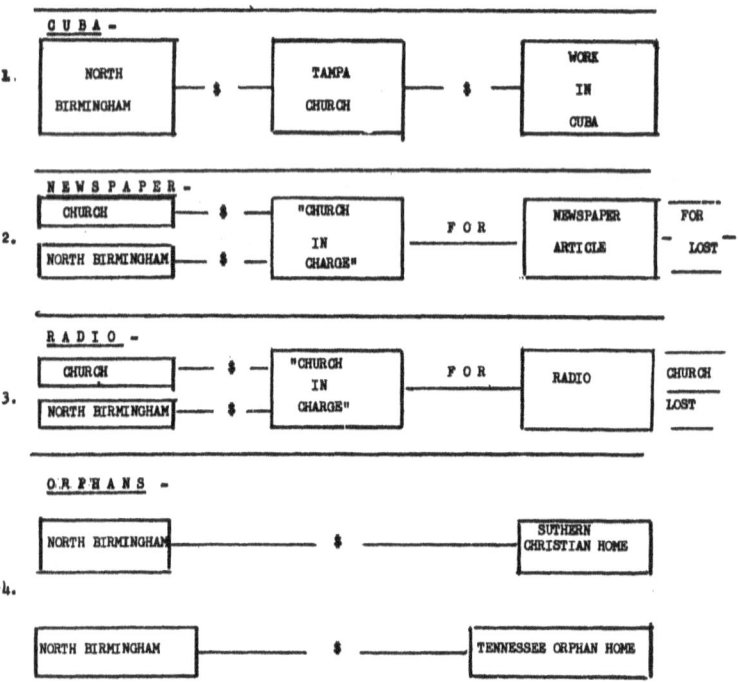

ence is, Brother Cogdill? I ask you this, if you endorse chart no. 45, and if so will you explain to us the difference?

Let us have next, please, chart no. 43. No. 43 please. We'll get that first, if we may, please, brother Roy. Now here, friends, here is the type of cooperation that's been followed repeatedly in Birmingham. Here, if you please, is the Cuba work, which was conducted some years ago when the North Birmingham congregation, which Brother Cogdill represents tonight, sent money to the T a m p a church, and the Tampa church handled it for the work in Cuba. Here is the newspaper ad of which we just spoke. Here is the radio work that was carried on for several years by North Birmingham participating according to the pattern. Now here if you please is the work, up until a few years ago at North Birmingham regarding the Orphan Home. They sent money to the Southern Christian Home. They participated in each one of these. That is, in the newspaper ad, in the radio work, and in the sponsoring work of the Tampa church for the Cuba work. Now let's have please chart no. 42.

CHART NO. 42.

JOHN T. LEWIS AND "THE LORD'S PLAN"

- "......MR. KENDRICK AFTERWARDS QUIT THE SOCIETY AND WENT BACK TO THE LORD'S PLAN OF DOING MISSIONARY WORK."
  - JOHN T. LEWIS, <u>VOL OF P. ON I. M. AND SOC.</u>, P. 70.

- "......SEND THE FUNDS TO THE ELDERS OF SOME CENTRAL CONGREGATION, WHO WILL DISBURSE THEM WISELY AND JUSTLY: ...."
  - C. KENDRICK, <u>LIVE REL. ISSUES</u>, P. 445.

I have shown you first, the general practice of the brotherhood. I've shown you Brother Cogdill's practice. I now show you the practice of the brethren in Birmingham. Brother John T. Lewis is recognized and p r o p e r l y so throughout this entire section. In his book on the Voice of the Pioneers, page 70, he made this statement. "Mr. Kendrick afterwards quit the society and went back to the Lord's plan of doing missionary work." Now let's see what the Lord's plan was according to Brother Lewis. In Live Religious Issues, page 445, Mr. Kendrick says, "That the funds are to be sent to the Elders of some central congregation who will disburse them wisely and j u s t l y." Now Brother Lewis says that's the Lord's plan. At least, he said it when he wrote the Voice of the Pioneers, said that's the Lord's plan of doing missionary work. Does he think so tonight? Does Brother Cogdill? Brother Cogdill do you endorse Brother Lewis' and Brother Kendrick's plan which they say is the Lord's plan for doing missionary work?

Now I've show you this, friends, and this has been the pattern for this speech tonight. 1. We've shown you our obligation. To prove that the Herald of Truth is right. 2. We've shown you what kind of a program it was. 3. We've shown you that that pattern of cooperation is part of Acts 11:27-30. 4. We've shown you that that's been the general practice of the brethren in following that pattern. We then brought it down to Brother Cogdill. We've shown that he's followed that pattern. We then came to Birmingham. We've shown that it was the pattern of the Birmingham churches until comparative recent years to follow that pattern. And we've shown that Brother Lewis called it the Lord's plan when he wrote the book. Now then has the Lord's plan changed, or has somebody in Birmingham changed? That's the question that is before us tonight. And I submit, friends, that there's no excuse for Brother Cogdill not dealing with these arguments. There's no excuse for him not taking these charts up. I've given him the number. He has a copy of the charts. What is this? Did you say the time was up?

Cogdill's First Negative

Gentlemen moderators, Brother Woods, Ladies and Gentlemen:

I'm very grateful for the good providence of God that makes it possible for me to be here upon this occasion and for this fine audience assembled, for your interest in the study of the issues at hand because I believe them to be very vital to the church of our Lord Jesus Christ and to the will of God. I wonder if this is a little too loud now. Can you cut it down a little please? I've got a lot of thunder as well as lightning, and I don't want to hurt anyone too badly with it. Brother Woods has made a speech, that from my point of view, is very interesting from two or three points. He spent most of his time talking to us about recent things, and what the brethren have practiced. Given us a lot of recent examples of the thing that he says is being done in the Herald of Truth, and spent mighty little of his time giving us any scriptural proof. He seems to think that his proposition reads: That because the brethren, in recent years, have been practicing this thing that he's talking about, therefore, it's in harmony with the scripture. But friends, that isn't any proof of what's in harmony with the scriptures at all. The appeal that he needs to be making is to New Testament example. Now Brother Woods, go back about 1900 years and give us something from the New Testament that begins to look a little bit like what you're doing, and you'll be making some headway on the proposition that you're under obligation to affirm. What the brethren have been practicing and what they say, in their testimony, about what they are doing, constitutes no evidence at all as to the scripturalness of a thing, and everybody in this auditorium knows that's so. Everybody. What Highland says about that work they're doing, and what the churches that contribute say about it, and what their intention or purpose is have no bearing whatever on the thing that you've agreed to affirm. And I'm going to insist as we go along, in this discussion now, just like I have in the part that's gone by, that you stay with your proposition. Let's don't bring any human testimony to the witness stand

and try to prove that a thing's scriptural by what the eldership of some church thinks about it. You know, Jesus Christ came on the scene 1900 years ago, and the elders of the Judean church, the Jewish Church, thought a lot of things were all right. They thought that the washing of hands before eating meat was all right. They had observed it as religious ceremony. They sought to bind it upon others. I don't know how many years they had observed it. I don't know exactly how many generations they had kept that thing. They came to Jesus and criticized him and condemned him because he didn't teach His disciples to observe it. The Lord simply pointed out to them that it was the tradition of the elders that made that thing acceptable in their minds, and not the law of God. And He uncovered the law of God, and the commandments of God, from the tradition of the Elders and pointed out to them that by their tradition they made the word of God of none effect. You can find that in Matthew 15. He refused to meet the demands of their traditions. He refused to bow in submission to them. He refused to teach them. He refused to put them on a par with the word of God.

He refused to allow His disciples to so regard them. But He taught them that the traditions of men made void the word of God whether they bind or whether they loosed. When they bind where God has not bound, they make void the commandment of God. When they loose where God has not loosed, or where God has bound, they make void the word of God.

Now if your appeal in this discussion is to be to tradition of the elders, the tradition of the brethren, then we ought to just mark out of your proposition the fact that it's in harmony with the scriptures because that has no bearing whatever to do with the matter. Now he brings up several charts on that point. Chart No. 42, Brother John T. Lewis, and the Lord's plan.

He wants to know if I endorse it. Well now, whether I endorse that or not would not have anything to do with the scripturalness of it, would it? Endorse it or not endorse it. That doesn't have anything to do with what the Bible teaches, Brother Woods, and you're under obligation to prove your proposition, not by endorsement, but by what the word of God says about the matter. That's what you agreed to do. That it's scriptural. Are you going to prove that it's scriptural by Roy Cogdill's endorsement? I don't know whether I endorse exactly what brother John T. Lewis said or not. There's only a scattering statement or two here about it.

I'll tell you what I would say about it, if it included in any sense the idea of one church handling the funds of another church, and receiving money from it, another church, when it was not a destitute or needy church receiving the money, I wouldn't endorse it. I wouldn't endorse it whether John T. Lewis said it, or Roy Cogdill had said it or whoever might have said it. If all the brethren said it, and it isn't in the word of God, I still wouldn't endorse it, and it wouldn't make any difference if I did, and it wouldn't do any good, with the matter of being scriptural or not scriptural. Brother Lewis is emminently able to take care of himself on that matter. What he had in mind, I don't know. But I want you to keep in mind, in any of these recent things that he's talking about; chart no. 43, the Cuban work, the Birmingham newspaper ad, the radio program concerning or that involved North Birmingham, the orphans, the fourth part in that chart 43 that involved North Birmingham; these matters I'm not familiar with in detail. I don't know what the facts are.

But I know what the New Testament principle is. The New Testament principle is that no church ever sent out of its treasury a contribution to another church unless the receiving church was destitute. Now, Brother Woods, if these instances violate that principle, then these instances are wrong and I wouldn't endorse any of them, if I knew what the facts were, and they did violate them. Because that's the ground upon which I stand. The teaching of the New Testament is that whenever a congregation contributed money out of its treasury to another church, another congregation, always the receiving church was in need. And now let Brother Woods find the exception to that. Concerning the Birmingham newspaper ad, the congregations of this city that were taking part in it, that had decided that it was not in harmony with New Testament principles, quit it because they decided that it was. They wouldn't engage in it anymore. North Birmingham, that invited me to represent them in this discussion, is one of them. They wouldn't engage in that kind of a cooperative effort again because they believe it violates the principle of one church handling the money of another church, or one church becoming a sponsoring church and the agent of another congregation.

Then he goes to the Music Hall meeting in Houston. Wants to know if I'll defend that. Now, Guy, as much as you've read the Guardian, you ought to know that that was repudiated a long time ago. And by the way, I'm glad you read it as much as you do. I hope you keep on. Maybe eventually it will start edifying you in spite of yourself. The Music Hall meeting was repudiated by me so far as the manner in which the money was handled, a long time ago. I said it not only in the Guardian that I wouldn't take part in that kind of a meeting again because it would be misused, and I have said publicly all over this country, in Houston where it happened, as well as in many other places, that I would not be a party to any kind of congregational cooperation where one church handled the money of o t h e r churches, such as was done in the Music Hall m e e t i n g. Now that happened a good many years ago. That's like the incident he brought up last night. That happened back before many of these brotherhood-wide promotions grew so big and began to attract so much attention. And before some of us had to re-study the application of New Testament principles to them.

Back in those days, there weren't any churches promoting nation-wide and international radio p r o g r a m s. There weren't any churches, in that day, in the Music Hall meeting day, that was trying to do a work for the whole brotherhood. That wasn't what the Music Hall meeting was. It didn't start as even a city-wide meeting. That wasn't the purpose of it. It was a Norhill meeting, principally and primarily to begin with. The mistake we made in it was when we allowed other churches to have a part in it by sending to the Norhill eldership their funds. I would not be a party to that again. Why? Because, having re-studied the application of New Testament principles, for which I've always tried stand, I've determined that it's a violation of them; that it's wrong and I would not practice it again. Now if that isn't plain enough concerning my attitude toward it, I'll try to make it a little plainer. And if you think it embarrasses me, to the least degree, to acknowledge that I made a mistake in the manner in which that thing was handled, you are wrong about it. I'm sorry the mistake was made. I'm trying to avoid it now. And if you'll be just as honest in admitting the mistakes that you've made, we'll make some progress in helping you in this debate. You've made mistakes and made changes, you haven't been perfect in your application or in your position either. You taught a lot of things, Brother Woods, back through the years, that I don't believe you believe now. I believe that you changed your position on a lot of things in spite of your denial. And you ought to be honest and honorable enough to get up here and admit it instead of denying it like you did last night.

Then he comes on down to chart no. 37. 38 is the next one, I believe. That chart no. 38 on types of cooperation. Is there an exclusive pattern? And he has several instances of cooperation listed. Between individuals 2 Timothy 4:9. One individual to another individual Romans 16. A christian family and needy individuals I Corinthians 16:15. Well those have nothing to do with his proposition. We're talking about churches—congregations—not christian individuals. So that much of his chart and time was wasted.

Now then, he says disciples and elders, in Acts 11:27-30. And you can put him on both sides of that. Oh, he says I think all right that that's a church sending to needy brethren in other churches. I think that's what it was, but that isn't what the Bible says, so you couldn't prove anything so far as the pattern is concerned. Well I'll tell you what kind of a pattern you can prove, Guy, and you'll admit it. You prove the pattern of how and when churches received help from elsewhere. They sent it to the elders. That's a pattern in New Testament teaching of how churches received help when they needed help. Whether it was a church giving or not. And does it have to say that it was a church, in order for it to be a pattern? Does it? Why you know he accepted the pattern of the Lord's supper on the chart last night. Didn't he? Give us that first chart again.

In the group next to you there, Bob. He accepted the pattern of the Lord's supper in Acts 20:7. Now, Brother Woods, does that say the church? Acts 20:7 says that the disciples came together on the first day of the week. Is that the church? Is that a pattern of worship? Does it have to say the church? If it has to say the church, don't ever preach the pattern of observing the Lord's supper from Acts 20:7 again, Brother Woods. But that's beside the point so far as Acts 11 is concerned. Whether it was done as individual action, and I've always been under the impression that when the disciples, in a community, in a locality, pooled their resources, their contribution into a common fund, that that would likely be a congregational treasury. That would likely be it, wouldn't it? If the members of a congregation contributed into a common fund, whether they did it on the Lord's day or some other day it would be a congregational fund, then. Wouldn't it? And they sent it by messengers to the brethren which dwelt in Judea. Paul and Barnabas, individuals, being the messengers, and they delivered it into the hands of the elders. That's the way they helped needy churches. They delivered it into the hands of the elders. What elders? The elders where the need and the work was being done.

Well, he says don't they deliver it into the hands of the elders out at Highland? Yes. But does Highland fit the pattern of Acts 11? Is Highland a needy church? Oh, he said, these people over here, they were just feeding hungry bodies there. Well, they were feeding hungry bodies in the church where the contribution was made. In the church where the relief was sent. That's where the hungry people were. Now then, the hungry souls that you help when you send to Highland, are they in the needy church at Highland? Is it a needy church? Is it a destitute church? And are you sending to that destitute church just to help hungry souls in the Highland church? Why he knows that isn't so. That doesn't follow the pattern in any manner or means. Not ever in the church receiving.

Well, he goes on over on his fifth point on that. Says churches and needy saints in Jerusalem—2 Corinthians 8 and 9, and the point there is that churches sent, but the saints received, as if they went down there and distributed their benevolence among the saints and ignored the church. Why you know how they received it from Acts 11. That's the only pattern of how the church received relief that you find in the New Testament. Specifically, it was delivered into the hands of the elders. Does the Jerusalem incident follow it, or is it an exception to it? If it's an exception to it, where do you find the exception? Where do you find the exception? But whether the church received it or not, I Cor. 16:1, 2· 2 Cor. 8 and 9 involves churches sending. So, in both passages we have *a pattern of how churches sent their money.* In Acts 11 you have *a pattern of how churches received the help.* In I Cor. 16 and 2 Cor. 8 and 9, by his admission, you have a pattern of how the church sent. Now you have a pattern on both ends of the line, Guy. Now all on earth you need to do is just to get the two ends together, and you've got all you need. And the Highland church and the Herald of Truth won't fit either one of them.

Well, Acts 15:1-32 is not a pattern—is not a pattern of the church sending help to anybody, so far as that part of it's concerned. Why the apostles rendered a decision in Acts 15. Paul consulted them. He went up by revelation. The letter was written by James, an apostle. They called the elders of the church in, and made known unto them, they concurred in the matter. The letter, written by James, an epistle was sent out unto all the churches. That's divine revelation, Guy. That's neither evangelism nor benevolence. You missed the point on both there. You don't have an example of either. There's a decree of the apostles of our Lord, dictated by the Holy Spirit of God, and he's trying to make that a matter of evangelism on the part of the church or benevolence. And he missed the point completely.

Well, he goes to chart No. 39, No. 37, the Great Commission. Chart No. 37, the Great Commission. And he says that in the Great Commission, we are under obligation to go into every nation in the world. And we're under obligation to go into every city in every nation and we're under obligation to preach the gospel to every person in every city in every nation on earth. Well nobody, of course, is denying that. But you know there's an obligation in that Great Commission that he needs to underscore. There are two parts to it. Jesus said, in Matthew 28:18 and 20 that you're to go teach all nations, baptizing them into the name of the Father, and of the Son and of the Holy Spirit, teaching them to observe all things, whatsoever I have commanded you. Now there's where your proposition comes in. You're trying to teach the church to do something that no apostle ever taught it to do. You're trying to teach the church to do something that no apostle ever received from the Lord. Where did any church ever become a sponsoring church, a brotherhood agency in the New Testament period?

I want my chart here on centralization.

Adams: You have the copies of those charts to give to them.

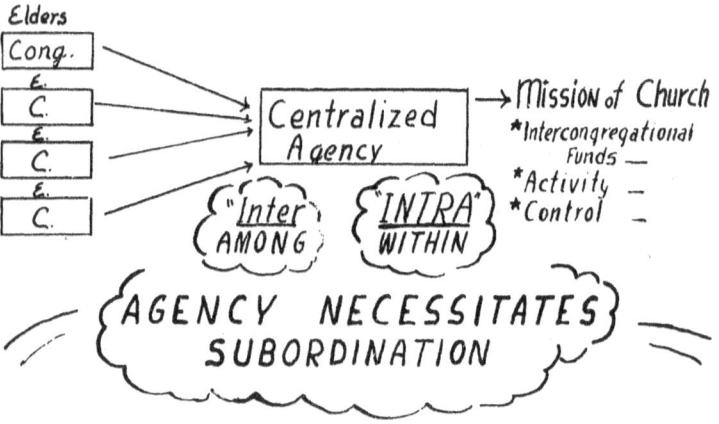

Cogdill: Well I don't have them over here, I don't believe. Maybe I do. Yes, here they are. All right centralization versus equality and autonomy. You know, this matter of centralization is a matter that isn't just occurring. It occurred a long time ago. This trouble has been repeatedly recurring in the church, and you can find historical reference for it. In your History of the Christian Church, by Philip Schaff, vol. 2, pages 142 and 143, in an article entitled the Episcopate, he said; "We do not therefore assume any strict uniformity, but the whole church age tended toward centralization. It, everywhere felt a demand for compact solid unity. And this inward bent amidst the surrounding danger of persecution and heresy, carried the church irresistibly toward the episcopate. In so critical and stormy a time the principle union is strained. Division of weakness prevails over all. In fact the existence of the church, at that period, may be said, to have depended a great measure on the preservation and promotion of unity, and that in an outward, tangible form, suited to the existing grade of culture. Such a unity was offered in the Bishop, who held a monarchal, or more properly, a patriarchal relation in the congregation." You could multiply statements of that kind. "That a system of fraternal equality in the relations of the community to each other, would, independent of these determine if circumstances have answered best the spirit of Christianity, and been most promotive of its free uncorrupted manifestations. Those circumstances soon gave rise to a system of subordination in the mutual relation of the community to each other." Then he said, "When the church system of subordination had become established, so the c o u n t r y churches were now accustomed to receive their presiding officers from the city," and he said, "they must have entered into a struggle with those of the city for the preservation of their independence." That's from Neander's church history of the Christian religion, vol. 1, the translation of Joseph Corey, page 202, the edition of 1851.

Then John Lawrence Mosheim, translated by Maclaine. "There reigned among the members of the Christian church, however distinguished they were by worldly rank and title not only an amiable harmony, but also a perfect equality." He says the churches in those early times, were entirely independent. None of them being subject to any foreign jurisdiction, but each governed by its own rulers and its own law. The tendency toward centralization grew into the episcopacy in the New Testament. Here you have the centralization agency, in this instance, the Highland church running the Herald of Truth radio program, where the funds of many churches, a thousand of them, are combined, and pooled, centralized under the control of one eldership.

Directed exclusively by that eldership in the doing of the work. That makes it an inter-congregational fund when they receive the combined funds of many churches. Here's an inter-congregational activity because it is supported and cooperated in according to their contention by many. And it is centralized in its control in one congregation and under one eldership. It is not an intra, within the church, arrangement. It is an inter-congregational arrangement. and you know when a matter becomes an inter-state matter what happens to it? It goes under the supervision of a super government. When a project involves or traffic involves more than one state then it becomes an inter-state, and one state government does not have jurisdiction. Now, in spite of all that he read from the Highland elders in that letter, you have them on record, and you know Brother Wood's position is already repudiated, denied, disproved by everything E. R. Harper contended for in his two debates with Yater Tant. And everybody that heard them knows it. He argued that when you send the money to us, it's ours. This is our work. It isn't anybody's work but ours. Get the Harper-Tant debate and read it. That was the very bone of his contention. It becomes ours. So Brother E. R. Harper, poor fellow, is not here to represent himself. He could have a debate with Brother Woods on that point unless he has been converted by some of these recent contentions. Fact of the matter is, they have a thing they don't know how to run. They don't know whose work it is. Just like a lot of these other human promotions. They have something, they don't know what it is, and they don't know how to run it. Listen: "The Herald of Truth radio program is a work of the church of Christ at 5th and Highland, Abilene, Texas. The elders of this congregation direct and oversee every phase of this work from the preparation of the sermons to the mailing of printed copies of these sermons. The Highland elders have never delegated any authority to any person. But as a unit, have directed this work." That's what they said in this book they put out, *"That the Brethren May Know."* And I'm glad they put it out.

But there's another matter in his speech to which I want to call attention. You know . . .

Brother Adams: Five minutes.

Brother Cogdill: Our Adventist friends have contended all along that I Cor. 16 was not a general fund, that it could not be used as a general fund, that it was not even a congregational fund, that it was the disciples laying by in store individually. Now I've met that in the Adventists all over the country. Those of you who've discussed with them know that's so. That each man laid by himself, individually, and that it was, therefore, a restricted matter. I want Brother Woods to produce one other plan given in the New Testament, after divine revelation on the point was made, for the church raising money for anything—one other way. Why that's the only way divine inspiration has ever given God's church to raise money for anything. It contributed money to evangelistic work. How did it get its money? The only way the New Testament enlightens us is that the disciples individually, when they came together, contributed into a common treasury, on the first day of the week, in order that out of that treasury, the church might meet its obligation. And that included preaching the gospel right along with benevolence. And we'll have to turn you over to the Adventists if you don't learn better than to argue that it was only for benevolence and couldn't be used.

You know he thinks preaching the gospel is charity work. He puts the preacher on the basis with the orphan to which you contribute. Why, he did that in his last appeal last night. Why, yes, he'd include evangelism. You k n o w Brother Warren argued, in his debate with Brother Douthitt, his moderator, that benevolence is evangelism. Brother Woods is reversing that. He's arguing and did argue that evangelism is benevolence. He makes every preacher in this audience a subject of charity. I resent it. I earn what the brethren pay me. Sometimes a whole whale of a lot more than I get. I'll tell you that. There isn't any charity connected with it. And the clothes that I buy out of the money that I get for preaching the gospel, are not clothes that have been given to me either. I bought them and paid for them with the wages that I received from the brethren, and the word of God says that in preaching the gospel, I had a right to them, Guy. In preaching the gospel, I had a right to them. That complements his speech.

I want him to tell us about this centralization matter. You know he'd leave the impression that there are just a few brethren, just a few of them, just in recent years that have taken up this matter of opposing these centralized projects. Well, we can just easily convince you that that isn't the case. I happen to have a little pamphlet here published *Reprints and Excerpts from the Gospel Advocate*. And by the way there couldn't any of them be printed anymore under the policy that he announced last night. Not a word of any article in this and I could furnish you a copy of it, if you want it. Be glad to see that you get one if you want it. *The Truth Between Extremes*, an article by Foy Wallace, Jr., published in August, 1930, when he was editor of it, republished in September 28, 1939, by B. C. Goodpasture, and commended by Brother Goodpasture himself. He said "It reflects our present sentiments on the matter in question." Foy E. Wallace said, "On the same principle, if the elders of one congregation, solicit the funds of other congregations for general distribution, then the elders of one congregation u s u r p the functions of the congregation, whose funds they receive and disburse. It is the same in principle as if a society or individual should do. How then, and to what extent may churches scripturally cooperate? Fortunately, we have a New Testament example. The prophet, Agabus prophesied of a famine that should come over all the world, the Jewish world. And the disciples, at Antioch, every man according to his ability determined to send relief unto the brethren which dwelt in Judea, which also they did, and sent it to the Elders by the hands of Barnabas and Saul. The disciples at Antioch cooperated with the churches in Judea through the elders in relieving an emergency in Judea. For one church to help another church bear its own burdens has scriptural precedent but for one church to solicit funds from other churches for general distribution, in other fields or places, thus becoming the treasury of other churches is quite a different question. Such procedure makes a sort of society out of the elders of the local church and for such there is no scriptural precedent or example." Now did the Advocate print error? If so, you ought to correct it. Brother Goodpasture endorsed that. He ought to join the column of the changers in the Gospel Advocate.

Then right on over another statement. This time from F. B. Syrgley, who was a writer for the Gospel Advocate, in an article published in 1932. "Every New Testament church was a complete body within itself. Was independent of all other churches. Not centralized with them in anything. That's the idea. No church had any authority over any other. The authority of the elders stopped at the church in which they lived and labored. These elders had no authority to take charge of the missionary money or any other money or means of any church, except the one where they were elders."

Wood's Second Affirmative

Brother Moderators, Brother Cogdill, Ladies and Gentlemen:

I am before you now for the second time this evening to continue the affirmation of the proposition under consideration tonight; that is, the scripturalness of such cooperative efforts as that characteristic of the radio program that's conducted by the Highland church of Christ.

Brother Cogdill, with typical sectarian practice, made mention of the fact that I spent a little time tonight in discussing some current practices. I made it very clear to you why I introduced these letters. I showed him first that it was my obligation to show what kind of program it was that I was defending. It was necessary first for me, first, to identify the program, establish its characteristics. Otherwise had I started producing scriptural evidence for it, Brother Cogdill would have come and said, "Well granting that what you say is the truth, you haven't identified that with your program." It was the fact that I did identify the program that disturbed him.

I've shown you what the brethren who contribute to that program think that they're doing. I have shown you what those who are conducting the program say that the program is. Brother Cogdill denies that either know what they are talking about.

Now, of course, in the final analysis of this or any other matter, if it's to be settled at all scripturally, it must be settled by the scriptures, and on that basis alone do we make our appeal. He said what people say about the Herald of Truth has nothing to do with the proposition. But it has all to do with it insofar as the type of the proposition is concerned. He tells us that I cited the tradition of the Elders. I offer none of this in proof of its scripturalness. I offer it to identify the program. Don't you be deceived by such a matter. What disturbs Brother Cogdill is the plain simple reasoning that was characteristic of our scriptural appeal.

Now he says that what Brother Cogdill says and what Brother Lewis says is not involved in this proposition. Of course, I do not regard them as scriptural authority. But I do accept them as competent witnesses in testifying what they themselves have said is scriptural. I've shown that what my practice obligates me to prove is in harmony with the Bible. I've shown that they themselves conform to a practice which is identical and which they themselves say is scriptural.

Now he says he doesn't know about the North Birmingham congregation's practice. He ought to acquaint himself with it. I want us now to put on the screen. Turn the lights out please. My chart, 43.

CHART NO. 43

COOPERATION - AS PRACTICED BY NORTH BIRMINGHAM FOR MANY YEARS

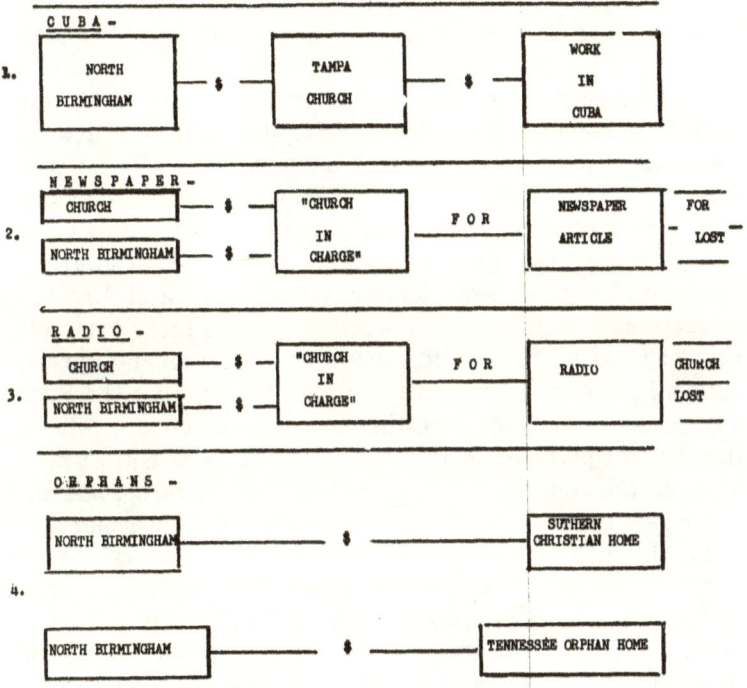

Brother Cogdill has told us that whatever is the practice or has been the practice of the North Birmingham church, that if it involves a practice other than that of a church in abundance or possessing ability to give, and sending to a church not in need that he repudiates it without hesitation. He thus repudiated the work which was characteristic of North Birmingham involving the work in Cuba. That's all wrong. That's all wrong. That eliminates then forevermore any other work along that line. That makes it wrong for them to support and maintain this newspaper type of cooperation which Brother Douthitt defended in the debate with Brother Thomas Warren on the ground that Brother John T. Lewis was over here and wouldn't let anything go wrong. Now Brother Cogdill says that this is wrong, therefore; it goes. That eliminates the type of work that was characteristic of the radio program. It was sponsored and maintained a few years ago in that fashion. And, of course, it cancels out the type of work that was done by the congregation in the support of orphans. Why? Simply because there is no pattern, no express pattern for this he says.

Carl Ketcherside says that tnere isn't any pattern for the located preacher. Why, Brother Cogdill, will you give up the located preacher? Ervin Waters says there's no pattern for the communion service. That is in individual cups. And you can't find one in the Bible yourself. When are you going to give up the individual cups? Alva Johnson and Van Bonneau, anti-Sunday school men, and Brother Abercrombie in this section somewhere says there's no pattern of class teaching, and there isn't so far as an express, detailed pattern. When are you going to give up the Sunday school? Step by step, then these brethren are following the anti-pattern. And I can point you to case after case all over the country where congregations have become indoctrinated with this hobby. Formally splendid congregations, the influence of which reached afar, and now drawn within their shells and have ceased the practice of that which was formerly characteristic of them. Why is it that he opposes this? Because it doesn't follow the pattern of Acts 11:27. What is the pattern of that passage? One church sending money to another church for the purpose of supplying their need. Now watch, please, it was sent to the elders. Brother Cogdill says that's the only reason why it is that one church may send to another church. He repudiates brother Tant on that subject. Brother Tant's position is that we may send to another church for evangelism as for example in the Montana work. Brother Cogdill, in his desperate effort to try to sustain a position tonight before you here, has fixed upon Acts 11:27, and says it's the only pattern. How may a church send to another. Only when it's sent to the elders. It follows then that regardless of how much in need a church might be that has no elders, no money could be sent. The people would starve to death.

Brother Cogdill, now it's not funny, just put it down and answer it; that will be more impressive than laughing.

And tell us when you come before us, could one congregation send to another if there were no elders there? He says it must be sent to the elders. Now if he says that such a contribution may be made, then you are going to have to find a pattern. But if you would have to follow the pattern then it follows that he's wrong on his exclusive pattern.

Well now, you watch how he shifts from this pattern. Let us have chart No., I'll have it. Just a moment here, chart No. 40.

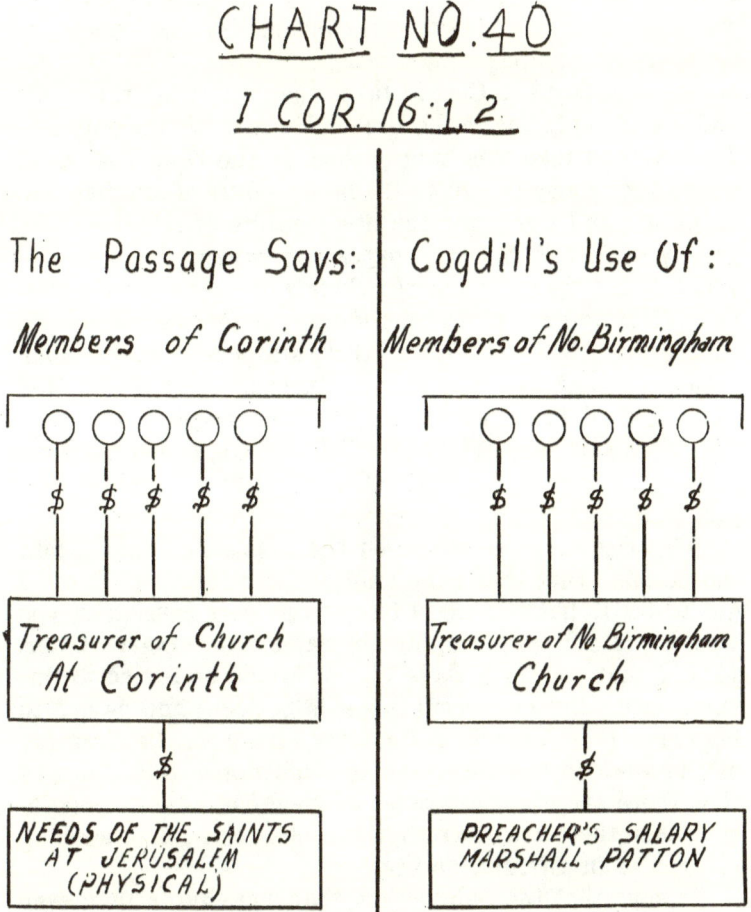

Here, friends, is I Cor. 16:1, 2, where Paul admonished the church in Corinth to lay by in store upon the first day of the week as they had been prospered, that there be no gatherings when I come. What do we have here? Here are the members of the church in Corinth. What are they doing? Contributing to the treasury of the church in Corinth. For what purpose? To use that money for the needy saints of another congregation—not their own, but another. Now, ladies and gentlemen, Brother Cogdill has told us that that's the only instance in the Bible we have of money being raised. I ask you now: Why, if his argument upon Acts 11 is an exclusive pattern, then why isn't this? What do we have here? Members contributing for the benefit of members of another congregation, not their own, but another. Yet Brother Cogdill takes the pattern on this chart and it's the only one in the Bible. He says it's the only one. That we can take this only pattern in the New Testament where the money is sent to the needy saints of another congregation and use it for the needy saints of the same congregation, use it for the purpose of paying the preacher, which is not there, of course. This was. And for the purpose of building a church building and for the purpose of edification. Now, friends, if there's a person in this audience that can't see the glaring inconsistency of Brother Cogdill, then I'd be surprised. Brother Cogdill, deal with this when you come before us. Tell us. Oh, you got up here and said, everybody knows that we don't have to follow this, just in the matter of benevolence. Well, why not?

He's tried to leave with you the impression that I take the position that that's the only purpose for that. Now, I don't take it, but you ought to. If you were consistent, you would. If you would apply the same reasoning to I Cor. 16:1, 2 that you do to Acts 11, you would be forced to this right here. But he rejects this as a pattern; and he denied here that it is the only pattern for giving on the first day of the week in the Bible and if you'll notice this, the fact that there are other examples of New Testament cooperation, then there are others in the Bible. Now, Brother Cogdill you're in dificulty on that.

He says that the only reason that one church may send

money to another church is when the church is in need. Now when he says that, he contradicts Brother Tant. I'm not interested, tonight, in Brother Tant's consistency. But inasmuch as he seeks to inject these matters, we just might as well let him harmonize himself with what Brother Tant said in the Harper-Tant debate p. 50. Let us have the next chart, the one on Montana. "He wanted to know what was wrong with preaching the gospel in Montana, which I defended over a radio program. I have urged brethren to send money to Montana to preach the gospel there." Let us have the next chart, the one on Africa. These two go together, they are the same point. It is flashed on the screen,

All right, we're ready to go. "What about sending money to Montana and to Africa to preach the gospel over the radio stations that reach out beyond the area which we're trying to support." Now listen, "I have urged churches to send money to Montana to put on a radio program to build up the cause of Christ in Montana." Yet Brother Cogdill says tonight that that's wrong. That the only purpose for which it can be sent is to help the needy saints of another Congregation. Now, Brother Cogdill, you're in serious trouble there. You and your fellow editor need to get together on that.

Now let me give you another example. In Acts 15:22, we have an account of the church in Jerusalem sending out these brethren to the Gentile churches. Brother Cogdill sought to leave the impression with you that that was purely an apostolic matter, and that's dangerous argument. That would eliminate Paul's case of when they sent direct to the preacher. Paul was an apostle. You're not an apostle. Are you going to reject this because it was an apostle? Where I asked for an example, you gave me only an example of money being sent to a preacher. Now you can't establish that. That's ridiculous reasoning, in the first place. And you watch him repudiate it when he gets to sending money down to Paul, but it just so happens that this case doesn't say it was the apostles. It says it was by a local church including the apostles and elders. And so he's in difficulty on that question. Then he comes back and says that he has repudiated the Music Hall meeting. Let's have the lights on, please.

Warren: 15 minutes.

Woods: Thank you. But do you know, friends, when he repudiated that meeting, he repudiated it right here tonight for the first time. He seeks to leave the impression with you that he has repudiated this meeting earlier. He repudiated his relationship to Boles Home, last night here. He has repudiated this matter here tonight for the first time. I want you to listen. Here's what he said with reference to it: "I have thought, and still think, that there is a vast deal of difference between a congregation undertaking in its own city a work for which it feels responsible and obligated and allowing others to help it do that work, and that same congregation promoting a program of work for the whole brotherhood for which it is no more responsible than any other congregation and expecting all the churches to finance that work for it, a work that it could not bear and would not undertake of itself alone, and then electing themselves to oversee such a 'Brotherhood program' for the church universal. If there were no more difference than the size of the thing, it would be much more dangerous because of its size. It has proved so difficult though to show the difference that I think I see in that to some of the brethren who seem determined to justify themselves in forgetting the New Testament pattern of the independence and equality of New Testament congregations that I have long ago surrendered the ground and henceforth will hold no more such meetings lest I lead my brethren into sin." The reason that he's opposed is to keep his brethren from sinning. He said tonight it was to keep from sinning himself or to that effect. Back there he saw a difference, but his brethren weren't smart enought to see it. Tonight it is because he would be sinning if he should do it. Back there he saw a difference in the two. Now it's wrong because it's just like Herald of Truth. The first time you've repudiated it is right here tonight.

Now there, friends, is the matter. He said that the difference would be that Norhill started that work, back

SPONSORING CONGREGATIONS

yonder. Well, it's not a question of who started it, it's a question of what's going on. That's what determines the scripturalness of a thing. What differences does it make? Now he raises this question: he says since Acts 11:27-30 is the pattern, what is it that can be proved from it? Well, 1. That the money was raised by a church that had it and that it was sent for the purpose of helping others and it was spent by the elders. Now he couldn't prove that if his life depended on it. That is, the last one. It was sent to the Elders, but he couldn't prove it to save his life that those elders took over and the brethren managed the needy homes in which that money was put. There, if you please, is the basic error of his reasoning all the way through. He says that a church can't contribute to that which it can't run. I asked the question, Brother Cogdill, did those elders follow those fellows all the way? You answer. And that again reminds me, you are expected to tell us what happened to a needy church that had no elders. Brother Porter, don't let him forget it, please.

Now, friends, with reference to Acts 11, he says now that Brother Woods says he has no hesitancy in saying that's the church, but it doesn't say so. That's right, it doesn't say so. In the first place, it says the disciples, not the church, but the disciples. Now Brother Cogdill says that he thinks it's likely that where all the members of an area make a contribution that that's a congregational contribution. Now he couldn't prove that, if his life depended upon it, that all of the disciples in that area made the contribution. But he says that when a situation of this kind exists that it's the church doing it. When all the members make a contribution to something that's the church doing it. Suppose out here in some little town of 300 people where there's a church of a hundred members and a representative of Abilene Christian College should be out here soliciting for a contribution and each one of these families that was a member of the church down here decided to give in a body to Abilene Christian College, would that be the church doing it, sir? I'm going to be interested in his answer to that. It'll be significant.

Oh, he says, it means the church because it says the disciples. Don't you know that the disciples constitute the church? We read in Acts 9:26 that Paul assayed to join himself to the disciples in Jerusalem. Hence, Paul tried to join the church in Jerusalem according to Brother Cogdill. Now he'll reject that reasoning and rightly so because it is an error to assume that necessarily the word disciples even taken in a collective sense involving activity not congregational in its nature, that such constitutes the church. Oh, he says in Acts 20:7, the record says the disciples came together. Yes, they came together. That's what constituted the assembly of the church. It was the coming together. Did the church exist before the disciples came together in its congregational capacity?

And again, friends, do you not see the vulnerability of Brother Cogdill on this matter?

Warren: Ten minutes.

Brother Woods: Thank you. He says that in these instances now, that in every case where this money was sent and, of course, there's only one case in which he builds his pattern, that the hungry souls were fed. Why yes, some elders, and I know that group of elders was doing their best that you endorsed to get them out of their oversight. Now how are you going to harmonize this with Brother Tant's editorial position here? You're the last man on earth that ought to be talking about somebody being consistent with somebody else. Then next he said, the only possible way to raise money is that which is designated in I Cor. 16:1, 2, and the only way by which one church may send money to another church is as that which is indicated in Acts 11. That's his pattern, his exclusive pattern. That eliminates sending money for the building of a church building. That eliminates sending any assistance such as that that was characteristic of Acts 15:22. In Acts 15:22 the preacher was sent from one church to another, that was for the purpose of rendering assistance. Now it wasn't for the purpose of helping a needy church either. Do you endorse Acts 15:22, Brother Cogdill? And let me call your attention to this, please. In Acts 15:22, the expression there in the original

Greek, where it says that it was sent to these people, is exactly the same as that in Acts 11:27, when it was sent by the hand of Barnabas and Saul. Exactly the same. They were sent by the hands of the church in Jerusalem. This money was sent by hand of Barnabas and Saul. Exactly the same expression in the original Greek. He shouts long and loud about a central agency. Now he offers no proof that the radio program is a centralized agency. The churches which contribute to the Herald of Truth deny that it is a centralized agency. The congregation that is promoting or putting on the program denies that it is a centralized agency. Brother Cogdill ought to prove that it is a centralized agency. He merely asserted it. Assertions are not competent evidence in this court, sir. Give us some proof if it, and when you do, you'll simply claim that you know more than the Highland elders like you know more than the Tennessee Department of Public Health.

Then next, friends he says that history, history reveals the danger of apostasy. Nobody questions that there are lessons to be learned from history. But let me emphasize please that history does not exist and is not designed for the purpose of trying to keep people from doing right. I submit to you that the abuse of a thing is no argument against its proper use. I have shown you, first of all, from the Great Commission, the need of evangelism. I have shown you the necessity of cooperation in that field. I have given you an apostolic example of such and I've shown you that Brother Cogdill applies the same reasoning in the matter of I Cor. 16:1, 2, all of which he rejects, arrays himself not only against Brother Douthitt but also against Brother Tant.

He says that Brother Harper took the position, as do these brethren at Highland that the program is the work of the Highland elders. I know that they do. That is the purpose of the letter I read; to show you that these brethren have stated that they mean by "the work" simply putting on the program. That's what they mean. And I've shown you that both those brethren and the contributing churches believe that they are carrying out their own program under the Great Commission, and that's all it is.

Now, Brother Cogdill, you haven't met the issue here. No. I haven't taken the position of the Adventists. Your position would necessitate the acceptance of it, though. I believe that I Cor. 16:1, 2 is an apostolic example of meeting a need. Now get this, ladies and gentlemen. There a need existed, it happened that in that particular case it was a physical need involving benevolence. But evangelism is as much of a need as benevolence was. That's the way the apostolic church met one need, then another legitimate need could be met in the same way. Both of us agree on that. But when we come over to another situation that is where one church came to the assistance of another, he rejects the same kind of reasoning exactly, and makes the same argument as the anti-Sunday school people on the cups and the classes. Exactly the same.

Warren: Five minutes.

Woods: Thank you. He says that the Gospel Advocate contained a reprint, involving a statement by Brother Foy Wallace, that points out the dangers of centralized control. You listen to this, ladies and gentlemen. That article by Brother Wallace was with reference to matters that were not violated in the Music Hall meeting because according to information I have, I think I'm correct on this. If I'm not, he can tell me the exact year. That article was written in 1939. But the Music Hall meeting was held several years after that. Brother Wallace held that meeting which he would now say is unscriptural after he wrote that article. Now does that sound like Brother Wallace was condemming what Brother Cogdill admits is parallel to the Herald of Truth here tonight? Well, obviously not. All of this is about the missionary society and so we must not do as you have done, just go down the line and start repudiating one thing after another on the basis of which the church has today reached its present growth, and reduce it to a second rate hobbyistic sect. Exactly what you brethren will do if you were to succeed.

He said he doesn't know about Brother Lewis' Lord's

plan. Well I'll give him a little more information. Let's have that chart again, please. Chart no. 42.

CHART NO. 42.

JOHN T. LEWIS AND "THE LORD'S PLAN"

- "......MR. KENDRICK AFTERWARDS QUIT THE SOCIETY AND WENT BACK TO THE LORD'S PLAN OF DOING MISSIONARY WORK."
    - JOHN T. LEWIS, VOL OF P. ON I. M. AND SOC., P. 70.

- "......SEND THE FUNDS TO THE ELDERS OF SOME CENTRAL CONGREGATION, WHO WILL DISBURSE THEM WISELY AND JUSTLY: ...."
    - C. KENDRICK, LIVE REL. ISSUES, P. 445.

All right, Brother Lewis says, in the *Voice of the Pioneers*, which is an excellent book containing much valuable information, that Mr. Kendrick, he was the man that espoused the missionary society, then repudiated it. Mr. Kendrick, afterward quit the society and went back to the Lord's plan of doing missionary work. But what was the Lord's plan? Well, on page 445, here is the expression, I'll just read the entire context. "If we follow these examples then all the congregations in a given region will raise funds under the prompting of some agent or agents like Paul and Titus will choose messengers and send the funds to the Elders of some central congregation, who will disburse them wisely and justly. And when serious difficulties disturb or threaten the peace and prosperity of the church, messengers will be chosen by the several congregations, who will meet with some one congregation to consult and confer as to what may be scriptural and best." He said further on page 444 and 445, "We are to say that congregations cooperated in raising and distributing funds for the relief of the poor. The Elders, in Jerusalem, receiving the funds at the hands of the messengers and dispersing them to the poor in Judea, not in

Jerusalem only." That's the Lord's plan of doing mission work according to Brother John T. Lewis, and I hope that no quote "peanut" unquote will rise up and question Brother Lewis as an authority in this section. And I'm not referring to Brother Cogdill in that statement, I'm just quoting Brother Lewis. All right, now friends, that covers his speech, how much time do I have?

Brother Warren: You have about 2½ minutes

Brother Woods: All right, now one more chart here to be introduced. Chart No. 47.

CHART NO. 47.

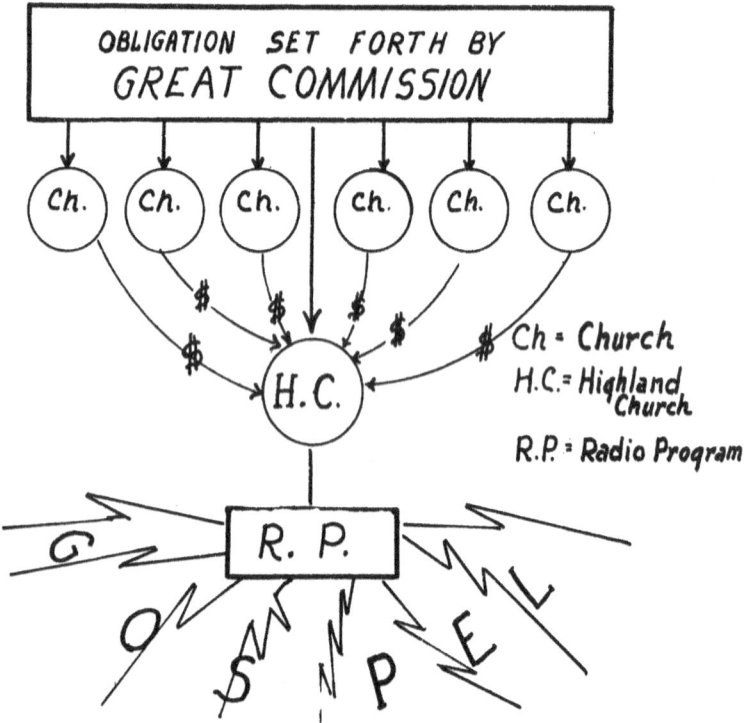

Chart No. 47. Now here, friends, is exactly what I'm defending tonight. And what I've given you an apostolic example of. Here is the obligation set forth by the Great Commission. These are the churches. This represents the money. These sent to the elders of the participating churches. And will you remember, please, that our position is that the Herald of Truth is nothing more than the cooperation of New Testament churches where one of the cooperating churches takes care of the details. And now here it is sent for the purpose of preaching the gospel to the world. And it's sent out to the world by means of this radio program. That is what I am defending here tonight. And I rejoice to know that on the basis of this type of cooperation, the church has had its most phenomenal growth. Today from the rockbound coasts of Maine to the shores of sunny California there exists the noblest brotherhood that the sun ever shone upon. That it's not limited merely to our country, and to our land, the gospel of Christ has crossed the seas and gone to the islands thereof and today countless thousands of people enjoy and appreciate the victories and blessings of the gospel of Christ because of this type of cooperation. Let me tell you what is being done by the Herald of Truth. It started on 85 radio stations. It's now on 260 stations. And it's being conducted on more than 100 TV stations, at least it has been over that many TV stations. It's also going to the Phillipine Islands, and by short-wave to Singapore, Hongkong, and parts of Japan. And by a conservative estimate it's now preaching the gospel, this program is, to from 7 to 10 mission people every Lord's day, at a cost, approximately of one cent per person for thirty minutes. And it has the offer now, the program has, of a half a million dollars of free time on TV if the funds can be provided.

Cogdill's Second Negative

Gentlemen moderators, Brother Woods, Ladies and Gentlemen:

I'm sorry that Brother Wood's time ran out on him because if he had had just a few more minutes in the kind of speech he was making, at the conclusion, he would have justified the missionary society in spite of himself. That sounded exactly like John Briney, didn't it? In the Otey-Briney debate, how much good is being done. Look at all the good we're doing. That justifies anyway on earth you want to do it whether you can find it in the Bible or not. Now that's some argument. Look at how much good the Herald of Truth is doing. Well now if you're going to put it on the basis of judgment, I could take even a few "peanuts," Brother Woods, and the same amount of money, and support more gospel preaching, and establish more congregations, in more towns and communities in the United States and throughout the world, than you can do with the Herald of Truth to save your life.

In the first place, how in the world are you going to plant a congregation anywhere on the radio? That's like trying to conquer England by air. You've got to have some ground forces. All of that claim of good that's being done, we have heard their own testimony about that. I haven't heard of so much good being done. And I'm like the colored boy before they put him in jail, I've been in circulation around over the country, and I know a lot of people that don't know a thing in the world about it. And I know a lot of people that never have heard it. And I know that about 60 per cent of the stations over which they preach are in places like Dallas, Texas, and Birmingham, Alabama, where the local congregations are doing a first rate job of preaching the gospel, and the Herald of Truth isn't needed. I know that, too. And you can get their own list of stations and find out for yourself. It's the old idea of 90 cents out of every dollar that they spend, being promotion. They admit that twelve and a half per cent of its goes in for office work. And we have their own statement for it. When you begin to consider the overhead of that thing, and you want to put it on the basis of the abuse of it, and the judgment that's exercised in it rather than the scriptural basis, you won't get along any better than you're getting along on the scriptures; you had better stay with your proposition, and try to prove it by the word of God.

If it weren't for human testimony you couldn't have made your first speech, much less the second. I know why you're introducing all of it. He got up here and tried to explain why. You didn't need to tell us that, you didn't have any Bible. That's the reason you introduced all of that human testimony. If you had had a passage like you can find for baptism for the remission of sin when you meet D. N. Jackson, you wouldn't have to go to all of that trouble, would you? Now honestly, would you? If you can find in the word of God like you can find singing when you meet a digressive you wouldn't have gone away around by Jericho to find Jerusalem, would you? Why all you need is just some Bible, and that's what your proposition obligates you to use. You forgot in the first three nights of this debate and you know he can't forget about the first three nights. He' still trying to fix up the legal matter that he got into. He got up last night and bragged about being a lawyer. I haven't said anything about being one. I've got a degree in law and am licensed to practice before the United States Supreme Court, as good a one as anybody in the country. But I hadn't brought that up. I've made no reference to it. I'm not especially proud of it. Not especially proud of it. But I wouldn't confess that if I wanted to practice law that I'd be a second-rate one. I'd try to beat that. I'd try to beat that. I can tell you that. And I wouldn't try to cite what some bureau said and palm it off on somebody as a statute, as the law. Why, he thinks that the Department of Public Welfare in Tennessee is the state legislature of Tennessee, a law-making body. That's just how accurate he is in all of the rest of the evidence that he tries to use. Now, Guy, I'd forget about that, if I were you. You've blundered badly on that, I'd leave that out of the rest of this debate. And you're the one that brought it up again.

Paul said, concerning the good the Herald of Truth does, "Shall we do evil that good may come?" It isn't a question of how much good is being done. It's a question of whether or not God is pleased with what is being done. That's the question. And the only way on earth you can prove that He is, is by divine testimony, not by what the elders at Highland say about it. They're not God's law making body. Nor are the elders at Hillsboro.

Nor is the editor of the Gospel Advocate. It isn't his province to determine what the truth is for everybody even that reads that paper either. And you know he talked about they didn't want to teach any error. No, and they don't want to correct any misrepresentations either. They'll say anything on earth that anybody will give it to use, nearly, against almost anybody that is opposed to them. Then you try to get it corrected when it isn't so. Now we can talk about that a little bit if you want to.

But he says Cogdill's repudiated Tant, and he's repudiated John T. Lewis, and he's repudiated North Birmingham. He says he doesn't know what they're practicing at all. Well, I have an idea that I know what they're practicing now on the Herald of Truth, and on everything like it. They won't support it. That's the reason they got out of some of those things that they got into back there, and that's the reason I got out of some of the things that I got into. I've learned better. That's what you need to do. If we can just get you to repudiating some of the things that you've said and done, we'll be making some progress. Now you know that thing works both ways. Two can talk about that. I wonder if he will repudiate Guy N. Woods? You listen to him: "In line with the fact that our lesson today deals with the autonomy of the church." That's what we're talking about, isn't it. That's what's involved in this discussion. "We point out that the contribution here alluded to was raised wholly without the high pressure organizational methods characteristic of today. There was no organization at all. The churches in their own capacity raised the funds and were gathered by brethren especially appointed for the purpose. This is the Lord's method of raising money. And it will suffice in any case. There is no place for charitable organizations in the work of the New Testament church. It is the only charitable organization that the Lord authorized or that is needed to do the work the Lord expects people today to do." Now listen. "Here, too, we see the simple manner in which the church in Philippi joined with Paul in the work of preaching the gospel." Get it now, this is Guy N. Woods. And by the way, it's Gospel Advocate literature. "This is the manner in which the church at Philippi joined with Paul in the work of preaching the gospel. There was no missionary society in evidence. None was needed." Why? Why wasn't it needed? "The brethren simply raised the money and sent it directly to Paul. This is the way it should be done today." Now what do you know about that? And he hasn't changed. He's the most unchangeable fellow I ever saw. Why I wouldn't get up here if I'd made a statement of that kind and occupy the position that he does tonight, get up here and deny that I had changed. No sir. No sir.

"This is the way it should be done today. No organization is needed to do the work the Lord has authorized the church to do." Why? Why now? Why isn't an organization needed? "Because the church that made up the money sent it directly to Paul." Don't you let him get away from that statement when he gets up here and tries to worm his way out of that. Why didn't they need some kind of an organization . . . a centralized agency? The answer is because they sent it directly to Paul. Now, Brother Woods, I want to know: how did they get that money they sent to Paul? How did they get it?

He said, you know Brother Cogdill said that the only example of a church taking up a contribution is in I Cor. 16, and that that's the only pattern. Yes that's the only pattern of the way the church raised its money. That isn't the only pattern of how the church *used* its money. That's what you're trying to make me say. And that isn't what I said. The only way that God ever gave the church to raise its money . . . "let each one of you." "Each one of you." By the members of the church. Do what? "Lay by in store on the first day of the week." Why? "That there be no gathering when I come." What did you want them to get it together for, Paul? The church had promised the contribution for the relief of the poor saints in Jerusalem and he wanted them to have it ready. How are they going to get it ready? By each one of you contributing on the first day of the week. But here is a church, according to Guy N. Woods, sending money that they got together somehow. They got it together some way. And they sent it to paul. There's another thing that the church used its money for. They sent it to Pau! to help him preach the gospel of Jesus Christ. Where did they get it? There isn't any other pattern of how God told the church to raise its money to do anything. They used the money that they did raise to do something else. And he got up here and tried to misrepresent me on the point I made on that.

You know he's disregarded the burden of proof. He's tried to shift it. I knew he would. I knew he would have to. He's tried to put me in the position of affirming a pattern. I'm not in the affirmative business tonight, Guy. You're affirming, tonight. You're the one that's obligated to find the pattern and you haven't found it. Not in the word of God, you haven't. Oh, no, you haven't found it in the word of God, and that's exactly what your proposition obligates you to do. Now he's under obligation, from the New Testament, not from some other source, but from the New Testament of God's word. He's under obligation in his proposition. And I'm going to hold him to it all the three nights that we're on it.

Your proposition says that it's in harmony with the scriptures. There are only two ways to prove it, Guy. Just two. Only two. And you can understand the two I'm about to give you now because they're legal. One of them is a statute authorizing, a statute making it the law. The other is an approved example or a case in point. And you can find that in only two ways as we have pointed it out on the Lord's supper, one of them, by the actual approved example of the thing or a necessary inference that must follow. Now either produce your statute, find your case in point, from the New Testament, or yield your proposition. That's what we want. That's what we want. And what we want in your pattern has to be a church sending to another church that isn't in need. Highland isn't a church in need. They send to everything else on earth nearly. They're not in need. That isn't destitute. Go out and look at their meetinghouse and you can tell that. They pay two or three of their elders to run around over the country and spread their propaganda about the Herald of Truth and stick their foot in the door of every church that they can get it into and try to get their hands into the treasury of every congregation in this country that they can get into. They're not a church in need. Don't tell me they are, brethren. They aren't. You're under obligation to find a congregation contributing to another congregation when it wasn't in need. That's what your proposition demands. I'm going to remind you of it everytime I get up here whether you like it or don't. He doesn't like my style of debating. He's told you that over and over. He says that when a man says that another fellow is not meeting his proposition and is not doing this or that, that's an evidence of the weakness of his position. Well, he's the worst one at that I know of. And he turned right around last night after he'd said it and did the very same thing. After I'd mentioned argument after argument that he'd illustrated on his charts, he complained constantly about the fact that I hadn't said a word in the world about anything he'd said. So he just turned right around in the same speech; he can't make a thirty minute speech without contradicting himself. I've seen Baptist preachers in that shape on the plan of salvation, and the reason they get in that shape is because they don't have any Bible for what they're preaching. That's the reason they get in it.

Well, we want a case in point. A case from the supreme court, Brother Woods, the apostles of our Lord. Jesus said, in the Great Commission, "Teach them, those whom you've baptized, to observe all things whatsoever I have commanded you." Paul said, Phil. 4:9 that what things you had heard and received, and learned and seen in me, these things do. What Jesus Christ commanded the apostles, what the apostles taught the churches, and that's what he needs to find. Jesus said to the apostles, "You shall sit upon twelve thrones judging the twelve tribes of Israel." That's what they were doing in Acts 15: That was an apostolic decision. Brother Woods knows that. He tries to make a case of one church helping another church, out of Acts 15. I deny that he's correctly applying the passage. He's wresting it exactly like he does the rest of the passages that he uses.

You turn back to Acts 15 and see what it is. "Then pleased it the apostles and elders, with the whole church." I want to know whose decision was it to send these brethren? He says the church sent, and he leaves the apostles of the Lord out of it. What had they done in Jerusalem? They had rendered a decision. Who had? The apostles had. Paul says, "I laid it before them that were of repute." Why did they? "Lest by any means I had run in vain." They carried a question to the supreme court of the church of God in the city of Jerusalem. That's what they had done in Acts 15. And when the decision was rendered, it was reduced to writing, and it was that writing that was sent by the hand of these brethren that he mentioned. Of course, they carried it. Just like they carried the relief. But was it relief this time? No, it wasn't benevolence, in the sense of food and clothing or money to supply physical need. Well, what was it? Divine revelation. A decision of the supreme court that the churches might know what the will of the Lord was. And he said it wasn't to churches in need. You mean those churches didn't need the decision of the apostles? How ridiculous can a man get? They weren't in need of it? Didn't need what the apostles decided in the city of Jerusalem? Brother Woods, I'd be ashamed of that.

Now he's already introduced this matter of the history of this business. And I've given you some of his history. He says Cogdill repudiates Tant and he repudiates his own associate editor, and so on down the line, and Cecil Douthitt, well I haven't got them in the shape you've got poor Brother Harper in. I want you to know right now, I feel sorry for Brother Harper. He represented the Highland church in two debates. That debate's in print. E. R. Harper took the position, and everybody that's read the book and everybody that heard the debates knows that he defended the Herald of Truth, representing the elders of the Highland church, the elders themselves, he defended them on the ground that it was *THEIR* work. And he argued with Brother Tant that when I give you a dollar, that dollar's yours. It belongs to you. The money that's sent to us is ours to use and we use it and the elders themselves say that we control the work. It is our work. That's what they say about it. And they are a centralized agency. Why, look here at the chart up here.

HOW DOES H. of T. OPERATE?

(1) DO MANY CHURCHES CONTRIBUTE MONEY? <u>YES.</u>

(2) DOES HIGHLAND RECEIVE ALL THE MONEY? <u>YES.</u>

(3) DO ELDERS OF HIGHLAND EXERCISE EXCLUSIVE CONTROL? <u>YES</u>.

16. *16.*

How does the Herald of Truth operate? In the first place, do many churches contribute money to it? Where does the money come from? From many churches, Will he deny it? Question no. 2. Does Highland receive all the money? Will they deny it? Question no. 3. Do elders of the Highland church exercise exclusive control over the money? Over the program? Over the preaching? Over the stations. Why, they say they even inspect the manuscripts of the sermon before they're ever preached. They say where they'll be preached. How many stations and where the stations are. Now if that doesn't constitute a centralized agency through which many churches are working and I challenge him to deny those three facts. Everybody in this crowd knows that's so. You know they're so. A thousand churches contributing money. Who gets it? The Highland elders get it. Who controls it? They do. They do. They select the preacher. Well, the preachers at first selected them. They've gone to selecting them now, though. But they said that we were on the wrong side of the table to do the selecting. We didn't do the picking; they picked us. They didn't born the thing, it was already born when they got it.

It was already started. It was promoted by promoters par excellent. One of the best and most outstanding promoters that I know anything about promoted that nationwide radio program. He is a promoter, and he did a good job of promoting that thing. I'll give him credit for it. He did an excellent job of it. And then he promoted it into the hands of the Highland elders, and all of a sudden it became theirs. I deny in fact that it is the work of one congregation. It's the work of many churches, but it's controlled by one, that's the point. That's what's unscriptural about it.

Now he said Brother Cogdill didn't repudiate the Music Hall meeting until tonight. You don't know what you're talking about. You're as wrong about that as you can be. You read one statement that I made years ago when this thing first began to be discussed among the brethren and you don't know what else has been said about it. I've said that I would never, anytime, anywhere, be a party to one church handling and disbursing the money of other churches, knowingly. Knowingly. Now if that isn't a repudiation of it, how am I going to repudiate it? Anything wrong in repudiating what you're convinced to be wrong? No, Guy Woods needs to do some repudiating if he's sincere in the position that he occupies tonight. If he's contending for what he believes, and I'm not saying that he isn't. Then he needs to repudiate some of the things that he says. He said, well, if they had to send it to the elders now if that's the pattern in receiving. Well there isn't any *if* about that. That is the pattern. That's the pattern of how churches received. He wanted to know if the elders took charge of the home. It doesn't say anything about the homes, Brother Woods. I don't know what they did about the homes. You are the one that put that in there. You've been trying to get the home, the private home in there ever since this thing started.

SPONSORING CONGREGATIONS

He can't see anything but the private home. He won't open his eyes and see an institutional home and whenever you begin to talk about the church doing some benevolent work under its elders, he thinks of a private home and runs. Runs from what the New Testament says about it. Well now did the elders receive it or didn't they. He says, well who's going to receive it if they don't have any elders, Brother Cogdill? Now you're in real trouble. How's the church going to do *anything* under the elders if they don't have any? How are they going to meet on the first day of the week under the supervision of the elders, if they don't have any. I guess they couldn't do that either under the supervision of the elders. Haven't got any elders. Haven't got any elders. And the church couldn't support any gospel under the supervision of the elders. Don't have any elders. And a church, therefore, couldn't receive any help if it was in need, if it didn't have elders. Well, that would just about eliminate a church that didn't have elders, wouldn't it? It just couldn't do anything because everything the church does, it does under the supervision of the elders. That's God's plan, Brother Woods. That's God's plan. Now you find in the New Testament how to operate the church without elders and I'll tell you how they received help when it's sent to them when they don't have elders.

But I want to point out another thing or two. We just started reading from Brother Syrgley awhile ago. You know the Gospel Advocate and Brother Guy Woods, and Brother B. C. Goodpasture, and I've got nothing personal against them, don't you misunderstand my attitude. If there's any enmity in my heart against anybody, I don't know it. And I pray that God may help me find it out. And I'll get rid of it. I'm not mad at Guy Woods, not a bit on this earth. But I'm going to be pretty rough on him because I'd like to help him. My mother used to be awfully rough on me because she loved me and that's the reason I get rough with him. I'm trying to help him. I will if he'll let me. The Gospel Advocate's printed a lot of things that you couldn't get in it now. It wouldn't print what Brother Srygley now. He said, "but here's what Foy Wallace meant." I know what Foy Wallace meant and I know what he's preaching all over this country. And he's condemming the Herald of Truth just like I am. Don't you misrepresent him either. He's preaching against it everywhere he goes, and against the institutional orphan homes as institutions of the church. I know where he stands on it. And you can find out if you want to know.

"Every New Testament church was a complete body within itself. Was independent of all other churches. No church had any authority over any other. The work of the elders stopped at the church in which they lived and labored." Brethren, that's New Testament teaching. Peter said, "Tend the flock of God which is among you." That's the only flock any eldership has any control over. They're the only members that they have any control over. You know what he said about Acts 9:26 was shocking to me. Honestly it was. He said, why Brother Cogdill said that Paul was trying to join the church. That's exactly what Brother Cogdill preaches about that. Just exactly what he preaches about it. He was trying to identify himself with the congregation in Jerusalem that he might have fellowship with them. They wouldn't have him until Barnabas came forward and commended him. The congregation controls its own fellowship, Brother Woods, you ought to know that. They didn't have to accept Paul. They knew his past history. They were afraid of him. They wouldn't receive him into their fellowship until he was commended. He was assaying to join himself to the disciples in Jerusalem and they are the church in Jerusalem. No, the church didn't have to assemble in order for the church to accept. And he missed the point on the chart over there. He said: "Didn't the church exist before that?" Yes, the church existed before that. Don't try to confuse this crowd with what you did. What did you do? You said that because the church was not mentioned, the text didn't say the church, and Antioch did it, therefore, it could not be proved that it was the church. It has to say the church to be a pattern. There's your argument, Brother Woods. That was your argument. And

I pointed out to you in Acts 20:7. It doesn't say the church. No, I didn't deny the church existed. It doesn't say the church. That's what you were trying to make it say. Yes, it was. Don't nod your head that way, because these folks heard you say it. They heard you say it. You said Acts 11:27, doesn't say the church did it. It isn't a pattern because it doesn't say the church. The tape will show you said it. That's the point we're talking about, and I replied to it by showing that Acts 20:7, not Acts 11:27-30 this time, but Acts 20:27, doesn't say the church, therefore, you couldn't prove it, that it is a pattern for the church to break bread according to Guy N. Woods. Then he gets up here and tries to confuse you by saying, didn't the church exist before it came together? That's some way to deal with a matter isn't it? You can be the judge about that.

Let's read what Brother Syrgley said. "Churches should never be tied together. Even in as good a work as preaching the gospel to the heathen." Would the Gospel Advocate print that without Guy N. Wood's explanation of it today? Reckon they would? They would turn F. B. Syrgley down just like they did Roy Lanier. That's what they'd do with him if he lived today. Because he doesn't agree with B. C. Goodpasture, the editor. No freedom of expression. You can't print anything in it that B. C. Goodpasture doesn't believe and then they want to sell it to the brethren. B. C. Goodpasture's creed. You get all the churches out of all their treasuries to subscribe for all their members, so they can read what B. C. Good pasture and Guy N. Woods, and his editoral staff has passed on, and determined to be the truth. Talk to me about centralization and concentration of power. And you're going to have to line up with them on the school question or you'll get hung before it's over with. Sure as you live. You don't need to worry about me and my position on the school question. I can state that and I will if it disagrees with everybody connected with the Gospel Guardian. And if preaching my convictions, and writing my convictions kills the Gospel Guardian before midnight, I'd still preach and write them and it could die.

It's the word of God and truth of God's word that's important. Not the position of some editor of some paper or of some eldership or of what brethren might say what they intend to be the case.

That doesn't determine the truth on anything. Brother Syrgley said no churches should be tied together even in as good a work as preaching the gospel to the heathen. All the good that you can do won't justify doing it. Elders of one church should not try to get hold of the money that has been contributed by others to direct for them in foreign fields or other places. I don't know if Brother Cawyer and Brother Reese and those elders are in this audience tonight or not. If they are, I want to recommend F. B. Syrgley to you and what the Gospel Advocate used to stand for. Brethren, this is not any cranky notion that originated in the last five years. Don't you let Guy Woods tell you it is. It isn't so. It isn't so. Why, I hear F. B. Syrgley saying that an individual can send his means directly to the preacher who's on the field preaching the gospel, and so can a church. And that's what Guy Woods said in the Gospel Advocate Commentary, 1946. That's the way Philippi did it. That makes it right. And I say amen. Guy, will you shake hands with me on that statement in 1946, or have you changed? Now honestly, do you still stand? Is that the way it ought to be done ..... the church send direct to the preacher ..... Montana or anywhere else? Is that what you believe about the matter? Will you shake hands with me on that statement now? You ought to, or you ought to have to admit that you've changed. Sure as you live you ought to. You talk about consistency, and I'm the last man that ought to talk about consistency. Listen I'm not worried about being consistent. I'm concerned about trying to be right. And you ought to be. I'm not concerned about consistency. It's what the word of God teaches that concerns me. Time up? I thank you.

FIFTH NIGHT
Woods' Third Affirmative

Brethren Moderators, Brother Cogdill, Ladies and Gentlemen:

In view of the fact that on last evening I gave a detailed definition of the terms of the proposition which I am affirming, and inasmuch as there seems to be no question regarding their significance, I shall waive the formality of further definition tonight. Just suffice it to say that it's my obligation and responsibility to prove that cooperative efforts such as that characteristic of the Herald of Truth Radio Program is scriptural in its nature, and that it's entirely in order for the churches of Christ to participate therein.

I desire to review briefly that which was presented on last evening, and hence I'm going to ask for my chart No. 37. We'll turn the lights out please, while we examine this chart. Observe that this sets out the obligation of

CHART NO. 37.

GREAT COMMISSION

"......INTO ALL THE WORLD............"

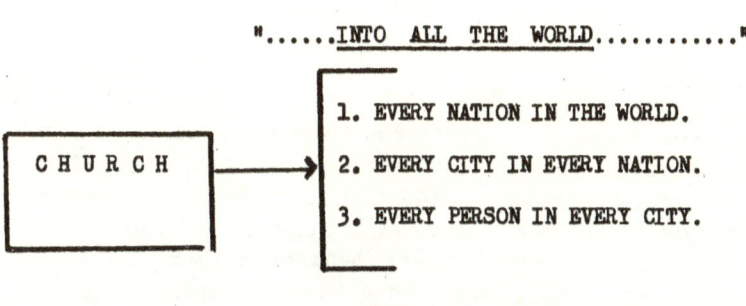

"........PREACH THE GOSPEL............."

the church under the great commission, that in Mark 16:15,16, our Lord said, "Go into all the world and preach the gospel to every creature. He that believeth and is baptized shall be saved, he that believeth not shall be damned." This requires that we go into all the world.

That means to every nation, and into every city of every nation, and then contact every person in every city in every nation on the earth, and then preach the gospel to each person under those consideration. I argued last evening, and it wasn't questioned that it would take the resources of the federal government to carry that out, and that since the church did carry it out, it must not and could not have possessed the resources of the Federal government, that there was cooperative effort on the part of the churches of the apostolic age.

CHART NO. 38.

TYPES OF COOPERATION

IS THERE AN EXCLUSIVE "PATTERN"?

1. BETWEEN INDIVIDUALS - 2 TIM. 4: 9.
2. ONE INDIVIDUAL AND SEVERAL OTHER INDIVIDUALS - ROM. 16: 1, 2.
3. CHRISTIAN FAMILY AND NEEDY INDIVIDUALS - 1 COR. 16: 15.
4. "DISCIPLES" AND "ELDERS" - ACTS 11: 27-30.
5. CHURCHES AND NEEDY SAINTS IN JERUSALEM - 2 COR. 8, 9.
6. CHURCH AND CHURCH - ACTS 15: 1-32.

WHICH IS THE EXCLUSIVE PATTERN???

Now may I have chart No. 38, please. Here, you will observe, we argued that there is no exclusive pattern. We called attention to the fact that there is cooperation taught in the Bible between individuals, between one individual and several others, between a Christian family and a needy individual, and between disciples and elders, and between churches and the needy saints in Jerusalem, and between churches and churches; and that, therefore, there is no exclusive pattern.

We called attention, in the light of that fact, to this: that it is absurd to argue for an exclusive pattern when so many different ways of cooperation is thus indicated.

SPONSORING CONGREGATIONS 253

Now, let's have chart No. 39. This matter is to get before you matters of last evening. We have here in Acts

CHART NO. 39.

ACTS 11: 27-30.

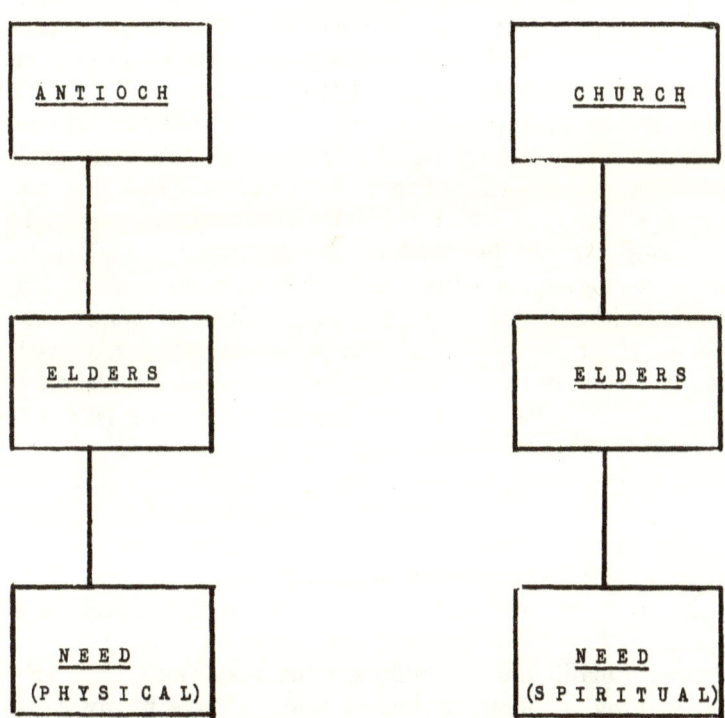

11:27-30 that which was set out with reference to the famine in Judea, and we're told that the disciples at Antioch determined to send relief, which they did, sending to the elders by the hand of Barnabas and Saul. We pointed out that there the need was physical in its nature, and that that's an exact parallel in the matter of the churches sending to another church for the purpose of meeting another need that is spiritual in its nature. And that if it's right to meet a physical need in this fashion, and this is an admitted case of church cooperation, that then, since is a need just as much as is this, that is, that the spiritual need is as great as the physical need, then it's proper to meet it in that fashion; and since there is no exclusive pattern taught in the Bible, and since this is a type of church cooperation, that it's eminently scriptural in its nature.

Now it might be said that in this instance it was only one congregation that was cooperating. In the great contribution of 2 Cor. 8 and 9, we have the churches of Galatia and the church in Corinth and the churches of Macedonia and Achaia participating. It's not the number of the churches that participate that determine the scripturalness of it. As a matter of fact, if it's right for two churches to cooperate, then under the same circumstance ten could cooperate, or ten hundred or ten thousand. And when brethren become alarmed and disturbed because of the number, it's simply that they are willing to admit that it's all right to do things in a little way that are good, but it would be wrong to do good things in a big way. That is the basis of such an objection, and we reject it without hesitation.

Now, I'm going to show you that brother Cogdill has utterly refused to deal with these matters and yet in spite of that fact he tells you that I have not sustained my proposition. It's up to him to prove that I haven't. I'm going to show you, and I'd like to have that chart back if I may, just for a moment, I'm going to show you that brother Cogdill himself endorses the very thing that he's condemning; at least, he has so said. I have in my hand here *The New Testament Church*. That's a book that brother Cogdill wrote. On page 39 of this book he has this to say, under point number 4, "Cooperation of local churches. Local churches cooperated in doing their work" ..... listen now ..... "but such work was always under the supervision of a local church and its eldership". What? Churches always cooperated, that is churches cooperated, but they always did so under the supervision of a local church, and its eldership, and he cites Acts 11:28-30, the very instances that I have given here. Now, according

SPONSORING CONGREGATIONS 255

to brother Cogdill in this book, that's a scriptural method of church cooperation.

Brother Cogdill chooses to ignore these charts, and refuses to have them put on the screen, notwithstanding the fact that he has a copy of each chart presented. And Brother Deaver will be happy to put them back on the screen for him at any time. Now evidently, brother Cogdill has decided that the best thing to do is not to look at them. Brother Porter attempted to, and brother Cogdill heard the debate. So now he has decided that he'll just not have the charts before us. Let us have No. 49.

CHART NO. 49.

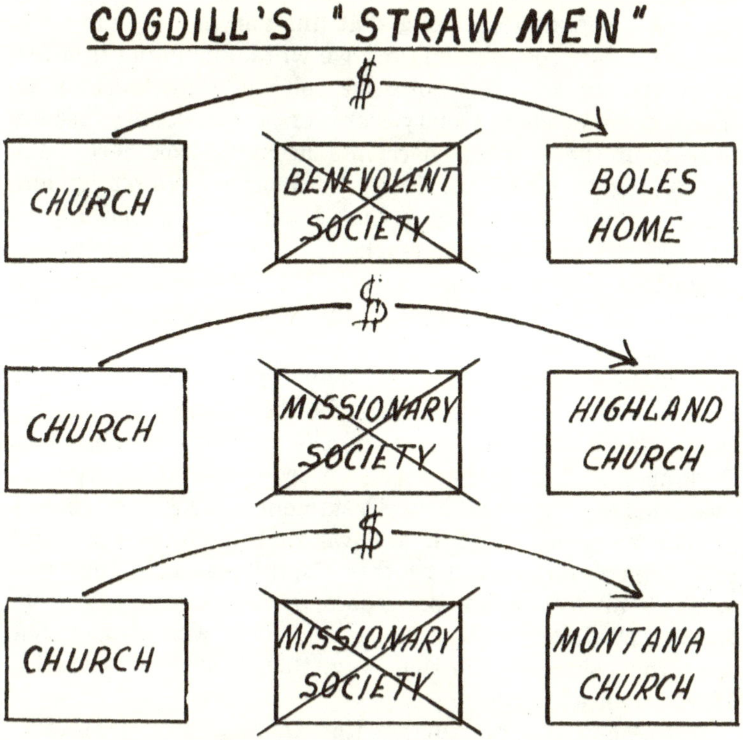

COGDILL'S "STRAW MEN"

CHURCH → $ → ~~BENEVOLENT SOCIETY~~ → BOLES HOME

CHURCH → $ → ~~MISSIONARY SOCIETY~~ → HIGHLAND CHURCH

CHURCH → $ → ~~MISSIONARY SOCIETY~~ → MONTANA CHURCH

Now this is a new chart and if you will you may make it available to brother Cogdill. Here is the basic difficulty that is characteristic of him, and here's his straw man.

Observe here. His claims declare and I am using this series of illustrations because I want to get before you the three matters under consideration here. He claims to oppose Boles Home because he says there's a benevolent society between the church and the home. Well, he goes on to say that there is a parallel here in that he claims there is a missionary society between the churches and Highland congregation that directs the Herald of Truth Broadcast. And yet you can see friends, its actually the same type of cooperative effort in the Montana work and brother Tant did not see this alleged institution in the same, despite the fact that the money is sent in exactly the same way for the same purpose. He argued that he didn't see a thing wrong with that and he endorsed it. Of course, I haven't heard the latest repudiation along that line and he may have. If he hasn't, he probably will and we will be listening in a few moments for it. Now observe, please, that there is no more a benevolent society here or a missionary society here than there is one here and he says, look here. I'm not trying to prove one thing by another. Don't let him come up here and tell you that I am, but he and I both agree that the scriptures teach this and that the scriptures teach this, and since this here is just like this, this being under consideration tonight, then it follows that it is scriptural also. And he says this—he says it in his book, the *New Testament Church.* And may I emphasize that that's exactly right. And watch, friends, there isn't anything between the Highland Church and the contributing churches. As a matter of fact, there isn't an organization of any kind over there except the New Testament church. If there's anything wrong, then it follows that a New Testament church is wrong. And brother Cogdill has said that this work is always under the elders of a local congregation. Said it was always that way. Then if it was always that way, then since this is that way, then this must be right. If not, then why not?

Let us now observe further that this has been characteristic of these brethren through the years to accept that type of reasoning. Let's have No. 45, please. Now understand, this is not an appeal to tradition. He'd like for you to think it is, but we believe that was right. He believed it was right and says it's still right in his book. Let's see

CHART NO 45
BIRMINGHAM NEWSPAPER AD COOP.

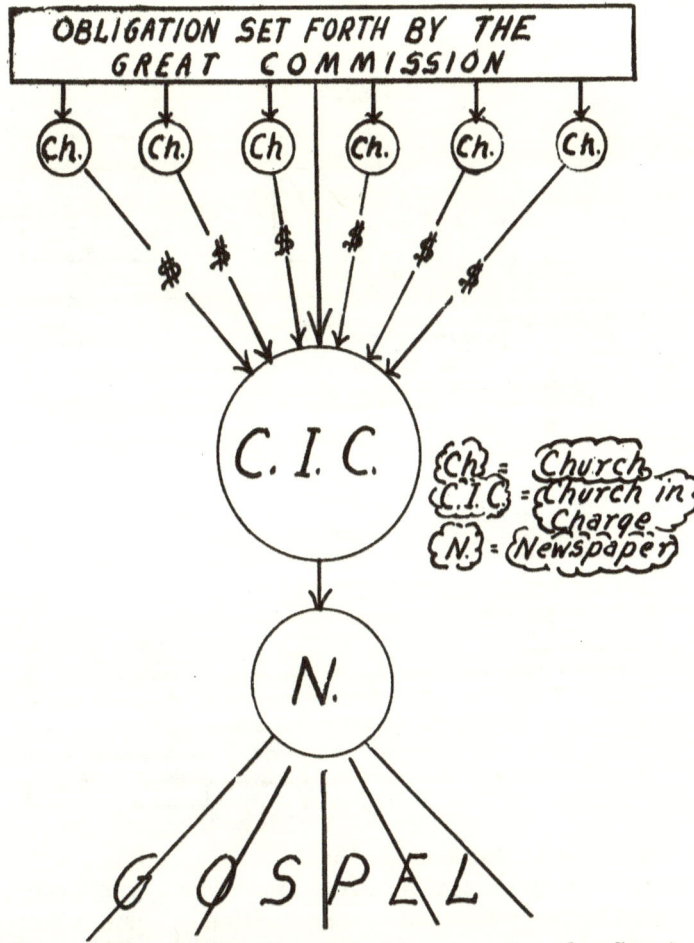

now here: Here is the situation set out under the Great Commission, the Birmingham Newspaper Ad. The churches participating merely sent to the church in charge, and that's the very phraseology. The money was then spent. And bear in mind, please, that this was practiced by these churches which are today following the line of brother Cogdill, having switched their position. They participated in it, and they thought it was right back then. And now since he's changed, they've changed. On this practice they were right and that's in harmony with what I'm defending.

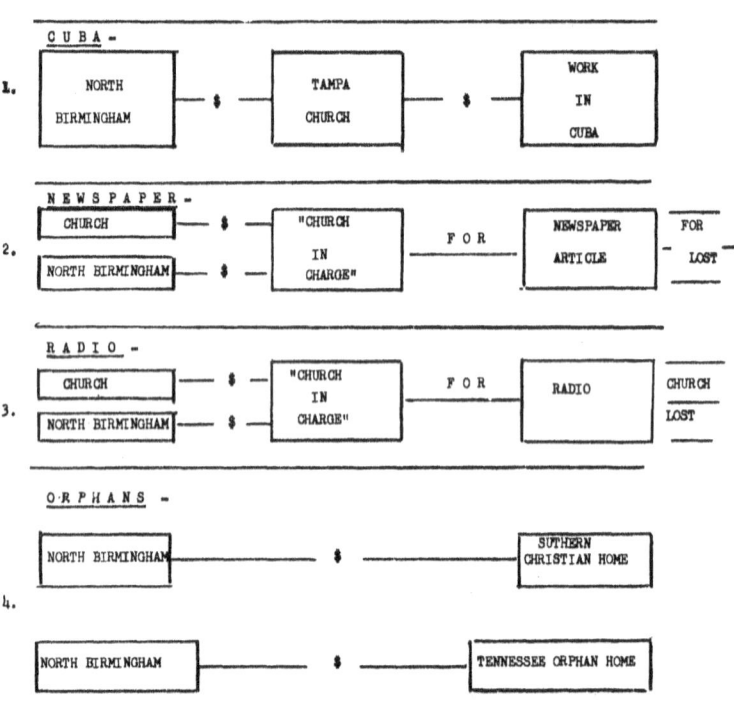

Let's look next now at No. 43. Here is this cooperation that was practiced in Birmingham, and particularly by the North Birmingham congregation. Some years ago, and may I emphasize please, this was back when North Birmingham was cooperating, back in that day they sent money to a Tampa church for the work in Cuba. They believed that was scriptural. In the case of the newspaper ad which I have just presented, the money was gathered from the churches here and was sent to the church in charge of the newspaper ad. Will somebody please explain to me where the difference is in this and that which I am defending? In the case of the radio program, the money was sent to the church in charge and it was spent.

Now I want to read to you exactly a matter along that line that you may see the churches that participated. Here is a statement that I have from 1939 through 1943: "Several churches of Christ of Greater Birmingham cooperated in preaching the gospel over the radio. At times the radio station would be changed, but each years the plan was identically the same. The West End church would be responsible for the program, making the contact with the company, be responsible to the company, pay the bills, and the cooperating congregations would participate by sending their checks to the West End Church treasury, who would pay the bill in one check drawn on West End Church. Some of the congregations now objecting to the Herald of Truth Broadcast participated in this plan, patterned exactly after the Herald of Truth plan, showing that they are the ones who left the former ground of churches of Christ in this area." Here is a list of the churches participating, the years in which they did:

1939: Ensley, North Birmingham, Tarrant, Woodlawn, West End. 1940: Ensley, North Birmingham, Tarrant, Woodlawn, Bessemer, Sandusky, Gardendale, Park View, Fultondale, Brookside, West End. 1941: Ensley, Bessemer, Woodlawn, Gardendale, West End. 1942: Ensley, Woodlawn, Central, West End. 1943: Ensley, Gardendale, now Mount Olive, Fairview, Central, Woodlawn, West End. That evidently was the Lord's plan back then. When did it cease to be the Lord's plan? Was it a missionary society in embryo? Was it a centralized church agency exercising dominion over the churches in Birmingham and destroying the autonomy of these local congregations? Was it? Ah, it will take a lot more than merely getting up here and saying that some of you folks are now in digression that are teaching this, and back in those days all of us taught that, and all of us practiced that.

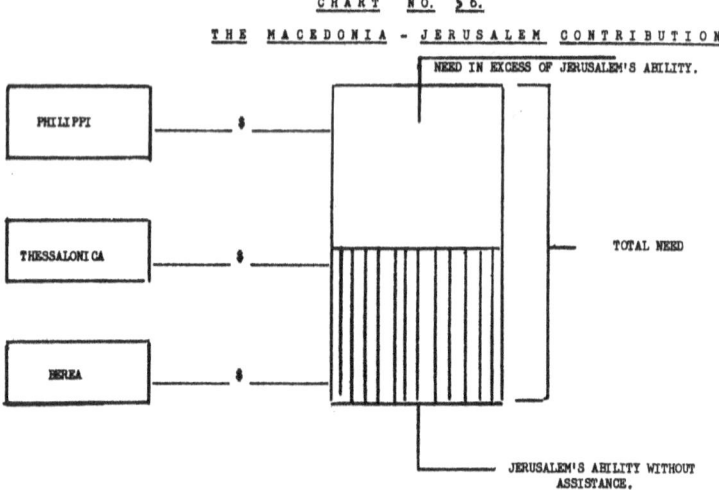

CHART NO. 56.
THE MACEDONIA - JERUSALEM CONTRIBUTION.

SAME PRINCIPLE IN HERALD OF TRUTH

Now then next, let us have chart No. 56. I'm going to show you now that what the brethren were doing back then is exactly what was done back in the apostolic age; and hence, it's scriptural. Watch here: This is the great contribution set out in 2 Corinthians 8 and 9. The Churches of Macedonia, Phillippi, Thessalonica and Berea, just these for example now, they sent to Jerusalem. Here, if you please, was Jerusalem's ability without assistance. And here is the amount contributed in excess of her ability and the total amount constituted the work that was done. Now here we have money that was sent from these churches to, so says brother Cogdill, to the Jerusalem Church. Now I ask you, is there something in here between these churches and that? Now was there a benevolent society or was there an evangelistic society? Did this church here take over the control of the churches? Was there a centralized agency? Either there was or there wasn't. If there was, then the centralized agency couldn't be too wrong if the

Jerusalem church practiced it. If this is not a centralized control there, then there is no such thing as that in the

CHART NO. 41
INTRODUCING GOD'S PROPHETIC WORD

During the winter of 1944 and 1945 the Adventists had carried on a campaign in the city of Houston as they had elsewhere, taking advantage of the war situation to arouse interest in their speculative and false doctrines concerning the Second Coming of Christ. They had conducted two or three services weekly in the Music Hall and had carried on an extensive advertising campaign in connection with these services and had attracted quite a lot of attention as a result. The Norhill Church of Christ in Houston thought it proper and wise to follow up this campaign of false teaching with a campaign to preach the gospel on these Bible themes free from speculation and deception. Originally the meeting was arranged with the idea of holding it in the Norhill building but the reception given the idea of such a meeting soon indicated far too great an interest for any one church auditorium in Houston to accommodate the crowds that would want to attend. It was decided, accordingly, to arrange to hold the meeting down in town and invite the cooperation of all the congregations of the Church of Christ in the city.

In order that the meeting might be carried out on a scriptural basis and without provoking criticism, the Norhill Church decided to sponsor the meeting, guaranteeing all expenses incurred, and simply extend an invitation to the other Churches of Christ to have whatever part in the meeting, financially and otherwise, they wanted to have. With this arrangement in mind the Music Hall was contracted for and the preacher and singer engaged for the time decided upon. When the invitation went forth to the other congregations of the city to cooperate in whatever way they could, the response was almost unanimous and was so hearty that the success of the meeting, the first of the kind ever undertaken in the city of Houston, was guaranteed from the beginning.

Brother Jack Meyer and the Heights Church were asked to plan and supervise the advertising of the meeting and that they did their work in fine fashion was amply evidenced by the widespread interest and attendance provoked. Brother F. F. Conley and the Milby Church supervised the ushering at all of the services and received splendid cooperation from the other churches of the city in that work and the large audiences were handled in a fine way. Brother Frank Smith and the church at Pierce and Baldwin had charge of the entertainment of visitors from out of the city and homes were provided for all while attending the meeting. Never has an effort of this magnitude been carried to completion with any better cooperation, finer spirit of unity, or less friction than this one. That was an outstanding feature of the meeting. Twenty churches worked together as one throughout the effort and the Chruches of Christ in Houston demonstrated the practical side of Christian unity and above all sufficiency of the Lord's church in the accomplishment of His work without the interference of human organizations. All of the funds were handled through the treasury of the Norhill church and all the bills incurred paid out of that treasury with a complete report furnished each congregation assisting. That this arrangement worked to the satisfaction of all is attested by the fact that in a city wide gathering of brethren after the meeting was over, the unanimous request of the churches cooperating in the first meeting was that Norhill congregation take the lead in the second meeting to be held the ensuing year.

Herald of Truth. Ladies and gentlemen, that's exactly the same. Don't let people deceive you on it. Exactly the same in principle.

All right, further, let me have now chart No. 41. Chart No. 41. Now this, friends, is the introduction to the book, *God's Prophetic Word*, which brother Cogdill, in which he endorsed the Music Hall Meeting. Let's have the next one, please. The actual chart on the Music Hall Meeting. Now here we are friends. He said, "Twenty churches worked together as one throughout the effort. And the churches of Christ in Houston demonstrated the practical side of Christian unity and, above all, the sufficiency of the Lord's church in the accomplishment of his work without the interference of human organizations. All the funds were handled through the treasury of the Norhill Church and all bills incurred paid out of that treasury with a complete report furnished each congregation assisting in the meeting." Why, you couldn't describe the Herald of Truth better than that. Let's have another one. The next one, now. No, I beg your pardon. Yes, that's it now.

Now then, brother Cogdill tells that that's no longer right. He has repudiated that; and that today he rejects the idea of the Music Hall Meeting, and he would lead you to think that his repudiation of it has been some time in the past. Now, brother Cogdill, we want simply to arrive at the truth with reference to this matter, and I'm going to prove to this audience that the date of your repudiation of that meeting was last night. Now you watch me and see if I don't do it. And I insist that there be some reply to it.

He hadn't rejected it in 1945 because that's when the meeting was held. He hadn't rejected it in 1950 because I have the bound volumes of the Gospel Guardian over here in which he argued with brother Wright and in which he maintained it was on a scriptural basis. It wasn't in 1951 because brother Tant in that year quoted Cogdill in the Gospel Guardian as having endorsed the Music Hall Meeting. Bear in mind that that was some six years after the meeting was held. He hadn't repudiated it then. He hadn't repudiated it in 1954 because that's the time when he made the statement that he wouldn't practice it any more, but he

CHART NO. 46
MUSIC HALL MEETING

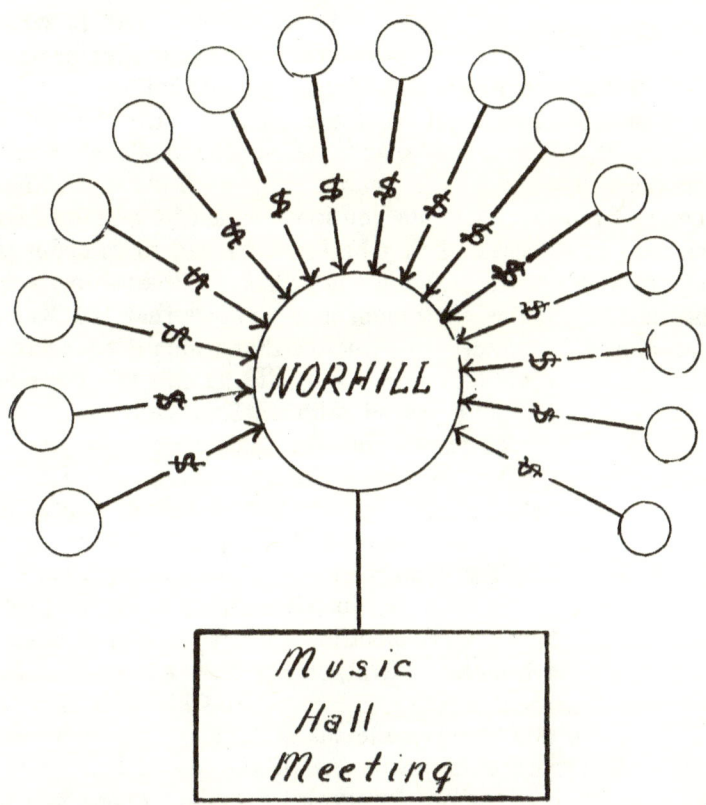

could still see a difference between it and that which he opposes in the Herald of Truth. He hadn't repudiated it in the Abilene Debate. And I'm going to show you that I'm not misinterpreting his statement. If I am, then his closest buddy likewise doesn't understand it, because here is what brother Tant said about it in 1955:

After quoting the statement which brother Cogdill made in 1954, on page 76, and I am quoting, "Brother Harper, Brother Cogdill for the sake of unity was perfectly willing to surrender that which he thought was right." Listen further: "Are you willing for the sake of unity to surrender an arrangement that you think is right, yet which is almost certain eventually to divide the church of our Lord?" Now what does he say here? He says brother Cogdill still thought it was right, that is when brother Tant made this statement, he thought that brother Cogdill then thought it was right. He was willing to forego it on the ground of expediency, but he still thought it was right. When was that? When the Abilene Debate was held. He believed it was right up until last night, November 21, 1957. And do you know when he quit it? On the very first occasion that he knew he had to in order to stay in this debate. That's the reason. Because anybody that has any logical judgment at all knows that the Music Hall Meeting is exactly in principle that which is characteristic of the Herald of Truth. Why did he quit it? Because he was running like a scared rabbit. That's all.

There's some of them, though, that don't run. Let's have now chart No. 48, chart No. 50. (laughter) I have an interesting statement here friends, that I want to read to you. Give brother Cogdill that chart, please. Now, here if you please, is the Music Hall M e e t i n g represented. Brother Foy E. Wallace, Jr., justifies and accepts the principle of the Music Hall Meeting. I have a signed statement here and I quote: "Brother Foy E. Wallace, Jr., in a lecture program at Tenth and Francis in Oklahoma City in 1957 (that's this year) made the statement that he would not let the brethren run him off of the Music Hall Meeting, and that he would engage in a similar arrangement again if the brethren selected him as their speaker." Harvey Pearson, Alstone L. Tobor. S i g n e d by these two brethren. And I was present in a group last night when one of the elders of the Tenth and Francis congregation stated that it was his impression that that's exactly what brother Wallace's feeling is regarding this matter. Now where is brother Cogdill? Here he is. He's pushed back

SPONSORING CONGREGATIONS   265

CHART NO. 50

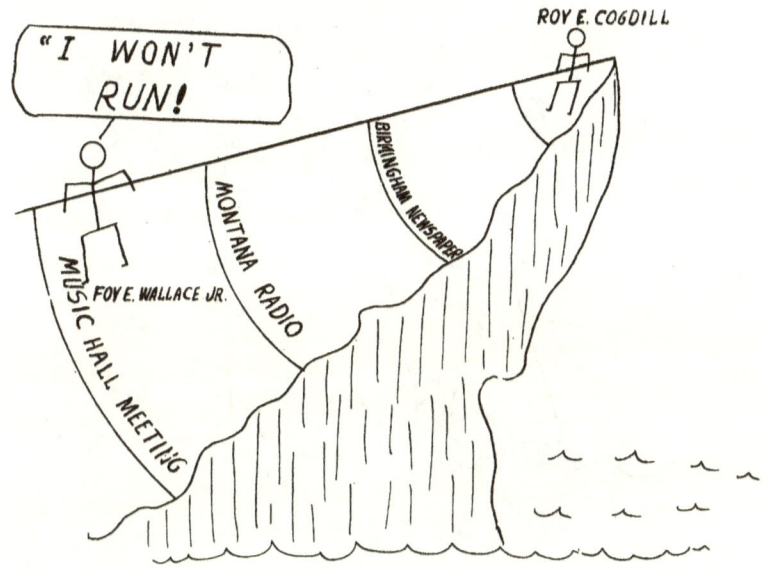

from the Music Hall Meeting, and from the Montana radio program, and from the Birmingham newspaper ad. He's standing over here now. Brother Wallace says, "He won't run me away from it." Yet brother Cogdill took for tall timber the very first time that he was faced with it. There is the situation, friends.

Let's look further. How much time now? Look at chart No. 48. Let's look at what extremes of antism to which these brethren have gone. Here is the Herald of Truth. Watch right here please; here is the Music Hall Meeting. Brother Foy Wallace says, "That's as far as you're going to push me." Well, let this represent the battle lines right here, please. Here is brother Wallace standing over here saying, "You're not going to run me into antism. I've gone as far as I'm going." Here's brother Tant over here says, "I'll make my stand on the Montana Radio cooperation program." But here is brother Cecil Douthitt and John T. Lewis. They are backed up behind that, and they say, "We'll take our stand here." Now understand neither one

CHART NO. 50A
TO WHAT EXTREME OF ANTI-ISM?

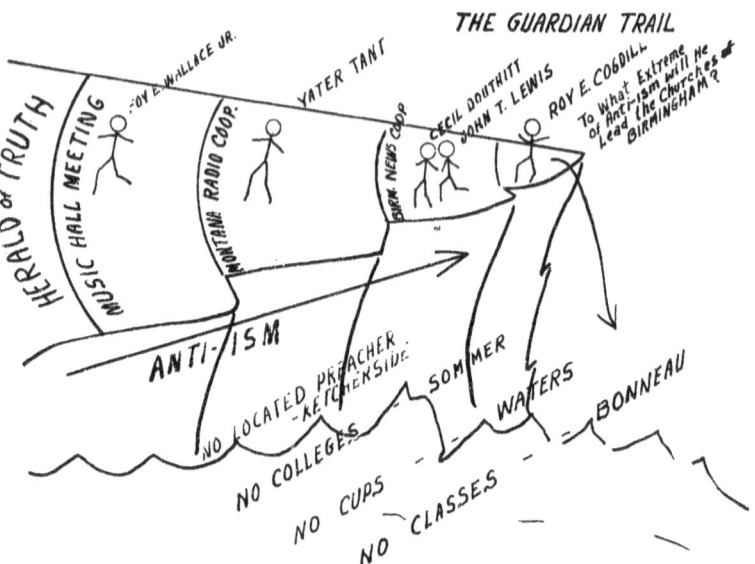

of them have repudiated this. Therefore, I know that that's their position right now, but brother Cogdill; he repudiated this; he's backed off behind that line; he's back off from here. Here he is now. Now then, where will he stop? Where will he stop? And where will you stop, friends? Ensley, North Birmingham, these other congregations, where are you going to stop? You have followed him to this point right here. Are you going on? You might as well, because the same principle that caused you to repudiate those will cause you to repudiate this.

In fact, he made a speech last night that is a carbon copy of what Carl Ketcherside makes all over this country with reference to these matters. Where is he going to stop? Are you going to let these men lead you into complete extreme anti-ism? There must be a stopping place somewhere. A few years ago you were back over on this line here conducting a program smilar to this. Now then, why have you changed? What is it that's led you to this? I tell you, ladies and gentlemen, this is the picture that's characteristic of them, and I make this prophecy: that it will not stop where it is today. You wait and see. The same considerations that prompted the repudiation of this will lead finally to the role of complete anti-ism and extreme radicalism.

I can't believe that the hundreds of good people in Birmingham are willing to follow men who will lead you in such devious courses as to repudiate such. Brother Cogdill has made a plea in this discussion for unity and harmony and I would like to see it. But I raise this question: Churches are now divided over cooperative radio programs and over benevolent work. Do you know when they started dividing? They didn't start back yonder in 1939. You know when they started? They started when these men moved away from their position back then. That's when they started. Are you to continue to follow them along that line? That, friends, is a question you must decide.

Now listen, there is a break in fellowship. And it will continue to become more and more so. If you think there is not, listen to this statement in the Gospel Guardian. In 1957, Bob Crawley, who gives as his address 1604 43rd Street, Birmingham, Alabama, says here, "The contribution is running regularly from $350 to $400 weekly. We have promised support to Quentin McKay to stay in Huntsville and try to reclaim what the digressives have taken away. There is very little question hereabouts regarding fellowship with the institutional crowd. The lines are already drawn and we would not do right to ignore them. Bit by bit all contact with them is being broken." Do you hear what he is saying? Because we're practicing exactly the same things that Ensley, North Birmingham, West End, and these other congregations practiced in this cooperative radio program, they are now telling us that our maintaining such a position that they are drawing the lines on us and that the fellowship is being slowly broken. I ask you, where are you going to stop, friends? Where are you going to stop?

Let us look further. Let us have now chart No. 51A. Here, if you please, is the Corinth radio program. Brother Cogdill maintains that this is not parallel to the Herald of

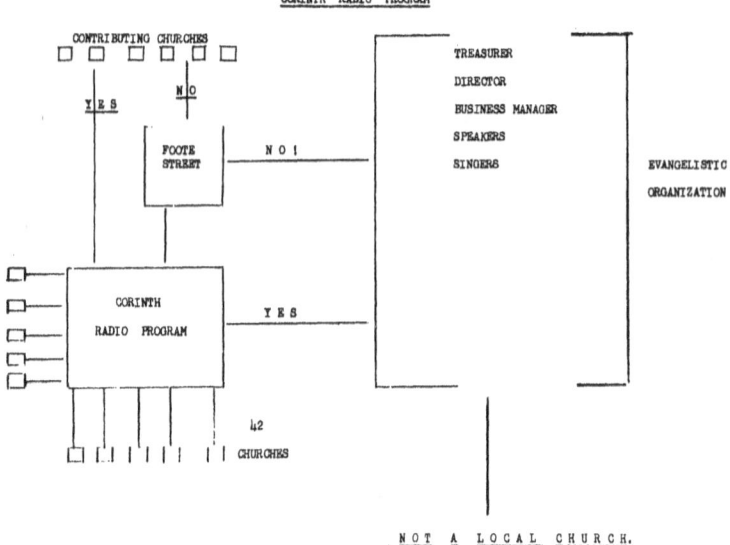

Truth radio program simply because he says the money is not sent to the Corinth radio program. We find that the brethren charged that the practice that is practiced in preaching on that program is identical with the Herald of Truth program; but he said, "No, the money is not sent to the Foote Street Congregation—allegedly the church conducting that program—but it is sent rather to a treasurer who, in turn, pays for the radio program." Now then, there are 42 churches as I understand it that are contributing to that. Now, I don't know how many people are involved in it but it has a treasurer, director, business manager, and probably more; besides that the speakers and singers. Now what is this, friends? It's not a local church. It's an evangelistic organization. Here's what happens: when men move away from the truth, it drives them to set up that which they cannot sustain, because let him describe the difference between this and a missionary society. What is the difference? In order to avoid the practice of many churches contributing under their local eldership, do you know what he's doing? He's setting up an evangelistic organization which is not the church. Oh, they say this is scriptural here because it's sent to the treasurer, and not put under the elders of the Foote Street Church. I ask brother Cogdill this question, and you watch now and see if he answers it: Suppose that instead of the money here being sent to the elders at Highland, it was sent to brother Harper, the preacher there, and that brother Harper handled all the funds just as the elders there are handling them—would you accept it, brother cogdill? Now, friends, you watch and see if he answers that. He accepts it here. Suppose that instead of being the Corinth Radio Program, it was the Herald of Truth with brother Harper as the preacher. I'll just make this prediction, that he'll never answer that.

Now, friends, a few things that he said on last evening that necessitates a brief reply, since I have had no opportunity to reply. In the first place, he cites brother Srygley as allegedly being opposed to that which I am defending. Brother Srygley sat on the platform and had a part in arranging the Hardeman Tabernacle meetings in Nashville, Tennessee, which these men now say are unscriptural. And so he can't cite brother Srygley and he misrepresents brother Srygley's statement in the Advocate, anyway. He said further with reference to how the scriptures establish things, he said there are two ways to prove a thing. He said one of them is by statute, and he said the other was by teaching and example. Where's your necessary inference? See, he's scared off of that too. Where is your necessary inference? Only two ways you said last night. You know why he has to eliminate the inference? Because you've got to have an inference where you have no pattern. Now he's down to two ways; two ways. One of them is statute and one teaching and example.

Well, he said Highland is not in need and that, therefore, it is not parallel to that which was characteristic of the church in Jerusalm. He needs to get together with brother Tant. Brother Tants says they are on the verge of bankruptcy. Now which one of them is telling us the truth about it? One of them says they are in need, the other says they are on the verge of bankruptcy. There's not a word of truth in that, and I'm prepared to prove it.

Then he says with reference to brother Harper that brother Harper is in a position contrary to what I hold. That, too, friends, is a misrepresentation. I subscribe exactly to the same view that brother Harper has. Brother Harper means by the work of that congregation, the operation of the program, the conduct of that program. That's exactly what he means by it, that's exactly what I mean by it. Brother Harper in the illustration of the dollar says, "Here is a dollar. You take it and go and buy gasoline with it." He designated the purpose for which the money was to be spent. That's exactly what's done at Highland. There is no loss of autonomy. The churches themselves determine how much they'll send, how long they'll send, when they'll stop, and the elders at Highland have no control over that whatsover. It's simply a figment of the imagination. It's objecting to other matters what he practices.

Now he reads from me in 1946 and misrepresents me completely. In that statement, I was discussing which organization ought to raise the funds for the New Testament church and I reasoned like this: That the churches of Christ are the only organizations that ought to raise the funds. And in that particular passage or place I had reference and made reference to Paul's example and mentioned that in that instance the money was sent to Paul. My point was this: that in that case there is a clear illustration that no other organization save the New Testament church was involved. Of course, I believe tonight that it's correct and proper to send money to preachers from the churches. That wasn't the point under consideration. I do not know why these brethren misrepresent me.

Further, he cites, in his antagonism towards the Gospel Advocate, he shouts out a wild intemperate statement about it that has nothing whatsover to do—If you want to talk about misrepresentation let me tell you this: For the last three or four years I have been one of the chief targets of the Gospel Guardian writers; and I can tell you truly that in no single instance that I can recall have they ever correctly represented me. In not one single instance have they done it. They always misrepresent me, by taking statements out of their context, or by making statements with reference to me which are not so. To give you an example, on two occasions their writers have published a statement that I was promoting hospitals for the churches of Christ; when I never at any time or place, under any circumstance, publicly or privately, orally or in writing, or otherwise, urged, suggested, encouraged the building of any kind of a hospital—public, private, or otherwise. I wrote to one of the writers of one of those articles demanding a correction and I received no reply to my letter. That's the kind of man that talks to you about the misrepresentations.

Now further, he says here that the Herald of Truth is not accomplishing what it ought to do because he said he could establish more than they are doing with what they do it with. I showed you that they preach to from seven to ten million people every Lord's Day and at approximate cost of one cent per person for thirty minutes. He comes up and says he could do more than that. Brother Cogdill, I like the way they are doing it better than the way you are not doing it, sir. I do, indeed. Get busy and show us. I think if you'll get busy and show us that you'll reach that many people every Lord's Day we'll quit the Herald of Truth and take up your method provided it's a scriptural one. But until you've started, don't claim that.

He says he doesn't know of much good. He doesn't know of much good. Suppose that man is charged with murder. He denies it and brings into the court four men who testify that they didn't see anybody kill anybody else. What would you think of that kind of testimony?

I thank you.

Cogdill's Third Negative

Gentlemen Moderators, Brother Woods, Ladies and Gentlemen:

By the grace of God we are permitted again to assemble on this occasion for a continuation of the study of the proposition that we discussed last night in the light again of what the Bible teaches. That is, that's what we're supposed to be discussing.

Brother Woods has introduced a lot of scripture in the last speech, hasn't he? Did you count the passages. Did you actually make a check? Did you watch him to see what kind of evidence he's trying to present his case and prove his proposition? Now he's complained a lot in his last speech about things that have been introduced in this debate on this proposition. He's the one that took the course. I've followed him simply where he's gone. That's all. He complains about where I've been travelling and it's because I've been walking in his footsteps. He's the one that introduced the Gospel Guardian into this discussion. And you know when you bring things of that kind in, and when you bring these things that men have done and what they have practiced and their inconsistency and things of that sort, I wonder if he thinks, I wonder if he thinks that there isn't any right to make any reply to that sort of a thing. I sat and thought while he was talking about a law-suit on record over in Henderson, Texas; it's a matter of court record over there where a man was injured and suing on the ground of personal injury, and of course, the insurance company was defending. Mr. White, a very capable, fine lawyer in Dallas was the attorney for the plaintiffs. He, of course, had the last speech to the jury. The attorney for the insurance company was very much concerned about what Mr. White was going to say in that last speech. And he warned the jury against his eloquence. He said that by his eloquence he will try to get you to disregard every bit of the evidence that has been presented in this case, and decide it purely upon the basis of emotion. And he said I don't want you to let him do that; that he is a very eloquent man. He'll soar like an eagle among the stars.

Well, when Mr. White came up to make that last speech he referred to that incident, and he said, "Gentlemen of the jury, my plaintiff's case would certainly be worthy of the very best representation that I could give it. If I were as eloquent as the attorney for the defendent thinks I am, I would use all of the eloquence that he attributes to me because I believe that the plaintiff's cause is just and would certainly justify the use of it. And if I could soar like an eagle among the stars, that's exactly what I would do. But there's one thing I wouldn't do. I wouldn't swoop like a buzzard to pluck the entrails out of an injured man." When he made that kind of a reference, the attorney for the insurance company immediately jumped to his feet and objected—very strenuously objected. And when he objected the old judge pulled his glasses off and looked down at the two lawyers and he said, "Gentlemen, who is that brought the birds into the court house anyway?" (laughter)

Now, brother Woods, if you don't like the things that were brought up in the discussion last night, just remember that you're the one that brought the birds into the court house. If you hadn't tried to establish your case by what Roy Cogdill has done, or by what Roy Cogdill has repudiated, or by what somebody else has done that's inconsistent with what they're doing now, you wouldn't have had any time to use. You couldn't have used fifteen minutes on the Bible that you've produced in all of the speeches that you've made.

Now where is the example? Where is the New Testament pattern for what he is preaching, and for what he is trying to defend? Where has he gone in the word of God? Where did he go to find many churches contributing to one church to help that one church under its eldership or through a board to do a good work, promote a big work? Why, that's what he's trying to justify. One congregation under its eldership drecting a brotherhood project. A radio program, not only national but international, to preach the gospel of Jesus Christ, not only in the mission field but all over the country where the churches are, to preach it not only out yonder for the heathen and to the people who haven't heard it, but to preach it even for the churches and for the brethren. All over the Southland w h e r e the churches of Christ are planted and where they are doing a good job of preaching the gospel themselves. Even locally, taking the money from the congregations all over this country in order to bring the gospel right back into their own community for them, because they are more capable of managing the affair than any other eldership? Because God has put upon them the responsibility for doing it? Because in the Bible there is a pattern of any congregation anywhere promoting a work that it is not able to sustain and sending it's representatives out with all kinds of high-powered promotional methods to get their fingers and their hands into the treasuries of all the churches? They are reaching everyone that they can.

If the Highland elders could have their way, and all of you that know anything about it, the kind of propoganda program that they're putting on, and the determined effort that they make to get into the churches all over this country, whether they're wanted or not, and there are many instances of that. There are brethren in this audience by the dozens that could testify to it, insisting upon an appointment to present their view of the matter, and insist upon congregations contributing to them.

Now, brother Woods, what you need to do is get a little Bible in this discussion. Go to the word of God to prove that it's scriptural. Find something like that in the New Testament. And you've made a miserable failure of finding it, and nobody knows that any better than you do.

He talks about witnesses in the court room in a murder case that didn't see the man commit the crime. Well, that's exactly the kind of testimony you've offered. That's exactly the kind of testimony you've offered. You've produced no Bible evidence to sustain a Bible proposition. Where is his pattern? You know the only one he's offered? Acts 11. He introduced it. He's the one that introduced it on his chart. And he's terribly disappointed because I don't show you all of those ridiculous pictures that he has up there again. He wants to look at them again himself. He thinks, evidently, they are very instructive and very pretty and it would take you thirty minutes to figure out what on earth that thing represented if you didn't have him to tell you what it was about. And how many passages of scripture on the most of them? Why, the only thing on earth they do is make his point the more ridiculous. Where in any one of them was there any Bible proof or Bible example of anything that begins to look like what they're doing in the Herald of Truth? I said last night, and I proved it, that it's a matter of centralized agency. It wouldn't make a bit of difference in the world whether it was a congregation or whether it was a board. Brother Woods would be under obligation to accept it either way it went.

You know on one of his charts he brought out a parallel, a parallel between the matter of benevolence and the matter of evangelism; spiritual needs and physical needs. It's chart No. 39. "Now," he said, "Cogdill's not paying any attention to my charts." I've answered every chart and referred specifically and dealt with every chart that he's introduced in the affirmative. I wasn't under any obligation to do it when I was in the affirmative, and he tried to lead me off from my affirmation. I didn't do it then because I wasn't under any obligation to do it. But in the negative I've referred to every chart specifically that he's mentioned, and he knows that's so. If I haven't now, if I've overlooked one unintentionally, drag it out and I'll deal with it. I'll deal with it. But in order to answer it, have I got to put it back here on this thing? Have I got to put it back up here? Now you can look at it if you want to. I don't object to brother Deaver finding them and showing them if he wants to. That's his part of the business.

But let me show you something. He says these two are parallel. Brother Woods, this doesn't represent your position. What you need in here is a home, not the elders of the church. You don't believe that the physical needs can be taken care of by the elders of the church. And you denied it for three nights and this audience knows that you did. (laughter) Why, of course, you did. You put it under a board and said it wasn't the business of the church to take care of physical need. Now get up here and deny

CHART NO. 39.

ACTS 11: 27-30.

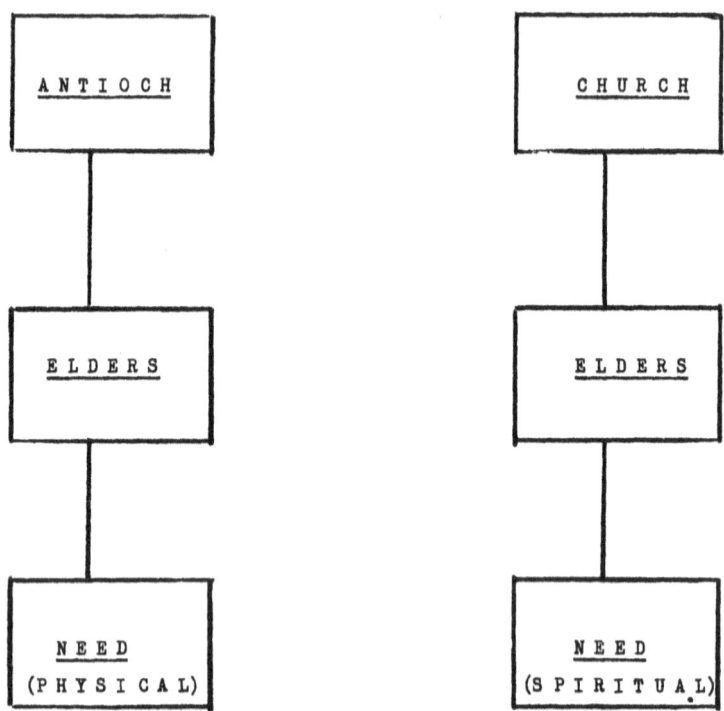

that and everybody in this crowd will know that you've given up your first proposition, your first position. Would you agree to the same thing over here that you've got over here, in what you teach and what you practice? Would you put the work under a board of directors and incorporate it? In spiritual needs? If you won't Guy, then your chart isn't worth anything because your parallel fails. You don't have any parallel there at all between those two matters. Why, certainly not. He said that brother Cogdill doesn't believe, he doesn't believe that scriptural needs are as great as physical needs. Well, now, that's a misrepresentation, and you take his misrepresentations away from him, even in quoting me, in the speeches that he makes, not one time out of every twenty-five does he correctly represent what I say about anything. And those of you that have been listening know that that's so. You know that that's exactly the case.

When you turn to the pattern that he offered to us in Acts, Chapter 11, we find the proposition that was given over here concerning the relief of needy saints among the brethren in the churches of Judea. He admits that it was sending to churches, but he admits also that it was sent to the elders of the church in matters of benevolence there. That it was sent to elders of the church. Then he wants to take the elders of the church in that case and prove Highland receiving money from many congregations to evangelize. He's mixed up in his pattern. That's the whole point about it.

Why, I read to you and he says I misrepresented it. Well, I didn't; I read it exactly like it was. And exactly like it is. I dare you to take the book and find a single word in it that is misread. Where ought to go when the gospel is preached? I'm letting Guy Woods speak for himself. Guy, if this is a misrepresentation, you misrepresented yourself. I'm not representing you; I'm reading what you said. Let me read it again. "Here, too, we see the simple manner in which the church in Philippi joined with Paul"—And get me my chart, brother Adams, while I'm reading this, on the Philippian Church. Just under that one, I think— "We see the simple manner in which the church in Philippi joined with Paul in the work of preaching the gospel. There was no missionary society in evidence. None was needed." Well, why wasn't the Missionary Society needed now? Of course, he was talking about the Missionary Society. But why didn't they need one? Well, you listen. "None was needed. The brethren simply raised the money and sent it directly to Paul." Directly to Paul. And what else did he say? "When men become dissatisfied—this is the way it should be done today. No organization is needed to accomplish the work the Lord has authorized the church to do. When men become dissatisfied with God's arrangement and set up one of their own, they have already crossed the threshold to apostasy." Guy, you've stepped through that door, just as sure as you live. Why? Because churches in the New Testament, when they supported the gospel, sent it directly to the preacher. That is the exact way that God limited that matter. To keep one church from becoming a centralized agency through which many churches operate.

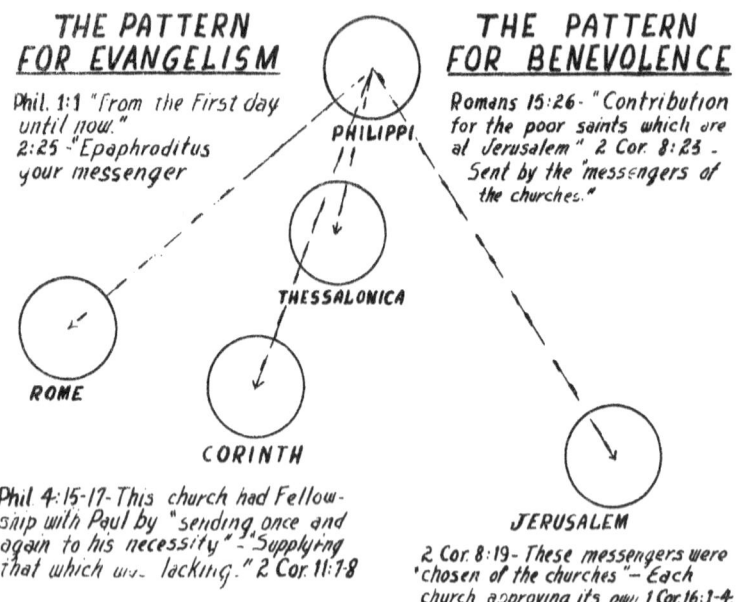

Why, here you have the pattern of benevolence. Rom. 15:26, a contribution for the poor saints at Jerusalem. 2 Corinthians 8. It was s e n t by the messengers of the churches. Those messengers were chosen of the churches. Each church furnished its own. I Corinthians 16:1-4, Paul said, "Him therefore whom ye approve by your letters him will I send . . ." Who selected the messengers of the Corinthian Church? They did. What was his purpose? To send their money, their contribution to Jerusalem, that he might become their agent. That's the way it was done in matters of benevolence. How did they get the money? Why, by their contributions on the first day of the week.

SPONSORING CONGREGATIONS

Then it was sent by their messengers directly to the church in need—*to the church in need*. Not for the church to do a work somewhere else, but for that church to care for its own needy members. That's the way it was done in New Testament days. But how did they support the gospel in New Testament days? Why, they sent contributions. Paul said, "From the first day until now ye have had fellowship with me in the furthering of the gospel." In Phil. 2:25, "Ye sent Epaphroditus as your messenger." In Phil. 4:15-17, he said the church had fellowship by sending once and again to his necessities, supplying that which was lacking. They were one among *churches*, plural, 2 Cor. 11:7-8, who supported him while he was preaching at Corinth. But how did they support him? They sent directly to the preacher. They sent to him in Thessalonica and supplied his wants. They sent to him in Corinth and supplied that which he lacked. They sent to him even when he was in prison in Rome.

Now, brethren, listen to me. That, I know, is right. That, you know, is right. Is Guy Woods going to get up here and tell us it's wrong to do it that way? Is he? There's New Testament example for that. What more do you need to prove to you that it's right to do it that way? Now if he wants to ridicule a congregation sending money to preach the gospel directly to the preacher, just let him say all about it he pleases. It's still a New Testament example. What I want him to find and what he's under obligation to find is where a church ever sent money in the New Testament to preach the gospel that it didn't send it to the preacher. Now find it, Guy. You tried last night and you failed. You went to Acts 15 and tried to make a matter of divine revelation, in Acts 15, where the apostles had made a decision; where that decision was reduced to writing by James, the Apostle; sent out to all the churches. That as the decree of the apostles and elders it might be observed and the will of God might be done. The first part of the New Testament ever reduced to writing and he tried to make that parallel to that matter of supporting the gospel, and to the matter of doing benevolence today. But he missed the point in it, and misrepresented the passage and wrested it entirely. He hasn't found any thing that begins to look like a congregation sending to another congregation to help it preach the gospel anywhere. They sent preachers. They supported the preacher. They sent direct to the preacher in his support. Where is the New Testament example? Where, oh, where? Why, instead of drawing some of those ludicrous, ridiculous illustrations up there that it would take a man thirty minutes to figure out heads from tails about it unless you pointed it out to him, and then he didn't make it too clear? Why didn't you jut put a simple passage on it, Guy? Just give us a simple passage, showing where a congregation ever sent money out of its treasury—that's what you're affirming—where a congregation ever sent money out of its treasury to any church to help that church preach the gospel. Now you find it, and I'll just admit defeat and quit and go home. You find the passage. If you think I won't accept the word of God, you're just wrong. You don't know me. If it's in there, I haven't found it Morever, I want you to find the congregation that sent a contribution out of its treasury to a church even for benevolence or for any other reason, *when that church was not in need.* Find it for us. And if you'll find that, I'll accept that. This audience out here will give it a lot more consideration if you'll just put the passage of scripture up here on the machine, and on the board, just what God's word says about it, rather than some of your illustrations.

There's another matter I want to deal with, lest I forget it. You know, you talk about misrepresenting. And you talk about dealing unfairly with a man. He's done that in one of the most marked ways I've ever seen. Last night he referred, and I didn't think too respectfully, to Brother John T. Lewis. I have no defense of John T. Lewis. He's a man who has been eminently able all of his life to defend himself. Last Lord's day, he began his 51st year right here in the city of Birmingham; the father of the cause of Christ, in this section. Came down here when they were meeting in a little rented hall and has been here laboring through the years. And you people know him and you know what he stands for. John T. Lewis wrote a book a number of years ago, *The Voice of the Pioneers, on Instrumental Music and Societies*. It was written and published back in 1932, copyrighted by the Gospel Advocate Company. Guy Woods, last night, put a chart—and if you can find it, Brother Deaver, put it up there. I don't object to him looking at it, but I don't have time for you to hunt for it. Guy Woods put a chart up here and he quoted from John T. Lewis' book. The first time he gave a specific reference here on page seven. Well, he didn't give all the quotation on page seven. Let's read it. "President Loos frequently spoke, in his pamphlet, of the part that Carroll Kendrick took in the convention, without stating the fact that Mr. Kendrick afterwards quit the society and went back to the Lord's plan of doing missionary work." Now then, here's the part he left out. What is the Lord's plan? "To the intent that now unto the principalities and powers in the heavenly places might be made known through the church the manifold wisdom of God, according to the eternal purpose which he purposed in Christ Jesus Our Lord."

Now then, this part of the quotation, where did it come from? Is this out of that? Did John T. Lewis endorse this? Can you find this in John T. Lewis' book? No, that didn't come from John T. Lewis' book. John T. Lewis was talking there about Kendrick quitting the Missionary Society. That's what he was talking about in that quotation. And he takes that quotation concerning Kendrick's quitting the Missionary Society and tries to put brother Lewis in the position of endorsing every thing that Kendrick said. And he turns to 445 of Kendrick's book to get the quotation. Of all the unfair representations of a man that I've ever known in my life, Guy, that caps the climax. That caps the climax. Because John T. Lewis commended turning away from the Missionary Society to preach the gospel through the church, and the question of church or congregational operation had not even entered it, and I challenge you, sir, every inch of you, all over, up and down and throughout, to find where John T. Lewis ever introduced the use of the passage that you quote concerning Jerusalem distributing that benevolence among all the congregations. Find this endorsement of it, or get up here and apologize for misrepresenting a man that everybody who knows, loves and respects. I never have in my life, I'll tell you frankly, I haven't seen a man go to such desperate depths to try to destroy somebody's influence.

Why, the whole attitude of the institutional movement among the churches of Christ today is line up or get out. Line up or get the yellow tag of quarantine pinned on you. You either get in line and do what we want to do, and help us promote it, or you're an old anti, *anti*. Guy, are you anti anything? Are you? Are you anti anything? Are you anti-sin? Are you? Are you anti-missionary society? Is there anything you oppose? I begged him in the first proposition we discussed to tell us what kind of a benevolent organization the churches of Christ could build that would be unscriptural. He was as silent as the grave about it. I'm begging him now to tell us what kind of church cooperation would be unscriptural. How could congregations cooperate unscripturally without forming any organization except the church? Oh, he said that's all they have, that's all Highland is, and Roy Cogdill said in his book, *The New Testament Church*,—and I'm glad he reads my book—he said in his book, *The New Testament Church*, that it was always under an eldership. That's exactly right. The work of the church in every place was always under an eldership—that's God's order. That's exactly what God said about it. "Elders in every church." Well, he said that's all Highland is. That's all Highland is. They're just an eldership and a congregation. Yes, but they occupy a perverted position. Get me my chart on centralization again. They occupy a perverted position, and you're preaching a perverted gospel.

I'm not denying that the Highland organization so far as the congregation is concerned is scriptural. A church under an eldership is scriptural to be certain. Nobody is denying that. Nobody is disputing it. But they are functioning in an unscriptural manner. Why, you've made a brotherhood agency out of a congregation. You have taken the resources of a thousand churches and centralized the power and the control over them in the hands of one congregation. A thousand churches. Now, Guy, you want to know where

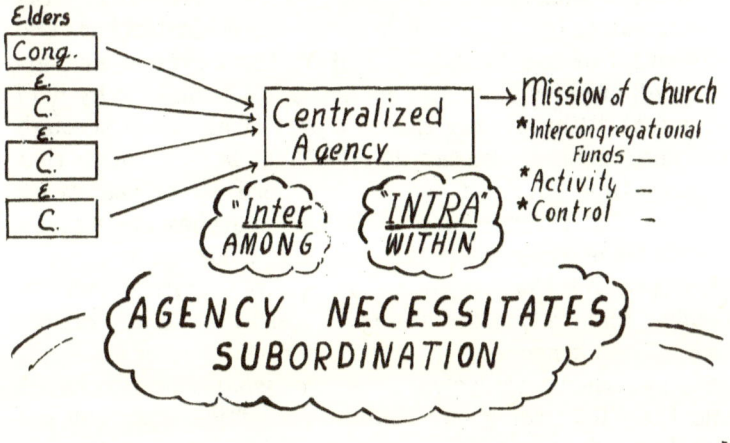

12.

to stop. He says where is this opposition going to stop? Well, what I want to know is, where is the promotion going to stop? Where are you going to stop? How many churches can do their radio preaching through Highland? If a thousand can, then ten thousand can. He says it isn't the size of the thing. Ten thousand can. Well, they say that's how many congregations we've got. Would you oppose every congregation of the Lord all over the world sending it's money to Highland to preach the gospel over the radio program? And if they can send their money, a part of it, they can send all of it, and they can send all of it for the gospel preaching over the radio, and then they can send all of it to Highland for the benevolent work and let them run an orphan home and old folks home for the whole brotherhood. Some of the elders, including one at Broadway in Lubbock, is trying to do that. They've really branched out. They've got them a school out there, and a brotherhood orphan home as well as a brotherhood missionary program, one eldership. Well, let's just concentrate in Highland or in Broadway. Both elderships are eminently capable, evidently, so let's just send all of our money to one congregation—either Broadway or Highland, or some of the rest of these sponsoring churches. Let them do not only all of our radio preaching but let them do all of our evangelistic or missionary work. Why not? Let them do all of our Bible school training for our teachers and publish all of our literature, and let them oversee and arrange all of our classes and oversee our schools? Why not? Why not? Why, if they can do a part of our work through that congregation, we can do all of our work through that congregation. And if we can do here all of our work through that congregation all of the churches everywhere can do all of their work through that congregation. And when you get that universal, centralized agency, you remember that he said the size of it doesn't make any difference. Then when you've done it, turn it all over to Highland, and then elect you a pope and what will you have? And there'll be somebody running for office when you get that far. There will be a man available campaigning for it. There always has been; there always will be.

Where is the stopping place? Guy, you raised a good question. I'm glad you suggested that. I'm glad you suggested it. He said the Gospel Guardian has always misrepresented him. Well, I'm not responsible for everything that goes in the Gospel Guardian. I knew nothing about the letter that you wrote to the fellow that said you were promoting a hospital. I don't know that you aren't. And if you aren't, I don't know why you aren't. Why would you oppose it? (laughter) Why would you? Get up here and tell this crowd why you're against the hospital. Now I want you to do it. You said the church can do these other matters through that kind of an arrangement. What would be wrong with a church of Christ hospital? And one brotherhood hospital? We've got a brotherhood Old Folks Home down in Houston. Why don't we start us a church of Christ hospital, and why don't we just get together and build us one big board to run all of our benevolent institutions? Why don't we do it? Put it all under one board, or if you want it, get you a board and put them under an eldership, and let that one eldership run the whole thing. There are organizations like that in the world and they do big things in a big way.

SPONSORING CONGREGATIONS

I can point out one to you—the biggest Protestant Orphanage in the entire country — an arrangement of that kind: The Christian's Children Fund. They are taking care of twenty-one thousand and they have in thirty-four different countries, orphanages. A Protestant Organization. What's wrong with it, Guy? Let's just get this thing on a sure enough big plan. You can blow that thing up until it really gets big. The things that are being done on that wouldn't be a drop in the bucket with what can be done. Put it all under one big board, or put it all under one eldership. Where is the stopping place?

You say, "Well, what's wrong with this?" It's an intercongregational affair. That's what's wrong with it. It crosses congregational lines and you are putting concentrated power and resources in the hands of one congregation, and they're keeping their propoganda mill grinding. They are sending out literature by the thousands of pieces Their printing bill runs up into the thousands of dollars. Could they do it alone? No, sir. But when you put thousands and thousands of dollars in the hands of one eldership, they can do it. They can really become a promotional agency; and they can keep some of their men constantly on the road, sticking their foot in the door of ever church that they possibly can force their way into, and reaching in with their hands into the treasury to get the thing under control. And there isn't any stopping place to it. You've already surrendered. You've crossed the threshold and you need to back up and turn around. That's what you need to do.

In addition to admitting that you've changed. Well, he said this is just a recent affair. "Why, brother Cogdill, he misrepresents us all. He misrepresents the Advocate and he misrepresents the opposition to this thing." I want to read you something that David Lipscomb said. He said, "I do not read Warlick's paper because he will not publish both sides of a question." He would not have made that statement, evidently, if he had not known what he was talking about. He went ahead and said, "I ceased to read his paper and we get along so peaceably. The Guide adopts the same plan"—talking about Daniel Sommer's paper—"The

Guide adopts the same plan. I treat both alike." Now listen: "I'm recognizing in all of these things the purest and best of motives to all—Warlick, Sommer, and all—and the effort to keep the church free from wrangles and fusses. We kindly tell them that in doing this they are violating the most sacred principles of fairness and right, approved by both God and man and must make themselves appear unfair and unjust to those so treated, I would like to see all of us get along pleasantly and harmoniously in obeying the commandments of God. But"—listen to it now, friends—"if the Gospel Advocate were to adopt this policy of criticizing others and refusing to let them reply, I would cease to read it." He couldn't read it now, could he? He couldn't read it now, because they don't believe in letting both sides of the question be presented. Oh, no. No, sir! We're just going to print what the editor believes to be the truth. I'm glad the editor of the Advocate doesn't determine the truth.

Is my time up?

Wood's Fourth Affirmative

Brethren Moderators, Brother Cogdill, Ladies and Gentlemen:

I'm now before you for the second affirmative of the evening and I'm exceedingly grateful for the fine interest that continues to characterize the debate. Glad to note brother Cogdill's enthusiasm and the very fact that he waxes warm evidences the pressure under which he is laboring in this debate.

Now he tells us here about a lawyer. He gave us a very interesting discussion of a lawyer and of a case to which he listened some time ago. When I reflect upon the manner in which he's been passing up my arguments, I was reminded also of a lawsuit that occurred in Kentucky many years ago before an ignorant Kentucky magistrate. When after the plaintiff had presented his evidence and the defendant got ready to start his, the magistrate said, "Hold on here; I don't want to hear any more. If I listen to any more it will confuse the court." So he doesn't want to listen to my side of it because it tends to confuse the court. But I insist that I'm still in the case and I must be answered.

Now he says, How many passages of scripture have I used? Well, I've read a number of passages. But if I didn't have but one, that would be enough. Just one would be sufficient. How many times does he think the Bible has to say a thing to be so? That was a pure appeal for prejudice, and anyone that's influenced by that type of reasoning wouldn't be likely to listen anyway. How many times does the Bible say that baptism is f-o-r the remission of sins? Only one time, and yet we think that's enough, don't we? And I have given you a clear, detailed case of church operation, and I've cited brother Cogdill's statement in endorsement of that, showing that he applied it both to benevolence and cooperation, in evangelism. And so, friends, it makes no difference whether there is one or one hundred passages, just so there is one passage that sustains it. I've introduced a good many, but one would have been enough.

He says for me to show a single example of where one church ever assisted another church at all in preaching. Now you get the full import of that, ladies and gentlemen. Evidently, his intention is to say that if I cannot produce an example of such, that therefore it's wrong. In which case it would be wrong for one church to send another church a New Testament. Now Roy Cogdill has taken the position of believing that it would be sinful for one church to send another church a New Testament. Now I ask him to clarify that. If he says, Oh, no, that's not correct, well all right, one church can cooperate with another in preaching the gospel. And so his implication that if there is no such example in the New Testament, therefore, that such would be wrong, then it would be wrong for one church to send tracts to another church.

Now brother Cogdill, you've dodged every question that I've asked you. Now that's one of them I want you to answer. I asked him the question plainly and clearly. Suppose the brethren out at Highland would simply place in the hands of brother Harper, the preacher, the reception of that money, and eliminate themselves from it, and let brother Harper handle the money, would he accept it? And do you know what he said about that? As silent as the grave. Why didn't he talk about it? He didn't know anything to say and hold on to his present position.

He talks about the activity of the Highland elders. If they are any more active in getting around over the country than these brethren are from the Guardian in trying to spread its teaching and its influence, then they are going some, I'll have to say. And I would like to call your attention to this fact please, that the shame and tragedy of church division, the heartaches and the sorrows that are characteristic of a once happy, united people, are to be found on the trail they themselves have already m a d e. Churches were not divided over these matters until these men began to preach these things. Back yonder when these brethren here in Birmingham were practicing these things, did someone write a statement in the paper and say the lines of fellowship are being drawn? Why, no. We were all together. Well, I'm still where I was back yonder. Who is it, friends, that gives the occasion for such? He brings it up.

Let me have chart No. 12. It's over here and how many scriptures are on that for a change? How many scriptures are on that, brother Cogdill? Yet here he says I haven't answered his argument. I introduced a chart on this proposition here. I called his attention to 2 Corinthians 8 and 9. Did you hear him mention 2 Corinthians 8 and 9 in the speech he just made?

I said if this is a centralized agency, then when the churches of Macedonia sent this money to Jerusalem it was centralized control, because it is just like this here because the money was spent by one congregation, but if it is not centralized control in the case of the Jerusalem and the Macedonian churches, then it's not when the same thing is done here. Now, friends, be honest with yourself. Don't be deceived and deluded about this. Just ask yourself a simple question. What is the difference between congregations of Texas, Oklahoma and Tennessee sending money to the elders of the Highland Church in carrying out an obligation that's common to them all, and the churches of Corinth,

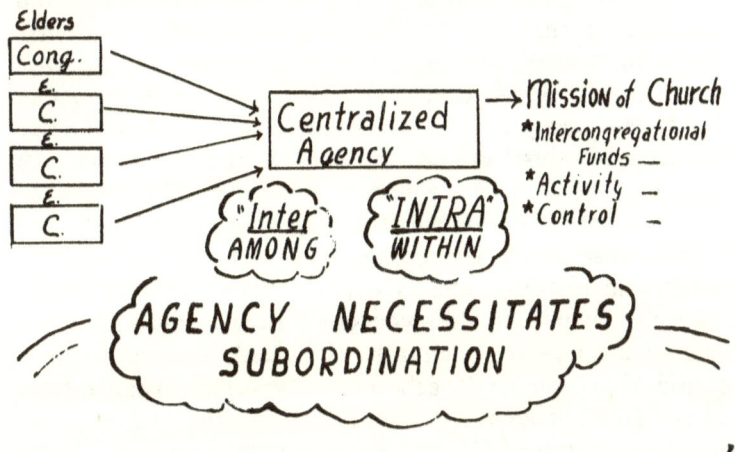

Achaia and Macedonia sending money to, he says, the elders at Jerusalem for the purpose of carrying out an obligation that they all sustain? Now you tell me what the difference is. One of them is centralized control. One of them is a sponsoring church arrangement. One of them is a missionary society and the other one is scriptural. Now where is the difference? There isn't any difference. Now the only way in which there could be anything wrong with this is for there to be another organization. The question is: Is there an organization out there at Highland that is unscriptural? The only organization they have is a New Testament Church. Why, all you have out there are the elders exercising authority over a preacher and a group of singers. They are exercising control over exactly the same thing that West End exercised control over when Ensley and North Birmingham is cooperating with them. Exactly the same.

Now let me have please, chart No. 39. My chart No. 39. Brother Cogdill is so confused that he thinks we're still on the orphan home question, but I'm glad to accommodate him in the matter in question. He comes over here and says, Well, this is not like your case here, because he said you object to the idea of elders receiving the money. Of course, I don't object to money being sent to elders. How on earth did he get that idea? The only question, ladies and gentlemen, is this, and this is the one that he persistently refuses to discuss, did these elders take over and operate these homes to which they gave the money that was sent to them? He says yes. In which case, they as elders were operating two institutions, the church and the home. In which case he puts the elders in business. Did you ever find out what that was over there on that chart No. 8 that he had—over in the corner here where he says food, and shelter, and clothing, etc. Everyone knows that it wasn't a church because he said you can't turn a church into a home, or a home into a church. It wasn't a home, because he said that you can't establish any other organization. Did you find out what that was? I never did. I even tried to find the address of it, and he gave me the wrong address because he gave the address of the Blytheville church, but he had already told me it wasn't a church. What was it?

Now, ladies and gentlemen, remember this: Here is the matter of a home and a church. He asked me this question: Would I accept the same situation in the field of evangelism? No, I wouldn't. No, I wouldn't. And the reason that I wouldn't is that we have God's divine institution for the purpose of evangelism, and the missionary society takes the place of the church and does its work. When the missionary society does its work, there isn't anything left for the church to do. The missionary society displaces the church. But when the orphan home does its work, the church has got just as much to do as it had to start with. If the church were it's own orphan home, like it's own missionary society, you wouldn't need the orphan home either. What is the missionary society? It's not an orphan home. Therefore, you've got to have a home for child care and you've either got elders over that or you don't. Did you ever find out what that thing was over there in the corner? It's still not to late, sir, to tell us. You listen for it.

Let me have that Annual Lesson Commentary. I want to show you that these men are persistently (turn the lights on, please) misrepresenting me even after I correct them.

What was the page that you were reading, Roy, so that I won't have to look for it? Now this is a Lesson Commentary that I wrote in 1946. Now, friends, here is what I was discussing here. The question of what organization is to do the work which God ordains for the church to do. Now listen: "In line with the fact that our lesson today deals with the autonomy of the church, we point out that the contribution here alluded to was raised wholly without the high pressure organizational methods characteristic of today. There was no other organization at all. The churches in their own capacity raised the funds and they were gathered by brethren especially appointed for that purpose." What am I talking about in this entire section here? About how to raise money for the church. What's the organization for raising it? The church. Now here's the next statement he quotes from me: "Here, too, we see the simple manner in which the church in Philippi joined with Paul in the work of preaching the gospel. There was no missionary society in evidence. None was needed. The brethren simply raised the money and sent it directly to Paul. This is the way that it should be done today. No other organization is needed"—listen now—"to accomplish the work the Lord has authorized the church to do." What am I saying? We don't need a missionary society because we've got the only one that we need, the church. Now I didn't have under consideration any thing there except the matter of what kind of an organization raises the money and in what fashion is that money to be raised. But it does look like people could see that. I believe every word of that. If I was going to write it tonight, I'd write it exactly like I did. Then I'd put a P.S. down here and say, "Now you fellows that write for the Guardian, take notice here that that's what I mean, or do I have to spell it out in words of one syllable for you." I think it would be necessary to do so. I see no reason why it is necessary to go over that, friends. Even if they were right in their misrepresentation of me that doesn't prove that I have not established my prposition.

Then he raises the question with reference to his chart No. 13. Where is his chart? He wants to know if I'll accept the **pattern** here in the case of the church at Philippi

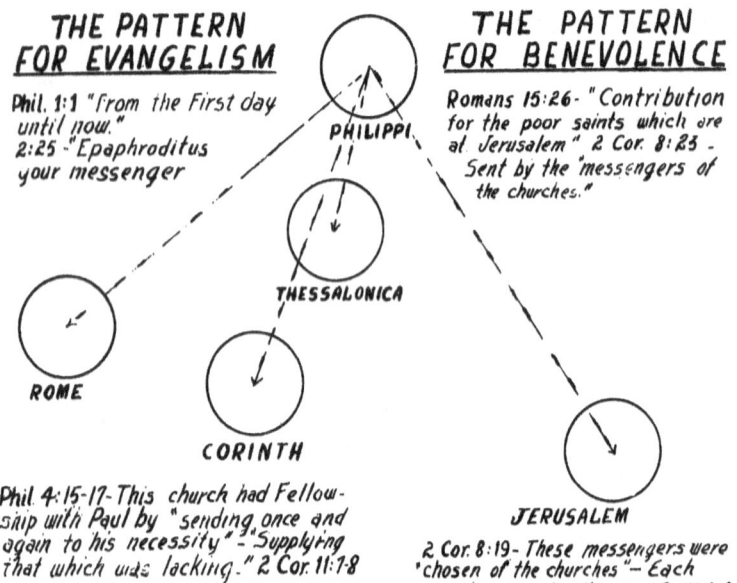

sending to Paul at Corinth and Rome—if I'll accept that pattern. I'll gladly. Do I endorse that kind of cooperation? Why, of course I do. Now you watch, friends. His pattern isn't even on here. Now, look. Here is Rom. 15:26, contributions for the poor saints which are at Jerusalem. That doesn't say a word about being sent to the elders. There is no passage of scripture that hints at the idea. He infers that that's what it was. Now you watch. You look at this, please. This passage says that it was sent to the poor among the saints. In this pattern over here, the money has to be sent to the preacher. It was sent to an individual, a saint. Now in the case of Paul, it can't be to the church. Must not be. For he said it was sent to the preacher. It can't be to the individuals, though it says individuals here, because this is supposed to be to the church, in order to fit his pattern. In the matter of evangelism, it must go only to the preacher. In the matter of benevolence, it must go only to the church. Well, this doesn't say the church. He reads it into it. So his pattern breaks down here, in Romans 15.

He wants me to cite a single instance of where one church ever sent another church any money whatsoever in the matter of evangelism. Well, he simply puts himself—I think I'll let brother Tant do it. I think I'll just let brother Tant satisfy him on that. Brother Tant said in the Gospel Guardian of June 15, 1949, or rather 1950 I should say, page 9, "Let us keep the issue clear. The Gospel Guardian is absolutely committed to the idea of churches cooperating with one another either in benevolence or in evangelism that is right and scriptural." Now, brother Tant, give him the verse; he wants it awfully bad. Brother Tant says that he's committed to that view and brother Cogdill demands the passage.

Now he refers to my ridiculous charts. I think they're rather pretty. I'm proud of them. It isn't the fact that they are ridiculous that disturbs him. It's what's on these charts. And I submit, friends, that it would be far better and more in keeping with his obligation in this debate to answer those. I've met a lot of men in debate, and I never saw a fellow that could explode arguments without even mentioning them. He's the first one that I ever saw even claimed it, much less attempted it. And there are going to be people that will go away from here night after night wondering why it was that this man was brought all the way from Texas to come over here to ignore my arguments.

Now I have a great deal of respect for brother John T. Lewis. I think I have more respect for him than brother Cogdill has, because I believe that brother Lewis is too intelligent a man to be influenced with that shallow, ridiculous appeal to prejudice that was made here tonight. I think that he is too intelligent a man to be influenced by such. Now I do not know what brother Lewis' position is, but I do know this, that here is what he said in his book: "Mr. Kendrick afterwards quit the society and went back to the Lord's plan of doing missionary work." Well, I can't learn from that what he went back to. I have to go somewhere else, because he didn't tell what Mr. Kendrick claimed that plan was. Nor did he say what he went back to when he quit the society. If he meant Eph. 3:10 to mean that that teaches that the church there, that it says in that passage that the church there was to preach the gospel to the world, he's got the wrong verse. He's got the wrong interpretation of it. Now don't misunderstand me. I believe that the church is to preach the gospel to the world. But Eph. 3:10 doesn't teach it. That's a misinterpretation of that passage if that's the reason he cited it. This says, "Unto principalities and powers in heavenly places be made known." In some fashion or the other it shall be made known to the angels and the heavenly powers. If he intended that to say that the church is to do it to the world, he missed the point. Now I don't know why he cited it because it didn't fit the passage, the instance.

Now I had to find out some way what Mr. Kendrick's position was. He said he went back to what he thought was the Lord's plan. I want to see what he thought the Lord's plan was. Well, what did I do? I took his book in which he makes a tremendous attack upon the Missionary Society after he quit. And in this book in which he discusses his position, after he quit the society and did what brother Lewis says that he did, went back to the Lord's plan, here is what Mr. Kendrick thought the Lord's plan was: "We've seen that congregations cooperated in raising and distributing funds for relieving the poor. The elders in Jerusalem received the funds at the hands of the messengers and disbursed them to the poor at Judea, not in Jerusalem only." Now that's what Mr. Kendrick said that he thought was right and Brother Lewis said that he went back to the Lord's plan, and this what he said he thought, and according to brother Lewis and brother Kendrick, this is the Lord's plan here of doing what we're talking about over here. Now anybody that can't see that is in need of more instruction than I could give on this occasion.

If brother Lewis wants to repudiate that and say he doesn't believe it, let him do it. In fact, I think you ought to have a confession column in your paper. And while you're at it, let each one tell what level he's on. Now while we're on that, let me have, please, the chart . . . . . Warren: "You have 12 minutes." . . . . . All right, thanks. Yes, that's the one I want right here. Here, please, we

CHART NO. 48

GOSPEL GUARDIAN CONFUSION ON "PATTERN."

UPHELD BY:	I T E M	CONDEMNED BY:
1. WALLACE	1. MUSIC HALL MEETING	1. COGDILL
2. DOUTHITT LEWIS	2. BIRMINGHAM NEWSPAPER ADVERTISING	2. COGDILL
3. LEWIS ("LORD'S PLAN")	3. BIRMINGHAM - CUBA	3. COGDILL
4. TANT	4. MONTANA ROGRAM	4. COGDILL
5. DOUTHITT	5. MEETING HOUSE WITH PREACHER'S QUARTERS	5. COGDILL
6. DOUTHITT	6. BIRMINGHAM RADIO	6. COGDILL
WHERE DO	**Y O U S T A N D,**	**B R O T H E R ?**

have the Gospel Guardian confusion on the pattern. Now with reference to the Music Hall Meeting, brother Wallace still upholds it. Brother Cogdill condemns it. Brother Douthitt, with reference to the Birmingham newspaper advertisement, he upholds it. He said brother Lewis over here wouldn't let anything go wrong over here, so he thought it was right. Brother Cogdill says it's wrong. He teaches it's wrong. Brother Lewis, who upholds the Lord's plan of missionary work endorses the Birmingham-Cuba work. Brother Cogdill has repudiated it. Brother Tant believes that it's all right for one to send money from one church to another in evangelism, as illustrated by the Montana program. Brother Cogdill says you can't prove where there's any instance where one church ever sent money to any other church for evangelistic purposes. Brother Douthitt says that the meeting house is scriptural, with private quarters for the preacher, of course. Brother Cogdill would repudiate sending money for that purpose, because you can't send money for any purpose except to a church in need.

Brother Douthitt endorsed the Birmingham radio program, and brother Cogdill repudiates it. Now, where do you stand, my brother? Which one of these do you accept? Some of you have started following them. Some of you are farther over the cliff than others. Now where are you going to stop? Where are you going to stop? That is a question. And while I'm on that I might say this: Brother Cogdill, who was it converted you to your present views? I'm certain that it wasn't brother Wallace, because brother Wallace doesn't stand with you. I'm certain that it wasn't Douthitt and Lewis because you don't agree with them. It wasn't brother Tant because you and brother Tant are in conflict. Who was it? As a matter of fact, your position is exactly the same as that of Carl Ketcherside, in so far as you've gone. You haven't gone quite as far. Now, Carl, you're here tonight, I believe. You're welcome to him. You can have him. And, friends, I don't want to leave the impression with you that this is to a frivolous thing. Brother Cogdill is already there, in so far as these matters are concerned that I've discussed. Now how far are you going? How far are you going?

I want to deal just a moment with a thing (let's have the lights back on, please) brother Cogdill wants to know, then here again now he's off the subject. But he wanted to know just what kind of an organization it would take to have something comparable to a missionary society in benevolence. He wanted to know what it would be. Well, I'll show you what it would be. Let these represent contributing churches. (He drew a diagram on the blackboard). Let this represent, please, the organization that under its board of directors is receiving funds from the churches. Let this over here, please, represent Boles Home, and this Childhaven, and this Tennessee Christian, and this Potter, and this Southern Christian, and so on. And this organization here sends the money. The Benevolent Society receives the money from the churches and with them establishes and maintains these homes. Now what is actually done? Here is what is actually done. Let this represent the churches and this represent the homes. Now let us suppose that it's a needy home, a private needy home, has in it three children. We believe that when these churches send money to this home, brother Cogdill

WOODS' BLACKBOARD DIAGRAM ILLUSTRATING THE THING HE WOULD OPPOSE AS UNSCRIPTURAL IN BENEVOLENCE

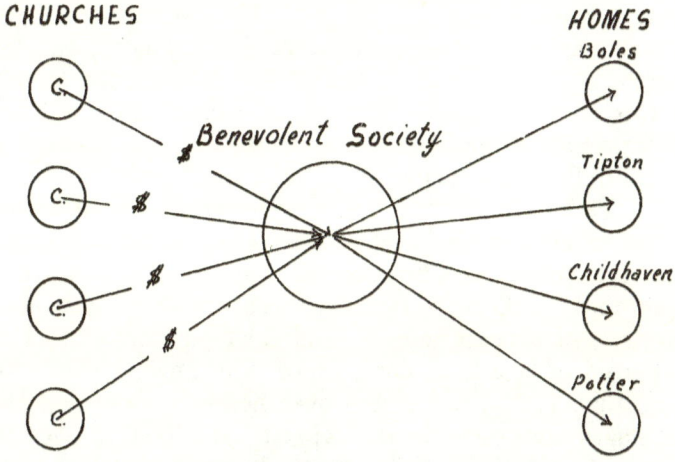

agrees, that that's scriptural. Suppose that instead of three children, it becomes thirty children, it's still just as necessary. Suppose that instead of being a man and wife that it's two women or it's two men, two brothers in the flesh, or two brothers in the spirit, or six brothers in the spirit who are operating this home, where did the sin begin? Now why didn't he ever tell us? That, friends, is exactly what's being done today.

Now, brother Cogdill, on your chart No. 8, you tell us if that's the home. We may get together on the home. I would be glad to see it since you brought this up, I would be glad for him to tell us what that is and remember, that's his explanation for what is done in the matter of providing benevolence by the church today. (Cogdill, "I think you have the wrong chart.") Woods: It's No. 2, No. 2. Now, I call your attention that this is what he says is the purpose of the home. I have asked him repeatedly the question, "Brother Cogdill, what is this?" It's not the church because you said we couldn't put the church in this business. I have here a wonderful statement, we think, I have here a splendid statement that was put out by Earl Dale, "The Church in Business". He says, and makes reference here to this: "The home is built and is maintained to care for children that "Churches of Christ" and "individual Christians" recommend and send." Now, I want to know if this describes this, and if not, why not? He's contending for a home . . . . . a church of Christ home. On that lovely farm the 'church of Christ grass' feeds "church of Christ cows'. These cows provide 'church of Christ beef' and give 'church of Christ milk'. The 'church of Christ hogs' provide 'church of Christ ham and bacon'. The 'church of Christ cotton' brings in 'church of Christ profits' while 'church of Christ hens' lay 'church of Christ eggs'. Now what do you think about that? All right friends, these are the things characteristic of orphan homes. You can't put the elders over that kind of work. I don't know why anyone would try to do that . . . . . put elders over homes. Now men that are elders may serve in the capacity of directors over the home. And I think it is eminently scriptural and right for the same men who are elders to perform those duties. You can't put the elders over two homes. Now he's the fellow that brought that up.

Now he wants to know, where will this promotion stop? He wants to leave the impression with you that some of us are trying to lead the church into digression, and that we're practicing matters that were not formerly characteristic of us. Will he designate one single thing that we're practicing today that he didn't practice ten years ago? It couldn't be a cooperative radio program, because we had here in North Birmingham, whom he is representing, participating in such. It couldn't be that which is operated on the basis of the Newspaper ad, churches combining their efforts along that line. He couldn't say that's a promotion. He couldn't say that it's the orphan homes, because he admitted the other night that he had used the facilities of one of them, and what I thought was a truly commendable thing, and I commend him for his interest in it, and I wouldn't try to reflect on him in the least on that. I wouldn't want anybody to get that idea, because I would do the same thing if I had been in his place.

Now what is it that we're promoting, friends? He

SPONSORING CONGREGATIONS 299

wants to know: Where now does it stop? Where does it stop? Now I want my chart there that shows the, what was that number that shows the preacher under control? No. 51, yes, No. 51. Chart No. 51. Turn the lights out, please. Now, friends, here, here is what we are contending for. Here are the contributing churches,

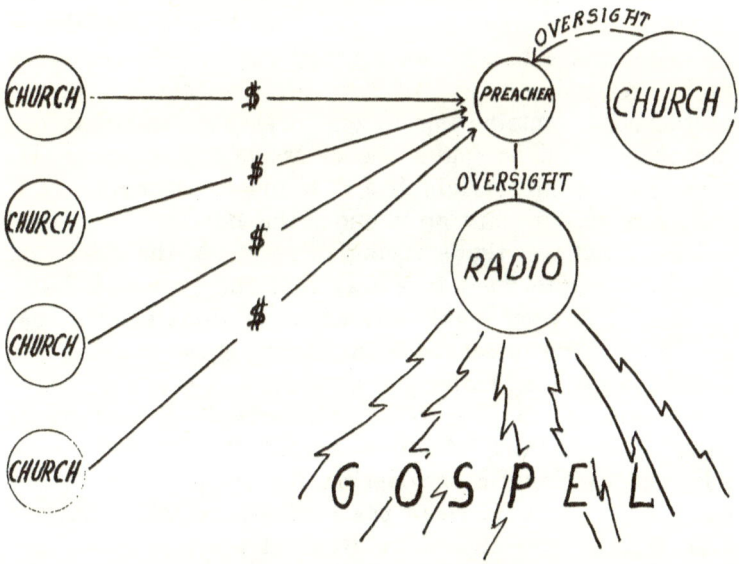

let this represent the Highland congregation right here. Now this is the way that we say it should be done and the way it is being done, in harmony with Acts 11:27-30. We have an exact picture of what's done there here, except in that instance, it's in the field of benevolence, and we are arguing in the field of evangelism. But we showed the other night, to which he never referred, that he used I Cor. 16:1, 2, which is money gathered in the field of benevolence, for evangelism. So we made his own argument for him. Now then, he says it would be wrong for the money to be sent to the church, but he says it would be all right for it to be sent to the preacher. Now he wants to know if many churches could send it to the Highland elders, if ten hundred or ten thousand, couldn't all of them. Now you let him tell us where to stop. Watch it please: He says that the right way to do it, and the only way to do it, is to send to the preacher. Now if one church could send to the preacher, could ten churches send? Could ten hundred? Could ten thousand? Where's the stopping place, brother Cogdill? You remember this, ladies and gentlemen, he's got the same problem right here that we have here. Exactly the same. And bear in mind, please, that he has said that this should always be under the elders of some congregation. So according to his reasoning, then we have all the churches in the brotherhood contributing to one preacher, and that one preacher would be under the elders of one church. He says that would be right but it would be wrong to do it the other way by putting it under the elders.

Now I tell you that's trying to set aside the eldership. That's trying to do it in a way that the Lord didn't put it. And I've been highly suspicious of these efforts that are being made to set aside the elders of the church; and I want to say this, ladies and gentlemen, and you get this: I go over the brotherhood continuously. I hold about twenty-five or thirty meetings a year, and I've held three hundred meetings in the last twelve years. And there's not been a single place in the brotherhood where there's been trouble over this thing where the elders stood pat. I have come to a new appreciation of the eldership of the church of our Lord as a result of that. I've seen exactly what the apostle Paul meant when he said to elders of the church at Ephesus, "I know that after my departing shall grievous wolves enter in among you, not sparing the flock." And I've seen the vital importance of men who have the souls of people under their care to have guarded them against men who would lead them away from the truth. "The spirit speaketh expressly" . . . . . I Tim. 1 . . . . . "that in the latter times some shall depart from the faith." It's the function of the elders to protect. Is it any wonder that men would seek to lead them

SPONSORING CONGREGATIONS   301

away from the elders of the church and put the work under a preacher?

From the floor: You've got two minutes if you want to get that extreme chart.

Woods: All right, then, let me have chart No. 50A.

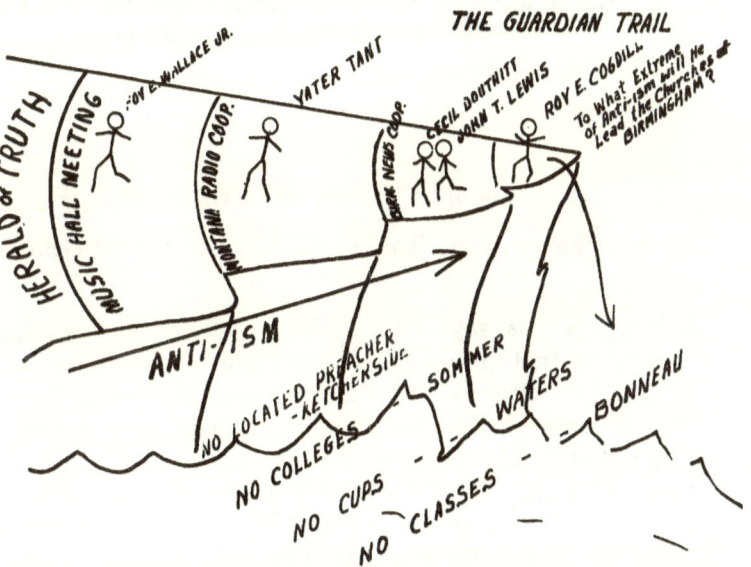

Chart No. 50A. Here we are friends. Now you watch, please. I've already discussed this phase of it. I've showed you that these brethren have been driven back step by step like an army retreating. They've gone back step by step. One rung at a time. Brother Cogdill stands right here. I want to ask him this question: What will be the end of it? Will he stop with the located preacher? Will brother Ketcherside wind up with them? He might as well, because the same arguments that sustain and justify brother Cogdill in his present view, in his opinion, may be used against the located preacher. Can you find the pattern of a located preacher in the Bible, in the sense of a detailed pattern? You can't. I say it's right, but it's right because it's taught generically, and not because there is a pattern. Will he stop here with Sommer and no colleges? I ask him: Will he stop with no cups? Where is the pattern detailing the example of the cups? Will he stop with no classes, and with Bonneau here? Where are you going to stop, friends? On the basis on which you've reached these conclusions, then these follow logically. On the basis on which he reached this. Well, he claims there is no exclusive pattern for what we're doing. But there's no exclusive pattern for the located preacher, and for the cups or the classes. Where are you going to stop, I ask you?

Cogdill's Fourth Negative

Gentlemen Moderators, Brother Woods, Ladies and Gentlemen:

Brother Woods says that if he produced one passage of scripture that is enough for the word of God to say a thing. I'll agree to that. If he'll produce one in favor of the proposition that he's holding to and that he's trying to prove, I told him a while ago that if he would just produce one, just one. He hasn't done that yet. But if he'll produce just one that shows where any congregation in the New Testament ever sent money to another church that was not destitute, just one, I'll quit this debate, admit that I'm wrong on the proposition and go home. Now find it, Guy. Get busy. You've got a job to do. You've made two speeches tonight and you've made no effort to point it out.

Just one time, the nearest thing to it that he came, was in his speech last night when he referred to the letter that was sent out by the apostles from the city of Jerusalem to the churches. That is the nearest example that he's found and he said they didn't need it, they weren't in need. And I pointed out to him that they did need the divine decision that was sent to them and he's made no further reference to it. It wasn't, of course, a case in point. It missed the point entirely.

He says that Jerusalem is exactly the same kind of an arrangement. The church at Jerusalem, when the congregations of Macedonia and Achaia (get me my chart on the pattern, if you will, that example) that when they sent their contributions, the churches of Macedonia and Achaia, to the church at Jerusalem, that they sent it to the poor saints. They didn't send it to the elders. Now you know the trouble with him is that he isn't satisfied when the word of God says a thing once. You know I pointed out to him last night that there is an exclusive pattern, that in Acts 11 they sent the relief to the brethren in Judea to the elders. They sent it to the elders, that's the way in which the churches received money. What has he said about it. Not a word in the world. An exclusive pattern? Yes, there's an exclusive pattern. For what? For churches receiving help. When did they receive it? When they were in need. How did they receive it? The elders received it. He wants to dodge the issue, by raising the question on one of his charts: Were the elders then over the home? How the elders did it I don't know. Neither do you. They weren't in charge of any private home; you can be certain of that. How they distributed it, I don't know; but the elders received it and they had the over sight of its distribution. And that's the only pattern of how churches ever received help. Now, Guy, find another one if it isn't exclusive. When the Bible gives you an example of a thing being done a certain way, and no other way, what more does it have to do to give you an exclusive pattern? Why, I pointed out to you that you have an exclusive pattern on the matter of raising money. There is an exclusive pattern on it. The congregation raised its own money by the contributions of its own members. The only one. The members contributed. That's where their money came from.

There isn't an example of any church in the New Testament raising its money by going out and begging other churches for it. You find that. They raised their money in the New Testament by the members contributing into the treasury of the church on the Lord's day. And he said Cogdill didn't say a thing in the world about 16:1,

2. That's just like a lot of the rest of his charges. He comes up here after I've spent a half a speech on some misapplication of some point or some misrepresentation of something and says he didn't say a word in the world about it. If you were here last night, you know I did say something about it. What did I say about it? That I Cor. 16:1, 2 is the only example, *the only example,* in the New Testament that God ever gave us for a church raising money to do anything, in the way of the work that God assigned it. The only way that any congregation ever was told to raise its money to do its work was by its members contributing. He came up and tried to say that I was making that an example and I ought to recognize that it's an example of how the church spent its money. Oh, no, there's more than one example of how the church spent its money. There's an example of benevolence ..... the church sending to the saints in Jerusalem and raising the money by the contribution of it's own members. Well, then there's an example of the church spending it's money when Philippi sent to Paul. How did they get that money? And what has he said about that? Do you remember hearing him saying anything about it? Do you remember him saying anything about the fact you have two examples of how the church spent its money? There's *one of how it raised it.* That's exclusive. Now, Guy, I just supposed that you knew as anybody else ought to know that if there is just one example of how a New Testament church did a thing that excludes everything else. If there are two examples of how it did it, then either of them would be permissible. Anybody ought to know that. If you'll find an example of a church meeting on any other day of the week than the Lord's day, I'll admit that there are two days when you can meet and break bread. But as long as you find just one example in the New Testament of the church meeting on the first day of the week and no other day, then that's an exclusive pattern, it's an exclusive example. If they met on two different days, then at least two and maybe more would be permissible. But they met on just one.

You've got an exclusive pattern of how to raise money.

No church ever raised it any other way. You've got a pattern of how they spent the money. How did they do it? Well, *when they sent to a church in need* that's the only time that a congregation ever made a contribution out of its treasury to another church. *The church was in need.* Now just what violation of that principle or example has he found? You tell me. Where's the one violation of the fact that no church ever sent a contribution out of its treasury to another church unless the church was in need. Jerusalem? Was the Jerusalem church in need? It was unable to supply the needs of its own members. It was destitute enough that it couldn't take care of its own. He says that's just like Highland, and he had a chart up here comparing the Jerusalem church to the Highland Church in Abilene. Now, friends, you can see that there's no point in that comparison. Why he got a little bit excited about the fact that Yater Tant said that they were practically in bankruptcy. Why, he said, I know that isn't so and I'm prepared to prove it. Well, I wouldn't ask you for the proof. I don't think they are either. I don't know whether Yater said that or not. But if he said it, he ought to stop and look at the meeting house they've got., unless that does bankrupt them. He ought to look at their financial statement to see what all they are contributing to. You know if I were helping a man that claimed that he was in need and I found out that he was sending what I was helping him with to everybody else in the country, I think I'd stop and do a little investigating about his need. The Highland Church receives from all the churches they can get to contribute to them and then sends out to anything that they are disposed to support, I suppose that they can find themselves able to support. No, they are not in need. They are not comparable to the Jerusalem church. Certainly they are not. The Jerusalem church was destitute enough that it could not take care of its own.

Brother Reese is sitting down here. He wouldn't tell you that the Highland Church is unable to take care of the needs of its own members. He won't tell you that. Why get up here and compare it with Jerusalem then?

It's not in the condition that the Jerusalem church was in.

Well, where is the example of a church sending out of its treasury to another church unless that church was in need? Was it the brethren in Judea in Acts 11? Why, the record says they sent "to the relief" of the brethren, to the aid of the brethren. The brethren were in need because of the famine that arose. And the brethren in Antioch determined to send relief unto them, to send help, that they needed, to the brethren which dwelt in Judea, "which also they did" Why did they send? Because they were in need. When the need was a benevolent need, to whom did they send it? We pointed it out to you in the example, on the church at Philippi. They sent it to the elders of the church. When the church was unable to take care of its own, to supply the needs of the saints in that church, they sent that benevolent contribution to the elders of the church. And Acts 11 says so. You have an exclusive pattern then in supplying the need of a congregation when it comes to benevolence. To whom do you send it? To the elders of the church. Why? Because they are in charge of the distribution of benevolence among the members of the congregation where they are elders. That's the reason you send it to them. It's their obligation to see after the flock, and you put it in the hands of the elders. Well, when the church needed from the viewpoint of hearing the gospel, when it was a community where the gospel had not been heard, then what did they do? They sent a preacher, Barnabus from Jerusalem in Acts 11:19, was sent up to Antioch. What did they send? Money? And let the church select its own preacher and be responsible for his preaching? No, sir. What did they send? They sent the preacher. They sent the preacher. He said, Well, now will brother Cogdill agree that one congregation could send another one a New Testament? Would he agree that one could send another one a tract? I'll tell you what brother Cogdill won't agree to. Brother Cogdill won't agree to the appointing of the elders of the Highland Church a receiving treasury for the money from all the congregations to furnish all of the congregations with all of their New Testaments and all of their tracts. That's what brother Cogdill won't agree to. And that's what brother Cogdill is opposing. And that's what you're under obligation to prove. That's right. Get busy and do it. You haven't even started.

Whenever you find one congregation receiving money from all of the churches in order that they may send tracts out and Testaments out to all of the churches, like a church in Dallas, Texas, sending money to Highland elders in Abilene in order that the Highland elders in Abilene may come right back to Dallas, Texas, and buy time on the Dallas radio and preach the gospel in Dallas for the Dallas churches. Now that's what's being done. That's what the Herald of Truth is. Churches all over this country sending money to the Highland elders in order that the Highland elders may come right back to Birmingham and buy time on the radio station in Birmingham to preach the gospel right here in Birmingham. When they sent for the preaching of the gospel, they sent the preacher. When they sent money to support the preacher, they sent it to the preacher. And you haven't found an exception to it, Guy, and you know you haven't. Now get busy on it.

Talk about an exclusive pattern . . . . . Yes. There's an exclusive pattern. When the need was benevolence, they sent it to the elders. When the need was evangelism and they cooperated in the work of evangelism, they sent it to the preacher. Oh, he said, when would that stop? Why if one church can send to the preacher, and a dozen churches send to the preachers, then a thousand could, and ten thousand could. No, no, there isn't any difficulty about the stopping place if you send it to the preacher. It'll stop when he gets his need met. Now if he starts in hiring other preachers to preach under him, it would never stop. That's the reason you can't stop it when you get Highland's set-up. Why the more money you furnish, the wider they are going to want their work to be. They're working all of the time and begging all of the time to enlarge their program. They want it to be bigger, and bigger and bigger and bigger, and more and more churches to send them more and more money so they can have more and more preaching done. And there isn't any stopping place to that, because they will never be satisfied. Never on the face of the earth.

When the preacher's need is met, that's the stopping place. And he ought not to get another dime. Somebody said, "Well, but he's liable to get more money than he ought to have." Yes, but I've got as much confidence in the preachers among my brethren as I have the elders among my brethren. Some of the elders are liable to get more than they ought to have. I've known elders in the church with sticky fingers. That's no reflection on elders, either, as a whole. I thank God for the eldership of the churches, all over this entire country. And the ones that I've labored with and worked with I honor, and insofar as they are keeping with the word of the Lord, I wouldn't be for one moment disrespectful toward them, or rebellious. But I'm saying I've as much confidence in the preachers as I have elders. And if a preacher can get too much money, an eldership can. The same objection exactly would lie. Churches ought to know what they are doing. When they support a preacher, they ought to know how much money he's getting. God intended for there to be a very direct connection between the church that supports the preacher, and the preacher whom they support. They are responsible for what he is preaching; they ought to know he is preaching the truth and they ought not to support one that isn't doing it. That's the reason a very direct connection has been preserved in God's order, by the church sending directly to the preacher. That's the point. God evidently intended that such should be the case.

But he said, you know what he's objecting to is the size of it. And I finally got him after five nights to try to describe an unscriptural benevolent organization. And look what he gave me. He said, why brother Cogdill, it's not the size of the thing that makes it wrong. Well, what's this wrong for? (Pointing to blackboard drawing) What's this wrong for? You know the Shultz-Lewis Home, by their charter, the board at Shultz-Lewis has the right to maintain more than one home. And I can read it in the

SPONSORING CONGREGATIONS

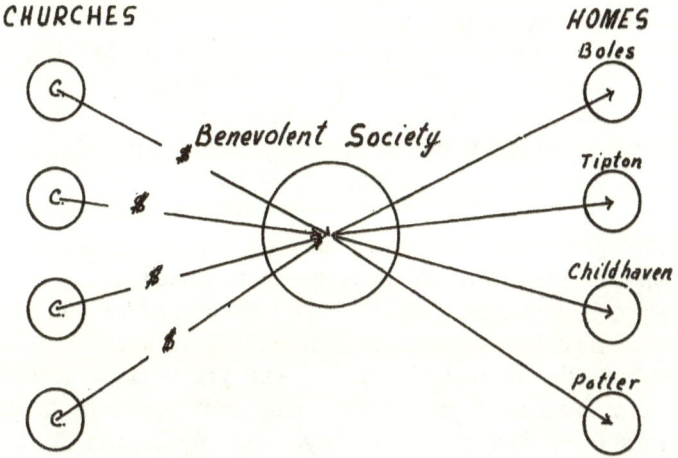

WOODS' BLACKBOARD DIAGRAM ILLUSTRATING THE THING HE WOULD OPPOSE AS UNSCRIPTURAL IN BENEVOLENCE

charter if he denies it. They've got the right to establish other homes. Boles Home in effect is working out that kind of a program right now. They are working out a cottage type. They are working out a cottage type. They are taking them out of dormitories and putting them into separate cottages as separate families. Well, suppose they move one of those cottages across the road. Now both of us can do some supposing. Suppose they moved one of those cottages across the road, Guy. And suppose when they move that cottage across the road, and put that family under the matron or the man and his wife who run that cottage, that they move another one across the road in the other direction; or a quarter of a mile down the road. And the same board runs all of those cottages and all of those family groups in those cottages. That's in effect and in fact what they're doing. Would that make it wrong?

If, if a benevolent society that has more than one home is unscriptural, then it's the size of the thing that makes it unscriptural. And he's gone back on his very statement about that. But there's another matter that I want to talk to you about. And that is his continued talk about the Music Hall Meeting. Now I told him that there are two reasons. I've given him two. I've given them repeatedly. He gets up here and insists on misrepresenting me every time he talks about it, when I told you and told him that there are two reasons why I would not engage in another meeting of that sort. That doesn't mean that there aren't any kind of arrangements where churches can cooperate in a meeting either. That isn't the point at all. And when he quotes Foy Wallace as favoring his position and implies because Foy Wallace favors a cooperative meeting of some sort or kind, and my information is that he said it would have to be modified, ... and I've got just as much right to my information as you have yours. And I know what he's preaching all over the country about the Herald of Truth. And you're misrepresenting him by implication, Guy. And you ought to be too honorable to do a man that way. Foy Wallace is opposed to the Herald of Truth and opposes it on exactly the same ground that I do, and there isn't any divergency between us on that. Not a bit on earth.

Well, he said, they are divided. Cogdill doesn't agree with Tant, and Cogdill doesn't agree with Douthitt, and Cogdill doesn't agree with brother Lewis. Cogdill doesn't agree with somebody else. And so they're divided. Well, Guy, nobody on earth is any worse divided than the institutional crowd. You can't even agree with brother Harper about whose work it is out there. Why brother Harper said it's our work . . . . . Ours. Nobody else's. It's ours. If you want to know whose work it is, he said, in that Abilene Debate, you find out whose paying the bill. Highland pays the bill. It's our work. Now you get up here and tell us what he meant. I suppose he meant what he said. If he didn't he ought to take it back, and correct it, and say what he meant. He preached it right here in Birmingham in exactly the same way in the speech that he made, and he's been preaching it all over the country and debated it twice, at Lufkin and at Abilene. Our work. And you say it isn't.

Oh, yes, what they mean by that is. . . . . . Well, now what do they mean by it? You mean they don't mean it? Is that what you mean? That's what they say, but they don't mean it. They say it's our work. And I read to you where the elders say, it is our work. We have the exclusive control. We haven't delegated any authority over it in any respect to anybody, from the preparation of the manuscripts right on down to the very last conclusion of it. It is our work. They said. Now you talk about a confession column, it isn't their work any longer and it belongs to all of the churches that are supporting it, then the elders at Highland ought to confess they were wrong about it. They ought to come to the altar, and if anybody on earth ought to join them at the altar, it's Guy N. Woods. He ought not only to confess that he's changed and been wrong, he ought to confess that he's tried to mislead you by denying that he's changed. That's the most dishonorable thing about the whole business. There isn't anything dishonorable about a man changing. No, no, not if he changes out of conviction. Not even if he changes from right to wrong, out of conviction, honest conviction. But for a man to get up here and say and read his own statement, and say now these brethren are misrepresenting me, when all on earth I did was to read what he said. I read what he said. This misrepresents Guy N. Woods. I want you to listen to it. "Philippi joined with Paul in the work of preaching the gospel. There was no missionary society in evidence, and none was needed. The brethren simply raised the money, (How did they do it?) and sent it to Paul." Now that's the kind of a statement that you attributed to John T. Lewis, brother Woods. He was talking about the missionary society, too. Wasn't he? Wasn't he? He was talking Kendrick changing from the missionary society. That's what he was talking about. It worked on this. Why wouldn't it work on him? Why don't you be as fair with him as you tried to be with yourself? I'd be ashamed of that. Get up here and continue to misrepresent him instead of apologizing for it. You need to make a confession, sir. You can be certain of that. John T. Lewis has no opportunity in this debate to speak for himself.

Oh, he said, but I was talking about the autonomy of the

church. That's what this debate's about too. That's exactly what this debate's about. That's what I'm talking about, and he said, "There was no missionary society in evidence and none was needed. The brethren simply raised money, and sent it directly to Paul. This is the way it should be done today. No organization is needed to accomplish the work the Lord has authorized the church to do. when men become dissatisfied with God's arrangement and set up one of their own, they have already crossed the threshold to apostasy. Let us be satisfied with the Lord's manner of doing things." All right. I am.

How did they send money to evangelize? They sent it to the preacher. Now you show us some other way. Show us another example. Show us the passage in the New Testament that gives us another example. See if I won't accept it. Produce it. Produce it. Show us where one church ever sent to another church when it wasn't in need. Show us that they sent to anybody else except the elders when they sent to supply the need. Show us that when they sent to evangelize that they sent to somebody besides the preacher. Just find it, Guy. You haven't begun to even look for it yet. You'd rather talk about something else.

Oh, he said, this is just a bunch of anti-ism. He said these fellows are just exactly like brother Ketcherside. And you know, I don't know brother Ketcherside, you ought to stay away from these debates. Guy can't keep you off his mind. (laughter) You ought to stay away. You disturb him tremendously when you attend these debates. He's mentioned you in almost every speech since you've shown up down here, some sort or kind of—You talk about running. What in the world is there about Carl Ketcherside—he's a pretty nice looking kind of a fellow. What is there about his presence that disturbs you so that you can't talk about anybody else hardly? Why he said when brother Cogdill finds an exclusive pattern for a located preacher, when he finds an exclusive pattern for the number of containers, when he finds an exclusive pattern for this and for that, for the Bible classes, then he said, he'll have something that's worth considering. But he can't find an exclusive pattern for that any more than he can for this.

You know he has the idea, and I haven't used the word digressive. I've tried to avoid ephitets. I've tried to avoid any nicknames. My mother taught me better than to call somebody something that he didn't like to be called when I was a boy. And I'm grateful to God that she did it. I don't call people by religious nicknames or anything else, that they object to. No, sir. Well, when you find an exclusive pattern, then what? If I couldn't find any more authority, if I couldn't find any more authority for a preacher laboring with a church under an eldership and preaching the gospel; if I couldn't find any more Bible authority for Bible classes teaching the word of God; if I couldn't find any more authority for an individual communion set than you find for the kind of cooperation that you are preaching, I'd accept the position of those brethren who oppose them and go along with them. But I can find more for it. If Carl Ketcherside thinks I can't, let him give me a chance. Let him give me a chance. And if the anti-Sunday school brethren think I can't, let them try me. I asked you repeatedly, would you endorse the same kind of an arrangement for the Sunday school than you do for the Herald of Truth. Would you be willing for the churches of Texas to put their Bible school arrangement under the elders of the Highland Church, send their money to Highland, let Highland train their teachers? Let Highland d i v i d e their classes and grade their students? Let Highland publish their literature and furnish the literature. If not, why not? What did he say about that? He conveniently forgot it. Conveniently forgot it.

Well, on this chart over here, the principle illustrated, 2 Corinthians 8 and 9. The next one, brethren in Macedonia and Achaia sending to Jerusalem. It's in front of that. Those churches made up their own money. 2 Corinthians 8 and 9, I Corinthians 16 shows it. The church at Philippi, the church at Thessalonica, the churches of Galatia, the church at Corinth, they made up their own money. They sent it to Jerusalem. Now the Herald of Truth plan is for Corinth, Philippi, Thessalonica and Galatia to send the

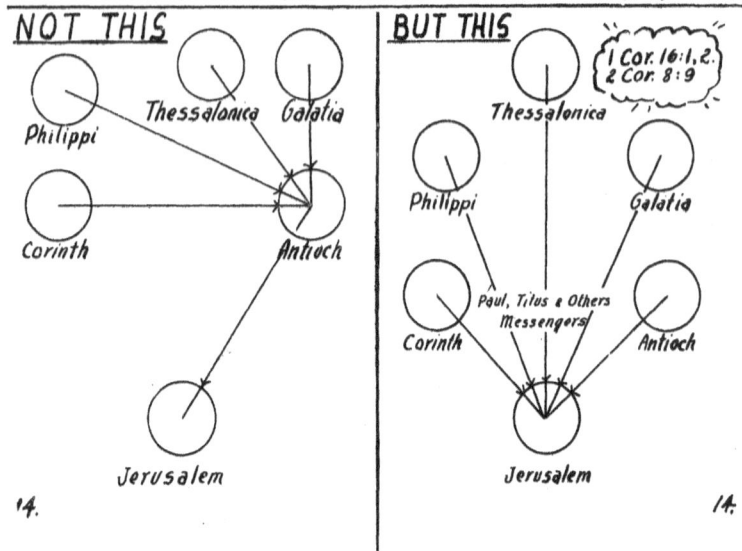

money to Antioch, and let Antioch do the work in Jerusalem. Oh, I'm not talking about Antioch sending the money on to Jerusalem. Just send it to Antioch, and let the Antioch elders do the work of benevolence in Jerusalem. That isn't the way it was done. There wasn't any sponsoring church. There wasn't any congregation as a centralized agency that received money from other churches. He can't find that in the passage of his life depended upon it. And he knows he can't. And he won't try it because it isn't there. They didn't send it to Antioch and let Antioch take charge of the work that was done in Jerusalem. They didn't send it to Antioch in order that Antioch might do a work for which they were all responsible. They sent it to Jerusalem. Here is the way it was done over here. Jerusalem was the church in need. The church in Jerusalem was obligated to take care of its own. They had more needy than they were able to take care of. They needed the help of others. The other churches sent out of a sense of obligation, because from Jerusalem the gospel had gone out. Treasuring up their own money, each church getting its money from its own members, from the giving of its own members. They selected their own messengers. (I Cor. 16:14; 2 Cor. 8 and 9) say so. They selected their own messenger, entrusted their own messenger with their own money and that messenger became the agent of that church to carry that money contributed by that church to Jerusalem, for the relief of the saints. That's the way it was done.

Now will he deny that Jerusalem is a church in need, and will he affirm that Highland is? That's what I want to know. Give me the next one now. Acts 11, you have the

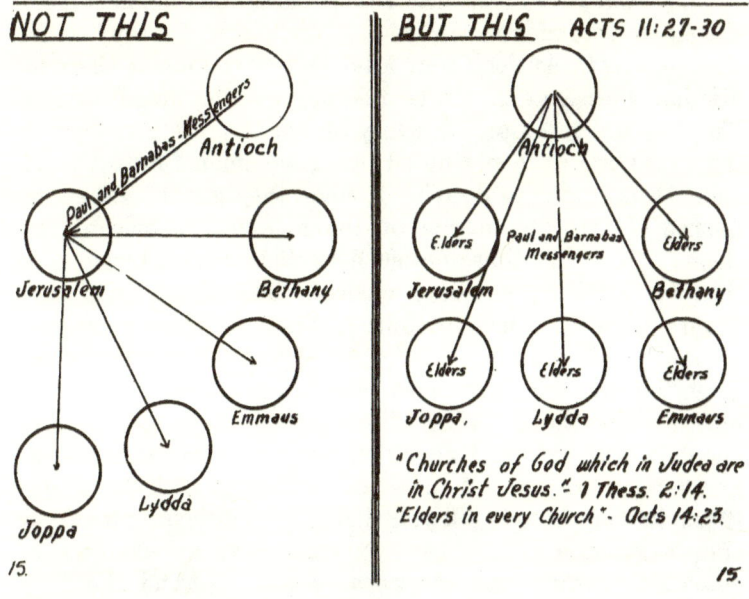

same thing exactly. You have one church sending to many churches. There was more than one church in Judea—a church at Jerusalem, another one at Joppa, Lydia, Emmaus, and Bethany, maybe others, but the churches of God in Judea are implied. I Thess. 2:14. The brethren in Judea were divided into more than just one congregation. How did the church in Antioch send their money? Did they send it to Jerusalem and let Jerusalem take charge of the distribution among the other churches? Are we ready for it?

Are you ready for the eldership of one congregation to oversee a general program of benevolence among all the churches of any size district? Is that his position? Is that what he's trying to say? Are you ready for the conclusion? How are you going to oppose the Methodist Episcopacy when you reach that conclusion? The fact of the whole matter is the man doesn't live—Guy Woods won't try to find that kind of a thing in the word of God. Whenever he does, I've got him on record on the other thing right here in this 1946 Annual Commentary. Of course he'd do that just like he did this other. He'd say that's not what I'm talking about. But it is what he's talking about.

They sent it to Jerusalem in one case, and they sent it to the elders in Judea in the other. Well, how did they do it? The church in Antioch sent Paul and Barnabas as their individual messengers. How did they get the money? Just like they did in I Cor. 16, every one of the disciples according to his ability contributed into a common fund at Antioch. What did they do with it when they got it? They delivered it into the hands of the messengers selected by them? What did these messengers do? They carried it to the elders. To the elders where? The elders in Judea. Where were the elders in Judea? The New Testament tells us that God's ordained order is, elders in every church. Then tell me that there isn't a New Testament example of how to contribute. Why if you even take what he says about it, and he's just as wrong as he can be, the one example is an example of churches sending to churches. But if you let Guy Woods tell you that it isn't an example of one church sending to another, you still have an example of *churches sending and churches receiving.* And the New Testament tells you how. I thank you.

SIXTH NIGHT

Wood's Fifth Affirmative

Brother Moderators, Brother Cogdill, Ladies and Gentlemen:

I'm now before you for the final evening and the first affirmative thereof on this proposition which has just been read, and about which we have been studying for the past two evenings. Again I do not see the need of any detailed definition or analysis of the proposition. We're all agreed with reference to the terms thereof and the only issue is: Is the program under consideration in that proposition a scriptural one? I decided tonight in this final session of the debate to set out evidence which I regard as irrefutable in its nature as I've already done in earlier evenings of the debate. However, before I begin, I should like to express briefly my appreciation to the Homewood congregation, to its Eldership, and to Brother Jack Meyer, the preacher, my sincere gratitude for the confidence imposed in me in the invitation that was extended me to represent the position which we believe to be the truth in this debate. And they have treated me in most magnificent fashion, and their preparation for the debate has left nothing wanting. I am indebted to Brother Thomas B. Warren who preaches for the Eastridge congregation in Ft. Worth for splendid assistance as a moderator and for the art work in the charts, and to Brother Roy Deaver who is President of the Ft. Worth Christian school for operating the projector, as well as many valuable suggestions, and to Brother Tom Gardner who is a member of the Eastridge congregation for taking care of the equipment as well as many others who have participated in most marvelous fashion.

It is my sincere hope that in this debate good has been accomplished. And I can truly say that I have no feeling of animosity toward Brother Cogdill, or toward any person in connection with the debate regardless of the side he may be on. It is my sincere hope that unity may prevail and that all of us may be one in the matter.

And now I'm going to introduce the evidence upon which I shall rely this evening. Let us now have chart no. 58.

CHART NO. 58.

1. **MY SCRIPTURAL PROOF:**

    (1) MT. 28; MK. 16.

    (2) ACTS 11: 27-30; 1 COR. 16: 1, 2.

2. **COGDILL'S OBJECTIONS FALLACIOUS.**

3. **CONSEQUENCES OF COGDILL'S THEORY - CHART NO. 54.**

4. **TO WHERE DOES "THE GUARDIAN TRAIL" LEAD? - CHART NO. 50A.**

You may turn the lights out please. You will observe that I have here on this chart the procedure that's to characterize our discussion this evening. I have designated first of all my scriptural proof that's already been introduced in the debate. First of all the Great Commission set out in Matthew 28 and Mark 16, in which place our Lord said go into all the world and preach the gospel to every creature. I gave an analysis of that Commission and to this very moment Brother Cogdill has made no effort to answer the argument made thereon. I insisted that the commission itself necessitates cooperation between New Testament churches in the carrying out of its obligation. That, in the very nature of the case, it would be impossible for churches operating independently of each other, in one generation, to preach the gospel to every creature in all the world, as was done in the apostolic age. That there would of necessity be conferences and contacts and assistance of various types and kinds rendered, all of which is cooperation between New Testament churches. That remains unnoticed, in fact, untouched.

I then made an argument from Acts 11:27-30 into which there's no need to enter tonight. Suffice it to say that that's an exact picture of cooperation between New Testament churches. Now in proof of that, let me have please, my chart No. 56. Chart 56 please.

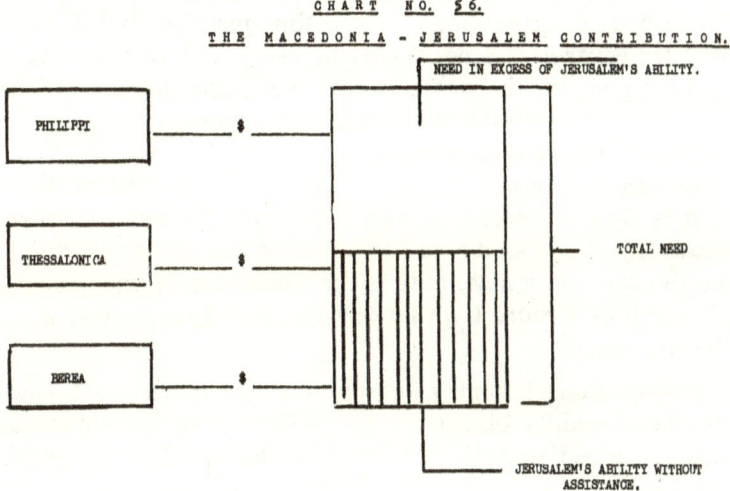

CHART NO. 56.
THE MACEDONIA - JERUSALEM CONTRIBUTION.

SAME PRINCIPLE IN HERALD OF TRUTH

I think we'd like to have the lights in the center out, those in the ceiling please. Now friends, this is an exact picture of New Testament cooperation in the case of the great contribution an account of which is found in I Corinthians, the 16th chapter, verses 1 and 2, and in 2nd Corinthians chapters 8 and 9, and in Romans chapter 15, and verse 26. I have, however, merely designated the churches of Macedonia, at least some of them, Philippi, and Thessalonica, and Berea in the contribution to be sent to Jerusalem, letting this represent, please, Jerusalem's ability and this that which was supplied by the cooperating congregations. These the total of it, that which is accomplished. And that, I insist, is exactly what I'm defending here tonight. Brother Cogdill has not attempted to so much as to point out any difference between that and the Herald of Truth program as it operates today.

What do we have here? New Testament congregations sending their money, so Brother Cogdill says, to the elders of the Jerusalem church. Now he can't prove that it went to the Jerusalem Elders. But he inferred that that was the case. And if so then we have the picture here of the elders of the Jerusalem church handling the money that was sent by various congregations. I ask this question, is this centralized control? If not then why decry a similar arrangement regarding the preaching of the gospel here. And if this is centralized control, then why oppose it today? He says this was to meet a need. In that case it was physical. Today there is a need which is spiritual in its nature. Now if it is right to meet one need which we all recognize, then what objection can be had in meeting another need which we likewise recognize, that is the preaching of the gospel? Now it'll take more than merely ignoring that to deal with the argument.

I wish to call your attention further to the fact that Brother Cogdill's objections are fallacious in their nature, and in connection with that let me have chart No. 60. Chart No. 60.

While we're getting this, let me ask that the lights in the center, up in the ceiling, be turned out. Those are the ones and turn the others on around the wall. Now this friends, is the chart upon which I want to call your attention tonight. That we have outlined Brother Cogdill's false pattern. His argument upon the subject involved, in the matter of this cooperation of Acts 11:27.

Here is what we have here. We have disciples sending money to elders. You're familiar with that matter, it's been before us for two or three evenings. How that a great famine was about to occur in Judea, and how the disciples in Antioch determined to send relief unto the brethren who dwelt in Judea, "Which also they did sending it to the elders by the hand of Barnabas and Saul." What do we have here? We have disciples sending to the elders Brother Cogdill says, notwithstanding the fact that the passage doesn't say it, that it constitutes the church. He says it must have been the church and that this is an exclusive pattern. Ob-

SPONSORING CONGREGATIONS

CHART NO. 60

COGDILL'S FALSE "PATTERN" ARGUMENT ON "SUBJECTS."

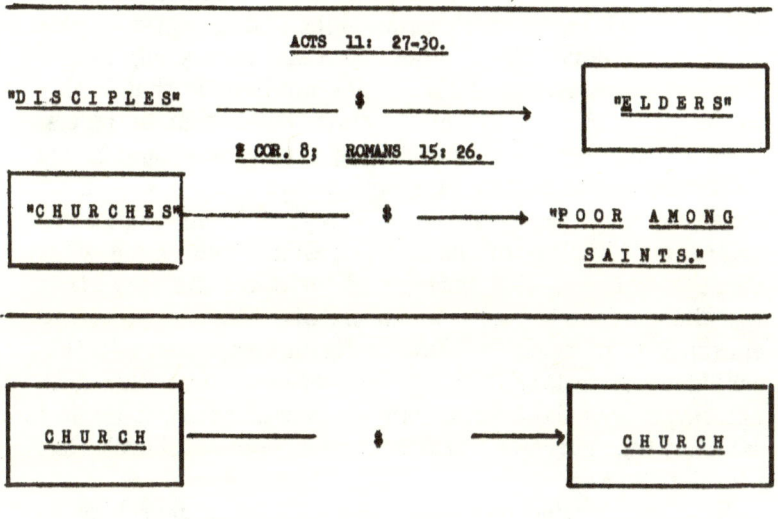

serve please that his pattern is that a church may send to another church only in a case of physical need.

But now in the next case which is presented, 2 Corinthians 8, Romans chapter 15, verse 26, the text plainly says that churches sent to the poor among the saints. Now get this please, it doesn't designate the church here. Brother Cogdill inferred that that's what it was, that it was sent to the church. The Bible doesn't say it. It says the poor among the saints, and that implies that there were some saints who were not poor. The mere fact that there were poor among the saints implies that some of the saints were not poor. It does not mention the church, it simply says the poor among the saints. And you watch please his breakdown here. His pattern is that it must be a church to a needy church. But in this case it does not mention the church, it simply says that churches sent to the poor among the saints. Oh he infers it, that this was the church, and he infers that if it was done that way here it must have been done that way here; and that's begging the question, that's assuming the very point that's to be proved; for example, (Moderator says something), Brother Woods: Thank you. I start out tonight in an automobile, to Memphis, I'm driving a Buick automobile, I arrive in Memphis in an automobile. Does it logically and necessarily follow that because I left here in a Buick automobile that I plan to arrive in Memphis in one? Now that's what he infers. Because that was true in one case, that it was sent to the elders, he thinks that in every other case it must also mean that whether it says it or not. Now that friends, is an unwarranted handling of the word of God. You watch what he needs. He needs a passage of scripture that says that the church sent to another church, and that the receiving church was in need, destitute in its nature. Actually this case does not establish it for two reasons: first, this does not say it was the church. In the second place, it doesn't say that the church in Jerusalem constituted a church that was destitute.

Now here is what he needs. Get it please, a church sending to another church that is destitute. And he couldn't find it if his life depended upon it. Now I've shown you this, that here are two different instances of cooperation. Both of them different in their nature. And so his argument fails.

Now let me show you, please, what's missing from his argument. Here are the characteristics of this activity in Acts 11, verses 27 to 30. There is a famine involved. Each disciple participated according to his ability. It was sent unto the brethren, that is to those outside the church in Antioch. It was sent to the elders. It was sent by the hands of messengers. And its purpose was to supply physical need. Now then if that's a pattern—and that's the one upon which he bases his contention; it's the only one in the Bible upon which the case of a famine of emergency or some catastrophe. In the second place, disciples could never give beyond their ability. They'd have to give only according to their ability. That's what this says they did. But we know that that's not a pattern because we know the Macedonians gave beyond their ability. In the next place, the church must provide relief for brethren only. In the next place, these brethren must not be members of the congregation providing the relief. Couldn't even help your own brethren from this pattern alone. Why it would have to be the brethren of some other congregation. That in order for a church to be the proper subject for assistance it would have to be elders. Couldn't help any congregation that didn't have elders. In the next place, you'd have to send the contribution by the hand of two men, and in the next place, one church could send assistance to another church only in connection with physical need.

Now is Brother Cogdill prepared for those conclusions? Let us have next, please, chart No. 55. I want to show you what his proposition does for him.

Now this is chart No. 55. Not the next one in order, but 55. Watch this friends, Brother Cogdill's theory kills radio work in the preaching of the gospel. Now notice please, let this represent, please, congregation A. The gospel goes into the area of congregation B and C. Now on last evening he said that he objected to the Herald of Truth because this preaching that comes into the Birmingham area by the Herald of Truth over which locally there is no control, but that's characteristic of every radio broadcast in the country. Everyone of them goes into areas where there are congregations. Hence, if his objection to the Herald of Truth be valid then it would destroy and make unscriptural every radio program in the country. Why if any program went into an area where the elders of the congregation then according to Brother Cogdill that would make it unscriptural.

CHART NO. 54
COGDILL SHUTS DOORS OF COOPERATION

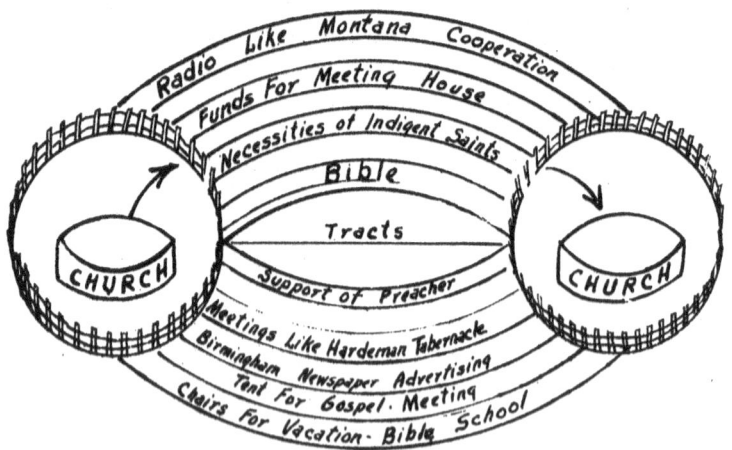

Let us have, please chart No. 54. I want you to note, friends, what his position leads to. Now bear in mind the respective position that one church may assist another church only when the giving church possesses ability to give and the receiving church is in need, physical need mind you. That's his position. And let this represent now the giving church and this the receiving church. And let this represent roads that lead from one to the other. There is but one road open. What is that? The necessities of indigent saints. That's Brother Cogdill's position that one church may send assistance to another church only when the other church is in physical need, physical need mind you. Now watch please what that excludes. That would make Brother Tant's Montana cooperative effort null and void. He can't travel that road with it. Remember, please, that sometime back Brother Tant made an appeal for churches in the South to send money to a little congregation in Montana to enable that congregation to put the gospel on the air up there. Well, that will eliminate that because that's not physical need. Brother Cogdill's pattern, which he alleges necessitates a contribution only in case of physical need. That will eliminate funds for a meeting house. You couldn't send a little group up in Montana some assistance to help them build a meeting house. If the only reason is for indigency.

In the next place, that would eliminate sending a Bible. It would eliminate sending tracts. You couldn't send assistance in that respect because that's not physical need. In the next place, you couldn't send support of a preacher that's the very part he denied. You couldn't conduct any more meetings like the Hardeman Tabernacle meetings. That's out. In the next place, you couldn't send assistance to conduct meetings upon the same basis as the Birmingham newspaper ad and that is accepted by the brethren right here. And Brother Cecil Douthitt said that it must be right because Brother John T. Lewis was over here and he wouldn't let anything go on that was wrong. So Brother Lewis endorsed it back when it was going on because Brother Lewis wouldn't let anything go on that wasn't right. Now that's out because that's not physical assistance.

In the next place, you couldn't send chairs for a Vacation Bible School if one Church wanted to borrow them. The chairs that another church had in order to conduct their Vacation Bible School they couldn't let them have them because that'd be assistance that wasn't physical.

In the next place, you couldn't send a tent. One congregation couldn't loan another congregation a tent. Not if this man's argument has any merit, the only reason that one church may send money to another is to eliminate the need. Needs of indigent saints. Now friends, I insist that he answer this. I'm either right or wrong on this one or the other.

Brother Cogdill, either I have represented this correctly, or I haven't. Now if I haven't represented it correctly, I want to know it. I want you to tell me if there are any of these needs that may be met. Please do that, for the sake of the cause of Christ, deal with this particular chart here. Let us have please, chart No. 53.

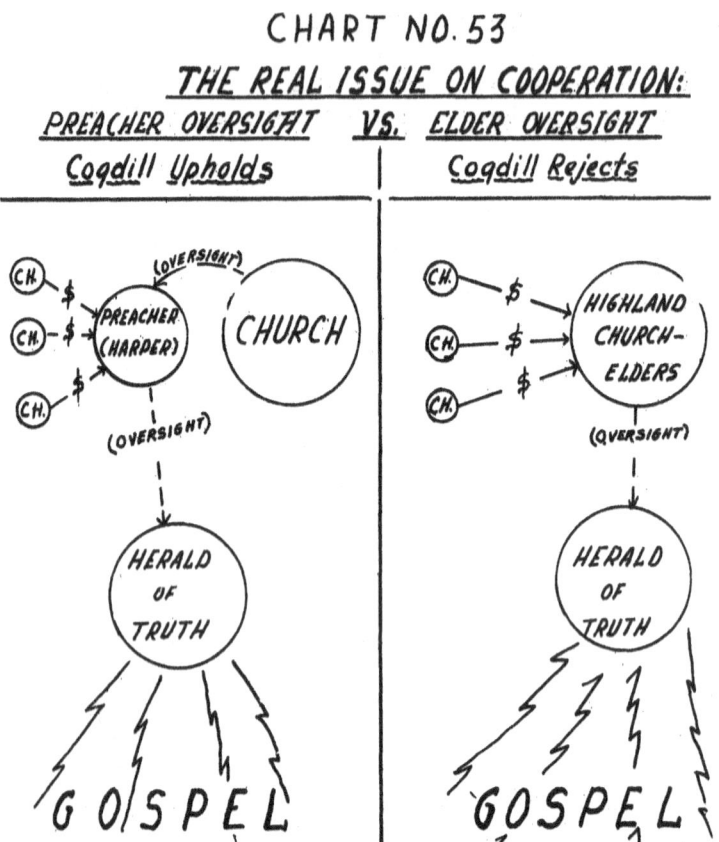

Now friends, here is a very important matter, and I want you to watch this carefully please. Here is the real issue on this cooperation question. It is actually a question of preacher-oversight versus elder-oversight. It is question of who will direct the work of the Lord, the elders or the preachers. This is what Brother Cogdill upholds. He's taken the position that it would be right for churches to send money to a preacher in order to operate a radio program. Now over at Corinth, Mississippi, sometime back there was a radio program conducted over there which some of us thought was exactly like the Herald of Truth, but when this matter was introduced in the Tant-Harper debate in Abilene, it was insisted that the money was not sent to the church but rather to the preacher and that the preacher operated independently of the church, and that it was not a church program but was simply a program directed by the preacher. Of course, the preacher was under the elders, but it was not sent to the church but was sent to the preacher and that that's what made it right. Now ladies and gentlemen, I ask this question with all seriousness and candor—I asked it last night and I got no answer. I hope Brother Cogdill you'll answer tonight. Suppose that the elders of the Highland church go back to Abilene and report to the others over there, there are three of them here, and seven others at home; suppose that these three elders go back over there and report to the other seven that there's a way to reach harmony and that is to take this program out from under the oversight of the elders in the Highland church and place it under the control of Brother Harper. Will you cease your objection? Now then, put it down, will you cease your objection? If this program is taken out from under the control of the elders and placed under the control of the preacher, will you cease your objection?

Secondly, if these brethren should see fit to make a change in their preacher, and you, and other circumstances were agreeable, would you be willing to conduct that program, Brother Harper, or rather Brother Cogdill, in Brother Harper's place under the same circumstances? That is, would you be willing to receive the funds sent to you instead of being sent to the church, and would you take the oversight of that program and would you preach on that program? Now friends, that's pertinent to this issue. We insist that there must be an answer.

Now let me have chart No. 50.

Chart No. 50A. This, friends, is the chart last night which we presented to show you exactly what's affirmed. These brethren have fought a retreating battle every since

CHART NO. 50A
TO WHAT EXTREME OF ANTI-ISM?

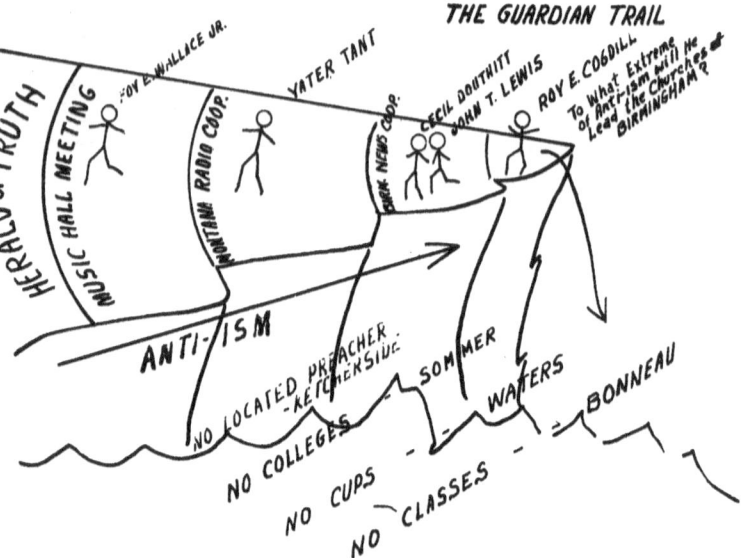

this thing started. One by one they've pulled in their battle lines until now they're on the very verge of extreme anti-ism. For example, the first thing that they ran away from, at least as far as Brother Tant was concerned, was the Music Hall meeting. He didn't hesitate to repudiate it. It then became necessary that he take his stand here on the Montana cooperative radio effort. But now in principle Brother Cogdill has repudiated that. And next, the stand was made here. These preachers here in Birmingham practice this. But now, that, too, has been repudiated at least by some of them. And now then, here Brother Cogdill stands out here on this point. Now how much further is he going? There is exactly the same basis for the opposition that is offered to the located preacher by Ketcherside and to the colleges by Sommer, and to the cups by Waters, and to the classes by Bonneau that there is to this. He tried to leave with you the impression last night that there is a pattern for this in the New Testament an exclusive and specific pattern. I deny it, and I challenge him to produce it. Now do not misunderstand me. It is a fact that the New Testament teaches that a preacher may locate but there's no specific detailed pattern of it like you insist that there must be for the Herald of Truth. There isn't, in the New Testament, any instance of individual cups, as such being used. I do not hesitate to say, that generically speaking they are authorized, but then according to his demand for a pattern, there is no pattern. So also are the classes. You can't find a Bible School set-up in the New Testament following the pattern that is characteristic of our activity today in that detailed, specific fashion that he demands for the Herald of Truth. Yet friends, up till now he has adopted a manner of arguing this question and he has occupied a position that is comparable to this. He said it seems these debates makes me think of Ketcherside. Of course, they do, because he's making Ketcherside's speeches for him. He said, well he'd debate Ketcherside. Well, if Ketcherside's smart, he'll just wait a few days. Because Ketcherside won the battle at Paragould, without firing a shot. Because over there five years after they challenged him for a debate on the very question, five years later they endorsed the preacher that was defending the very thing that Ketcherside would have defended had they had the debate with him just five years later. They allowed themselves to be pushed back until they are occupying the very position that Ketcherside had challenged them on earlier.

Now then, friends, I want to make brief mention of some matters last evening to which I thus far have had no opportunity to reply. Brother Tant and Brother Cogdill need to get together on the condition of Highland financially. Brother Tant has just jublished in the paper that they're virtually on the edge of bankruptcy, or words to that effect. Whereas, Brother Cogdill says that they are in splendid condition. Now one of them said today, in my presence, that they weren't quite as bad off as Brother Tant thought they were and they certainly weren't as well off as Brother Cogdill thinks they are. In fact, they must be somewhere between those two extremes.

They sought to leave the impression with you that the Herald of Truth is operated in some fashion as to assist the local congregation at Highland. Let me emphasize this, friends, not one penny that the churches of Christ send to the Herald of Truth program goes into the treasury of the Highland Church—not one penny of it—insofar as their operating treasury's concerned.

Moderator: Five minutes.

Brother Woods: It's kept in a separate treasury and it is used solely and only for the Herald of Truth program. Even this literature, for example, this that's been exhibited in the lobby of the Bankhead hotel here was provided for by the Highland Church and not from the treasury, and that is composed of the money put together for the purpose of preaching the gospel. And so such statements as that are misleading and fall short of the truth. On last evening, some matters were said with reference to brother John T. Lewis. I cited a statement from him proving that Brother Lewis, at one time, thought that what Mr. Kendrick came back to was the Lord's plan, and I cited Mr. Kendrick to see what he thought the Lord's plan was. If I were to say that some fellow left the Baptist church and went to Adventism, it'd be legitimate for me to determine what he went to, and the only way I could find out what he went to is to find out what Adventism is. So when he said he took up the Lord's plan of doing mission work then I looked to see what Mr. Kendrick thought that plan was, and the truth of the business is that that's what Brother Lewis believed back then because that's exactly the basis that was characteristic of this Birmingham cooperative radio program and newspaper ad. The principle's exactly the same. Now Brother Lewis may repudiate that if he wishes and he can have time in the debate if he wishes to do so. Now that, friends, is a matter that I want you to consider carefully. I want you to realize this that we're not trying to defend or establish something that is without scriptural merit. We are not affirming that people may abandon the scriptures. On the contrary, we insist that we must conform to them. But you remember this, please: a creed is just as objectionable though it may be unwritten or though it may have been adopted by our brethren as from a denominational source, and that these brethren stand in the unhappy position of advocating that which they themselves would have condemned just a few years ago when such matters were defended by the hobby-riders and those who were dividing the church over the question of classes and cups and located preachers and so on. I want you to remember please that these practices are taught in the Bible. Taught in the Bible in the same fashion that we establish authority for our Bible schools. Taught in the same fashion that we establish authority for the individual cups. Taught in the same way that we believe that a located preacher is scriptural. And I resent such implications that we have espoused any kind of position in recent years, because these are matters that have been accepted by us all through the years. I stand exactly where I stood on these matters ever since I've been preaching, more than a quarter of a century. I read the sermons that came from the Tabernacle meetings published in the Nashville Banner, or it could have been The Tennessean, at the time that Brother Hardeman preached them, and I have endorsed and supported such cooperative efforts and participated in them through the years. We're just as loyal to the word of God as anybody. We resent and reject an implication of any other nature. I want you tonight to remember this, please, that we ought to recognize that we are brethren, that we ought to realize that the peace and harmony of the church must be involved in any consideration of these matters. And that it's not in harmony with practices of Christian courtesy to impute to somebody a position which he does not hold, and I do not intend to do that to Brother Cogdill and I resent his implication that any of us have abandoned the truth. On the contrary, some of us are still contending for the truth, still insisting for that which Brother Cogdill stood for until comparatively recently.

There, friends, is the real basis of the matter. Now, Brother Cogdill, there's three or four things to which I want you to give attention. One: Please tell us whether or not my chart on the roads from church to another represent your position in this debate. Whether I have it correctly represented that there is but one reason that one church may send assistance to another church and that is when the receiving church was in need, in physical need, mind you. That is when its members are destitute. I want to know further whether if the brethren of the Herald of Truth broadcast will take that out from under the control of the elders and place it under the control of the preacher, whether or not you would accept it as a scriptural program? I want to know if you will not do so why you won't. Did you tell me my time was up? Moderator: yes. Bro. Woods: Thank you.

Cogdill's Fifth Negative

Gentlemen Moderators, Brother Woods, Ladies and Gentlemen:

It's a real privilege to me to be back again before you tonight for the purpose of replying to the things that have been advanced in the speech that you've just heard and some things that perhaps may have been advanced prior to the speech that you just heard.

Brother Woods has gone back over the same ground in this speech that he covered last night in both of his other speeches. He hasn't changed the argument a whit as those of you who were here last night well know. He's drawn some new pictures, some new illustrations, some new cartoons of the same arguments that he has made in both other speeches to illustrate the arguments that have been advanced, the things that he's had to say. So in replying to the things that were said in the speech to which you have just listened will be in effect answering the things that have already been answered. And before I get into that there are some other matters that I want to present to Brother Woods.

I have here several statements concerning things that he's introduced in the debate that I'd like for him to tell us

SPONSORING CONGREGATIONS

about. I know of no better way than to simply present the statements to them and ask him to sign them if they represent his convictions. If they don't, to tell us why. Will you sign the following statements and let me give you a copy of them so you can follow them as we read them:

No. 1. "I endorse the following statement from C. Kendrick, *Live Religious Issues*, page 445, quoted in my chart No. 42, as being a correct picture of the operation of the Herald of Truth conducted by the Highland elders at Abilene, Texas. Quote: "Send the funds to the Elders of some central congregation who can disburse them wisely and justly." Unquote. And the entire paragraph, which I read in my first speech including the applications made of Acts 11:27 and 30 concerning the Jerusalem elders distributing the funds contributed by Antioch throughout the Judean churches." Now that's simply asking him to endorse what he read and what he quoted from Dr. Carroll Kendrick's book. He attributed that to Bro. Lewis. And I'm asking him, since he compared it to the operation of the Herald of Truth, if he's willing to endorse it. If he isn't, he can say so. And I'd appreciate him telling us why. If it's parallel to the Herald of Truth, how can he keep from endorsing it?

No. 2. "I believe the members of a congregation have the right to circulate a petition to oust the elders by majority vote if they will not put the Orphan homes and the Herald of Truth in their budget." Now why would I ask him to sign a statement of that kind? Because last night he introduced the East Huntsville matter, and that's exactly what occurred in that congregation. They tore that church up; circulated false charges and a petition against the elders because the elders would not put in the budget the support of the orphan home. That's what happened up at East Huntsville. I have a statement from a lot of good brethren concerning it. Brother Woods either endorses their action or he doesn't. He introduced the matter, I didn't. I'm simply asking him, do you agree that they acted scripturally when they circulated the petition against the elders, called a meeting and voted the elders out by majority rule and took the church over. *Not* in order to get the orphan home *out* of the budget, but in order to get it *in* the budget, in order to get the church to support it. It was not doing so.

Now then No. 3. "The elders of a congregation have the scriptural right to put the Herald of Truth in the budget whether the membership of the congregation can conscientiously contribute to it or not, and should do so." Do you believe, Brother Woods, that if the Elders of a congregation think the Herald of Truth is scriptural, but the members of the congregation cannot conscientiously support it, that they ought to commit that congregation against the conscience of those brethren who cannot contribute to it? I'd like to have an answer to that, and know what your attitude about it is.

No. 4. "Every preacher who opposes the Herald of Truth is an apostate, and every church that refuses to support it is reduced to—quote, 'a second-rate, hobbyistic sect.'" Unquote. Now he's made those statements, I want to know if he's willing to stand on them. You know to get up here and make a sort of a sympathetic kind of a plea, like he did in the last few minutes of his speech while ago, that we ought to treat one another as Christians, and that we ought to recognize that we are brethren and that we ought to be united is not very well in harmony with calling those who do not agree with him on the question, who are just as sincere and conscientious as Guy Woods, or the elders of the Highland church ever dared to be, apostates because they don't agree, and calling congregations who oppose the Herald of Truth, accusing them of relegating themselves to a "second rate, hobbyistic sect". Now, Brother Woods, if that's your idea of the way to promote unity, among brethren, you've got a different notion to what I've got.

No. 5. "The support of the Herald of Truth and the orphan homes among us are matters of expediency but should be advocated and promoted even to the destruction of fellowship among brethren in Christ." Now they're either matters of necessity or matters of expediency. If they're matters of divine law and we have a pattern for them, then, brethren, there isn't any choice about, it, and the man who

SPONSORING CONGREGATIONS

doesn't support it, and the church who does not have it in its budget is apostate. But if it's in the realm of expediency, if it is a matter of judgment as to whether or not we do the work that way, then I want to know does Brother Woods believe that if anytime, anywhere, in any congregation, a matter of mere expediency ought to be pushed to the point of destroying the fellowship of brethren in Christ? Are you really interested in unity? That's what I want to find out.

No. 6. "It is unscriptural and wrong for an orphan home to be under the supervision and control of the elders of a church of Christ serving in their capacity as elders." Now, Guy, that's what you argued and you've introduced the orphan home back into this proposition. I want to know if you're willing to sign your name to it and stand on it. You're going to have a lot of your own orphan home brethren to convert. You're going to have to work on nearly all of them West of the Mississippi river, because they think, under Firm Foundation influence, they think, nearly all of them, that they're operating under an eldership. Even Boles Home claims to do that to some degree.

No. 7. "I am opposed to churches of Christ building and operating hospitals even for benevolent purposes." He said the Guardian had woefully misrepresented him when they said that he was in favor of hospitals or promoting hospitals or some such expression. I want to know what his position on the hospitals is. If you're not willing to sign any of the above statements will you explain whether or not they correctly represent your views and if not, why not? I believe I've already given you a copy of them.

Now, Brother Woods, if you're as good at answering questions as you are at asking them, and if you are as good at giving information as you demand somebody else to be, we're going to find out some things when you answer those statements or when you refuse.

I called your attention to another matter that he's under obligation to establish. You know we hear a lot from them about component parts. Well when you take his proposition apart, take it to pieces and look at it, there are some component parts, if you want to use that expression, that he's under obligation to establish. I want, briefly, to review them.

No. 1. Any eldership can promote anything that they deem to be a good work whether the congregation where they are elders is able or competent to do it or not.

No. 2. Any ambitious eldership can employ and send out their promoters and propaganda agents to gain admission to the treasury of every possible church, and secure all of their money possible.

No. 3. The funds of many or all of the churches can be pooled or combined in that one promoting congregation under the exclusive control of that one eldership.

No. 4. Thus the promoting church has a work that is exclusively theirs.

No. 5. This promoting church and its eldership is entitled to whatever part of the resources of other churches they need in order to do that good work which they have assumed.

No. 6. The propaganda agents and promoting representatives of this promoting church are entitled to insist upon admission to the services of every congregation in the land in order to have sufficient opportunity to promote these churches out of their money to help them support this good work which they have assumed to do.

No. 7. The more money they can thus secure and the more universal this promoted program becomes the better it will please the Lord.

No. 8. Any preacher that opposes such a program is an "anti", "hobbyist" and a "factionist", and should be marked and "quarantined".

No. 9. *The Gospel Advocate* and its editor and paid writers, with its great circulation, have the right to do the marking and branding.

No. 10. The editor of the Advocate has the exclusive right to determine the truth of all these contentions for everybody he can bring under his influence, and the influence of his paper without giving any opportunity therein for discussion unless it is favorable to his decision.

No. 11. If the eldership of the church will not submit to this program, the promoting brethren have the scriptural right to vote them out and take over, so they can support such a wonderful program.

No. 12. Any such church as will not be brought into line with such a wonderful work is thereby reduced to a "second rate, hobbyisitic sect", and that by official pronouncement.

Now those are statements, not that I have concocted, that he's made in this debate. And the tapes will show that they are the positions that he's taken by exactly what he said. Those of you who have been here listening to him know that it's so.

Well, what am I under obligation to do? You know he's pushing me for a pattern. He's forgotten completely that he is in the affirmative. Why, Brother Woods, you agreed, when you signed the proposition, that it is in harmony with the scriptures—you agreed to prove your proposition by the word of God. That's what you agreed to do; to prove your proposition by the word of God. To find the pattern, the authority for what you're doing and what *you're* advocating. You're the man that's under obligation to find the pattern and you failed miserably to do it. You haven't shown us any pattern of anything that looks like the Herald of Truth in the word of God. You have from your pictures but not from your Bible. What we need is a little scripture in support of your proposition. Nearly every chart he's put on this screen—nearly every one of them—has been noticeable by its complete absence of any scriptural reference whatever. How much Bible have you seen in those cartoons? How much? How many of them had any scriptural argument connected with it? How many of them was even based on a passage of scripture? To how many passages when he presented them and when he made his speeches did he refer? On the other hand, being interested not in just dealing with cartoons and answering illustrations, I have in the speeches that I have made thus far on this question tried to deal with it from a Bible point of view.

Let me point out to you what I have emphasized and what I have pointed out:

1. Each congregation is to finance its own work by the individual contribution of its own members. Where is the pattern for that? First Corinthians, chapter sixteen,

verses one and two. That's the way Paul told the Corinthian church to do it. That's the way Acts 11:27 and 30 says the brethren in Antioch did it—three new Testament examples.

2. That contribution, when made into a common fund, becomes a treasury of the church of the Lord, subject to apostolic authority, because figuratively laid at the feet of the apostles, Acts chapter two. They brought it in, chapter four, and laid it at the feet of the apostles, that which they had received by the sale of their lands and their houses.

3. I have shown you that the congregation is bound, by apostolic authority, in the use of those funds—by the authority of the Lord exercised through his inspired apostles. The elders of the church are bound to use that congregational treasury in harmony with the will of Christ. Only the apostles of our Lord had the authority to bind and to loose, Matthew chapter 18. Adams: Fifteen minutes. Thank you.

4. Congregations, in the New Testament, they contributed out of their congregational treasury to another church only when that church was in need. First Corinthians, sixteen, verses one to four; 2nd Corinthians 9, 2nd Corinthians 8, Acts 11. Why was the contribution sent to brethren in Judea? They were in need. Now, Guy, whatever caused the need is purely an incidental matter. The important thing is, the need existed, they were not able to meet it themselves, other churches helped them — the Antioch church. Or if you insist that it can't mean the church when it doesn't say the church, then the brethren in Antioch sent to the brethren in Judea. They sent it to the elders in Judea. For what purpose? To meet a need. *To meet a need.* They didn't send it down there without there being any need. I wonder what his point about Highland was. Is he trying to convince us—talking about what Yater had to say about it and what I had to say about it—is he trying to convince us that the Highland church is a church that has needy members in it that they can't help? Is that his point?

If it isn't, he has no point of comparison. Whatever their financial status may be, he has no point of comparison unless they have members within that congregation that they are unable to take care of themselves. That was the case in Jerusalem. That was the case in 2 Corinthians 8 and 9. It was the case again in Acts 11. In both instances, he found nothing to the contrary. Nothing to the contrary. Now, Brother Woods, you've got one more speech. I want to beg you with all the sincerity of my heart. You say you believe in going by the Bible. I want you to produce, in your last speech, you haven't done it so far, that example from the New Testament, that passage of scripture from the New Testament that either expressly states, that necessarily infers, or that gives an approved example of a congregation sending out of its treasury to another church, when the church wasn't in need. I tell you how liberal I'll be with you, you just find me an example of where even individual disciples sent to a church a fund that they made up as individuals unless the receiving church was in need. Just forget about church to church now, Guy. Find us a church, that from outside of its own members, received help in the New Testament when it wasn't in need. That's what I've been begging for for three nights now. Brethren, that's what he hasn't found. And when this debate goes into print, it'll still not be there. It will not be in the book, because it is not in *The Book*. And Guy Woods can't find it. He can draw pictures and illustrate things, but he can't find that, and that's what he's practicing, and that's what he needs to justify his practice.

Congregations, in the New Testament day contributed to a work of preaching the gospel only by sending out preachers and sending wages directly to the preacher whom they were supporting to supply his need. Philippians 2:25, 4:15 and 17, 2 Corinthians 11:7 and 8.

Now you know he deals with the idea of a preacher having a radio program under him, sending to the preacher in order that the preacher might use some other means out here somewhere. Last night I told you that the sending to the preacher ought to stop when the preacher's need stops. That's New Testament pattern, too. When congregations, in the New Testament, supported preachers, they supplied their need. They gave them what they needed in order to do their work and Paul said it was wages that he received. Support the ox that treadeth out the corn—that's one illustration that he uses—shall not be muzzled, and so on. "He that preacheth the gospel shall live of the gospel." That's what the Bible says about it. And when churches sent to a preacher and they always sent to the preacher, in the New Testament, when the purpose was to preach the gospel, they sent to the preacher, and I begged him for an exception to that. Where did a church ever contribute outside of its own local work to the preaching of the gospel, to the support of gospel preaching that it did not send to the preacher? Now that's what we want. That's what you need to sustain your proposition, Guy. That's what I'm begging you for. You've got one speech left in which to do it. You haven't done it yet.

When churches received benevolent contributions from others, such was received *only by the elders* to be distributed under their supervision, Acts 11:27 and 30. He said, well now how does Brother Cogdill know that they sent it to the elders of Jerusalem. Well, I'll tell you the reason I reached that conclusion. The only time the word of God tells you how they ever did it, it said they sent it to the elders. That's the only thing you find. Now find an exception to that. They sent for the poor saints in Jerusalem. But they sent to the relief of the brethren in Judea. How did they send to the relief of the brethren in Judea? They sent it to the elders. If they sent it to the elders when they sent to the relief of the brethren in Judea in Acts 11, to whom did they send it, in the absence of any further information about it, when they sent to the poor saints or for the poor saints in Jerusalem? Without any further information, would you be entitled to the conclusion that they did it in Jerusalem like they did it in Judea in Acts 11? Would they? Show me an example to the contrary.

When churches sent contributions to work elsewhere they chose *individuals only—never congregations* — as their agents or messengers and the reason pointed out to you on one of the charts was because agency requires subordination. You can't have agency without it. When one church becomes the agent of another church. it is subordinated to that church, serving that church, doing what that church tells it to do, or binding the other church by their consent in what they do. Agency means subordination. An individual can be an agent of a congregation. But when you make one congregation the agent of another congregation, you destroy the equality of the churches of Christ. That's the thing that's wrong with it. You exalt one and concentrate power in one congregation and one eldership that God never did intend for them to have.

If God had intended for us to have that kind of centralized power, don't you know that God is wise enough, in the all sufficiency of his plan, brethren—don't you know that he is?—that he would have given us the machinery with which to carry it out. Guy made this statement in his first speech down here in Birmingham at Central church that God gave to the church, the church has the machinery with which to do its evangelism. (How much time do I have?) The church has the machinery with which to do its evangelism. I want to know what it is. What is it, Brother Woods? He tells us that it isn't sufficient. The church doesn't have sufficient machinery as God designed it, with the organization God gave it. Give me my chart on the sufficiency of the church. I believe it's about number six. That there isn't a congregation on the face of the earth that's able to carry out the program of the Great Commission. Why he said, we're obligated to go everywhere into all the world. He'd have that thing pictured by saying or inferring, and I wonder if that's what he meant to infer that God meant for every congregation, at the same time, to go into all of the world itself. Is that your argument? Is that the point, that God intended for every church concurrently, at the same time, to preach the gospel in all of the world? He intended for the North Birmingham church to preach the gospel in all the world. And he intended for Homewood to preach the gospel in all the world. For both of them to do the whole job themselves. Who, on earth, ever advocated that? I tell you what he did do though, Guy. It started with one, didn't it? Didn't it? Did God plant many churches at one time so they could cooperate and carry out the Great Commission? How ridiculous can a man make himself in advocating a false position, and trying to justify an idol that he's got in his heart?

From Jerusalem the Gospel went forth into all the world, and in 30 years time, listen to me, in 30 years time, they preached to every creature under heaven, in the world known at that time. They carried out the Great Commission. Six millions of people, six millions of people, history indicates, within that period of time, heard and accepted, at least a form of the gospel of Christ. And they did it without one scintilla of evidence that any congregation became a centralized agency, in which the funds of other churches were pooled, and in which that money came under the exclusive control of one eldership. Where does he find it in the New Testament? They did it without it any such program as this brotherhood-wide business that these brethren are promoting on the church today.

But I call your attention to another thing. Contributions sent from congregations to work elsewhere, as we've suggested, was always sent to the work to be done. Never to a centralized agency; either a board or the promoting elders.

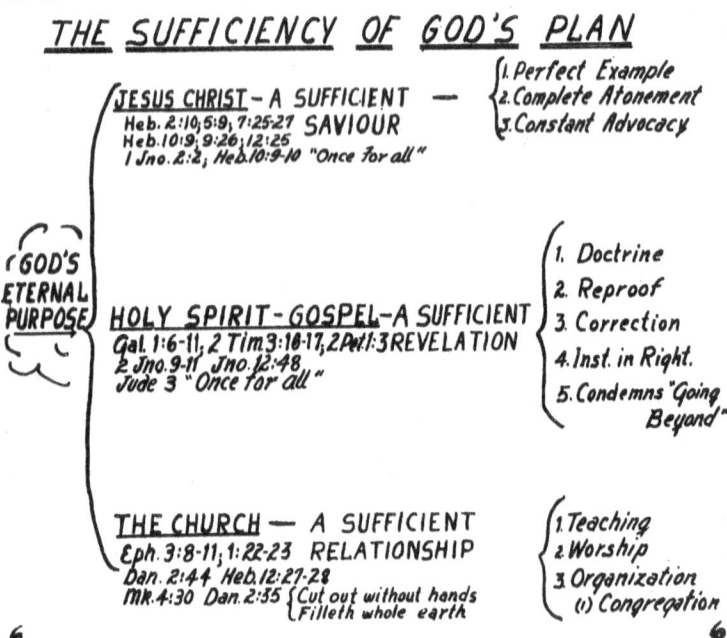

Listen to me, friends, there's the sufficiency of God's plan. We've introduced it and talked about it, Jesus Christ, the sufficient Savior. There'll never be another sacrifice made. The church or the gospel of Jesus Christ is sufficient revelation and it is sinful to go beyond. Oh, he said, we're not going beyond the Bible. We don't believe in going beyond the Bible. Well you are going beyond it. I didn't accuse you of believing in going beyond it, but your going beyond it is what this debate's about. That's what's creating all of the dissension. Friends, it isn't opposition that creates the division. Don't let him palm that off on you; you know it isn't so. Churches were not divided within your generation and mine over pre-millenialism because somebody opposed pre-millenialism. That wasn't the reason it divided churches. It was divided because somebody taught the false doctrine of pre-millenialism.

The church was not divided over the Missionary Society because of the opposition to it. Get me right on that. You said the other night, and misquoted me on it, I think it was unintentional, that I said it was the opposition that caused it. Well, it wasn't. It is the introduction of it that caused it. The churches were not divided by instrumental music, because of the opposition; it was the introduction of it without scriptural authority. And the churches are not divided over the Herald of Truth being opposed. They're dividing because it is being promoted in the church along with human institutions, and human arrangements without scriptural authority. Why, he said it belongs in the same class with the Sunday school, and literature, and the one cup. You'd better never debate any of these anti-brethren anymore. I'll tell you that. If you can't do a better job of producing Bible for your Sunday school arrangement, Bible classes on the Lord's day, under the elders of the church, if you can't do any better job in justifying the individual communion set because it comes within the scope of the thing God authorized. I believe it has authority. I wouldn't practice it if I didn't believe it had Bible authority. If I couldn't do any better job producing Bible authority for Bible classes, literature, women teachers and the individual communion set, the located preacher etc . . . than you can do for the Herald of Truth, I'd quit every lasting bit of it. And let somebody hollow change all they wanted to.

He said, Oh we've changed. Where's the change going to stop? Where the changing going to stop? We've changed. Everybody but Guy Woods has. Jack Meyer, the preacher over at Homewood; that had him down here for this debate, has. He's the unchangeable one of the whole outfit. Isn't that remarkable? I want you to know, brethren, that's remarkable. I tell you the difference between you and the rest of us. You just won't face the fact of it. You talk about running. No, you're not like Foy Wallace. You're not saying, "I'll not run", you're running like a scared chicken. And you're running from admitting that you've changed. That's what you're running from. And you ought to be ashamed of it. You ought to get up here and admit that you changed. I've introduced passage after passage from you that proves that you have.

Never did churches send to a centralized agency. Every congregation, under its own eldership, sufficient in God's plan. The Jerusalem church sent to Antioch. Jerusalem continued to send and Antioch continued to send from the day that they began. When the gospel was planted at Philippi, they sent out and never ceased to send out. And every time a congregation was planted it became responsible for planting others. It was a cumulative plan, but it began with the congregation, brethren, and ended there.

Woods Sixth Affirmative

Brother Moderators, Brother Cogdill, Ladies and Gentlemen:

I am now before you for my final speech of the debate. I desire to take up these matters, one by one, which Brother Cogdill introduced, deal with them fully and fairly. Because, if we know our hearts we have no other purpose in mind than simply to present the truth on these or any other matters that may be under consideration.

SPONSORING CONGREGATIONS

I should like to say, first, with reference to these statements which he has introduced that I am surprised that Brother Cogdill would attempt such a thing as this in this the final night of the debate and when I have no opportunity to reply. But the test is honesty now. I have some statements for him to sign, too. And when he indicates that he will sign these and give me an opportunity to comment upon his statements as he would upon mine then we'll sign them together and both of us make our statements to the audience. Now here are the statements:

No. 1. The only time that one church can send assistance to another church is when the receiving church is in want and the sending church is in abundance. Roy E. Cogdill.

No. 2. The scripture which proves the above statement is .... Then the place for him to sign it.

No. 3. The only purpose of the assistance which one church can send to another church is to supply the physical needs of the indigent saints of the receiving church.

No. 4. Radio programs under the oversight of preachers, while the preacher receives funds from some churches of which he is not a member, are scriptural.

And, of course, under each one of these a place to sign.

No. 5. next. If the elders of the Highland Church, Abilene, Texas, were to place the Herald of Truth under the oversight of E. R. Harper, Evangelist, with Brother Harper receiving funds from churches, as the Highland elders now receive funds, and spending the funds as Highland elders now spend the funds, such an arrangement would be in harmony with the scriptures. A place for him to sign.

No. 6. Elders, functioning as elders, have the scriptural right to provide and oversee such an institution for orphan children.

No. 7. Elders, functioning as elders, may provide and oversee a program of recreation for orphan children.

And then No. 8. The Herald of Truth Radio cooperation is parallel to the Missionary Society, and all who participate in such are guilty of digression, and are unworthy of fellowship faithful Christians.

No. 9. The passage which states that one church in abundance sent money to another church in want is .... Then the place for the reference.

No. 10. All of the orphan homes among us are unscriptural and all who participate in their support are digressive and are unworthy of the fellowship of faithful christians. If you are not willing to sign any of the above statements, will you explain whether they correctly represent your reviews, and if not, why not? Now, we believe in fairness, and we are going to insist on fairness in dealing with this matter.

Now, friends, I regret that Brother Cogdill has seen fit to introduce a matter which had no place in this debate. He tells you that on last evening I introduced the Huntsville, Alabama division. Why I did nothing of the kind. I merely read a quotation from Bob Crawley that made mention of the fact that they were sending money up to Huntsville. And I was careful about the statement and didn't read it for that purpose. I read it to show that Brother Crawley was saying and advocating the idea of withdrawing fellowship from these folks. And so anxious was he to get that matter in up there that he rubbed it in to that fashion. Now here is the statement that I read. This appeared in the *Gospel Guardian* of some weeks back. This year, within this particular year.

"We have promised support to Quinton McKay to stay in Huntsville and try to reclaim some of what the digressives have taken away. There is very little question hereabouts regarding fellowship with the institutional crowd. The lines are already drawn and we would not do right to ignore them. Bit by bit, all contact with them is broken." Now that's the extent to which I introduced the Huntsville matter. As a matter of fact, I do know something about that. And since he's raised just a word or two regarding it.

The East Huntsville congregation of some 350 members was at peace and enjoying harmony until the preacher who was responsible for and participated in the division espoused these views which Brother Cogdill tonight defends, and began to advocate them in that congregation.

SPONSORING CONGREGATIONS

When trouble arose it resulted in a break of fellowship. And today the preacher and a small group of the brethren are now out in a rented building — at least were a few weeks ago when I was in Huntsville, and there is no fellowship there. Now then, when did the break come? After the preacher espoused Cogdill's hobby. What was it that produced the division and the break of fellowship? The preaching of his hobby. When did the division come? When they espoused Cogdill's hobby. What is it then that produced the division? Cogdill's hobby.

Take for example the division in the church in Greenville, Texas. There, if you please, was a congregation that had an unbroken record of the support of the Boles orphan home. And they were agreed upon these matters fully. Then the preacher espoused Brother Cogdill's hobby and began to advocate it. The result was that a once peaceful and happy congregation is now divided. And division is there. What produced it? It was the preaching of these views which Brother Cogdill admits that he has espoused in recent years. When did the division come? It came after these views began to be preached. What was it that produced the division? The preaching of these views. Friends, do you want it in your congregation? Now it was Brother Cogdill that introduced this. I regret it. I wish we could get back to those days when we were all preaching the same thing. And that this division didn't exist. And if I had it in my power I would return it to those days. But these brethren have espoused positions that made the practices of the brethren right here in Birmingham digressive.

For example, they repudiated the newspaper cooperation ad. At least Brother Cogdill places it on the same basis, and would of necessity make it exactly of the same character as the Herald of Truth program.

Take, for example, the work that was done in Cuba, when the money was sent from North Birmingham to a congregation in Tampa, who sent it on the Cuba work. Would they endorse that now? No!

Now then, when these matters are injected and these changes produced division. What is it that causes the division? It's the espousal of that which is contrary to that which was formerly believed. And so it is over the country. There is a trail of divided churches wherever this business is preached. Bakersfield, California; Newburn, Tennessee; Greenville, Texas; Russellville, Alabama; Huntsville, Alabama; West Palm Beach, Florida, and so the ugly trail goes.

What produces it, friends? When did it start and who was there preaching when it happened? There is the question. I plead with you with all the earnestness that I possess and in the light of the judgment day to realize what the espousal of these things are doing to the cause of our Lord.

In the next place, he says that the position that I now advocate in this debate is that all of the churches should combine their control under one eldership and that this eldership should have its foot in the door of the treasury of each congregation and should get all the money from them that they can. Friends, I repudiate and reject such a description of it. I have repeatedly placed before you the Macedonian and Jerusalem contribution and have begged him to reply to that to which he's made no mention at all. No mention at all; hasn't so much as even dealt with it. I've shown you that if there's any centralized control in the Herald of Truth Radio program that the same condition existed between the Macedonian and the Jerusalem church. But that if there was centralized control on that occasion that then such must be right. Why doesn't he answer that? Why he thinks he can get up here and tell you that I haven't introduced any scriptures at all, and you'll believe it.

And while we're on that matter of how much scripture we've introduced, may I say to you this, friends, I don't think the Bible has to say a thing a hundred times to mean it. I have established my proposition by irrefutable evidence. I've engaged in a good many debates with Baptist preachers. I frequently, in a debate with a Baptist preacher on the design of baptism, will take up only one passage of scripture. I recall meeting a Baptist preacher in Texas one time in which during the whole debate, I took care that I didn't use but three verses of scripture: Mark 16: 15 and 16; Acts 2: 38; I Peter 3: 21. And you know what he did? He did exactly Roy Cogdill. He yelled and shouted and pleaded and plead for more scripture. Why? Because he needed more about which to quibble. It's not that I haven't presented enough scripture; it's just that Brother Cogdill's said all he knows to say on the arguments made, and he needs more about which to quibble. It's not that I haven't presented enough scripture, it's just that Brother Cogdill's said all he knows to say on the arguments made. And he needs more about which to quibble.

Moderator: 20 minutes.

Brother Woods: Thank you. He says that the Gospel Advocate today is doing the marking. I know of nobody that the Gospel Advocate has marked. The Gospel Advocate is simply contending for what we believe the truth to be. And if you want to put it on the basis of a quarantine, let me tell you this; I preach in meetings continuously; about thirty meetings or more a year and I've held about three hundred meetings in the last twelve years, and I keep more than a hundred meetings scheduled ahead. I've had 6 or 8 meetings cancelled as the result of the fact that I have preached and taught that the Herald of Truth is a scriptural program and that the orphan homes ought to be supported. And do you know why these meetings were cancelled? And do you know who got them cancelled? Somebody either directly or indirectly connected with the Gospel Guardian managed to get each one of them cancelled. And I have the evidence and I can prove it. Now they complain that others are advocating a quarantine when they are practicing it all over the country. If you need any evidence of it, listen here, "There is very little question hereabouts regarding fellowship with the institutional crowd the lines are already drawn, and we would not do right to ignore them." Who said that? A Birmingham preacher.

He said that the Gospel Advocate's editor decides what's right. Well it's a private affair. He owns the paper. If B. C. has the controlling interest in it, it is his, he has the right to say what he wants to go in it. Just as any man who preaches has a right to say what he's going to preach. And Brother Cogdill doesn't like him, evidently he doesn't, he can publish what he pleases in his own paper. But I have material down there that they will not publish. At least they once did, it's probably in the wastebasket now. Brother Thomas Warren has article after article down there, did have, that they won't publish. I know brethren that I could give you all over the country that have sent material to them that they won't publish, and yet they try to make you believe, some of you, that they publish both sides. They want to publish both sides, by telling you what our side is, and what their side is. That's the idea.

Now as to evidence of how irresponsible and intemperate Brother Cogdill can get in a speech, I was amazed to hear him make this statement. He said first, "Find an example in the New Testament where one church ever sent assistance to another church except that church was in need." Well, I did that the very first night. I called his attention to the fact that in Acts 15, that we have an account of the church in Jerusalem, at a time when he says that church was in need of assistance, that it sent assistance by sending preachers along with other material up to the Gentile churches, thus the Jerusalem church assisted them, and that in the field of benevolence, or rather in the field of evangelism when he says they were receiving help in the field of benevolence. You know what he says on that? Oh he says that that was simply revelation. Well now if you cannot send an inspired document without that being an example of revelation, then on the same basis you couldn't send, one church couldn't send a New Testament to another church. I asked him repeatedly to answer that. Did you get his answer? All right, now here is the intemperate statement: he said, "Find where members of one church ever sent money to another church other than one in need." Why he denied that members ever sent contributions to another church unless that church was in need. Do you know what that amounts to, friends? Think of that for a moment. He even challenges the idea of members, individual members, sending a contribution or making a contribution to another church. Do you know what that means? That means if some of you are visiting here and going to stay over night and attend worship here in the city, you can't make a contribution to a congregation where you don't have membership. How wild can a fellow get? One church can't send assistance or give assistance to another church. One individual can't. Oh, I don't know what he'll say next. He has said that the money was always sent to the preacher. Now then he believes that there's no such things as cooperation between churches then in evangelism. Isn't that what we've been telling you all along. I charge that these brethren do not believe in cooperation between churches in the field of evangelism. The only time that money can be sent and the only way for it to be sent is directly to the preacher, therefore, there isn't any such thing as cooperation between churches in evangelism. Therefore, one church can't send another church a New Testament. Now why didn't he frankly and plainly say that that's his position?

Let me have the chart please, chart No. 59.

CHART NO. 59
COGDILL REJECTS

BIBLE UPHOLDS
Col. 4:16; ACTS 15:22-32.

That's the one that I want you to see. Chart No. 59. Friends, I insisted that he give us a reply to this, and he refused to do so. Now here is his position. One church may send another church money only if it is in the field of benevolence and only if the receiving church is in need. What is his position? That this church might send to that church over there assistance only if that church over there is in physical need. That is, its members are hungry or need clothing or so on.

Now if that's right, one church could not send to another church a New Testament. For example, you couldn't even send a package of New Testaments to a little congregation over in Nigeria. You couldn't do it. Do you think, friends, that intelligent, sensible people are going to continue to follow these men into these ridiculous extremes?

Let us have please, the chart that shows the different roads. Chart No. 60.

Now, friends, I insisted that we must have an answer to the question that I raised upon this. He made no reply to it. Why not? Why doesn't he deal with these matters? It is the obligation of the man in the negative to reply to that which is presented. Here was the matter right here. I said according to Brother Cogdill's position and I said, "I want to be right on this, I don't want to charge him falsely." And I insisted that he tell me if I had it right that this represents the giving church and that that represents the receiving church. I said that according to his position, the only reason that one church could send funds to another church was for the purpose of relieving the needy or indigent saints, and of course, it must in such case have needy saints. That eliminates the possibility of any funds for radio cooperation. That would eliminate funds for a meeting house. You couldn't send Bibles. You couldn't send tracts. You couldn't help support a preacher. You couldn't help with meetings like the Hardeman Tabernacle Meetings or like the cooperative efforts of this City in times past. You couldn't loan chairs for a Vacation Bible School. Or you couldn't lend a tent if you had it, because that would be assistance in the field of evangelism. Why didn't he deal with that? What do you brethren think of it, anyway? What is the purpose of a debater anyway? Why is a man supposed to be a respondent to a speech if it's not to deal with what you present? I've seen a lot of fellows in a debate, but I've never seen a fellow that would run from argument as much as Roy Cogdill. I've met Baptist preachers that would make a far better effort to try to answer what was presented than this man. Why didn't he answer that?

Let us have, please, the chart that shows the position that Brother Cogdill holds with reference to sending to the preacher. Again now, I'll have to hunt for the number unless you can find it for me there. That is chart No. 53.

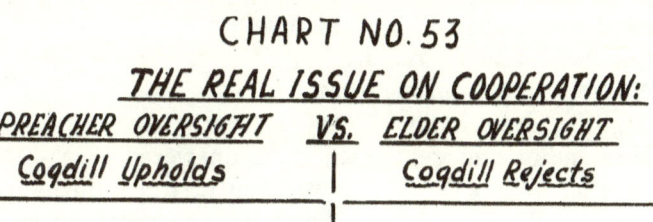

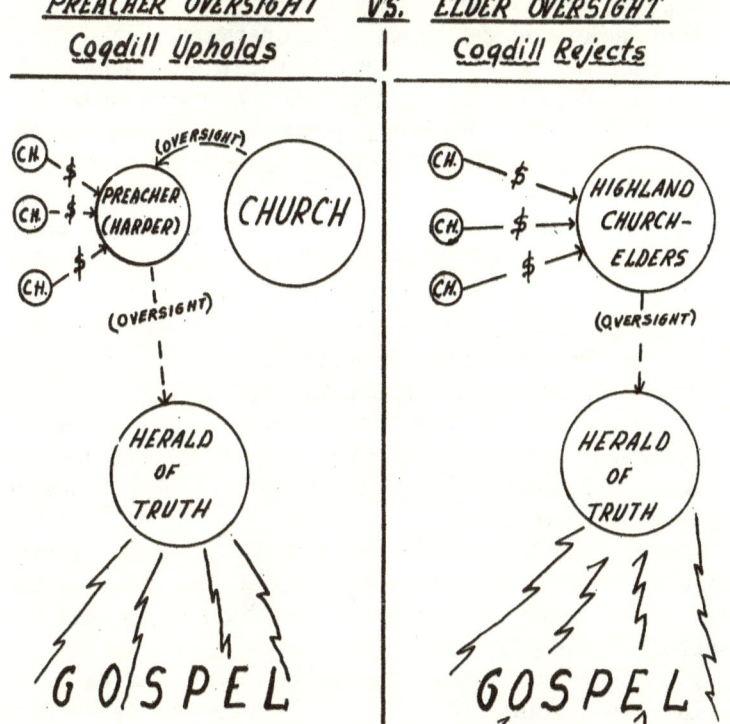

This is it friends. Here we have Brother Cogdill's position. You heard him say the only ground on which money may be sent from a church in the field of evangelism is directly to the preacher. Now he couldn't prove that to save his life. Because the very chapter that he has in mind, which he's never introduced is where it was sent to an apostle and an apostle is over the elders and the preachers. And insofar as that is concerned, it's not a parallel. Now look, I asked him this question, "Brother Cogdill, would you object to the radio program if they simply took the control of it out from under the elders of the Highland Church and put it under the preacher? Why didn't he answer that? Why didn't he answer it? Will you answer it now? I'll give you one minute of my time if you'll answer it right now.

Cogdill: I answered it.

No you didn't answer that.

Cogdill: Yes, I did.

Now ladies and gentlemen if he answered that —

Brother Warren: If he answered it, what did he say?

Brother Woods: Yes, I didn't hear any answer to it.

Brother Cogdill: I'll repeat it when I make my speech.

Brother Woods: Well, I have no reply to you, sir. Why not answer it now? Now's the fair time. Now, friends, we are brethren, and we ought to deal with each other honestly and fairly. This man intends to wait until I have no reply now to deal with these matters.

Brother Adams: May I say a word, Brother Woods?

Brother Woods: Yes, you may.

Brother Adams: He replied to your argument.

Brother Woods: I beg your pardon.

Brother Adams: He did reply to your argument.

Brother Woods: All right, what did he say? I didn't hear you say anything.

Brother Cogdill: Well, you weren't listening. I said that the preacher had his need supplied and that was the end of the congregation's sending to him. That was the support of the preacher.

Brother Woods: Then a preacher cannot receive . . .

Brother Cogdill: Well, I'm not arguing with you . . .

Brother Woods: Well, now you're not answering the question.

Brother Cogdill: I answered the question.

Brother Woods: Here's the thing. Here's what he's saying, ladies and gentlemen: He's saying that if this preacher's hungry that it would be all right for this church to send the money to feed him, but that's not the point under consideration. I asked him this: he said the only way a church may send money in evangelism, is to send it to the preacher. Now in that case it's not for the purpose of feeding the preacher, it's for the purpose of helping him preach the word. Now I asked him this question: Brother Cogdill would it be all right to send money to a preacher to conduct this radio program? Not to feed his hungry body. He knew that's what I asked. Why didn't he answer it?

Brother Warren: Brother Moderator: My contention is that Brother Cogdill hasn't answered the question posed on this chart. Do you say that he has answered the question posed here?

Brother Adams: Yes sir I do.

Brother Warren: Do you say that answer is yes or no?

Brother Cogdill: You can't answer it yes or no.

Brother Woods: All right . . .

Brother Warren: That's not the question here . . .

Brother Cogdill: I didn't answer it yes or no. I won't do that the next time.

Brother Woods: That Isn't what he's asking you; he's just asking you if you answered it.

Brother Cogdill: Yes, I answered it.

Brother Woods: He says he answered it. Now ladies and gentlemen I'm perfectly willing to leave it with you as to whether he answered it or not. This audience is sufficiently intelligent and has the ability to know whether that's an answer to this question or not. I tell you, friends, before I would allow myself to get into a position of that kind, and be forced to manuever in that fashion, I'll give up the hobby that I'm holding. I plead with Brother Cogdill (laughter) to have the courage. I certainly would. I certainly would give it up if I were him, and I know that the people in this audience feel ashamed that Brother Cogdill will not meet this question fairly. What are we talking about? Brother Cogdill if they were to place it under the preachers would it meet your pattern?

Brother Warren: You have eight minutes.

Brother Woods: Thank you. Ladies and gentlemen, he hasn't met the issue and you know it.

Now then that, friends, covers his speech. At least insofar as the matters that were introduced, and that I have done fully in times past. Yes, I want him to put first on the chart, on the board, chart No. 50. No. 50, please, or 50A, let's have 50A, I beg your pardon.

This now, friends, is the position that these brethren occupy and here is position right here don't you forget it, you remember that this is where you're headed and I hope that before you fall off into this down here that you stop before it's too late. Now I want to show you what this man has done by way of a summary of the arguments that he's introduced and the conclusions drawn. We may have the lights on now if we please. Here are some of the blunders, contradictions and inconsistencies of Roy E. Cogdill, in the Birmingham, Alabama debate on the cooperation of churches:

1. Brother Cogdill says he objects to the Herald of Truth radio program because the preaching is heard in the area served by the supporting churches. Yet often preachers on radio programs where the sermon is heard in a hundred or more areas where there are New Testament churches and elderships, which have no control over or endorsing what he preaches.

2. Such an objection, if valid, would kill every radio program in the South.

3. He holds that in spiritual matters money may be sent to the preacher and not the elders and fails to recognize that such a practice bypasses the elders, puts the preachers in charge, and is evangelistic control featured by Carl Ketcherside.

4. He intends to use 2 Cor. 11: 8 as an example of money sent to the preacher rather than the elders, but (1) cannot prove that this did not go to the church first;

and (2) if it did and not he disregards the fact that this was an apostle who was over elders and preachers.

5. Cogdill says a church can send money to another church only in connection with physical need which means that a church could never send a preacher, a tent, a songbook, a tract or a Bible to another church.

6. Cogdill and his group use 2 Cor. 11: 8 in an effort to prove that money was sent directly to Paul, a preacher. That was the great contribution designed for the needy in Jerusalem, he reasons that because it went to the poor among the saints it went to the church in Jerusalem, but he denies that when the churches sent to Paul, a saint, that it was sent to the church in Corinth. He thus refuses to apply his own reasoning on Romans 15: 26 to Cor. 11: 8.

7. 2 Cor. 11: 8 is cited to prove that money was sent direct to Paul, but fails to recognize that the design of it was to provide for Paul's physical needs in order that he might preach the gospel. He thus argues that a church may send to a preacher in connection with spiritual matters and yet the funds received by the preacher, would of necessity be used to supply his personal physical needs that he might render spiritual service.

8. His argument is forced into the conclusion that the church may assist only those that are members of the body of Christ, needy Christians, and that it would therefore be sinful for the church to spend a penny in relieving the distress of the people in the world, however great their sufferings might be.

10. He thus defies God's law of love (Mat. 5: 33) which is basic to the existence of Christianity, and is an adoption of the principle which the Pharisees taught.

11. His reasoning and position on the cooperation question is that a church, (a) may send money only (b) to supply physical need, (c) of Christians only, (d) in case of emergency only.

12. He holds that a church can send to another church of Christ in connection with physical needs only and which position means there could be no cooperation in spiritual matters at all.

13. Cogdill argues that one congregation can send to another in need, but fails to recognize that a congregation can be in need because it has available to it an opportunity, the accomplishing of which requires more money than it has at the present.

14. His position thus logically makes it unscriptural for one church to send money to another for the purpose of assisting them to build a house in which to meet.

15. He argues that a church can send to a preacher who needs a church but cannot send to a church that needs a preacher.

16. His position that a church can send assistance to another only in connection with physical need is materialistic in nature and elevates the body above the soul making it right to supply food to the stomach in this manner but wrong to supply the sincere milk of the word for famishing souls.

17. He disregards the fact that the mission of the church of our Lord is the salvation of souls and that we save souls by evangelizing, which may be done not only by what we say but also by what we do.

18. His entire position is based on an arbitrary between benevolence and evangelism, yet the Bible plainly teaches that we evangelize in benevolent activity. Jesus said, "Let your light so shine before men that they may see your good works and glorify your father, which is in heaven." By good works others are led to glorify the Father and this is evangelism by good works.

19. He insists that Romans 15: 26 is in harmony with his pattern of money sent from one church to another only when the receiving is in need, yet he ignores that fact that this contribution is not said, (1) to have been sent to the church, (2) that all of the saints were poor. That it was for the poor among the saints necessitates the conclusion that some of the saints were not poor.

20. He effects to know more than the elders of more than a thousand New Testament churches which contribute to the Herald of Truth program. He knows more about the Highland Church than its elders, so he claims, than they know themselves. And he presumes to tell all

SPONSORING CONGREGATIONS

of them in the whole world that they're not doing what they say they are.

21. Though he lives in Texas and does not practice law he tells the Chief of the Bureau of Child Welfare of the State of Tennessee that he doesn't know his own business when he says that in the state child care institutions of the type under consideration must be incorporated.

22. Though Cogdill has repudiated under the pressure of this debate the Music Hall meeting conducted by brother Foy E. Wallace in Houston, Texas, brother Wallace still upholds the scripturalness of it and is quoted as having said that he would conduct another were he invited. The absurdity of Brother Cogdill's position is (this is No. 23.) that it makes it sinful for one church to send a copy of the New Testament to another church.

24. Cogdill said, I had rather be right than consistent. Thus implying that one may be right without being consistent, which is, of course, wrong. Unfortunately he is both wrong and inconsistent.

Now, ladies and gentlemen, my affirmation has been that the Great Commission necessitates and requires church cooperation. That in the very nature of the case it would be impossible to discharge the obligation that it sets out without such cooperation. Secondly, that we have examples of such cooperation in the New Testament. As for example in the case of the Antioch contribution to the elders in Jerusalem. And that this contribution was from one church, so brother Cogdill says, to another church. Hence there is an example of cooperation between churches. But he argues that that is in the field of benevolence. Even so, in I Cor. 16: 1-2, the contribution that's used by us all for the purpose of building church houses, for the purpose of buying songbooks and literature and for paying the preacher. The purpose for which that contribution was raised, mind you, the purpose for which it was raised. He comes back up here and says that it's not question of how it was spent but how it was raised. Well, that's the purpose for which it was raised was in the field of benevolence. It was for the poor among the saints in Jerusalem and yet Brother Cogdill takes the passage that applies to the poor and applies it to the preacher and to evangelistic activity.

Cogdill's Sixth Negative

Gentlemen moderators, Brother Woods, Ladies and Gentlemen:

It is with a great deal of pleasure that I appear before you for the last time in this discussion in reply to the one which you have just listened to. There are a good many things that I want to call to your attention, and I trust that my voice will hold up for me until I am through. Getting warm has always made me hoarse, and I always get warm when I preach, if the building's warm especially.

Brother Woods has insisted that he believes very much in cooperation. So do I. It isn't a matter of cooperation. The issue in this debate has not been cooperation any of the time. The issue rather has been what kind of cooperation is scriptural. He's been under obligation to affirm the proposition called for— that the matter of churches of Christ contributing out of their treasuries to the support of a radio program, Herald of Truth, conducted by the Highland Church in Abilene, Texas, is in harmony with the scriptures. And I am certain this audience knows whether or not his appeal has been to the scripture. He's appealed to nearly everything else. And I want to begin tonight by pointing out to you that kind of evidence in this speech that Brother Woods has used.

He used an argument on the Great Commission that would justify the Missionary Society without any modification whatever, That we should go into all the world; that means into every city in the world; every city means every creature in every city, or the Great Commission means every creature in every city; that the method is not specified by which we are to go and do that preaching or teaching; therefore, his conclusion is that the Herald of Truth is under and in harmony with the Great Commission. That same argument exactly without any modification whatever has been made down through the years for the Missionary Society. It has always been the very point upon which they stood—that God tells us to go, and He tells us to preach, and He hasn't give us the specific method by which we are to go and are to preach. And I submit to you that if tonight it proves the Herald of Truth to be scriptural, then it proves the Missionary Society likewise to be scriptural and for that very reason.

He has handed to me a number of statements in reply to the ones that I gave him. He paid no attention to them. Now Guy likes to ask questions. I dealt with his question fairly. He's in print as saying that the way a man deals with questions in a debate determines the honest and forthright approach that he has in that debate. Now if that's so, I'm just going to leave up to you how honest and forthright he was. I asked him, simply as a means of determining whether or not he's willing to stand upon the things that he had said, and he utterly ignored them. Oh, "if he'll answer mine, I'll answer his." Well, you can't now, your speech is gone. When are you going to answer them now? Why weren't you fair enough to answer them, yes or no, or say why you wouldn't answer them? You didn't have to answer them, you didn't have to sign them. I asked you if you weren't willing to do it, to tell us why. Why didn't you tell us why? Now you're the last man in the world that ought to get up and brag about being fair in debate, because you've answered nothing in this debate as this audience knows. You know the other night, he said that when a man gets up here and tells you that his opponent has failed to sustain his proposition when he gets up and talks about the weakness of his opponent, that that's a sign of the weakness of his position. Well you gave us about fifteen or twenty minute's evidence of the weakness of yours in that last speech—bragging about what you had done and condemning what I had not done. Well the book's going to show that. And you good people that have listened to this discussion, night after night, know whether or not it's true.

But I want to show you, and I'm not introducing these charts for the purpose of replying to the charts. I've already replied to the argument that's on the chart—mentioned it over and over again. He isn't satisfied with answering the argument, he wants you to answer his chart. I want these charts put before you tonight, in the order in which I shall call for them, in order that we may see the kind of evidence that Brother Woods has used in an effort to sustain his proposition. That's what the charts are being introduced for. The first one, No. 42: John T. Lewis and

CHART NO. 42.

JOHN T. LEWIS AND "THE LORD'S PLAN"

- "......MR. KENDRICK AFTERWARDS QUIT THE SOCIETY AND WENT BACK TO THE LORD'S PLAN OF DOING MISSIONARY WORK."
    - JOHN T. LEWIS, VOL OF P. ON I. M. AND SOC., P. 70.

- "......SEND THE FUNDS TO THE ELDERS OF SOME CENTRAL CONGREGATION, WHO WILL DISBURSE THEM WISELY AND JUSTLY: ...."
    - C. KENDRICK, LIVE REL. ISSUES, P. 445.

the Lord's plan. And he attributes to John T. Lewis, an endorsement of a statement in another book, a statement to which Brother John T. Lewis did not refer in what he had to say, and claims that Brother Lewis endorses this thing concerning which he has not produced one syllable that Brother Lewis has ever written one word of endorsement that he has ever given. And I'm saying to you that that's about the most unfair thing that anybody could possibly do—attribute a statement in a book, a book that wasn't under review, a book that brother Lewis had not endorsed, and attribute a statement in that book, that he had never even referred to, so far as Guy Woods knows, he never had even read it. He's talking about what a man did up here, and Guy wants him to swallow what a man said down here. Now that's the kind of evidence that he's offered. If I were Guy N. Woods, I'd be ashamed to get up in public de-

SPONSORING CONGREGATIONS

bate and take advantage of a man who has no opportunity to reply, sitting in the audience, not engaged in the discussion, in such a willful misrepresentation as that. Guy, you ought to repent of it; you're going to face it in the judgment. That's the truth about that matter. And you know why he did it? I'll tell you why. He attributes the Birmingham congregations and their stand on these issues to Roy Cogdill. We'll see that in one of the charts in a moment. Oh, you're following Roy Cogdill. The congregations in this city were occupying the positions that they occupy right now so far as I know, and I'm certain that it's true, the very first time I ever preached in Birmingham. It's largely a tribute to the influence of one man, a man who's been the father of the cause of Christ in this city—John T. Lewis. It's his influence. And the reason that that thing was introduced was to try to discredit the influence of John T. Lewis. As he stood up here the other night and said, "quote: 'Peanuts' unquote." It's going to take a whole sackful of those "goobers" to destroy the influence of that man and don't you forget it. And you haven't done you or your cause any good by the use that you've made of that thing. You ought to be ashamed of it. If I were in your place, I'd repudiate it yet before this thing comes to a close. And you're generous with your time, I'll give you a minute of mine in order to get up and apologize for it.

Brother Woods: If Brother Lewis will stand up and say he repudiates that position, I'll take it down from the chart.

Brother Cogdill: Do you want to make a statement Brother Lewis and say that you want to say you repudiate it, he'll take it down? That's not the point. Will you apologize for using it?

Brother Woods: No, because . . .

Brother Cogdill: No, but that's what you ought to do.

Brother Woods: Let him repudiate it . . .

Brother Cogdill: You ought to apologize for misusing it. That's what you ought to do. You're attributing to him something you had no ground to attribute. You can't find where he ever made that statement. Where he ever endorsed it. Whether he ever read the book or not and a thing up here that he referred to that had no connection.

I'm glad you can see that. Don't tell me that you can't. If you'll open your eyes you can.

Chart No. 43. Where's the scripture on that first one 42? No. 43. I want you to look at the scripture on this one.

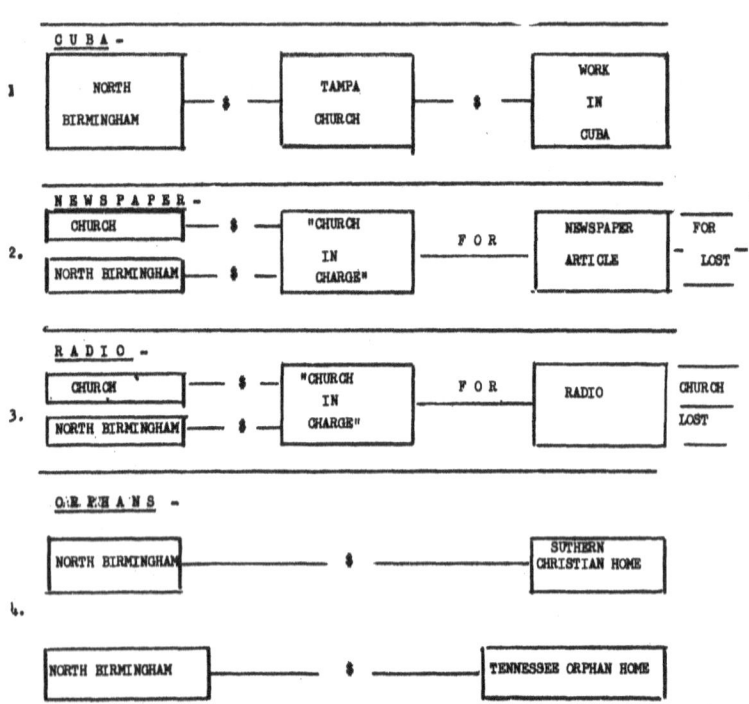

Here's Cuba and by the way you misrepresented that. He's got a Tampa church, Nebraska Avenue, as a sponsoring church. I happen to know that Brother C. W. Scott got a telegram and took it to Guy N. Woods, last night and he told him that the Nebraska Avenue church repudiated, by that telegram, the fact that they received any money. Another one of his misrepresentations. Where's the scripture on it?

Brother Warren: Brother Cogdill.

Brother Cogdill: I'm replying to what's been introduced.

SPONSORING CONGREGATIONS 365

Brother Warren: Well, I hadn't intended to say anything but that's new material that hasn't been in this debate...

Brother Cogdill: I've got a right to reply to what's been introduced.

Brother Warren: Now wait just a moment. I'm addressing my remarks to your moderator...

Brother Cogdill: Well, you addressed them to me.

Brother Warren: Brother Adams.

Brother Adams: All right.

Brother Warren: I'd like to say first of all that this is the first time that Brother Cogdill's ever had these charts on the screen...

Brother Cogdill: I'm showing you what I put them up there for.

Brother Warren: I'm addressing my remarks to Brother Adams. This is the first time these charts have been on the screen. It seems to me to be significant that they cover the time that Brother Woods had no reply. The information on this particular matter has not been introduced in this debate before. Now if Brother Cogdill insists on going ahead with the presentation of them, that'll be up to him. I'll not stand up and try to cause any more confusion on that point. But I do want it to be a matter of record in the book that it is new material.

Brother Adams: Well, we didn't object to your list of inconsistencies the other night and there was a lot of new material in it. I am going to rule on this, that Brother Cogdill just go on with his discussion and let the Nebraska avenue church matter go.

Brother Cogdill: All right fine. I'll withdraw it if they've got any objection to what I've said about it and apologize for it. I've no intention to introduce any new material.

Brother Woods: May I say just this word. Brother Cogdill, we have no objection to your mentioning it, if you'll just let me produce the proof that they were a sponsoring church. If you'll let me produce the proof...

Brother Cogdill: Do you have the telegram that shows they didn't?

Brother Woods: I have a statement . . .

Brother Cogdill: Did Brother Scott show you the telegram?

Brother Woods: May I say just this please? If you're addressing your remarks to me . . .

Brother Cogdill: You addressed yours to me, Brother Woods.

Brother Woods: Brother Scott came up here last night and said that's not the situation as it now exists. I said that I didn't say that it was the situation as it now exists because North Birmingham is not now sending that money. But back yonder when they did send it, the Tampa church, the elders of that church received the money, so that dates back to the time when North Birmingham was cooperating. Of course, they've quit cooperation now.

Brother Cogdill: They've quit that kind of cooperation, brethren. They're still cooperating. And not only has North Birmingham quit, but now since he made his speech, and you can count my time again from this point; since he made this speech, Tampa church has quit it if they ever did it. And he knows it because they sent the telegram last night. Now we'll just let that matter drop and I'll use the chart only for this purpose, if they haven't any objection to a reply being made to any of the rest of it.

You have here an illustration of North Birmingham sending to the church in charge for a newspaper article. And where's the passage of scripture that proves that the Herald of Truth is scriptural by that? If everything he said about the whole thing's so, I want to know, would you draw the conclusion, if you grant everything he said, would you draw the conclusion from it; therefore, my proposition is sustained; the Herald of Truth is in harmony with the scriptures.

Give me the next one, Brother Deaver. You have here another chart concerning the Corinth radio program. And that's been misrepresented. That's been misrepresented. But, of course, I can't deal with the misrepresentations now. I tell you why. But I say that if everything he has on that chart's so, if every bit of it were true, what would it prove about the Herald of Truth being scriptural? What

SPONSORING CONGREGATIONS 367

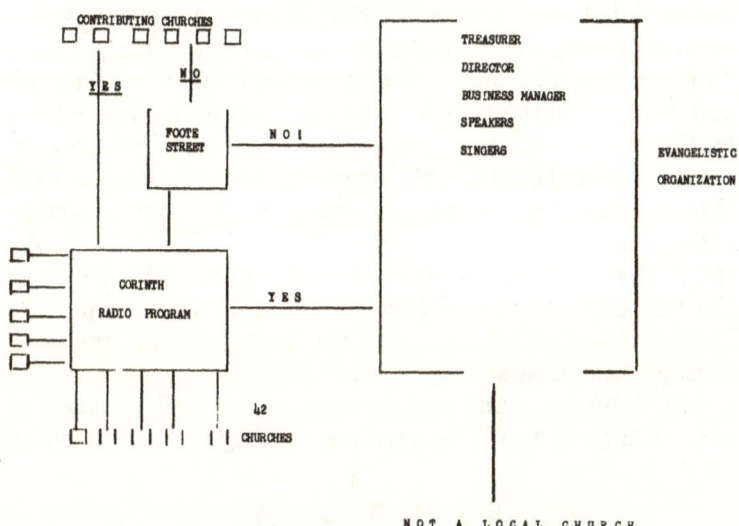

CHART NO. 51A

CORINTH RADIO PROGRAM

NOT A LOCAL CHURCH.

was the purpose of the argument on it? I'll tell you, it's to take the place of the fact that he had no scripture.

Give me the next one. Let's look at it and see if we can find any scripture on it. Chart No. 48. Here we have

CHART NO. 48

GOSPEL GUARDIAN CONFUSION ON "PATTERN."

UPHELD BY:	ITEM	CONDEMNED BY:
1. WALLACE	1. MUSIC HALL MEETING	1. COGDILL
2. DOUTHITT LEWIS	2. BIRMINGHAM NEWSPAPER ADVERTISING	2. COGDILL
3. LEWIS ("LORD'S PLAN")	3. BIRMINGHAM - CUBA	3. COGDILL
4. TANT	4. MONTANA ROGRAM	4. COGDILL
5. DOUTHITT	5. MEETING HOUSE WITH PREACHER'S QUARTERS	5. COGDILL
6. DOUTHITT	6. BIRMINGHAM RADIO	6. COGDILL
WHERE DO	YOU STAND,	BROTHER?

again, Wallace, and Douthitt, and Lewis, and Tant, and Douthitt and Douthitt, and over on the other hand, Cogdill. And in all of the erasures—and by the way you know Brother Woods said he'd be a second rate lawyer. Well, I want to know who did this cartoon? I don't know whether I'd rate his cartooning that high or not. My opinion about the matter is, for whatever it's worth to him, that he'd do a lot better job debating if he'd leave the cartoons of the Fort Worth brain trust aside and debate on his own material, **rather than listening** to their dictation. But read **everything** that's on it. Believe everything he said about it. Does it prove that the Herald of T r u t h is scriptural? That's the kind of evidence we looked at all the way through this debate.

And then we want another one. Let's look at another one. Chart 46A. When does the sin begin? Auditorium,

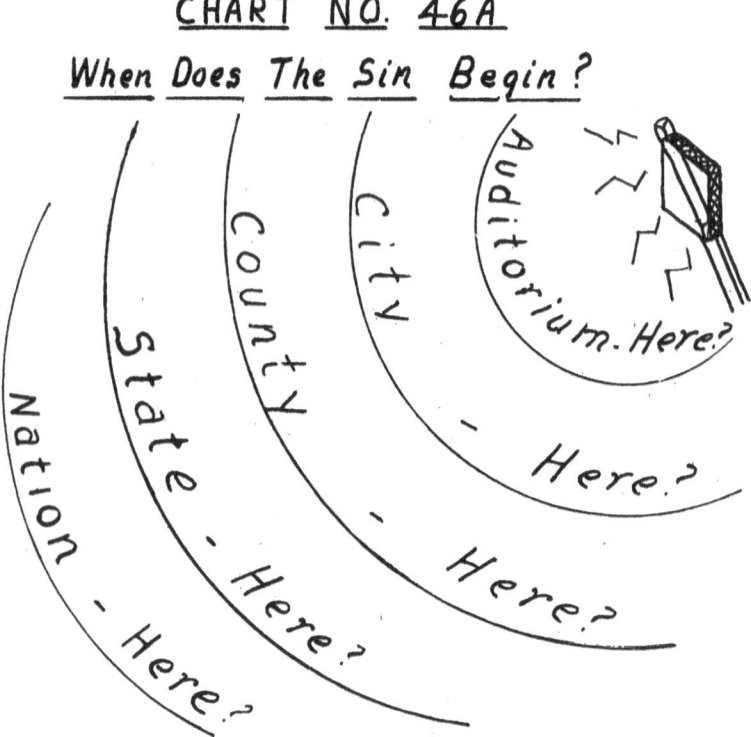

city, county, state and nation. Where does the sin begin? Therefore the Herald of Truth is scriptural. He's in the affirmative. It's in harmony with the scripture. What is? The Herald of Truth. What's bad about it? Well, you'll

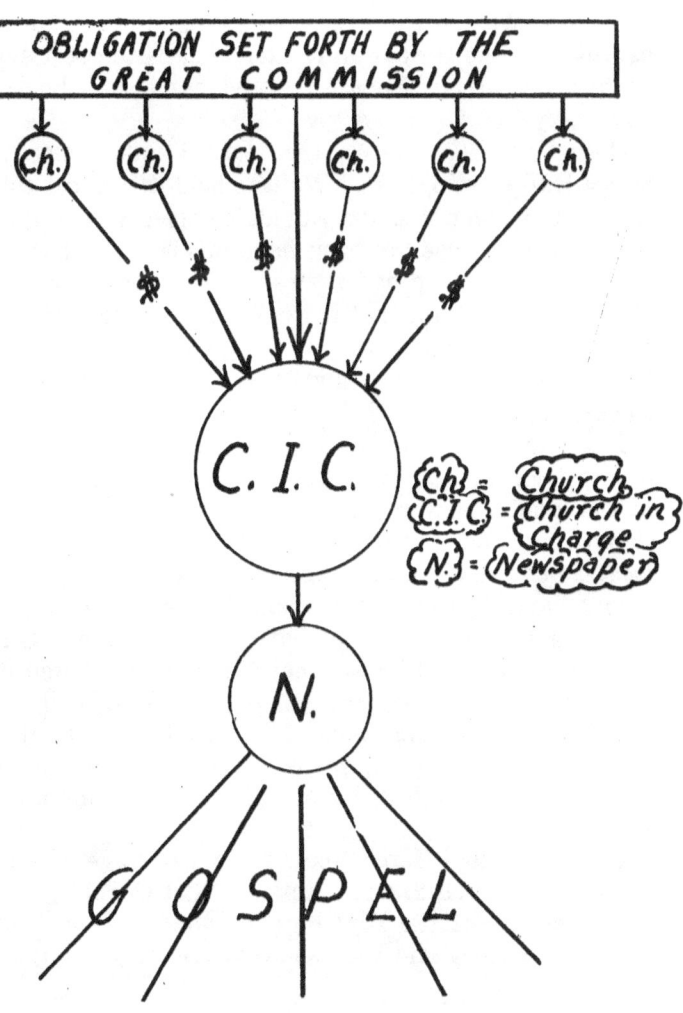

CHART NO 45
BIRMINGHAM NEWSPAPER AD COOP.

have to let him tell you. There isn't any Herald of Truth or Bible either on it. That's the kind of evidence that he's paraded up here from the very beginning.

Chart No. 45. And here you have the newspaper ad cooperative. And by the way, I'm going to say that Brother John T. Lewis told me that he never did endorse it. Never has had anything personally to do with it. Represented as having done so, Cecil Douthitt said he didn't know whether he did or not. That's the statement Cecil Douthitt made. But suppose that everything connected with it is so, and John T. Lewis did endorse it, which he didn't, what does it prove about the Herald of Truth? That's the best evidence he has, brethren. Honest to goodness it is. Look again now.

Chart No. 46. Here's the Norhill music meeting, or Music Hall meeting. Foy Wallace held it. And I told him way back yonder, I said I wouldn't engaged in it again for one reason because brethren have misused it. Even if the way that that thing had been done had been modified and changed to the point that it wouldn't have violated any other scriptural principle, they've misused it to justify brotherhood-wide promotions, and that isn't what that was. That's one reason.

I said another reason I repudiated it, would not defend it that I'd stated all over this country and there are people in this audience who have heard me say it over and over that I would not again be a party to one church, even in a local matter like that, handling the money of any other church, and I've said it a whole lot longer than just last night—a whole lot longer than just last night. And yet he gets up here and insists that I hadn't repudiated it until last night. And I say to you, Brother Woods, it isn't so, and you weren't fair about it. It isn't so. But if everything you said about it was so, it still wouldn't prove that the Herald of Truth is scriptural. It'd have nothing to do with that.

Chart No. 40. Here's one he has a passage of scripture on. 1st Cor. 16:1, 2, and points out that Cogdill misuses it. The members of the Birmingham congregation contribute into the treasury and they use that treasury to support the

CHART NO. 46
MUSIC HALL MEETING

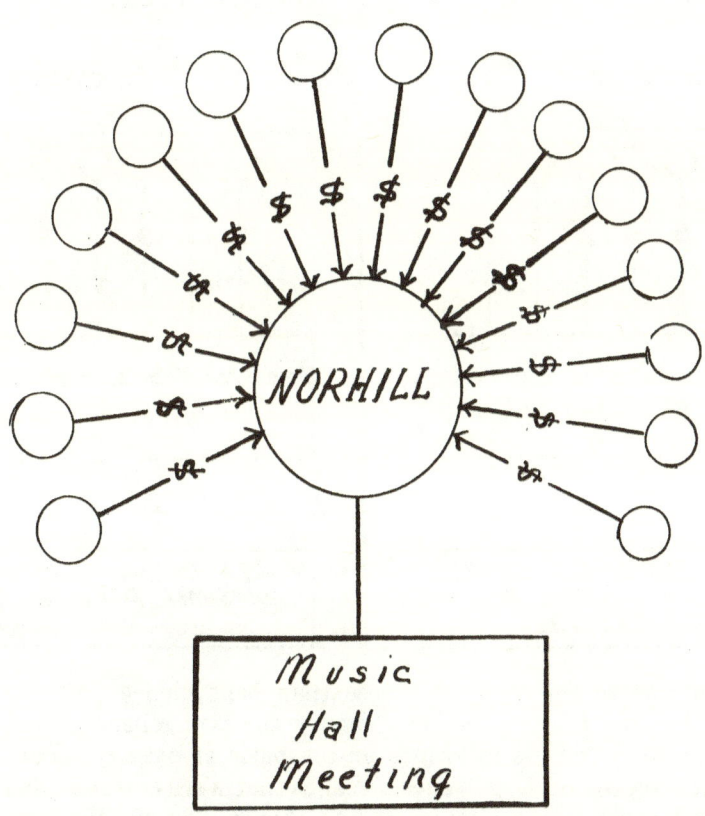

preaching of the gospel. I asked him last night and pressed him and he said, "He didn't deal with these things." I pressed him. Two different nights I have before tonight with the fact that 1st Cor. 16 is the only passage that tells any congregation in the New Testament how to raise its money—the only way that God ever gave. Yet churches

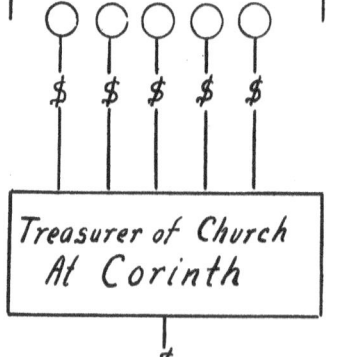

contributed for other purposes than benevolence. Where is the way they raised their money for evangelism if that isn't it? And his inference on the basis of charity. Paul put it on the basis of wages. Wages that were deserved like the laborer in the field or the ox that treads out the corn or the man that tends the vineyard.

Chart No. 47. Here has the obligation set forth by the Great Commission. And I'm glad to notice that here he has a chart that is exactly a duplicate of the thing that he put on the board. He said that this would be an unscriptural organization for the purpose of benevolence. (Illustration

CHART NO. 47.

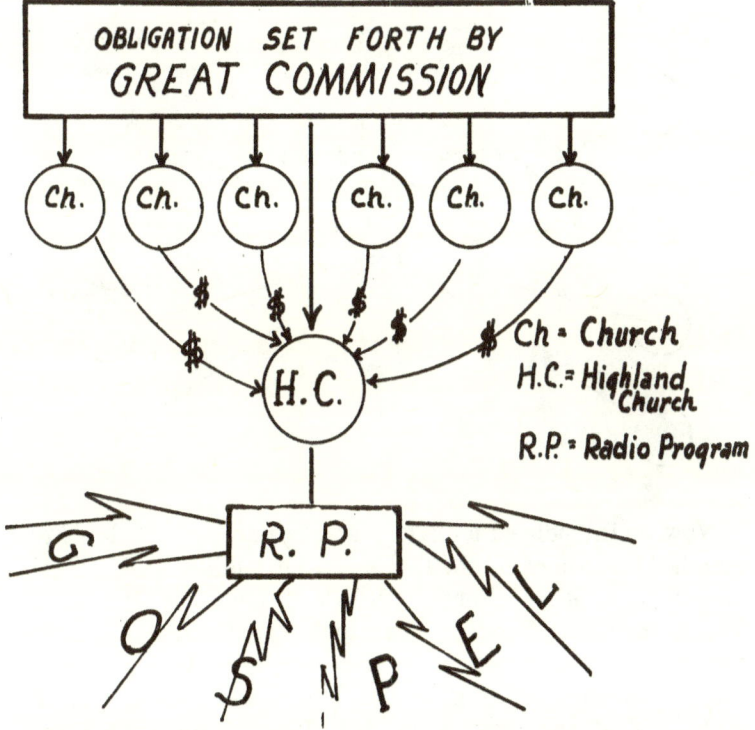

on blackboard) Why? Many churches sending to a central agency that it might send out here to establish other homes, several homes—a board here that would establish several homes—Boles and Tiptons and Potter's and so on. If that board established several institutions in the field of benevolence as a centralized agency, that'd be unscriptural. Do you see the difference between that one illustration and this one? Do you? Churches sending to a centralized agency. Why that's what we've been opposing from the very beginning. That's the reason the thing's unscriptural. The money, the power, the obligation of many churches, the control over their resources, the resources of many churches centralized in one congregation with that congregation exclusively expending those to send out the gospel.

WOODS' BLACKBOARD DIAGRAM ILLUSTRATING THE THING HE WOULD OPPOSE AS UNSCRIPTURAL IN BENEVOLENCE

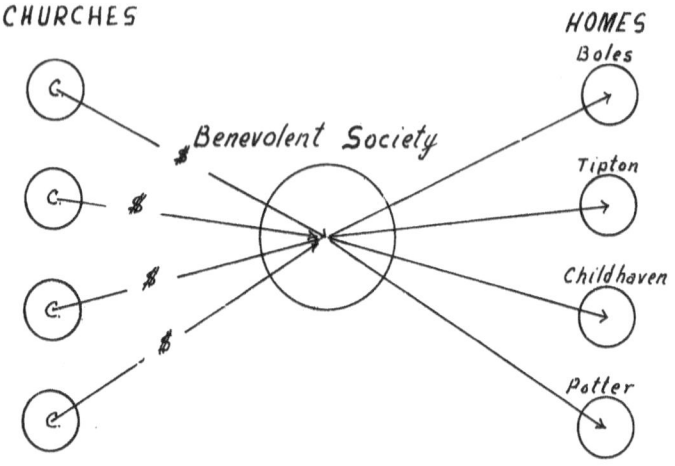

Now he introduced a chart just a minute ago. I don't remember the No. of it, about one church sending a New Testament to another church. No, that isn't the Herald of Truth, Brother Woods, That isn't the Herald of Truth. Let me tell you something. Here is the Herald of Truth. Many churches sending to the Highland church. To do what? That they may send New Testaments out all over the world. That's the Herald of Truth. Your illustration doesn't illustrate in the other chart.

Give me chart No. 51. Here's a preacher now. This church is sending money to the preacher in order that the preacher might have oversight of a program of preaching the gospel. That he might oversee a program. Well I don't read in the New Testament about preachers overseeing a program Nor do I read in the New Testament about churches that sent to a preacher funds with which to oversee a program of work. I read only in the New Testament, I dealt with that last night, I dealt with it in my other speech, that's the point that he said I didn't reply to. I said that that thing's not right. I wouldn't endorse it. Why? Because the New Testament churches stopped send-

CHART NO. 51
WILL COGDILL UPHOLD THIS?

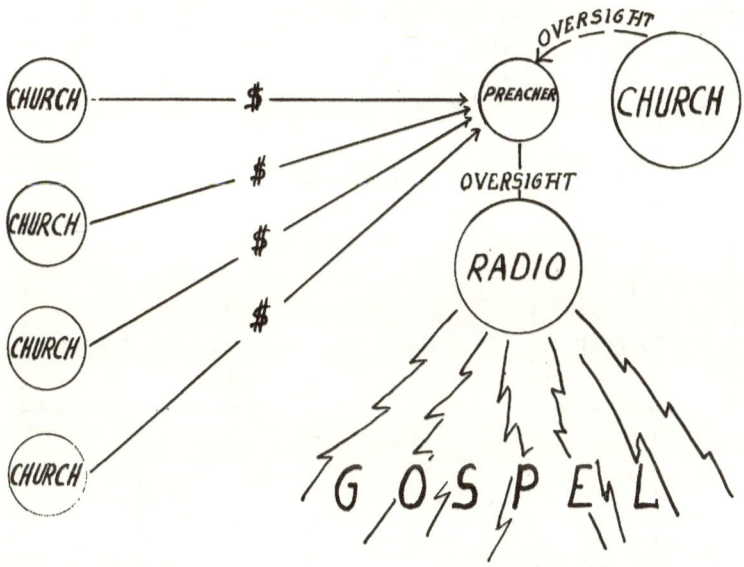

ing to a preacher when they supplied his need. And everybody that was here last night, and who's been here tonight, knows that I dealt with that. And he did that just like he's done everything else. You can get up here and answer what he has to say and his way of getting around your answer is to say that you didn't say a thing in the world about it, not a thing in the world about it. Well just grant everything he's got on the chart, what would that prove about the Herald of Truth? Why it would only prove if I endorsed that picture that my judgement is involved in the matter, not what the word of God teaches. That's the whole thing. I don't claim perfect judgment. I haven't always exercised perfect judgment.

Chart No. 39. I've made sometimes a miserable failure of applying the principles of truth that I believe to the problems at hand. I've done it in my own personal life. I've done it in the work of the Lord. I haven't changed my preaching. I've changed my practice, Guy. You've done it the other way. You've changed your preaching rather than your practice. That's the change you've made. You're preaching now what you haven't preached, and I've given you instance after instance of it. The inconsistencies of the man, denying that he's ever changed. He's not even preaching now what he did preach. And you know he got

CHART NO. 39.

ACTS 11: 27-30.

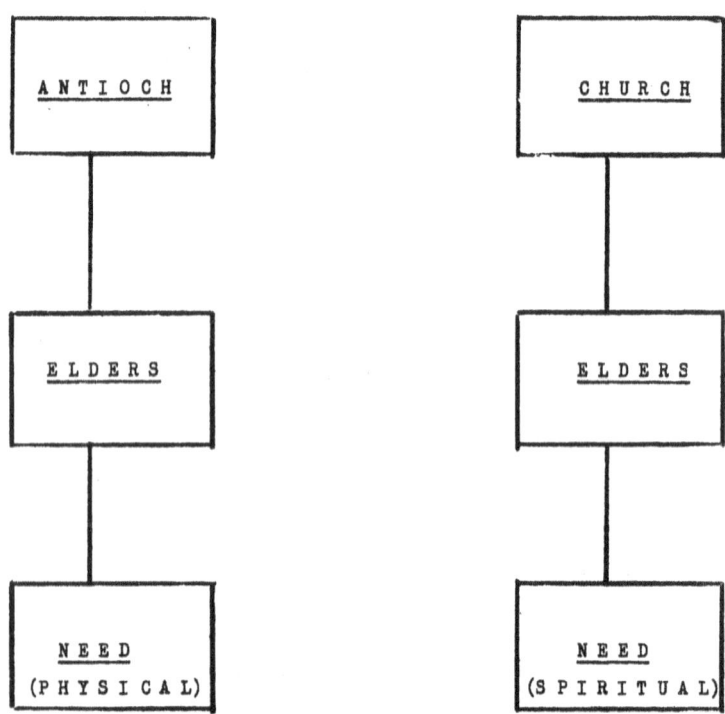

himself in trouble with this chart. He spent three nights up here denying that the elders of any church can oversee any kind of a physical need. Three nights he denied that. Why he said that involved the home. You can't supply the needs of people physically without a home. And elders can't oversee a home. Three nights he argued. Then he comes up here and draws a parallel to the Herald of Truth. Now, Guy, which time did you mean what you said? **Did you mean what you said about this when you were discussing the orphan home question? Or do you mean what you're saying about it on the Herald of Truth question?** You talk about a man getting mixed up, I wouldn't know how to mix a man up on it. The idea of condemning it in benevolence. It's impossible. That thing involves a home in benevolence. That's what he said about it. That thing involves a home in benevolence. You can't do it without a home he argued and those who have been in attendance know it. Then he comes right back and tries to parallel a Bible example with an unscriptural example in trying to find authority for what he is doing. He put the name of the church up here that did this. Why didn't he name the church in the New Testament that did that? Why didn't he give you the name of the church there like he did here? Get up here and try to create confusion in these two and by that kind of thing to keep you from seeing the truth You ought to be ashamed of it, Brother Woods. You ought to repent of it, because you've crossed yourself up and contradicted yourself world without end right there on that chart. Given up your whole position on the thing. I'm on chart No. 49. He did the same thing here.

Now you notice. He's got a church sending to a Montana church. And a church sending to Highland Church and a church sending to Boles Home, and he crosses these out. Why that's what he's defending. That's what he's defending. For three nights he argued here that the churches had the right to build that, that benevolent society, that benevolent organization. He argued for three nights that they had the rights to build that. Nobody denies the right to supply a home for the destitute. *A home, not Boles Home.* It's unscriptural in its organization because this is Boles Home in principle. That would have to be the place. This is the organization. That's the place where the work's done. This is the organization that does it. And if that is what he endorses then where in the world did you get this? Why don't put put this under a board? Why don't you organize

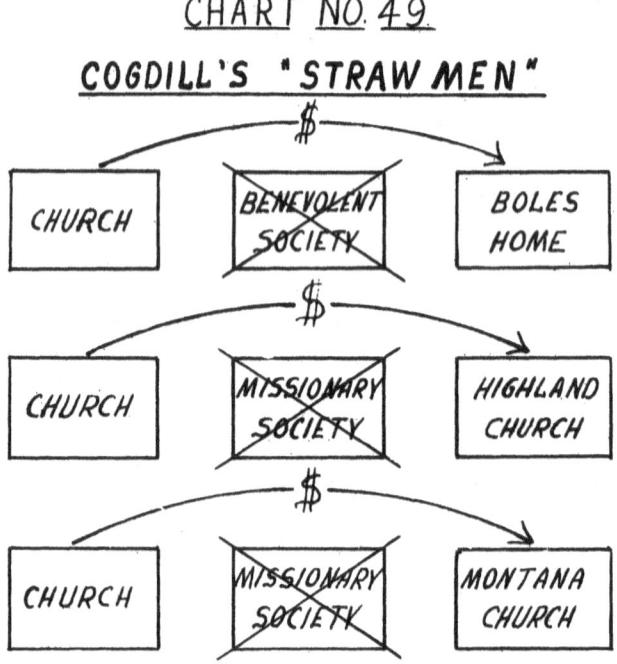

here what you've got up there? Why don't you? The elders of the Highland Church ought to take an object lesson from that. And if everything he said were true, if all of it were so, then I want to know how does it prove, how does that prove, how could that possibly prove, that the Herald of Truth is scriptural? Now, brethren, that's the best they can do. Guy Woods is as capable as any of them. There isn't any question on earth about that. He's an artist at confusing the issue. He's had wonderful experience in debating. And I've met a few, not many, not many, but he's as good as any man I ever saw in trying to cover up the issue.

Oh, he said, when I meet a Baptist preacher, use just three passages of scripture to prove that baptism's for the remission of sins, he hollows where's the scripture? Well if you had used three I wouldn't be hollowing. You haven't used three. You haven't even used one. Not one. I've begged you from the beginning of this debate on this proposition to point out the example of a church that sends to another church when the church receiving the money is not in need. Brethren, where is it? Where is the example of a receiving church? Oh, he said, Acts 15. Do you deny that they needed what they received in Acts 15? I asked you that last night. Why that was a divine decision. It was rule of the supreme court. It involved a revelation. It was a decision of the apostles of the church of our Lord. It was the word of God sent out by the apostles, not by the church. He misrepresents Acts 15 all up and down the line. It wasn't the church that made the decision. It wasn't the church primarily that did the sending. They concurred in the sending by the apostles as well as in the decision, but it wasn't the decision of the church. It wasn't a sending of the church primarily. It pleased the apostles, and the decision was the thing, that pleased the Holy Spirit. It pleased the Holy Spirit.

He doesn't have a case. There isn't an example of it.

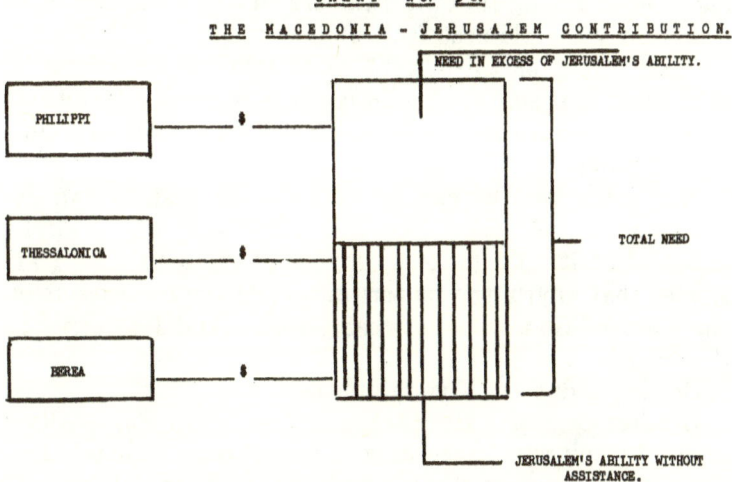

Then chart No. 56. The Jerusalem church. The Jerusalem church. Now what on earth do you mean by your representation here? I want to ask a question: Is the Jerusalem church, the church that wasn't in need? Was it a church wth abundance? He said Roy Cogdill said and it's in his inconsistency list, and he read it so fast that I couldn't hear them and I don't have a copy of them, of course. But I heard enough of them to know that about ninety-nine and ten-ninths of them were just not so. They were misrepresentations. They were misrepresentations. One misrepresentation was: he said that I said that a church in abundance sent to a church in need and that's the only way it ever happened. I didn't say it, Guy. Didn't say anthing *about a church in abundance.* You never heard me say it. The tape will show that I never said it. I said everytime a congregation sent to another congregation that the congregation receiving was a needy congregation that it had a need that it could not supply. I don't know what caused the need. I don't know how long it lasted. But however long it lasted and whatever caused it, it was a church in need. Anybody that would deny that the Jerusalem church had a need among its own members that it could not meet would deny the plainest facts of inspiration. Is that what he meant to do on this chart? And suppose everything he said about it is so. Where on earth is there any scriptural proof on it that the Herald of Truth is in harmony with the scriptures?

That's the best he can do. That's the best he can do. That's what he's done from the very beginning. I'd be ashamed of it. I'd make up my mind the next time I affirmed that anything was scriptural, I'd try to prove it by the word of God. That's what I'd do. And I referred to this chart . . .

Brother Adams: Five minutes.

Brother Cogdill: Here is a chart on which Foy Wallace says, "I won't run," according to Guy Woods. There's Roy Cogdill standing out there. And what's this down here. I suppose that's the sea of digression. There is the slipping among us? Where there's the worldiness that is rampant in the church today? Where there's the Modernism that's taking hold upon the church and the human institutionalism, the sea of digression. Roy Cogdill's standing out here

CHART NO. 50

where you fall off and doing his best to keep you from falling off—if you're not already gone. (laughter)

Now, brethren, let me tell you something. Turn the lights back on. The time's about gone. Let me tell you something and make an appeal to you in the last two or three minutes of this speech. There's an answer for that kind of thing if I had not been interested in trying to teach you and to preach and to show you what the word of God teaches. Don't you ever think I couldn't answer that kind of stuff. There's an answer to it. It's sophistry from the beginning to the end of it. Human sophistry. That's all there is to it, and no argument in it, and it's hatched up by a Fort Worth brain trust of young preachers who are trying to change the church, and Guy Woods ought to know better than to use it.

I've made my appeal to you on the basis of Bible Authority. Now where's my first chart? I illustrated it to you in the very beginning of this discussion. I kept it before you

HOW TO ESTABLISH SCRIPTURAL AUTHORITY
THE LORD'S SUPPER

(1) EXPRESS COMMAND — "This do in remembrance of Me."
(Observance)   I COR. 11:23-24

(2) APPROVED EXAMPLE — "And upon the <u>first day of the week</u>,
(Time of Observance)   When the disciples came together to break
                       bread."   ACTS 20:7

(3) NECESSARY INFERENCE — "The first day of the week...to break bread"
(Frequency of Observance) (Means as regularly as the day comes.)
                           COMPARE: "The Sabbath day to keep it Holy."
                                        HOW OFTEN?

EXPEDIENCY : ANY HOUR WITHIN THE FIRST
                 DAY OF THE WEEK.

from the beginning. That there are three ways of establishing Bible authority; one of them by express command, one by approved example, three — necessary inference. That the realm of expediency is within the realm of command, example or inference, and if you cannot find a command, or an example, or an inference that includes the thing you are doing it isn't expedient, it is unscriptural, it's without authority. He hasn't produced either one of them. Where's the example he's produced in the New Testament of one church receiving money from a thousand churches or even ten, when it wasn't a need and a destitute church? Where did he find it in the word of God? He hasn't found it. You know he hasn't found it. He knows he hasn't found it. He made a mighty poor excuse of even hunting for it. Then I pointed out to you that God excludes the human organization.

God excludes the human arrangement in the accomplishment of the work of the church. The only organization that God has ever given the church is a congregation. A local congregation under a local eldership. The obligation of that eldership extends only to that congregation, to its members and its work—"tending the flock of God which is among them." Whenever elders extend their oversight beyond the work of the congregation where they are elders, they have invaded God's realm of silence. They've transgressed and gone beyond the word of God. That's what they've done. And that's what Highland Church is doing in Abilene. They're operating in a field that no New Testament congregations ever operated in. Turn the chart over. That God's command when it becomes specific ex-

SCRIPTURAL AUTHORITY

Commanded	Generic	Specific
ARK (GEN. 6:14)	WOOD	GOPHER
WATER OF CLEANSING (NUMBERS 19:2)	ANIMAL	RED HEIFER WITHOUT SPOT
PRAISE (EPH. 5:18; COL. 3:16)	MUSIC	SING
EVANGELIZE (I TIM. 3:15; I THESS. 1:7-8)	CHURCH (I THESS. 1:1)	ORGANIZATION (CONGREGATION)(PHIL. 1:1)
EDIFY (EPH. 4:16)	CHURCH	ORGANIZATION (CONGRE.)
RELIEVE (I TIM. 5:16)	CHURCH	ORGANIZATION (CONGRE.)

3.   3.

cludes everything else. That the church, the congregation, that it is not only to carry on the relief of the destitute, but the congregation is the organization that God has given to evangelize the world. And its the only way. Guy Woods says it can't do it. God gave us an obligation and if it took all the resources of the United States of America to carry it out, and we just can't do what God said do. God said for us to do it, but we just can't do it. The organization isn't big enough. God gave us a job but he didn't give us something big enough to do it with, therefore, we've got to blow up and stretch out the one God gave us and give elders authority that God never assigned to them. Here

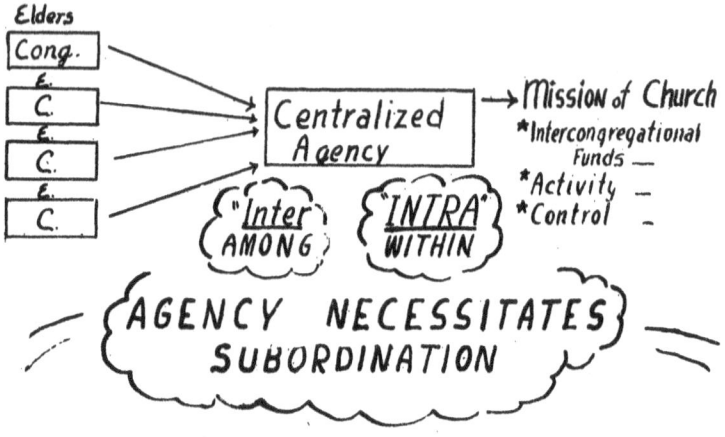

you have a centralized agency; in this case the Highland Church an agency controlled exclusively by their own admission, by the Highland elders. Yet, they are carrying on inter- congregational activity. They are a perverted order of God's organization—elders over the church, yes, but no church a brotherhood agency. No elders are a brotherhood eldership. That's the whole point. When they make themselves a centralized agency—give me the last one on that— that's when they go beyond the word of God and that's what God condemns. That's what Guy Woods needs to find Bible Authority for. How does the Herald of Truth operate? Why it operates first of all, by many churches furnishing the money. It operates by Highland exclusively controlling all the money; and they spend a lot of it for literature and propaganda, a lot of it for promotional agencies in order to increase the scope of their work. And I thank you.

HOW DOES H. of T. OPERATE?

1. DO MANY CHURCHES CONTRIBUTE MONEY? <u>YES.</u>

2. DOES HIGHLAND RECEIVE ALL THE MONEY? <u>YES.</u>

3. DO ELDERS OF HIGHLAND EXERCISE EXCLUSIVE CONTROL? <u>YES.</u>

16.   16.

CHART NO. 9

GAL. 4: 12.

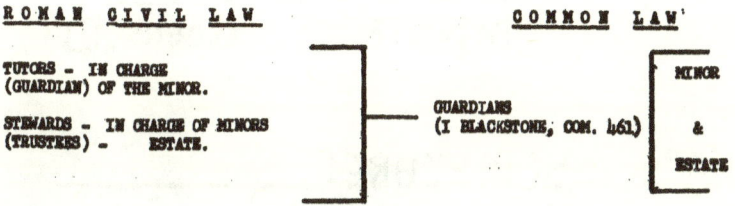

ROMAN CIVIL LAW   COMMON LAW

TUTORS – IN CHARGE
(GUARDIAN) OF THE MINOR.   MINOR

STEWARDS – IN CHARGE OF MINORS   GUARDIANS   &
(TRUSTEES) –   ESTATE.   (I BLACKSTONE, COM. 461)
                                                         ESTATE

<u>ESTATE</u> – BY (1) WILL, OR (2) GIFT.

<u>DURATION</u> – (1) FEE SIMPLE; OR (2) A TERM OF YEARS.

<u>ORPHAN HOMES</u> – ESTATE HELD IN TRUST FOR A TERM OF YEARS, BY TRUSTEES, WITH
                SUPERINTENDENTS IN CHARGE OF EDUCATION AND CARE OF FATHERLESS
                CHILDREN.

CHART No. 14
OVERSIGHT

- WHO IS AUTHORIZED TO HAVE OVERSIGHT OF (MANAGE):

    1. A CHURCH (CHECK):
       PARENTS ☐   ELDERS ☐

    2. A HOME (CHECK):
       PARENTS ☐   ELDERS ☐

    SCRIPTURE: _____

CHART NO. 20.

WHAT IS IT?

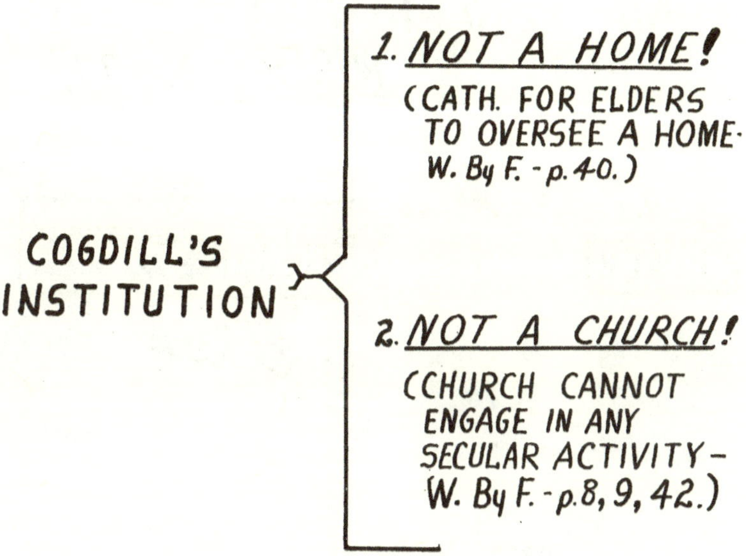

COGDILL'S INSTITUTION
1. NOT A HOME!
(CATH. FOR ELDERS TO OVERSEE A HOME· W. By F. - p. 40.)
2. NOT A CHURCH!
(CHURCH CANNOT ENGAGE IN ANY SECULAR ACTIVITY - W. By F. - p. 8, 9, 42.)

CHART No. 21

COGDILL'S POSITION

IF THIS-
WHY NOT THIS?
PARENTS
HOME
RE-ESTAB.
ELDERS
CHURCH
OFFICIALS
STATE
RE-ESTAB.
ELDERS
CHURCH
SCRIPTURAL POSITION
PARENTS
HOME
ELDERS
CHURCH
OFFICIALS
STATE
ELDERS
CHURCH

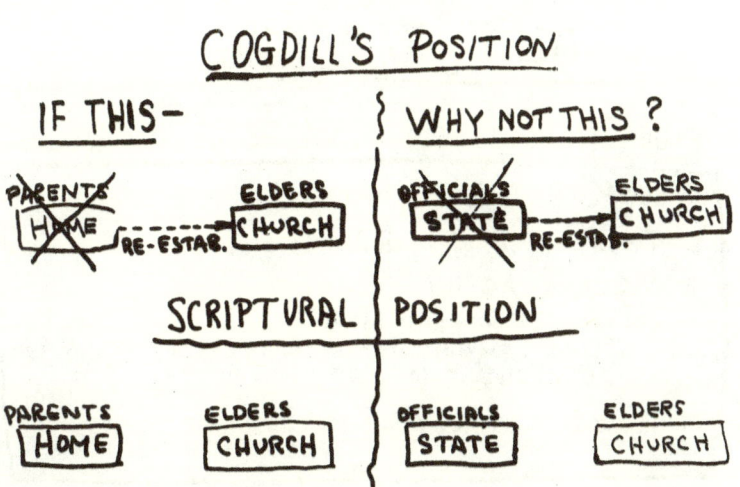

CHART NO. 22

COGDILL'S POSITION: CHURCH CANNOT BUILD ANYTHING BUT ANOTHER CHURCH   PAGE 77.

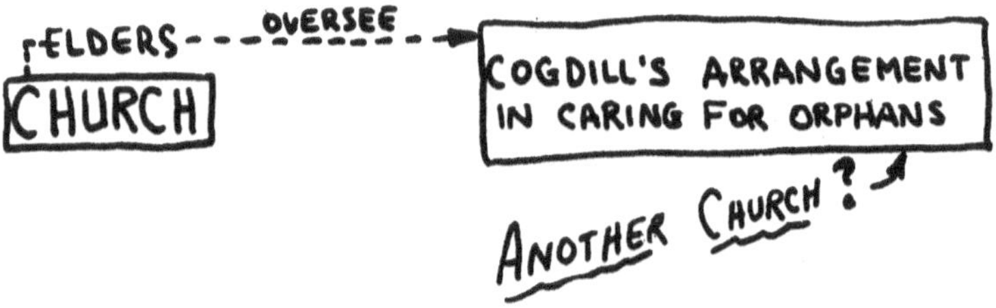

ELDERS - - - OVERSEE - - - →

[CHURCH]

[COGDILL'S ARRANGEMENT IN CARING FOR ORPHANS]

ANOTHER CHURCH?

CHART No. 23

COGDILL'S "ARRANGEMENT"

ELDERS, AS ELDERS, OVERSEE

1. LEGAL ENTITY (LICENSED)
2. THOSE NOT CHRISTIANS
3. SECULAR ACTIVITY
    RECREATION — PLAYGROUND
    SECULAR EDUCATION — SCHOOL (ELEMENTARY SCH, HIGH SCHOOL — COLLEGE — UNIVERSITY)
4. LEGAL CUSTODY OF PERSON

CHART NO. 28

COGDILL ADMITS AND DENIES

ORPHAN HOME	ITEM	FOSTER HOME
1. DENIES	1. A HOME	1. ADMITS
2. DENIES	2. NOT A CHURCH	2. ADMITS
3. DENIES	3. ANOTHER ORGAN.	3. ADMITS
4. DENIES	4. RECEIVES FUNDS FROM CHURCHES	4. ADMITS
5. DENIES	5. NOT MANAGED BY ELDERS FUNCTION AS ELDERS	5. ADMITS

CHART No. 52

II COR. 11:8

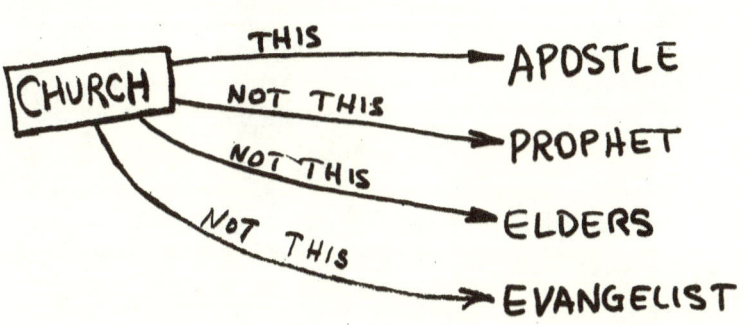

CHURCH
- THIS → APOSTLE
- NOT THIS → PROPHET
- NOT THIS → ELDERS
- NOT THIS → EVANGELIST

www.ingramcontent.com/pod-product-compliance
Lightning Source LLC
Chambersburg PA
CBHW032015230426
43671CB00005B/91